American Indian Policy in the Jacksonian Era

American Indian Policy in the Jacksonian Era

Ronald N. Satz

UNIVERSITY OF NEBRASKA PRESS · LINCOLN

For
my wife and children: Christa and Ani and Jakob
my mother and father: Gertrude and David Satz
my mother- and father-in-law: Berta and Jacob Ilgaudas

Library of Congress Cataloging in Publication Data

Satz, Ronald N
  American Indian policy in the Jacksonian era.

  Bibliography: p.
  1. Indians of North America—Government relations—1789–1869. 2. United
States—Politics and government—1829–1837. 3. Indians of North America—Land
transfers. I. Title.
E93.S27   970.5   73-94119
ISBN 0-8032-0823-5

*The publication of this book was assisted by a grant from the
Ford Foundation Ethnic Studies Publication Program.*

Contents

List of Maps

and Illustrations

Preface

THIS STUDY was undertaken in the belief that one of the central problems facing modern man, like his predecessors, is the difficulty of easing tensions that arise from ethnic rivalries and confrontations. If Americans can look dispassionately at the sources and results of ethnic conflict in the past, perhaps they will be able to deal more effectively with such tensions in the future.

The American Indians hold a unique position in American ethnic history. They alone were indigenous to this continent. Unlike Afro-Americans or Spanish-Americans or any other group of hyphenates, the American Indians have had their relationship with the larger society spelled out in "solemn treaties" negotiated between their leaders and the United States government. Today Americans are increasingly becoming aware of the existence of these treaties as well as the executive orders and statutes that have outlined the relationship between the government and the Indians. Such reawakened interest in the native Americans is refreshing, but much scholarly work on the origins, motivation, execution, and results of federal Indian policy must be done if we are to be able to put Indian-white relations in their proper perspective. This study is an effort to bring one short but critical period of American Indian policy into better focus.

While many historians refer to the Jacksonian era as a watershed in federal-Indian relations, there has been no systematic analysis of government Indian policy during this period. Although Grant Foreman's numerous publications in the 1930s and '40s provide detailed information about Indian removal and emigrant Indian life in the trans-Mississippi West, they offer little analysis of federal Indian policy. The only comprehensive monograph dealing with the topic is George Dewey Harmon's impressionistic *Sixty Years of Indian Affairs: Political, Economic, and Diplomatic, 1789–1850* (1941). Many other books and articles have made important contributions to our understanding of American Indian policy in the Jacksonian era, but a one-volume comprehensive analysis of the topic is lacking. This study represents an effort to fill that gap in the historical literature of the period.

During the course of my research, I have benefited from the assistance of a great number of people and institutions. It is a pleasure to acknowledge their contributions. Staff members at the National Archives, the Library of Congress, the Smithsonian Institution, the University of Maryland Library, the University of Tennessee at Martin Library, and the numerous historical societies and libraries listed in the Bibliography greatly facilitated my research. A special note of thanks, however, must be given to Robert M. Kvasnicka and the personnel of the Social and Economic Records Division at the National Archives for bringing pertinent manuscript collections to my attention and for their continued interest in my research.

Herman J. Viola, director of the National Anthropological Archives, granted me access to his extensive collection of Thomas L. McKenney correspondence. The following scholars shared their research findings with me either by sending unpublished articles or reprints of their studies or through conversations: Francis Paul Prucha of Marquette University, Joseph C. Burke of Duquesne University, Arthur H. DeRosier, Jr., of East Tennessee State University, Reginald Horsman of the University of Wisconsin at Milwaukee, Robert A. Trennert, Jr., of Temple University, and James Van Hoeven of Central College in Pella, Iowa. Although my own approach to federal Indian policy does not necessarily coincide with theirs, I have benefited from their thoughtfulness.

Professor David S. Sparks, dean of the Graduate School of the

University of Maryland, directed an earlier version of this study as a doctoral dissertation. I am greatly indebted to him for his insightful commentary, warm support, guidance, and encouragement during the years that I have known him. Professors Richard T. Farrell, David Grimsted, and Whitman Ridgway of the University of Maryland and Professor Francis Paul Prucha of Marquette University read earlier drafts of this manuscript and offered many helpful suggestions. The comments of political scientist Theodore R. Mosch of the University of Tennessee at Martin helped considerably to improve chapters 6 and 7. My understanding of the social-science concepts utilized throughout this study owes much to sociologist Paul J. Baker of Illinois State University and anthropologist Choong S. Kim of the University of Tennessee at Martin. Latin Americanists Winthrop Wright, Donald Giffin, and J. Benedict Warren of the University of Maryland broadened my understanding of race relations in the Americas.

My research has also been aided by financial assistance from two sources. The history department of the University of Maryland provided a fellowship in 1970 which permitted me to devote my full time to research at the National Archives and the Library of Congress. A Ford Foundation Fellowship in ethnic studies in 1971 made it possible for me to have access to manuscript collections outside the Washington, D.C., area.

I am indebted to Algis Ruksenas, Jim Carner, and Morris Solomon for their stimulating company during my days at Illinois State University and the University of Maryland. A special note of thanks is due my departmental chairman, Harry M. Hutson, and my colleagues at the University of Tennessee at Martin for their interest, comradeship, and encouragement during the various stages of the preparation of the manuscript. The students in my frontier history, middle period, Indian history, and minority history courses at the University of Maryland and the University of Tennessee at Martin contributed to this undertaking by challenging my ideas and by raising questions that led me to investigate additional areas of federal Indian policy.

Several cheerful, patient, and diligent women have helped me prepare this manuscript for publication. Early drafts were typed by my wife, Christa G. Satz, and Isabel R. McDonald, Leah Morris, and Wanda Vowell. The entire final draft was painstakingly prepared by Pat Williams. The secondary sources section of the Bibliography was carefully rechecked for accuracy by Kitty Cashion. I am grateful to all of the above for their contributions. Finally, I wish to express my deepest thanks and appreciation to the six very special people to whom this book is dedicated.

RONALD N. SATZ

University of Tennessee at Martin

Introduction

BETWEEN 1789 and 1829 the United States government managed to avoid confronting some of the most vexing and embarrassing legal, political, and moral problems of Indian-white relations. The executive department claimed the exclusive right to treat with the Indians, and Indian affairs were managed by War Department personnel in Washington and in the field. Anxious to placate settlers and speculators whose ever increasing demands for Indian land could not be ignored, government officials used force, bribery, deception, and threats, among other things, to convince Indian leaders to sign land cession treaties. By acknowledging tribal sovereignty to ratify formal purchases of land, the government found a convenient means of justifying its dispossession of the Indians. The purpose of the treaty-making process was to benefit the national interest without staining the nation's honor. Since the Indians generally responded to the pressure of advancing white population by emigrating farther west, there was little reason for officials to question the soundness of federal policy, even though the irresistible thrust of white settlement during the early 1800s was making a mockery of the treaty-making process.[1]

At the same time that the federal government was attempting to open Indian land east of the Mississippi River to white settlement, it was sponsoring attempts to "civilize" and assimilate such

1

eastern tribes as the Cherokees, Chickasaws, and Choctaws. The motivation behind these efforts was twofold. First, they expressed the sincere humanitarian desire of some government officials to bring the Indians the benefits of white society and to absorb them into that society. Secondly, they represented the deep-felt need of many citizens to put American expansion and dispossession of the Indians on a firm moral base by endeavoring to prepare the tribesmen for assimilation within American society while simultaneously relieving them of their land. Despite government attempts to civilize the Indians, the underlying assumption of American Indian policy was that the eastern tribes would continue to relinquish their land at approximately the same rate that whites demanded it. Civilizing the Indians for their assimilation into American society never took precedence over pushing them outside the area of white settlement; it merely justified it.[2]

By the 1820s, however, a new set of conditions brought about the need for a reevaluation of federal policy. Government-sponsored efforts to civilize the Indians began paying significant dividends during the decade. Several of the southern tribes, especially the Cherokees, benefited from these efforts and adopted many of the visible symbols of white society. Contact between these Indians and missionaries, government agents, and traders had led to the growth of a sizable population of mixed-bloods who frequently acted as intermediaries between their less sophisticated tribesmen and white Americans. Along with the accouterments of an agricultural economy and society, these mixed-bloods picked up concepts of property similar to the white man's and became owners of plantations, mills, and trading establishments. All of these factors, combined with the Indian's understandable nostalgic desire to remain on the land where his ancestors died, stimulated a growing resistance to additional land cessions. Thus the federal government found itself pursuing two goals simultaneously, with success in achieving one likely to impair fulfillment of the other.[3]

The Cherokees provide an outstanding example of the success of federal efforts to civilize the Indians. They had deliberately embarked on a program to adopt many of the patterns of white society in order to earn respect as a civilized nation and thereby preserve their tribal integrity and land against further white encroachment. Their efforts culminated in 1827 in the adoption of a written constitution modeled after the American Constitution. This document proclaimed the Cherokees an independent nation with complete sovereignty over tribal land in Georgia, North Carolina, Tennessee, and Alabama. While the federal government's recognition of Indian sovereignty had previously served as a convenient device for obtaining land cessions, the Cherokee Nation announced it would use its sovereignty to prohibit such actions in the future.[4]

The Cherokee Nation's declaration of its absolute sovereignty within southern states came at an extremely inopportune time. The John Quincy Adams administration had already quarreled with state officials in Georgia over their insistence on the immediate removal of the Creek Indians. Georgia officials had charged the federal government with reneging on its 1802 agreement to extinguish all remaining Indian title as soon as possible in return for the state's cession of its western land claims. The pact with Georgia conflicted with one made a decade earlier with the Cherokees which "solemnly guaranteed" them their existing tribal land. The government had reaffirmed its promise to these Indians as late as 1798. As years went by and the government took no action to fulfill its promise to Georgia, the state's political leaders decided to take the matter into their own hands.[5]

State officials in Georgia had long considered the Indians as mere "dependent tenants" subject to the will of the state, and they received added encouragement in this belief from Supreme Court Chief Justice John Marshall. In a well-publicized majority opinion in 1823, Marshall ruled that the Indians held their land by "right of occupancy" which was subordinate to the "right of discovery" that the United States had inherited from the British. The Cherokee Constitution of 1827 presented the threat of an *imperium in imperio* and was anathema to Georgia officials. Disgusted with President Adams's refusal to force the Indians to abandon their land and deeply angered by the intransigence of the Cherokees, the Georgia state legislature decreed on December 20, 1828, that all Indian residents would come under its jurisdiction after six months.[6]

Southerners in eastern Alabama, northern Mississippi, western North Carolina, southern Tennessee, and the territory of Florida closely followed the actions of Georgia. Residents of these areas eagerly sought the Indian land adjoining their communities for settlement, mineral deposits, and extension of their cotton culture. Some also had another important reason for seeking the removal of the Indians. Since the early 1800s, the flight of fugitive slaves into Indian country, especially in Florida, had constantly plagued southern plantation owners. The Seminoles and a few other Indian groups as well repeatedly refused to return fugitives, and the runaways themselves chose to remain with their more humane Indian masters. Petitions continually poured into Congress and the executive departments for the recovery of fugitives residing in Indian country, but the legal procedure for securing their return was cumbersome and costly. When frustrated plantation owners took action into their own hands, the result frequently was great bloodshed. A large number of southerners viewed the presence of fugitive slaves or stolen slave property in Indian country within their state or territory as a serious threat to internal security. Such havens for discontented blacks posed the danger of possible Indian-black cooperation against adjacent white communities at a time when northern abolitionist propaganda was causing great concern among segments of southern society. The extension of state law over tribes residing in the South would permit strict control of the Indians and, according to some politicians, would enable the region to increase its representation in Congress, thereby helping to offset northern antislavery votes.[7]

Many southerners were bitterly outraged when the Adams administration refused to comply with Georgia's demand for the immediate removal of the Indians and threatened to use the army to protect the tribesmen. Some southerners warned that if the federal government could defend the existence of Indian "nations" within states it could also interfere in the internal affairs of the slave states and emancipate slaves. President Adams was especially suspect by southerners since he had close ties with abolitionists and other "zealous bigots and fanatics in the free states." A serious constitutional crisis was at hand by the end of 1828.[8]

Before leaving office, Adams and leading members of his cabinet agreed that removing the Indians to the trans-Mississippi West was the only feasible solution to the critical situation confronting the nation. Adams, following the advice of his able Secretary of War Peter B. Porter, recommended exchanging uninhabited land

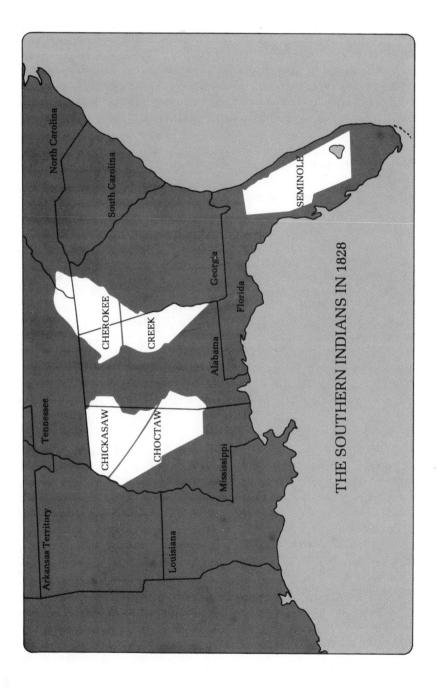

THE SOUTHERN INDIANS IN 1828

west of Arkansas and Missouri for eastern Indian land on a voluntary basis. This was not a novel plan.[9]

Virtually every American president since the formation of the government had seriously considered the feasibility of transferring the Indians to areas outside the geographical limits of the United States. George Washington envisioned a "Chinese wall" to keep whites and Indians apart. Thomas Jefferson, after the Louisiana Purchase in 1803, contemplated making a permanent exchange of vacant land in the newly acquired area for Indian land in the East. James Madison considered similar measures in his effort to pacify the Indians after the War of 1812. John C. Calhoun, James Monroe's talented secretary of war, was a strong advocate of Indian removal and convinced Monroe to adopt the policy in 1825.[10]

The idea of removing eastern Indians to a permanent location in the West also had the support of such enlightened figures in the 1820s as Calvinist clergyman Jedidiah Morse, Baptist missionary Isaac McCoy, and novelist James Fenimore Cooper. Generally, these men favored a policy of negotiation which respected the tribes' right to ratify or to refuse to sign removal treaties. It was this approach to removal, recommended by Adams, which brought the federal government into disrepute in Georgia and her sister states in the South prior to the election of Andrew Jackson.[11]

NOTES

1. Joseph R. Hayden, *The Senate and Treaties, 1789–1817: The Development of the Treaty-Making Functions of the United States Senate during Their Formative Period* (New York: Macmillan Co., 1920), pp. 1, 4, 11–39, 103; Reginald Horsman, "American Indian Policy and the Origins of Manifest Destiny," *University of Birmingham Historical Journal* [England] 11 (1968): 131–37.

2. *Warrenton Reporter* (North Carolina), October 4, 1825; R. S. Cotterill, *The Southern Indians: The Story of the Civilized Tribes Before Removal* (Norman: University of Oklahoma Press, 1954), pp. 225–26; Horsman, "American Indian Policy," pp. 131–37. For the meaning of the concept of *civilization* in its Jacksonian-era context, see chapter 9.

3. Cotterill, *Southern Indians,* pp. 223–30; Mary E. Young, "Indian Removal and Land Allotment: The Civilized Tribes and Jacksonian Justice," *American Historical Review* 64 (October 1958): 32–33; Alexander Spoehr, "Changing Kinship Systems: A Study in the Acculturation of the

Creeks, Cherokee, and Choctaw," Field Museum of Natural History, *Anthropological Series* 33 (January 1947): 221–22, 224–25.

4. Henry T. Malone, *Cherokees of the Old South: A People in Transition* (Athens: University of Georgia Press, 1956), pp. 57–173; Constitution of the Cherokee Nation, July 26, 1827, enclosed in John Forsyth to President Adams, January 26, 1828, Records of the Office of Indian Affairs, Letters Received, Cherokee Agency East, Record Group 75, National Archives, Washington, D.C. (hereafter cited as IA, LR or LS, RG 75, NA); *Niles' Weekly Register* 33 (January 19, 1828): 346 (hereafter cited as *Niles' Register*); Wilson Lumpkin, *The Removal of the Cherokee Indians from Georgia*, 2 vols. (New York: Dodd, Mead & Co., 1907), 1: 42–43.

5. Ulrich Bonnell Phillips, *Georgia and States' Rights: A Study of the Political History of Georgia from the Revolution to the Civil War, with Particular Regard to Federal Relations* (Washington, D.C.: Government Printing Office, 1908), pp. 34–35, 48–72; *Warrenton Reporter*, October 4, 1825; James D. Richardson, comp., *A Compilation of the Messages and Papers of the Presidents*, 10 vols. (Washington, D.C.: GPO, 1896–99), 2: 370–73, 415–16; Samuel Flagg Bemis, *John Quincy Adams and the Union* (New York: Alfred A. Knopf, 1956), pp. 79–87. For the agreement with Georgia and the treaties mentioned above, see Articles of Agreement and Cession, April 24, 1802, in Clarence E. Carter and John P. Bloom, comps. and eds., *The Territorial Papers of the United States*, 27 vols. to date (Washington, D.C.: GPO, 1944–[69]), 5: 142–46; Charles J. Kappler, ed., *Indian Affairs: Laws and Treaties*, 3 vols. (Washington, D.C.: GPO, 1892–1913), 2: 24, 40. Adams's views on Indian policy are discussed in the following article which appeared after this book was completed: Lynn Hudson Parsons, " 'A Perpetual Harrow Upon My Feelings': John Quincy Adams and the American Indian," *New England Quarterly* 46 (September 1973): 339–79.

6. *Johnson and Graham's Lessee* v. *William McIntosh*, 8 Wheaton 543 (1823): 587–91; *Niles' Register* 24 (March 8, 1823): 3, 25 (November 29, 1828): 222; Georgia Congressional Delegation to President Monroe, March 10, 1824, in *Georgia Journal* (Milledgeville), April 20, 1824; Resolutions of the Legislature of Georgia [December 1827], U.S., Senate, *Document 80*, 20th Cong., 1st sess., pp. 3–13; Charles Francis Adams, ed., *Memoirs of John Quincy Adams*, 12 vols. (Philadelphia: J. B. Lippincott & Co., 1874–77), 6: 255, 258, 262, 373, 7: 102, 136, 231–32; Georgia, State Legislature, *A Compilation of the Laws of Georgia Passed Between 1820 and 1829* (Milledgeville: Camack & Rayland, Printers, 1830), p. 198.

7. Governor of Georgia to General Gaines, February 5, 1817, George Perryman to Lieutenant Sands, February 24, 1817, Talk to the Creeks by Georgia Commissioners, December 29, 1820, Secretary of War Barbour to Delegation of Florida Indians, May 10, 1826, U.S., Congress, *American*

State Papers: Indian Affairs, 2 vols. (Washington, D.C.: Gales & Seaton, 1832–34), 2: 107, 155, 253, 698; W. Ward to Governor of Mississippi, January 16, 1826, January 1, 1827, Governors' Records, Mississippi Department of Archives and History, Jackson, Miss.; J. C. Mitchell to Barbour, May 1, 1827, IA, LR, Misc., RG 75, NA; Thomas L. McKenney to James A. Everett, June 8, 1829, same to David R. Mitchell, July 6, 1829, July 6, 1830, IA, LS, 6:1–2, 38, 495–96, RG 75, NA; *Senate Journal,* 21st Cong., 1st sess., p. 84; Alvin L. Duckett, *John Forsyth, Political Tactician* (Athens: University of Georgia Press, 1962), pp. 116–17. For additional references to the southern fear of Indian-black cooperation, see Ronald N. Satz, "Federal Indian Policy, 1829–1849" (Ph.D. diss., University of Maryland, 1972), p. 7 n–8 n.

8. *Warrenton Reporter,* July 8, August 16, October 4, 7, 1825; *Nashville Whig,* July 9, September 10, 1825; Richardson, *Papers of the Presidents,* 2: 415–16. James W. Silver, in his biography of *Edmund Pendleton Gaines: Frontier General* (Baton Rouge: Louisiana State University Press, 1949), p. 129, refers to the situation in Georgia as "a crisis between nationalism and localism which, though relatively unnoticed by historians, was hardly less grave than the later nullification controversy between the Federal government and South Carolina." Also see *Niles' Register* 29 (September 10, 1825):17–18.

9. Richardson, *Papers of the Presidents,* 2: 416; U.S., Secretary of War, *Annual Report* (1828), pp. 21–22; U.S., *Statutes at Large,* 4: 315 (hereafter cited as U.S., *Stat.*); Bemis, *Adams and the Union,* pp. 62, 84. Adams was willing to withdraw federal support from Indian missionary establishments in the East in order to encourage removal. See Annie H. Abel, "The History of Events Resulting in Indian Consolidation West of the Mississippi," *American Historical Association, Annual Report for the Year 1906* 1 (1908): 368–69; Richardson, *Papers of the Presidents,* 2: 416.

10. Washington to Secretary of State, July 1, 1796, in John C. Fitzpatrick, ed., *The Writings of George Washington from the Original Manuscript Sources, 1745–1799,* 39 vols. (Washington, D.C.: GPO, 1931–44), 35: 112; Abel, "Indian Consolidation West of the Mississippi," 241–343.

11. Jedidiah Morse, *A Report to the Secretary of War of the United States, on Indian Affairs, Comprising a Narrative of a Tour Performed in the Summer of 1820* (New Haven: S. Converse, 1822), pp. 82–83; *American Baptist Magazine* 6 (March 1826): 92, 9 (February 1829): 65; Isaac McCoy, *Remarks on the Practicability of Indian Reform, Embracing Their Colonization* (Boston: Lincoln & Edmands, 1827 and 2d ed., New York: Graz & Bunce, 1829); Albert Keiser, *The Indian in American Literature* (New York: Oxford University Press, 1933), p. 142.

1 /

Old Hickory Takes Command

THE GAUNT OLD GENERAL who entered the White House in March, 1829, had fixed views on Indian policy and sedulously employed the full powers of the presidency to have them adopted as federal law. The tremendous energy and perseverance Andrew Jackson expended in Indian affairs, however, was apparently not related to any feelings of animosity toward the Indians. Jackson was not the merciless Indian-hater most historians have portrayed. Although he was a ruthless opponent in battle, Old Hickory demonstrated great paternalism in his dealings with the Indians as territorial governor of Florida. He also openly sanctioned Indian-white marriages, adopted an Indian orphan, whom he treated as his own son, and counted hundreds of full-bloods as personal friends. Jackson was not an admirer of what he termed the "erratic" ways of Indian life, but his views on Indian policy were not governed so much by any personal negative attitude toward the Indians as by his overwhelming concern for the nation's growth, unity, and security.[1]

Old Hickory's policy toward the Indians was a natural corollary of his conception of the nature of the American Union and its needs. Upholding the old Republican doctrine of state sovereignty, Jackson envisioned the federal government as one of severely limited powers. Yet he was also a fervent nationalist. His synthesis of these two positions provided the theoretical base for his Indian policy. One of the most vital aspects of that synthesis was Jackson's vision of Americans from every state and territory in the Union indissolubly bound together in a common destiny unfolding before them by expansion across the continent without direction from the federal government. Jackson's fusion of nationalism and states' rights, however, left ample room for the use of the federal government to remove impediments to the fulfillment of the great destiny awaiting the nation. The southern tribes, according to the new president, constituted such an obstacle.[2]

During the fifteen years preceding his election to the presidency, Jackson had witnessed firsthand what he considered the contradictions and foibles of federal Indian policy. The government had frequently called upon him, in his role as an army officer and territorial governor during the years following the War of 1812, to aid in the negotiation of treaties and to remove white intruders from Indian lands. Jackson came to view the entire treaty-making process and the federal obligations stemming from it as "an absurdity" and anachronism.[3]

Years of experience in Indian affairs led Jackson to the position that the Indians had only a "possessory right" to the land they lived on and were thereby subject to American sovereignty. American "national security" demanded the removal of the Indians outside the nation's geographical limits in order to provide "a connexion of our territory by the possession of their claims" and to improve the defensive posture of the lower Mississippi Valley against any incursions by foreign powers. While he conceded that the government should never perpetrate "acts of injustice" against the Indians, he was even more concerned that it "should not heap injustice on herself and her own people." The problem, as he saw it, was to devise a plan whereby the government could provide for "justice to the Citizen, the interest and security of the United States, and the peace and happiness of the Indians."[4]

Jackson's solution to this vexing dilemma was a plan he formally introduced in his negotiations with the Cherokees in 1817. First, the Indians had to emigrate outside the boundaries of all states in the Union. This measure would prevent the anomaly of tribal governments existing within sovereign states. The Indians would receive permanent title to tracts of land in the trans-Mississippi

West in exchange for their eastern land. Secondly, those Indians desiring to remain in the East would receive individual allotments of land and become citizens of the states in which they resided. Jackson thought only a few of the most educated and property-minded mixed-bloods would choose to stay in the East, and they would have to acknowledge the superiority of state laws, thereby ending the necessity and contradictions of treaty making. Old Hickory asserted that these steps would consolidate the western frontier by opening vast areas of land to white settlement and benefit the Indian as well.[5]

Jackson argued that the Indians could only find peace and happiness across the Mississippi River. There the federal government would "circumscribe their bounds, put into their hands the utensils of husbandry, yield them protection, and enforce obedience to those just laws provided for their benefit, and in a short time they will be civilized." Jackson even went so far as to call for the consolidation of the southern tribes in the West, with the possibility of their becoming "a member of the United States, as Alabama and Mississippi are" after their children received sufficient education.[6]

President Monroe referred to Jackson's detailed plan as "very deserving of attention," and its outlines were readily discernible in the former's official announcement of the removal policy in 1825. In any event, Jackson had formulated what he considered a coherent policy to end the troublesome controversy between the southern states and the federal government over Indians. The seriousness of the clash between Georgia and the Adams administration only reaffirmed Jackson's dedication to these proposals.[7]

Jackson's enthusiastic support for Indian removal was undoubtedly one of the reasons he swept the southern states in the 1828 election. Following his election but preceding his inauguration, the legislatures in Georgia, Alabama, and Mississippi passed acts calling for the extension of state laws over the Indians in their midst. Politicians in these states hoped this action would disrupt tribal government and force the Indians to emigrate.[8]

Unlike his predecessors, Jackson entered the presidency facing a grave crisis in Indian-white relations. He had, of course, contributed to the growing tension by encouraging southerners with his proremoval rhetoric. Jackson hoped, however, to bring a quick end to the controversy. The president believed that the uncompromising positions of the southern states and the Indians would end in bloody conflict if the federal government did not mediate the dispute. Whereas Monroe and Adams had postponed taking any definite action during their administrations, Jackson had to act immediately in large part because he had helped to aggravate the situation by his position on Indian removal. The president was also aware that opposition to Indian tribes claiming sovereignty within their borders, the "abominable" tariff of 1828, and the mounting invective of northern abolitionists were causing southern states like Georgia and South Carolina to assume a belligerent character that could pose a dire threat to his beloved Union and undermine the southern wing of the Democratic coalition which had propelled him into office.[9]

Jackson's first official response to the growing agitation over the issue of the southern Indians came in his inaugural address in March, 1829. He told the enthusiastic partisan crowd assembled before him on the capitol grounds that "it will be my sincere and constant desire to observe toward the Indian tribes within our limits a just and liberal policy, and to give that humane and considerate attention to their rights and their wants which is consistent with the habits of our Government and the feelings of our people." This statement, together with the appointment of John H. Eaton, a Tennessee advocate of Indian removal, as secretary of war and John M. Berrien of Georgia, an advocate of removal and a staunch opponent of the tariff, as attorney general brought a brief respite from southern intransigence for the new administration.[10]

The president lost little time in maneuvering to secure widespread support of his views on Indian policy. He had little time to spare. Legislation approved in Georgia, Alabama, and Mississippi that extended state jurisdiction over the Indians would soon go into effect and tie the government's hands. At the same time, the Cherokees in Georgia were asserting their sovereignty with new boldness that infuriated southern politicians.[11]

A few weeks after his inauguration, Jackson urged the Creeks and Cherokees to abandon their eastern land and move outside the limits of the United States. He offered these tribes what he considered extremely generous terms. The federal government would reimburse them for all improvements on their old land, compensate them for any lost stock, grant allotments or reservations to those willing to remain in the East under state law, and place the Indians who moved to the West under its "paternal, and superintending care." Jackson warned these southern tribes that they would find no solace if they remained on their old land and continued their pretensions to sovereignty. "The arms of this country can never be employed, to stay any state of this Union, from the exercise of those legitimate powers which attach, and belong to their sovereign character," he told them. Following this forthright statement, Jackson sent his old friend William Carroll to Georgia to arouse sympathy among the Indians for removal. Carroll, an active gubernatorial candidate in Tennessee, had considerable influence among the southern Indians. Jackson asked him to seek out the men "upon whom, as pivots, the will of the Cherokees and Creeks turns" and convince them of the need to emigrate. The president also cautioned Georgia Congressman Wiley Thompson that intrusions upon Indian land would only aggravate the situation and impede the government's efforts to encourage the tribes to leave Georgia.[12]

The leaders of the Creeks and Cherokees responded to the president's exhortation with a reiteration of their steadfast refusal to abandon their native soil. The reaction of the American public, however, had a more important impact on the administration. Jackson's "talks" to the two tribes provoked an immediate challenge from numerous humanitarian groups, mostly in the Northeast, who saw themselves as the defenders of their beleaguered "red brothers" in the South.[13]

At the forefront of this vocal opposition was a prestigious benevolent association, the American Board of Commissioners for Foreign Missions. This Boston-centered missionary society, comprised largely of Congregationalists and Presbyterians, was the leading recipient of the federal funds allocated for civilizing the Indians. It used legal, moral, and religious arguments in defending the right of the Indians to remain unmolested on their ancestral land. The American Board received support for its attack on the president's position from humanitarian groups throughout the North which stressed the Indians' treaty rights to remain on their land and also from anti-Jackson politicians who feared Indian removal was a partisan move to "conciliate the South" while "propitiating the West." Both groups argued that Jackson's approach would stain the nation's honor.[14]

The vocal opposition to his "talks" with the Indians led Jackson to seek influential allies. He realized he could not afford to allow all the voices of religion and moral righteousness to speak out against his Indian policy at a time when his opponents were feverishly trying to undermine the coalition that had elected him. Jackson had won strong backing in 1828 from church groups, excluding the more conservative ones, and he sought to maintain that support by molding public opinion in favor of Indian removal. The president assigned that formidable task to Thomas L. McKenney.[15]

McKenney, one of the best-informed men in the country on Indian affairs and an acknowledged humanitarian, was a logical choice for the job. He had served as superintendent of Indian trade between 1816 and 1822 and became head of the Bureau of Indian Affairs in 1824. He was one of the members of the Adams administration who agreed that removal was the only means to promote the best interests of the eastern Indians and to assure their tribal integrity and prosperity. McKenney had accomplished a great deal for the betterment of the Indians during his tenure in the Indian Bureau and his reputation as a friend of the Indian was well established. At the same time, his preference for Adams in the election of 1828 and his earlier support for Calhoun in 1824 made McKenney eager to please the new president in order to secure his position within the administration. Jackson shrewdly took advantage of these circumstances and encouraged McKenney to court the nation's leading religious spokesmen and to persuade them of the virtues of the administration's Indian policy.[16]

A month after Jackson entered the White House, McKenney appealed to a leading New York clergyman, Episcopalian Bishop John H. Hobart, for a public endorsement of Indian removal. He asked Hobart to consider establishing a religious association that would promote removal as a step toward preserving the Indians. McKenney observed that such an organization could arouse public opinion in favor of the measure by pressuring Congress to support it. It could also promote interest among the Indians themselves by sending emissaries to the several tribes. Despite McKenney's vigorous defense of the removal policy outlined by Jackson and his eloquent plea for assistance, Bishop Hobart refused to take any initiative in the matter. This did not, however, deter McKenney.[17]

Early in May he launched a full-scale assault on the critics of the removal policy. He began by taking an open stand against the position of the prestigious American Board and its spokesmen. Next, he contacted Stephen Van Rensselaer, president of the Missionary Society of the Dutch Reformed Church and one of the wealthiest and most prominent men in New York, and tried to win him over to Indian removal as a humanitarian measure. McKenney told Van Rensselaer that "I am now convinced that our Indians can be saved; but there is not a moment to be lost," for "the *crisis* has arrived." The crisis, according to McKenney, was that "the General Government *will not* interfere (nor should it) to prevent the states from extending their laws over the Indians within them." Only two alternatives remained. "They must remove," he warned, "or perish!" McKenney permitted nothing, including his own frail health during the next several months, to interfere with his efforts to persuade Van Rensselaer and other prominent church leaders to advocate Indian removal.[18]

Working in close liaison with members of the Dutch Missionary Society, McKenney began organizing what came to be known as the New York Board for the Emigration, Preservation, and Improvement of the Aborigines of America. McKenney helped to create and direct the board with the specific "*understood invitation of the Executive.*" Federally subsidized out of the annual appropriation for civilizing the Indians, the board's sole purpose was to arouse a ground swell of religious support for Indian removal as a Christian policy before the opening of the Twenty-first Congress in December. As a center for disseminating propaganda, the board was to ensure, as Jackson put it in his inaugural address, that the "feelings of our people" on Indian removal matched the "habits of our Government."[19]

The New York Indian Board officially convened on July 22, 1829, and selected Stephen Van Rensselaer as its president. Its membership included representatives of the Dutch, Episcopalian, and Presbyterian churches. McKenney traveled to New York at government expense to supervise the organizational activities and the drafting of a constitution. He cheerfully reported back to Washington that the board comprised a "hotbed" of "the most thoroghgoing Jacksonites in the nation." At McKenney's prompting, the religious leaders drafted a constitution proclaiming that "this Board is pledged to cooperate with the Federal Government of the United States, in its operations in Indian Affairs; and at no time to contravene its laws." Consistent with the administration's position, the board acknowledged its support for the emigration, preservation, and improvement of the Indians with the explicit statement that only emigration could bring preservation and improvement. McKenney confidently advised Secretary of War Eaton that the board's actions would be "wide & deep—& will be a *shield & buckler* in the future."[20]

At a public meeting of the board on August 12, possibly attended by as many as six hundred people, McKenney presented what one Democratic editor called an "eloquent and judicious address" reiterating his position that removal was a humanitarian policy. An antiremoval editor, who suggested that the well-meaning head of the Indian Bureau was not aware of the administration's nefarious designs, conceded that the speech was one of "Humanity and Justice." McKenney, however, was eager to lend his reputation and rhetorical ability to the new administration's policies, and he worked hard to protect the new board from "all liability of being *imputed* as being a political machine."[21]

McKenney remained in New York to read the proofs of the board's proceedings. He wrote officials in Washington and secured federal funds originally allocated for Indian education to pay the expense of publishing approximately two thousand copies of a forty-eight-page tract which included the board's proceedings, the "talks" to the southern tribes, and his own address. This publication contained the first comprehensive public statement of Jacksonian Indian policy. Confident that he had helped to create an invaluable propaganda tool for the administration, McKenney wrote Secretary of War Eaton that "I think the blow is struck that will silence all opposers upon this branch of the clamors of the day." He boasted that "this sort of machinery can move the world."[22]

The New York Indian Board continued to operate after the publication of the government-financed pamphlet. McKenney arranged to have it openly solicit the president's views on Indian affairs. The plan was to provide Jackson with an opportunity to make a public statement that religious leaders on the board would warmly receive as a righteous and noble reply. McKenney was confident that this would leave "no grounds" for opponents of removal.[23]

The board also undertook other action to "make the billows roll the other way!" It furnished Democratic editors with notes concerning its proceedings, while the official organ of the Dutch church published articles extolling the virtues of the board's activities and the administration's policy. The board drafted a memorial for Congress which it sent to McKenney for his "inspection and free corrections, curtailments and emandations." It also prepared to undertake an extensive lobbying effort in Washington. While all these activities were going on, Lewis Cass, an ardent Jacksonian Democrat with sixteen years of experience in Indian affairs as territorial governor of Michigan, brought the board's activities and endorsement of removal before a wide audience in an unsigned article in the influential *North American Review,* published in Boston.[24]

The New York Indian Board proved a valuable ally to advocates of removal, but the administration desperately needed to enlist additional supporters. The antiremoval American Board was too influential a body to be offset by the New York Board. Jackson's political adversaries, moreover, were providing extensive press coverage for a series of articles designed to expose the "gull-trap" of McKenney and the New York Indian Board by demonstrating the legal right of the southern Indians to remain on their ancestral lands. Jeremiah Evarts, a Congregationalist leader and corresponding secretary of the American Board, writing under the pseudonym William Penn, was denouncing Indian removal as an attempt "to *drive* the Indians, by *force,* from their country." The wide circulation given his pithy essays, which began appearing in the *National Intelligencer* one week after the formation of the New York Indian Board, made it imperative for Jackson to step up his campaign for Indian removal.[25]

The administration found additional support primarily among the Baptists, who had a large southern and western membership. The Reverend Isaac McCoy had relentlessly pressured the Baptist General Convention into endorsing Indian removal. In May, 1829, McCoy began an eight-month campaign swing throughout the East Coast to win support for the measure. The *Columbian Star and Christian Index,* a popular Baptist magazine published in

Philadelphia by the Reverend W. T. Brantley, supported McCoy's effort. In addition to the work of the Baptists, the administration encouraged such diverse groups as the Moravians and the Methodists to speak out in favor of moving the Indians to a western haven. President Jackson was determined to use every available means in promoting widespread acceptance of his Indian policy.[26]

The discovery of gold in northeastern Georgia in the summer of 1829 added new complications to the controversy by bringing swarms of whites into the area claimed by the Cherokees. This invasion of Cherokee land aroused a ground swell of indignation in the North. Many religious groups joined Jeremiah Evarts and other anti-Jacksonites in demanding that the federal government protect the tribesmen from white intruders.[27]

President Jackson moved cautiously. He had already informed several southern governors that he shared their views on the Indian question. The War Department sent special agents to the southern tribes to encourage proremoval sentiment. At the same time, however, in compliance with existing federal law, the War Department issued orders to the army to remove all intruders from Indian country. Soldiers were to tell white squatters that, if necessary, they would be "forcibly removed, and their Cabins destroyed." Jackson wanted relations with the southern Indians to remain "quiet and peaceful" until the New York Indian Board and similar organizations could build sufficient public support for removal.[28]

One way in which the president tried to temper the increasingly volatile situation was to keep channels open with key southern leaders. Speaking in behalf of Jackson, Secretary of War Eaton cautioned the governor of Georgia that "any thing which might wear now the appearance of harshness towards the Indians, might have a tendency to drive [them] back from the course the Government are endeavoring to pursue." Such actions would only offset the work of the New York Indian Board and lead to additional "opposition and difficulty" in pushing removal. Eaton urged Georgia officials to do everything in their power to "unite with the Federal Government in avoiding even an appearance of practiced injustice towards the uncultivated and unhappy children of the forest."[29]

The opening of the Twenty-first Congress in December, 1829, presented the administration with its first opportunity to secure legislation promoting Indian removal. The efforts of the New York Board, the Baptists, and other sympathetic religious groups made administration leaders confident that there would be a favorable response to a presidential request for legislation calling for the relocation of the Indians. Jackson used his first annual message to Congress as a vehicle for outlining and winning support for his position on this issue.

Speaking from "the most deeply rooted convictions" of his mind, Jackson informed Congress that "I can not . . . too strongly or too earnestly . . . warn you against all encroachments upon the legitimate sphere of State sovereignty." While the president was anxious to preserve "this much-injured race" of Indians, he could only act "consistently with the rights of the States." Whatever the original reason for including Indian tribes within the boundaries of states and territories, the federal government could not permit a "foreign and independent government" to establish itself within a member of the Union.[30]

Jackson also used another line of reasoning to buttress his Indian policy. Minimizing the impressive cultural and agricultural advances of the Cherokees and other southern tribes, he called the Indians hunters and wanderers who had no right to "tracts of country on which they have neither dwelt nor made improvements, merely because they have seen them from the mountain or passed them in the chase." While extolling the virtues of the superior American society of cultivators, the president lamented that "surrounded by the whites with their arts of civilization, which by destroying the resources of the savage doom him to weakness and decay, the fate of the Mohegan, the Narragansett, and the Delaware [of the East] is fast overtaking the Choctaw, the Cherokee, and the Creek." To avert "so great a calamity," he proposed a policy of Indian removal "actuated by feelings of justice and a regard for our national honor."[31]

The president asked Congress for "an ample district west of the Mississippi, and without the limits of any State or Territory now formed, to be guaranteed to the Indian tribes as long as they shall occupy it, each tribe having a distinct control over the portion designated for its use." The Indians would have "governments of their own choice, subject to no other control from the United States than such as may be necessary to preserve peace on the frontier and between the several tribes." Across the Mississippi River, "the benevolent may endeavor to teach them the arts of civilization, and, by promoting union and harmony among them, to raise up an interesting commonwealth, destined to perpetuate the race and to attest the humanity and justice of this Government." Any Indians refusing to emigrate voluntarily would come under state jurisdiction for, by "submitting to the laws of the States, and receiving, like other citizens, protection in their persons and property, they will ere long become merged in the mass of our population."³²

These recommendations immediately became the subject of intense partisan warfare. While the administration, as expected, received support from the New York Indian Board, the Baptists, and the Dutch church, as well as from residents of the South and the Old Northwest, there was an avalanche of vehement opposition from the East, inspired by Jeremiah Evarts and the American Board of Commissioners for Foreign Missions. As Thomas McKenney observed, "the people, too many of them, seem to believe that it is merely a question of removal, a matter of policy to get rid of the Indians, of whom, when once rid, they are to be left where they may emigrate in all their ignorance, and to contend unassisted with all the calamities of the past." The administration also received a barrage of vitriolic criticism from its political opponents, who decried the government's "broken faith" with the Indians and urged religious leaders and the American people to flood Congress with petitions opposing removal. Such remonstrances began pouring into Congress before Democratic leaders could introduce legislation containing Jackson's proposals.³³

Immediately after the opening of the Twenty-first Congress, administration supporters began a concerted effort to enact into law President Jackson's proposals for large-scale Indian removal. Each house of the Democratic-controlled Congress referred the portion of the president's first annual message relating to the topic to its committee on Indian affairs. Democrats from Jackson's home state of Tennessee headed both committees. As early as February 22, Senator Hugh L. White reported out a bill from his committee calling for an exchange of land with all eastern tribes. John Bell introduced a similar proposal in the House of Representatives two days later. The long ensuing debate in both houses of Congress explored the constitutional and moral implications of Jackson's proposal and received widespread coverage in the nation's leading newspapers.[34]

White's bill was the main topic of discussion in the Senate from April 6, when it came up for debate, until the final vote was taken eighteen days later. The Tennessean, together with colleagues from Georgia and Mississippi, ably led the proremoval forces. Senator Theodore Frelinghuysen of New Jersey, a former president of the American Board of Commissioners for Foreign Missions, rallied the opponents of the bill.[35]

The debate in the Senate was quite spirited. Missouri Democrat Thomas Hart Benton called it "one of the closest, and most earnestly contested questions of the session." Benton, like most Jacksonians, claimed that Indian removal was "an old policy, but party spirit now took hold of it, and strenuously resisted the passage of the act." The Reverend Isaac McCoy, the leading Baptist proponent of Indian removal, agreed that the issue had really become "a test of the strength of the two great political parties." In any event, McCoy hurried to Washington to lobby for White's bill. At the same time, Jeremiah Evarts of the American Board was already hard at work in Washington circulating his William Penn essays and lining up opposition to the measure. Religious spokesmen as well as political leaders employed their skills in order to promote "right views" on the matter of Indian removal.[36]

On April 7, 1830, Theodore Frelinghuysen rose in the Senate and began a speech in opposition to White's bill that extended over three days and took six hours to complete. The eloquent rhetoric of this freshman senator from New Jersey moved abolitionist William Lloyd Garrison to write a poem praising him as a "Christian statesman." Frelinghuysen no doubt deserved the appellation, since he was a devout man with a long record of activity in humanitarian and religious reform, including Indian missionary work. The pious, fervently anti-Jackson senator undoubtedly envisioned his opposition to the Removal Bill as a way of promoting Christan benevolence for the Indians and simultaneously attacking what he referred to as Jacksonian hyprocrisy.[37]

Frelinghuysen's lengthy speech, reflecting the arguments of the William Penn essays of Jeremiah Evarts, upheld the right of the southern Indians to refuse to leave their ancestral homes. The senator voiced the feelings of his anti-Jackson colleagues when he cautioned that "the real object" of White's bill was "to remove all the Indian tribes beyond the Mississippi, or, in case of their refusal, to subject them to State sovereignty and legislation." The actual intent of the administration proposal, he warned, was to "rescind, modify, or explain away, our public treaties" with the Indians. Treaties granting tribes perpetual rights to their land were merely "plighted covenants" to those whose "insatiated cupidity" hungered for more Indian land "than we shall dispose of at the present rate to actual settlers in two hundred years."[38]

Senator Frelinghuysen particularly focused his attention on the Cherokee Indians and their struggle against the state of Georgia. He pointed out that the United States was bound by treaty stipulations to protect these Indians in "the exercise and enjoyment of their civil and political rights." Yet Georgia officials were proceeding to survey their "rich and ample districts" of land. Directly facing Senator White, Frelinghuysen asked, "Do the obligations of justice change with the color of the skin?" He turned then to his colleagues from the South: "Is it one of the prerogatives of the white man, that he may disregard the dictates of moral principles, when an Indian shall be concerned?" Frelinghuysen pleaded for the rejection of the "unwarrantable pretensions of Georgia" because the "rules of equity" demanded that "a rigid execution of the highest justice" be accorded the Cherokees, whose land title and sovereignty were recognized in "sacred" and "solemn" treaties.[39]

Frelinghuysen expressed utter dismay over the extension of Georgia law over the Cherokees. He pointed out that, "prompted and encouraged by our counsels, they have in good earnest resolved to become men, rational, educated, Christian men; and they have succeeded beyond our most sanguine hopes." Georgia, however, would nullify all of this. "We find," he said, "a whole people outlawed—laws, customs, rules, government, all, by one short clause, abrogated and declared to be void as if they never had been." Georgia's action was unprecedented. "History furnishes no example of such high handed usurpation," the senator

asserted, adding that "the dismemberment and partition of Poland was a deed of humane legislation compared with this." Warning that the passage of the Removal Bill would only encourage
Georgia and other southern states to continue "this disgraceful
system" to promote emigration, Frelinghuysen implored the Senate to uphold the treaty rights of the Indians. "Let us beware
how," he concluded, "by oppressive encroachments upon the sacred privileges of our Indian neighbors, we minister to the agonies
of future remorse."[40]

Anti-Jacksonite Peleg Sprague of Maine agreed with these arguments. Sprague echoed Frelinghuysen's contention that the passage of the measure would seal the fate of the southern tribes. He
especially feared that the Jackson administration would use any
appropriations attached to the bill either to pay for "glittering
bayonets" to intimidate the Indians or to pay for gifts to bribe
unscrupulous chiefs into disregarding the welfare of their people.
Sprague's fears stemmed from what he referred to as the bad faith
demonstrated by the Jackson administration. While the administration was promising the Indians a peaceful home in the trans-
Mississippi West, he argued, it was doing nothing to establish such
a utopia. The president was asking for authority to negotiate for
Indian removal but he was not making preparations for the subsistence or the security of the emigrants in their new homeland.
Only "gilded promises" were coming from the White House.[41]

Sprague's criticism of the Jackson administration was strongly
supported by an anti-Jackson colleague from Rhode Island. Ascher
Robbins, pretending to address himself to the Cherokee Nation,
asserted that the bill asked the Indians to "go far into the depths
of an unknown wilderness, there to abide the destiny which may
there await you, or to surrender your rights, and submit your-
selves" to the power of the states without enjoying the rights of
citizenship. In addition to the inequities that the passage of the bill
would bring, Robbins attacked the very constitutionality of the
proposal. Pointing out the government's long history of treaty
making with the Indians, he asserted that "if these Indian nations
are competent to make treaties, then this proposed law ... is
unconstitutional; for it is to make a treaty by the Legislature,
which can only be made by the Executive and Senate." For all of
these reasons, Robbins concurred with Sprague and Frelinghuy-

sen that the passage of the bill would bring "violated justice" and retribution from God.[42]

Supporters of the Removal Bill quickly responded to these attacks. John Forsyth, the former governor of Georgia, rose to defend the righteousness of Georgia's actions and White's bill. Forsyth, speaking just three months after the famous debate between Daniel Webster and Robert Hayne over the question of states' rights, suggested that his opponents' "zeal and industry in the Indian cause" stemmed from their eagerness to "arrest the progress of Georgia." While the Indians in New York and in New England were at the "tender mercies" of state governments, the southern tribes alone were singled out by opponents of the administration for protection against "anticipated oppressions." Forsyth argued that Indian removal was a necessary measure in order to dispose of a "useless and burthensome" people and to open new land to "survey, sale and settlement" for southern whites.[43]

To those whose humanitarianism led them to inquire as to the future fate of Indian emigrants, Forsyth made this pledge. "A race not admitted to be equal to the rest of the community; not governed as completely dependent; treated somewhat like human beings, but not admitted to be freemen; not yet entitled, and probably never to be entitled, to equal civil and political rights, will be humanely provided for" in the trans-Mississippi West. While "persons who have united, at this eleventh hour, in opposition to a project which has been steadily kept in view by three administrations" were filling the southern Indians with "vain hopes," the Indians had no alternative. The southern tribes "must remove, or remain and be subjected to the State laws, whenever the States choose to exercise their power." Georgia, following in the footsteps of New York and New England, would never "submit to the intrusive sovereignty of a petty tribe of Indians."[44]

Robert Adams of Mississippi agreed with Forsyth that every state had the right to "legislate over all of the population within her limits." Adams, moreover, charged that the opponents of the Removal Bill were unjustly maligning the intentions of its proponents. "The friends of this measure," he asserted, "do not wish to vest power in the President of the United States to assign [the Indians to] a district of country west of the Mississippi, and, by strong arm, to drive these unfortunate people from their present abode, and compel them to take up their residence in the country assigned to them." Adams claimed that he and other supporters of the bill only asked for "free and voluntary" removal. "I can see nothing in the provisions of the bill before us," he stated, "unbecoming the character of a great, just, and magnanimous nation."[45]

Senator Adams's arguments did little to persuade anti-Jacksonites that the Removal Bill would not lead to forced emigration of the southern tribes. David Barton of Missouri urged the adoption of amendments guaranteeing that neither secret negotiations nor intimidation would be used to secure the signing of removal treaties. Barton, who had bolted the Jacksonian faction in Missouri in 1824 to support Adams, stressed that he was not attempting to impugn the integrity or challenge the motivation of the Jackson administration. "It would be a feather in the cap of this administration," he argued, "to [declare], by a law, to govern all our public agents, President and Commissioners, that neither force, nor fraud, nor direct, secret bribery, shall be resorted to in acquiring the land of those helpless people, whose guardians we affect to be."[46]

On April 24, the last day of the debate on White's bill, opposition leaders Frelinghuysen and Sprague offered amendments to the measure designed to safeguard the rights of the southern Indians, should it pass. They wanted the government to openly acknowledge its obligation to protect the treaty rights of any Indians who might refuse to emigrate, and to guarantee those desiring to emigrate their perpetual right to any trans-Mississippi land granted them in exchange for their southern holdings, and, finally, to delay all removal operations until Congress had an opportunity to determine whether the proposed western sites were suitable to "the wants and habits of Indian nations." These amendments, however, were rejected by the Jacksonian majority. When the final vote was taken, White's bill passed by a margin of twenty-eight to nineteen. The voting pattern was overwhelmingly along party lines. The alignment of anti-Jackson men from Missouri and Ohio against Indian removal and of Democrats from New Hampshire, New Jersey, New York, and Pennsylvania for the measure suggests that propinquity to the frontier was not the decisive factor influencing senators from those states.[47]

John Bell's Indian removal bill had not come up for debate in the House by the time the Senate bill arrived for concurrence on April 26. Bell agreed to let White's bill take precedence. Debate began on May 13 and lasted thirteen days. Bell strenuously defended the proposed legislation and received able assistance from Democratic colleagues Dixon Lewis of Alabama and Georgia Congressmen Wilson Lumpkin, Richard H. Wilde, and James M. Wayne. The principal spokesmen against the bill were National Republicans William L. Storrs of Connecticut, Samuel F. Vinton of Ohio, and Massachusetts Congressmen Edward Everett and Isaac Bates. The passage of White's bill by the Senate meant that the debate in the House would be crucial to the fate of the Indians. Antiremoval spokesmen recognized this and focused their energies on swaying any uncommitted or wavering congressmen to their side. As a result of their efforts and the numerical superiority of the proremoval forces in the House, the ensuing debate was more virulent than in the Senate.[48]

Democrats saw the bill as the only way to prevent the creation of an *imperium in imperio.* They shrewdly reminded their critics that most of the New England states had already unburdened themselves of Indians. Southern and Western states should now have the same opportunity to promote their internal development by removing the Indians residing within their borders. Supporters of removal quoted the famous Swiss jurist Emmerich de Vattel to buttress their position that people usurping more extensive territory than they could commit to agricultural labor had "no reason to complain, if other nations, more laborious and too closely confined, come to possess a part."[49]

Critics of the bill demanded the enforcement of all treaty provisions guaranteeing the various tribes the integrity of their boundaries and protection from intruders. They absolutely refused to be a party to any measure permitting "sixty thousand human beings —the sick, the aged, the infirm, children, and infants—to be transported hundreds of miles, over mountains and rivers and forests" to a "western desert" by "those who will engage to perform the service for the smallest sum." Opponents of removal vigorously argued that Jackson wanted to dump the eastern "agricultural tribes" like the Cherokees and their neighbors into a desert wasteland swarming with "warlike tribes." Massachusetts Congressman

Isaac Bates, for example, quoted from an official report of Major Stephen H. Long of the U.S. Topographical Engineers, whose exploring expedition of 1820 helped to popularize the existence of a "Great American Desert" in the trans-Mississippi West. Bates read a portion of Long's report depicting the region as "almost wholly unfit for cultivation, and, of course, uninhabitable by a people depending upon agriculture for their subsistence." Bates and his National Republican colleagues warned that the administration's talk of civilizing the Indians in the West was merely a subterfuge for its nefarious intentions.[50]

The debate in the House of Representatives clearly demonstrated the prevailing lack of consensus on the geographical and geological nature of the country's western frontier. Since Major Long first reported the existence of a "Great American Desert" in the early part of the decade, there had been little agreement among Americans as to its composition or exact location. Many critics of Indian removal sincerely feared that the Democratic administration intended to resettle the advanced Cherokees and other similar "civilized" tribes on land lacking sufficient water and timber for their subsistence. Advocates of the measure, on the other hand, cited lengthy reports from the Reverend Isaac McCoy and others who had personal knowledge of the area. These statements indicated that the mixed forest-prairie area just west of Arkansas and Missouri possessed suitable resources for the Indians. Neither side was willing to accept the other's evidence as unimpeachable authority.[51]

Democratic leaders saw party politics rather than humanitarianism behind the intense opposition to Senator White's bill. They pointed out that the Adams administration had recommended a similar measure in 1828 and had praised the area designated for the Indians as "remarkable for salubrity of climate, fertility of soil, and profusion of game." Since many of the most vocal opponents of Indian removal in 1830 had supported the plan under the Adams administration, Jacksonians charged they were putting partisan politics above the national interest. The fact that it was Andrew Jackson who was sponsoring the measure did actually have a great deal to do with the mounting opposition to Indian removal. Jackson's political enemies equated his name with barbarism. Many of the staunchest opponents of White's bill agreed that Indian removal was desirable, but they believed that the federal government had an obligation to deal fairly and honestly with the Indians. These men were fearful that Jackson, unlike Adams, would use the measure to force emigration.[52]

Several leading National Republicans were maneuvering the debate in Congress over White's bill in such a way as to provide a useful issue for the 1832 presidential election. Henry Clay, a gifted politician from Kentucky who had served as Adams's secretary of state, was confident he could defeat Jackson in 1832 if he could raid Democratic strongholds in New York and Pennsylvania. The Kentuckian cheerfully noted that the bill was weakening the administration's strength in both those critical states, and he encouraged opposition congressmen to speak out forcefully against the measure. The prospect of stealing Pennsylvania from the Democratic column on this issue was especially bright since Quaker leaders in that state were already exerting tremendous pressure against it. Ohio and New York were also virtual battlegrounds as a result of public sympathy for the Cherokees. Opposition to the Removal Bill, therefore, became one means of expressing opposition to the administration and splitting the Jacksonian coalition.[53]

Some Democratic congressmen found themselves caught between their desire to demonstrate loyalty to the administration by supporting the bill and their eagerness to placate aroused public feeling in their states for the Indians. Joseph Hemphill of Pennsylvania, for example, considered himself a "sincere" friend of the president, but he could not ignore the strong antiremoval views of his Quaker constituents. Perhaps as a result of these two conflicting pressures, Hemphill argued that the question of Indian removal was too deeply involved in "both the political and moral character of the country" to become a mere party issue.[54]

Hemphill voiced the fears of many Pennsylvania Quakers when he pointed out that President Jackson had not precisely indicated the "mode and manner" he planned to use in carrying out his plans for Indian removal to the West. In order to correct the president's obvious oversight and to appease his constituents, Hemphill made several recommendations. First, he suggested that the president appoint "three disinterested commissioners" to help implement Indian removal. They would visit the various tribes, inform them of conditions in the western areas intended for their new homes, and ascertain tribal feelings about emigrating. Hemphill also cautioned that a thorough investigation of the western lands would have to be undertaken before any Indians emigrated, since the government's knowledge of "the character of the country, and the numbers and condition of the Indians there" was too "defective." The Pennsylvanian especially bemoaned the fact that while the government was anxious to remove the Indians, it was "almost entirely ignorant of the country required for from seventy to a hundred thousand Indians, who are contemplated to be removed."[55]

Another matter that disturbed Hemphill was the provision in the Removal Bill which stipulated that the government would pay individual Indians for any improvements they had made on the land they might relinquish in the East. This provision seemed to contradict another one guaranteeing that only "tribes or nations" would make the final decision concerning the advisability of emigrating. "Now," Hemphill remarked, "I wish to know the real meaning of the bill." He posed this question to the bill's sponsors: "If consent is not given by the tribe or nation, is it intended to go to individuals and purchase from A, B, and C?"[56]

Hemphill concluded his remarks by pleading that his colleagues do nothing contrary to the "practice and principles" of William Penn. The best way to assure such a noble course, he suggested, was to send out the commission he had recommended and to put off the drafting of a formal removal bill until the commissioners could issue a report and until such time as all the ambiguities in the present bill could be ironed out. The Pennsylvanian offered his proposals as an alternative to the administration bill and argued that "before we ... embark in this boundless and expensive project, the information required by the substitute [bill] is well worth obtaining." A delay of about a year, he stressed, would permit Congress to obtain sufficient information and to "take the responsibility on themselves, and lay down in detail the mode and manner of the removals, and let the President carry the law into execution." Since the white "race" was responsible for destroying Indian society, Hemphill argued that "we ought to act towards them with the strictest fairness, and attend to their glimmering existence with more than the ordinary humanity."[57]

The roll call vote on Hemphill's substitute bill resulted in a tie, ninety-eight to ninety-eight. Speaker of the House Andrew Stevenson, a Virginia Democrat, cast the deciding vote against the measure. Although Hemphill's proposals failed, the close vote clearly indicates that many Democrats had second thoughts about the Removal Bill.[58]

Following the defeat of Hemphill's alternative measure, John Bell adroitly maneuvered to bring the administration bill to a final vote. Bell assured wavering Democrats who had supported Hemphill that "no three living men could perform the duties proposed" by the defeated substitute bill in less than two years. Such rhetoric, together with increasing pressure from the administration, influenced three members of the Pennsylvania delegation and one member from Massachusetts who had supported Hemphill. These four Democrats helped to pave the way for the final vote of 102 in favor of the Removal Bill to 97 opposed. In spite of all the efforts to line up party support for the measure, however, a significant number of Democrats voted with the opposition, and several found themselves "constrained to shoot the pit," as Secretary of State Martin Van Buren remarked, and avoided voting at all on this controversial question. Democratic Congressman Pryor Lea of Tennessee admitted that the administration's victory came only after "one of the severest struggles, that I have ever witnessed in Congress." One of the interesting aspects of the voting pattern that emerged in both houses of Congress is that Jacksonians adhering to a political philosophy of states' rights, limited government, and retrenchment voted to provide huge expenditures for Indian removal, while National Republicans adhering to a political philosophy which encouraged federal expenditures bemoaned the "enormous expense" removal would bring. The issue of Indian treaty rights versus states' rights and the viscissitudes of partisan politics caused the Jacksonians and their opponents to momentarily trade positions concerning federal expenditures. In any event, the House returned the bill to the Senate for its concurrence on May 26.[59]

When the Senate took up the slightly modified House version, opposition leaders Frelinghuysen and Peleg Sprague of Maine once again unsuccessfully attempted to add amendments guaranteeing the Indians all rights provided by treaties and requiring the

executive department to furnish Congress with detailed information about the proposed western sites for the Indians before any
voluntary emigration began. John M. Clayton, a National Republican from Delaware, tried to restrict the bill to the state of Georgia,
but this, too, failed. Certain of success, administration leaders were
unwilling to compromise. They called for a final vote on the measure and obtained a victory for the president. On May 28, 1830,
Jackson signed the measure into law.[60]

The Removal Act of 1830 provided President Jackson with the
necessary congressional sanction to carry out the policy he had
outlined in his message to Congress early in December. He now
had authorization to exchange unorganized public domain in the
trans-Mississippi West for Indian land in the East. Indian emigrants would receive perpetual title to their new land as well as
compensation for improvements in the East and assistance in emigrating. Congress appropriated five hundred thousand dollars to
help the executive department carry out these provisions. This
legislation reflected what the president had long acknowledged as
"the habits of our Government and the feelings of our people"
toward the Indians, and the administration proceeded immediately to encourage the southern Indians to enroll for emigration.[61]

NOTES

1. Herbert J. Doherty, Jr., "The Governorship of Andrew Jackson,"
Florida Historical Quarterly 33 (July 1954): 19–21; Frederick M. Binder,
*The Color Problem in Early National America as Viewed by John Adams,
Jefferson and Jackson* (The Hague: Mouton & Co., 1968), pp. 152–54, 156;
James A. Hamilton, *Reminiscences* (New York: Charles Scribner & Co.,
1869), p. 73; Jackson to Major General Thomas Pinckney, May 8, 1814,
same to Secretary Crawford, June 10, 1816, same to [Monroe], March 4,
1817, same to Brigadier General John Coffee, September 2, 1826, Draft
of the First Annual Message, December 8, 1829, in John S. Bassett, ed.,
Correspondence of Andrew Jackson, 7 vols. (Washington, D.C.: Carnegie
Institution, 1926–35), 2: 3, 244, 278, 3: 312, 315, 4: 104. For a recent
attempt to rescue Jackson from the scorn heaped upon him by countless
numbers of historians, see Francis Paul Prucha, "Andrew Jackson's Indian
Policy: A Reassessment," *Journal of American History* 56 (December
1969): 527–39.

2. William S. Hoffman, "Andrew Jackson, State Rightist: The Case of
the Georgia Indians," *Tennessee Historical Quarterly* 11 (December

1952): 330; Major L. Wilson, "Andrew Jackson: The Great Compromiser," ibid. 26 (Spring 1967): 64, 75–76; Robert V. Remini, *Andrew Jackson* (New York: Harper & Row, 1969), pp. 128, 130. For a succinct statement of Jackson's position, see Jackson to Secretary of War [1831], in Bassett, *Correspondence of Andrew Jackson*, 4: 220.

3. Crawford to Jackson, January 27, 1816, Jackson to [Monroe], March 4, 1817, same to Secretary Graham, July 27, 1817, same to Secretary Calhoun, June 19, September 2, 1820, January 18, 1821, in Bassett, *Correspondence of Andrew Jackson*, 2: 227–28, 278–79, 308–9, 3: 27–28, 32, 38.

4. Jackson to Pinckney, May 8, 1814, same to Crawford, June 10, 1816, same to [Monroe], March 4, 1817, same to Calhoun, June 19, September 2, 1820, January 18, 1821, same to Colonel John D. Terrill, July 29, 1826, same to Coffee, September 2, 25, 1826, ibid., 2: 3, 244–45, 278–81, 3: 27–28, 32, 38, 308–9, 312, 315. For evidence that Jackson was familiar with John Marshall's decision in *Johnson* v. *McIntosh*, see Jackson to Secretary of War [1831], ibid., 4: 220.

5. Talk with the Cherokees, June 28, 1817, ibid., 2: 299 n; Jack E. Eblen, *The First and Second United States Empires: Governors and Territorial Government, 1784–1912* (Pittsburgh: University of Pittsburgh Press, 1968), p. 266. Also see Jackson to Robert Butler, June 21, 1817, in Bassett, *Correspondence of Andrew Jackson*, 2: 299.

6. Jackson to [Monroe], March 4, 1817, same to Calhoun, June 19, 1820, same to Terrill, July 29, 1826, in Bassett, *Correspondence of Andrew Jackson*, 2: 279–80, 3: 27–28, 308–9.

7. Monroe to Jackson, October 5, 1817, ibid., 2: 331; Jeremiah Evarts to David Greene, February 21, 1829, in J. Orin Oliphant, ed., *Through the South and the West with Jeremiah Evarts in 1826* (Lewisburg, Pa.: Bucknell University Press, 1956), p. 49; Francis Paul Prucha, *American Indian Policy in the Formative Years: The Indian Trade and Intercourse Acts, 1790–1834* (Cambridge, Mass.: Harvard University Press, 1962), pp. 232–35. For Monroe's announcement of the removal policy, see Richardson, *Papers of the Presidents*, 2: 280–83.

8. Florence Weston, *The Presidential Election of 1828* (Washington, D.C.: Catholic University Press, 1938), pp. 43, 185; Robert V. Remini, *The Election of Andrew Jackson* (Philadelphia: J. B. Lippincott Co., 1963), pp. 76, 124; Mary E. Young, *Redskins, Ruffleshirts and Rednecks: Indian Allotments in Alabama and Mississippi, 1830–1860* (Norman: University of Oklahoma Press, 1961), pp. 14–16.

9. U.S., Congress, *Register of Debates in Congress*, 20th Cong., 2d sess., pp. 22–23; Evarts to Greene, February 21, 1829, in Oliphant, *Through the South and the West*, p. 49. For an excellent account of the southern reaction to nothern abolitionism, see William W. Freehling,

Prelude to Civil War: The Nullification Controversy in South Carolina, 1816–1836 (New York: Harper & Row, 1966). The southern orientation of the Democratic party is discussed in Richard H. Brown, "The Missouri Crisis, Slavery, and the Politics of Jacksonianism," *South Atlantic Quarterly* 65 (Winter 1966): 55–72.

10. Richardson, *Papers of the Presidents*, 2: 438; Thomas P. Govan, "John Berrien and the Administration of Andrew Jackson," *Journal of Southern History* 5 (November 1939): 448; *Debates in Congress*, 20th Cong., 2d sess., pp. 22–23.

11. Tho[ma]s L. McKenney to Cherokee Delegation, April 4, 1829, IA, LS, 5: 393–94, RG 75, NA; Memorial . . . of the Cherokee Nation, February 27, 1829, U.S., Congress, House, *Document 145*, 20th Cong., 2d sess., pp. 1–3; Memorials of the Cherokee Indians, November 5, December 18, 1829, *House Report 311*, 21st Cong., 1st sess., pp. 2–9.

12. Jackson to the Creeks, March 23, 1829, Eaton to John Crowell, March 27, 1829, Eaton to Cherokee Delegation, April 18, 1829, Eaton to Carroll, May 27, 30, 1829, IA, LS, 5: 372–75, 410, 412, 442–43, 456–59, RG 75, NA; *Niles' Register* 36 (May 30, 1829): 231, 36 (June 13, 1829): 257–59; *Natchez Statesman and Gazette* (Mississippi), June 27, 1829.

13. Cotterill, *Southern Indians*, pp. 237–38; Abel, "Indian Consolidation West of the Mississippi," pp. 370–71.

14. R. Pierce Beaver, *Church, State, and the American Indians: Two and a Half Centuries of Partnership in Missions between Protestant Churches and Government* (St. Louis: Concordia Publishing House, 1966), pp. 61, 66–67, 71, 73, 75–76, 97, 103–11; *Quarterly Register of the American Education Society* 3 (August 1830): 60; M. D. McHenry to J. H. McHenry, April 2, 1830, Hardin Family Papers, Chicago Historical Society, Chicago, Ill.; Adams to Clay, April 21, 1829, in Calvin Colton, ed., *The Private Correspondence of Henry Clay* (New York: A. S. Barnes & Co., 1855), 227.

15. Francis Paul Prucha, "Thomas L. McKenney and the New York Indian Board," *Mississippi Valley Historical Review* 48 (March 1962): 636–37; Anson Phelps Stokes and Leo Pfeffer, *Church and State in the United States*, rev. ed. (New York: Harper & Row, 1964), p. 185.

16. Morse, *Report to the Secretary of War*, appendix, pp. 284–90; McKenney to John Cocke, January 23, 1827, same to James C. Mitchell, August 23, 1828, IA, LS, 3: 328–29, 5: 95, RG 75, NA; McKenney to Secretary of War, September 29, 1827, IA, LR, Misc., RG 75, NA; *North American Review* 63 (October 1846): 482; Herman J. Viola, "Thomas L. McKenney and the Administration of Indian Affairs, 1824–30" (Ph.D. diss., Indiana University, 1970), pp. 250, 276; Prucha, "McKenney and the New York Indian Board," pp. 637–38. One scholar contends that

"McKenney, seemingly oblivious of the change in administration [in 1829], continued to follow his policy of moderation." See Arthur H. DeRosier, Jr., *The Removal of the Choctaw Indians* (Knoxville: University of Tennessee Press, 1970), p. 101.

17. McKenney to Hobart, April 7, 1829, in Prucha, "McKenney and the New York Indian Board," pp. 639–40.

18. McKenney to Van Rensselaer, May 9, 1829, Simon Gratz Collection, Historical Society of Pennsylvania, Philadelphia, Pa.; *Magazine of the Reformed Dutch Church* 4 (July 1829): 118; McKenney to Reverend Eli Baldwin, May 21, 1829, IA, LS, 5: 439, RG 75, NA; McKenney to Eaton, [August 3, 1829], IA, LR, Misc., RG 75, NA; Prucha, "McKenney and the New York Indian Board," pp. 640–41.

19. McKenney to Baldwin, May 21, June 27, 1829, IA, LS, 5: 439–40, 6: 30–32, RG 75, NA; McKenney to Eaton, [July 22, 1829], same to Baldwin, July 30, 1829, enclosed in same to Eaton, August 3, 1829, IA, LR, Misc., RG 75, NA; *Magazine of the Reformed Dutch Church* 4 (August 1829): 159; *Columbian Gazette* (Georgetown, D.C.), August 25, 1829; *New-York Evening Post*, August 31, 1829. Also see *Documents and Proceedings Relating to the Formation and Progress of a Board in the City of New York, for the Emigration, Preservation, and Improvement, of the Aborigines of America* (New York: Vanderpoole & Cole, 1829); *North American Review* 30 (January 1830): 62–121.

20. McKenney to Baldwin, July 13, 1829, same to Eaton, July 15, 1829, IA, LS, 6: 46–49, RG 75, NA; Baldwin to McKenney, July 7, 11, 29, 1829, McKenney to Eaton, five undated letters, [July–August 1829], same to Baldwin, July 30, 1829, Van Rensselaer to [Dr. Westbrook], August 4, 1829, enclosed in McKenney to Eaton, [1829], IA, LR, Misc., RG 75, NA; *Columbian Gazette*, August 25, September 5, 1829; *Documents and Proceedings*, pp. 22–23.

21. *Documents and Proceedings*, pp. 28–42; *New-York Evening Post*, quoted in *Columbian Gazette*, August 25, 1829; ibid., August 29, September 1, 1829; McKenney to [Eaton], Private, [July 1829], IA, LR, Misc., RG 75, NA.

22. Baldwin to Eaton, August 14, 1829, McKenney to Eaton, August 14, 1829, Vanderpoole & Cole to Eaton, September 25, 1829, Bill of Lading, September 28, 1829, Eli Baldwin to McKenney, October 19, 1829, IA, LR, Misc., RG 75, NA; McKenney to Cashier of Bank of New York, September 16, 1829, same to Dr. John Clark, September 16, 1829, IA, LS, 6: 87–88, RG 75, NA.

23. McKenney to Eaton, August 21, 1829, IA, LS, 6: 70, RG 75, NA.

24. Ibid.; *Magazine of the Reformed Dutch Church* 4 (August 1829): 159, 4 (September 1829): 190–91, 4 (October 1829): 222, 4 (November

1829): 247–50, 4 (December 1829): 287; McKenney to Baldwin, October 8, 1829, IA, LS, 6: 105, RG 75, NA; Baldwin to McKenney, October 29, November 26, 1829, IA, LR, Misc., RG 75, NA; *North American Review* 30 (January 1830): 62–121.

25. *Daily National Intelligencer* (Washington), August 1, 1829 (hereafter cited as *National Intelligencer*); [Evarts] to Eleazer Lord, August 11, 1829, Papers of the American Board of Commissioners for Foreign Missions, Houghton Library, Harvard University, Cambridge, Mass. (material from this collection is used by permission of the Harvard College Library); *Columbian Gazette*, August 25, September 1, 3, 1829; *Daily Richmond Whig*, August 21, 1829; *Quarterly Register of the American Education Society* 3 (August 1830): 61, 4 (November 1831): 75–76. For an early indication of Evarts's strategy, see Evarts to David Greene, March 10, 1829, Papers of the American Board. Jeremiah Evarts's essays were shortly published in book form. See *Essays on the Present Crisis in the Condition of the American Indians: First Published in the National Intelligencer, under the Signature of William Penn* (Boston: Perkins & Marvin, 1829).

26. Beaver, *Church, State, and the American Indians*, pp. 95–99; Randolph O. Yeager, "Indian Enterprises of Isaac McCoy, 1817–1846" (Ph.D. diss., University of Oklahoma, 1954), pp. 395–424, 441, 479, 483; Lucien Bowle to [McKenney], May 9, 1829, IA, Registers, LR, 2: 40, RG 75, NA; H. Lincoln to McKenney, September 19, 1829, in *Magazine of the Reformed Dutch Church* 4 (November 1829): 247–48; *Columbian Star and Christian Index* 1 (September 12, 1829): 171–72, 1 (December 19, 1829): 388, 2 (February 13, 1830): 106–7, 2 (February 20, 1830): 120; *American Baptist Magazine* 10 (February 1830): 54–55, 10 (April 1830): 126–27; McKenney to Eaton, August 14, 1829, enclosed in Baldwin to Eaton, August 14, 1829, IA, LR, Misc., RG 75, NA.

27. Phillips, *Georgia and States' Rights*, pp. 72–73. Also see note 25 of this chapter.

28. Circular from Eaton to Governors of Tennessee, Mississippi and Alabama, May 21, 1829, same to Carroll, May 30, July 15, 1829, same to Hugh Montgomery, October 9, 1829, same to Governor John Forsyth, September 15, October 14, 1829, McKenney to Crowell, June 15, 1829, same to R. M. Johnson, December 11, 1829, IA, LS, 5: 438, 456–58, 6: 13–14, 49–50, 86, 107, 113–19, 190, RG 75, NA.

29. Eaton to Forsyth, September 15, October 14, 1829, ibid., pp. 86, 119.

30. Richardson, *Papers of the Presidents*, 2: 452, 457–58.

31. Ibid., pp. 457–59.

32. Ibid.

33. *Debates in Congress,* 21st Cong., 1st sess., pp. 507–11; *American Spectator and Washington City Chronicle,* February 6, 1830; *Columbian Star and Christian Index* 1 (December 19, 1829): 338, 2 (February 13, 1830): 106–7; 2 (February 20, 1830): 120; *Magazine of the Reformed Dutch Church* 4 (December 1829): 287; *Arkansas Gazette* (Little Rock), April 20, 1830; *National Intelligencer,* January 12, 15, 1830; McKenney to H. L. White, February 26, 1830, IA, LS, 6: 293, RG 75, NA; T. Frelinghuysen to Jeremiah Evarts, January 11, 1830, Evarts Papers, Library of Congress, Washington, D.C.; Ambrose Spencer and Henry Storrs to John Trumbull, January 25, 1830, Gratz Collection; [Evarts] to David Greene, March 31, 1830, Papers of the American Board. For the numerous petitions against Indian removal, see *House Journal,* 21st Cong., 1st sess. and *Senate Journal,* 21st Cong., 1st sess.

34. S 102, *Original Bills,* 21st Cong., 1st sess., Records of the United States Senate, S21A-B1, S21A-B2, RG 46, NA (hereafter cited as Senate Records); HR 287, *Original Bills,* 21st Cong., 1st sess., Records of the United States House of Representatives, HR21A-B1, HR21A-D112, RG 233, NA (hereafter cited as House Records); *Debates in Congress,* 21st Cong., 1st sess., pp. 305, 580–83; Theodore Frelinghuysen to Jeremiah Evarts, February 22, 1830, Evarts Family Papers, Sterling Memorial Library, Yale University, Hartford, Conn.; *Nashville Republican and State Gazette,* March 30, April 2, 1830; *Niles' Register* 38 (March 20, 1830): 67; *Magazine of the Reformed Dutch Church* 4 (March 1830): 383.

35. *Debates in Congress,* 21st Cong., 1st sess., pp. 305, 307, 309–20, 324–39, 343–57, 359–67, 374–77, 380–83.

36. Thomas Hart Benton, *Thirty Years' View; or, a History of the Working of the American Government for Thirty Years, from 1820 to 1850,* 2 vols. (New York: D. Appleton & Co., 1854–56), 1: 164; Isaac McCoy, *History of Baptist Indian Missions: Embracing Remarks on the Former and Present Condition of the Aboriginal Tribes, Their Former Settlement within the Indian Territory, and Their Future Prospects* (Washington, D.C.: William M. Morrison, 1840), pp. 397, 399–400; I. C. Bates to Evarts, February 26, 1830, Evarts Family Papers, Yale University; Dean Ray Montgomery, "Jeremiah Evarts and Indian Removal" (Master's thesis, University of Maryland, 1971), pp. 106–26.

37. *Debates in Congress,* 21st Cong., 1st sess., pp. 307, 309–20; Charles R. Erdman, Jr., "Theodore Frelinghuysen," in Allen Johnson and Dumas Malone (eds.), *Dictionary of American Biography,* 22 vols. (New York: Charles Scribner's Sons, 1956), 7: 16. Also see Frelinghuysen to Evarts, January 11, February 22, 1830, Evarts Papers, Library of Congress.

38. *Debates in Congress,* 21st Cong., 1st sess., pp. 309–12.

39. Ibid., pp. 312, 316, 317, 320.

40. Ibid., pp. 318–20.

41. Ibid., pp. 355–57.

42. Ibid., pp. 374, 377.

43. Ibid., pp. 325, 328.

44. Ibid., pp. 326–28, 332.

45. Ibid., pp. 359, 367.

46. Ibid., p. 381. For Barton's political career, see Edwin C. Reynolds, *Missouri: A History of the Crossroads State* (Norman: University of Oklahoma Press, 1962), p. 117.

47. *Debates in Congress*, 21st Cong., 1st sess., p. 383; *Senate Journal*, 21st Cong., 1st sess., pp. 266–68; S 102, *Original Bills*, 21st Cong., 1st sess., Senate Records, S21A-B1, S21A-B2, RG 46, NA. For statistical analyses of the roll call, see Satz, "Federal Indian Policy," p. 34; David J. Russo, *The Major Political Issues of the Jacksonian Period and the Development of Party Loyalty in Congress, 1830–1840*, Transactions of the American Philosophical Society, n.s., Vol. 62, pt. 5 (Philadelphia, 1972), p. 14.

48. *Debates in Congress*, 21st Cong., 1st sess., pp. 819, 988, 993–1120, 1122–36; Pryor Lea to Editor, May 27, 1830, in *Knoxville Register*, June 9, 1830.

49. *Debates in Congress*, 21st Cong., 1st sess., pp. 819, 988, 993–1120, 1122–36. For the use of Vattel's writings in defense of removal, also see Report of Bell, February 24, 1830, House Records, HR21A-D112, RG 233, NA.

50. *Debates in Congress*, 21st Cong., 1st sess., pp. 1047–48, 1067, 1069, 1071–74. Francis Paul Prucha erroneously asserts, in his "Indian Removal and the Great American Desert," *Indiana Magazine of History* 59 (December 1963): 321, that "opponents of removal offered little criticism of the policy on the basis of giving the Indians poor land in return for what they relinquished in the East. Nowhere did Long's report enter into the discussion." Prucha's article has received considerable attention, and Ray Allen Billington changed his interpretation of Indian removal in the recent edition of his widely used frontier history textbook in order to conform with Prucha's findings. Compare Billington's *Westward Expansion: A History of the American Frontier*, 2d ed. (New York: Macmillan Co., 1960), pp. 470, 820, and 3rd ed. (New York: Macmillan Co., 1967), pp. 470, 842.

51. McCoy, *Practicability of Indian Reform* (1827 ed.), p. 33, ibid. (1829 ed.), pp. 33–34; McKenney to Secretary of War, September 29, 1827, IA, LR, Misc., RG 75, NA; same to Eaton, April 6, 1830, IA, LS, 6: 373–74, RG 75, NA; *Columbian Star and Christian Index* 2 (February 13, 1830): 106–7; *American Quarterly Review* 8 (September 1830): 109–10; *Quarterly Register of the American Education Society* 3 (November

1830): 124; Terry L. Alford, "Western Desert Images in American Thought, 1800–1860" (Ph.D. diss., Mississippi State University, 1970), pp. 196–221, 316. For information on the region that Long reported on, see Richard D. Dillon, "Stephen Long's Great American Desert," *Proceedings of the American Philosophical Society* 3 (April 1967): 93–108.

52. *Richmond Enquirer,* February 26, March 12, April 30, 1830; *Debates in Congress,* 21st Cong., 1st sess., p. 1,122; John C. Fitzpatrick, ed., *The Autobiography of Martin Van Buren* (Washington, D.C.: GPO, 1920), pp. 282–83; John William Ward, *Andrew Jackson, Symbol for an Age* (New York: Galaxy Books, 1962), p. 43. The quotation is from Secretary of War, *Annual Report* (1828), pp. 21–22.

53. Clay to Francis Brooke, April 19, 24, 1830, same to J. S. Johnston, April 30, 1830, Daniel Webster to Clay, May 29, 1830, in Colton, *Private Correspondence of Henry Clay,* pp. 261, 263, 265, 274–76; Fitzpatrick, *Autobiography of Martin Van Buren,* p. 289; Martin Van Buren, *Inquiry into the Origin and Course of Political Parties in the United States,* ed. by his sons (New York: Hurd & Houghton, 1867), p. 323.

54. *Debates in Congress,* 21st Cong., 1st sess., p. 1132.

55. Ibid.

56. Ibid.

57. Ibid., p. 1133; *House Journal,* 21st Cong., 1st sess., pp. 716–17.

58. *Debates in Congress,* 21st Cong., 1st sess., p. 1133.

59. Ibid., pp. 1,133–36, 1,145–46; Fitzpatrick, *Autobiography of Martin Van Buren,* p. 289; Lea to Editor, May 27, 1830, in *Knoxville Register,* June 9, 1830; Charles G. Sellers, Jr., *James K. Polk, Jacksonian: 1795–1843* (Princeton, N.J.: Princeton University Press, 1957), pp. 161–62; Marie P. Mahoney, "American Public Opinion of Andrew Jackson's Indian Policy, 1828–1835" (Master's thesis, Clark University, 1935), pp. 96–98, 113–14. For statistical analyses of the roll call, see Satz, "Federal Indian Policy," p. 40; Russo, *Major Political Issues,* pp. 13–14.

60. *Debates in Congress,* 21st Cong., 1st sess., p. 456; *House Journal,* 21st Cong., 1st sess., p. 732; *Senate Journal,* 21st Cong., 1st sess., pp. 327–29; U.S., *Stat.,* 4: 411–12. For the proposed amendments to the bill in the Senate see S 102, *Senate Documents,* S21A-B1, RG 46, NA.

61. U.S., *Stat.,* 4: 411–12. A recent monograph by an ethnologist erroneously asserts that the Removal Act "gave the President the right to extirpate all Indians who had managed to survive east of the Mississippi River." See Peter Farb, *Man's Rise to Civilization as Shown by the Indians of North America from Primeval Times to the Coming of the Industrial State* (New York: E. P. Dutton & Co., Inc., 1968), p. 250. See the Appendix for the actual wording of the Removal Act.

2 /

The Political Response to the

Removal Act

THE INDIAN REMOVAL ACT of 1830 was too controversial an issue to win the acquiescence of anti-Jackson politicians or other friends of the southern tribes. Leading National Republicans were seeking to portray President Jackson as an ignorant, overbearing, military tyrant, prone to ruthlessness and vindictiveness, and the Removal Act provided an excellent propaganda vehicle for this purpose. Indian removal occupied a secondary but nevertheless prominent position alongside such momentous issues as the tariff, internal improvements, and the National Bank in the alignments contributing to the formation of a new two-party system in the 1830s.[1]

Henry Clay, Jackson's archrival, hoped to use the president's sympathy with the southern states on the Indian question and his extensive use of the veto power to build a substantial following for the 1832 election. Clay assured a close friend after the passage of the Removal Act that "measures have been devised, and are now in a train of execution, to give expression to public sentiment" disapproving of "the Veto, the Indian bill, etc." The Kentuckian encouraged the holding of public meetings throughout the nation to adopt "spirited resolutions" condemning the Removal Act and asserted that "our efforts should now be directed to the rejection of treaties negotiated in pursuance of that abominable law, and to the withholding of appropriations to carry it into effect." Partly as a result of Clay's efforts, petitions calling for the repeal of the Removal Act and the protection of the southern Indians poured into Congress from religious groups and humanitarian associations.[2]

Clay and other anti-Jackson leaders also urged the Cherokees to appeal to the American people and the Supreme Court in order to enlist their sympathy and expose the administration's base intentions. Jeremiah Evarts of the American Board helped the Indians by composing the "Appeal of the Cherokee Nation to the American People" which the National Republican press immediately reprinted. In the meantime, Massachusetts Senator Daniel Webster, Senator Frelinghuysen of New Jersey, and New York Congressman Ambrose Spencer persuaded the Cherokees to employ former attorney general William Wirt to carry their case to the Supreme Court.[3]

Although Congressmen Clay, Webster, Spencer, and Frelinghuysen worked closely together to prevent the removal of the Cherokees, their attitudes toward Indians and Indian rights were somewhat varied. Because these men were the leaders behind the antiremoval movement, their views deserve some attention.

Henry Clay had long held a low opinion of Indian character and had confided to friends that the tribesmen were justly doomed to extinction. The Kentuckian had also previously asserted that the United States had complete sovereignty over the Indians and the territory they occupied, but he believed that the government had to respect Indian treaty rights.[4]

Daniel Webster had contended as early as 1823 that the Indians had clear title to the land they dwelled on, but this belief apparently stemmed more from his close ties with land speculators than from humanitarian considerations. In the 1830s Webster was one of many politicians and businessmen who profited from the removal policy by investing in land obtained from the Indians in the Old Northwest.[5]

Ambrose Spencer maintained that his interest in the Cherokees was "influenced by a regard to the honor & character of the country, as well as by feelings of humanity towards a noble, but much injured people." Spencer hoped to "excite the deep sympathies of all christian people" and to undermine the faith of those who still

believed in "the wisdom or patriotism" of the Jackson administration. Yet Spencer's concern for Indian rights in the South did not
match his previous actions in New York. Eight years before the
passage of the Removal Act of 1830, Spencer, then chief justice of
the New York Supreme Court, had attempted unsuccessfully to
uphold the extension of state law over the Indians residing in New
York.[6]

Theodore Frelinghuysen was a devout man with a long history
of activity in humanitarian and religious reform, including Indian
missionary work. While possessing political ambitions, he also sincerely believed he was carrying out God's work on earth. Frelinghuysen was a strong anti-Jacksonite, but his sympathy for the
southern Indians was not out of character nor inconsistent with his
previous actions or utterances. He agreed with Clay, Webster, and
Spencer that the Cherokees had a right to maintain their independence in Georgia and other southern states.[7]

Jackson's adversaries were eager to demean his triumph in securing the passage of the Removal Bill. They called the president's
victory the result of "a corrupt juggle between the Executive and
some of the members [of Congress] with regard to other bills, the
Maysville Road bill, the Baltimore Rail Road Bill, &c." The opposition's greatest problem, as attorney William Wirt clearly recognized, was that "there are many well meaning men who think it
the interest of the Cherokees to remove." Thomas McKenney and
the New York Indian Board had apparently swayed some prominent men to espouse removal as a humanitarian reform and convinced others to reconsider their opposition to the measure. Some
anti-Jacksonians feared that McKenney and the New York Indian
Board had blunted the "great question of political morality" involved in the proposal to remove the southern tribes by painting
an idyllic picture of the proposed Indian home in the West. National Republicans were anxious to offset such propaganda, and
the legal defense of the Cherokees seemed the best approach.[8]

William Wirt undertook the defense of the Cherokees in the
summer of 1830 after Daniel Webster and other anti-Jackson leaders had convinced him that a legal decision in favor of the Indians
would embarrass the president politically. Although initially sympathetic to the proremoval arguments of Thomas McKenney and
the New York Board, Wirt quickly accepted the position that the

Cherokees had a legal right to remain in Georgia unmolested by
state law. He then began referring to Jackson's contrary opinion
as a "new fangled notion in opposition to those of Washington,
Jefferson, Madison, Monroe and John Q. Adams." Through an in-
termediary, he solicited Chief Justice John Marshall's opinion on
the matter and was tremendously encouraged by Marshall's strong
statement of sympathy for the beleaguered Indians. Wirt confided
to a friend that the chief justice would protect the Indians and
become "our political Saviour." His next move was to seek a test
case before the Court. Wirt and other opposition leaders believed
the president would refuse to enforce any Supreme Court decree
favoring the Indians. The idea was to make Jackson appear as a
nullifier of federal law, and the National Republicans quickly established a vast propaganda network to prepare a "Winter's Campaign" to accomplish that end.[9]

Jeremiah Evarts of the American Board of Commissioners for
Foreign Missions, encouraged by Clay, Webster, and Spencer, col-
lected the best speeches against the Removal Bill and published
them in a lengthy book. He also secured the reprinting of his
famous William Penn essays, helped in preparing editorials for
National Republican newspapers, and joined other anti-Jacksonites in soliciting aid from prominent intellectuals, ministers, and
educators. Clay helped Evarts persuade the *North American Review* to publish an article by the latter refuting an earlier
proremoval one by Lewis Cass that had appeared in that journal.
In addition to this aid, the Kentuckian urged Evarts to encourage
religious groups throughout the nation to support the Cherokees.
"The female sex is generally on their side," Clay noted, "and a
co-operation between that and the Clergy would have powerful
if not decisive influence."[10]

Anti-Jackson newspapers gave wide coverage to the president's
dismissal of Thomas McKenney from the Indian Bureau shortly
after the passage of the Removal Bill. Ignoring the political aspects
of his dismissal, they insinuated that McKenney had finally discovered the administration's true intentions and disowned them.
When McKenney, the guiding spirit behind the New York Indian
Board, began speaking out against the president's Indian policy,
it became much easier for Clay and his followers to court the major
religious organizations and to counteract the work of the New

York Indian Board in order to "rescue our Country from the foul stain which the execution of the Indian bill would bring upon us."[11]

Next to newspaper, magazine, and oratorical agitation, the opposition's main tactic was to forge a sufficient majority in Congress to repeal the Removal Act. Senator Frelinghuysen, for example, charged that the administration had "suspended public laws & thrown aside public treaties as if they were worthless rags," and encouraged the public to send antiremoval petitions to their representatives in Congress. Jeremiah Evarts campaigned in Boston for an antiremoval candidate during the congressional election of 1830 and urged voters to cast their ballots only for those men who would pledge to work for the repeal of the Removal Act. In the meantime, however, anti-Jacksonites encouraged intransigence among the southern tribes. "If the Indians remain firm and refuse to treat," Clay advised, "they will ultimately be successful." Clay cautioned National Republicans against being "too inactive," and they heeded his warning.[12]

The opposition brought together some of the nation's outstanding legal minds to consult on the best course to pursue in defending the Cherokees. James Kent, Ambrose Spencer, Horace Binney, John Sergeant, and Daniel Webster—all attorneys of stature—communicated with Wirt in behalf of the Cherokees and received funds directly from the Indians to promote their cause. While organizing the legal defense for the tribe, anti-Jacksonites in Congress also established a publicity committee during the winter of 1830–31 to direct a national campaign to repeal the Removal Act and to rescind any treaties made under its influence.[13]

Democrats reacted caustically to these efforts to make Indian removal a party question. Supporters of the measure argued that since removal was in the national interest as well as in the best interest of the Indians themselves, it should not be relegated to the realm of partisan politics. In Jackson's home state the proremoval *Nashville Republican and State Gazette* charged that the lamentations of the northeastern urban elite against removal were purely hypocritical cries of people knowing less about Indians than they knew about the indigent in their own cities. The president himself believed that "the course of *Wirt* has been truly wicked. It has been wielded as an engine to prevent the Indians from moving [across] the Mississippi and will lead to the destruction of the poor ignorant Indians." Wirt and his advisers had "deluded" the Cherokees into believing they could maintain their independence in Georgia. Jackson, however, warned that "an absolute independence of the Indian tribes from state authority can never bear an intelligent investigation, and a quasi independence of state authority when located within its Territorial limits is *absurd.*" Removal was the only way of escaping the tyranny of state law without disrupting tribal life.[14]

Jackson responded to the growing criticism of the Removal Act in his message to Congress in December, 1830. He maintained that the act fully "exonerated the national character from all imputation" while providing an "end to all possible danger of collision between the authorities of the General and State Governments on account of the Indians." Noting that "the waves of population and civilization are rolling to the westward," he asserted that "we now propose to acquire the countries occupied by the red men of the South and West by a fair exchange, and, at the expense of the United States, to send them to a land where their existence may be prolonged and perhaps made perpetual." Removal was a policy "so just to the States and so generous to the Indians—the Executive feels it has a right to expect the cooperation of Congress and of all good and disinterested men." Besides, asked Jackson, "what good man would prefer a country covered with forests and ranged by a few thousand savages to our extensive Republic, studded with cities, towns, and prosperous farms, embellished with all the improvements which art can devise or industry execute, occupied by more than 12,000,000 happy people, and filled with all the blessings of liberty, civilization, and religion?"[15]

While the president was urging support for his removal program, his opponents were busy undermining the policy. Under the guidance of William Wirt and other anti-Jacksonites, the Cherokee Nation filed suit in the Supreme Court for an injunction to stop Georgia from interfering with its rights. The counsel for the Indians argued that the Court had to defend the tribe's right to its soil and self-government since the United States had long recognized these rights in treaties. Wirt, in effect, asked the Court to challenge the president's Indian policy by issuing a restraining order to Georgia.[16]

Chief Justice Marshall's ingenious opinion delivered on March 18, 1831, accepted neither Wirt's contention that the Cherokees constituted a sovereign nation nor the administration's position that they were a subject nation at the mercy of Georgia. Marshall sympathized with the Indians and acknowledged that "the acts of our government plainly recognize the Cherokee Nation as a State, and the courts are bound by those acts." He noted, however, that "the relation of the Indians to the United States is marked by peculiar and cardinal distinctions which exist nowhere else," for "Indian Territory is admitted to compose part of the United States."[17]

The extraordinary relationship of the Indians to the United States government led Marshall to take a unique position. He viewed the tribes as neither independent nor subject nations but as "domestic dependent nations." According to the chief justice, "they occupy a territory to which we assert a title independent of their will, which must take effect in point of possession when their right of possession ceases. Meanwhile they are in a state of pupilage. Their relation to the United States resembles that of a ward to his guardian." While Marshall agreed that the federal government was responsible for the welfare of its Indian wards, he nevertheless rejected the Cherokee Nation's petition for a restraining order since the tribe had incorrectly filed suit as a foreign nation.[18]

Associate Justices John McLean, Henry Baldwin, and William Johnson concurred with Marshall that the Court lacked jurisdiction in the case. Marshall's obiter dictum, however, only represented his and McLean's views. While voting with Marshall and McLean in denying the Court's jurisdiction, Johnson and Baldwin —the former a South Carolinian appointed to the Court in 1804 by Thomas Jefferson and the latter a Jackson appointee—went on to deny that the Cherokees possessed any political or property rights in Georgia. Democrats viewed their opinions as a vindication of Jackson's Indian policy. Secretary of War Eaton confided to a friend that "the decision of the Supreme Court on this Indian question, will set all these Southern tribes aback. There was their last reliance and that now has failed them."[19]

The two dissenting justices, Smith Thompson and Joseph Story, viewed the Cherokees as a foreign state, but they did not deliver formal opinions in the case. As Jacksonians began publicizing the opinions of Baldwin and Johnson, however, the chief justice re-

gretted he had taken such "a very narrow view" of the case and
privately urged Thompson and Story to put their positions in writing, since "the public must wish to see both sides." Thompson
issued a written opinion and Story found it satisfactory enough not
to issue a separate one; this was after the Court had already rejected the Cherokee Nation's petition.[20]

Thompson's dissent had a tremendous political impact. It gave
the Indians new hope that the Court might rule in their favor in
a subsequent case, and it led the opposition to redouble their
efforts to discredit the administration. Richard Peters, the Court
reporter, aided the anti-Jacksonites by publishing a private edition
of the Court's proceedings for public sale. This publication, labeled a cheap partisan trick by the Democrats, contained the
lengthy briefs of the defense counsel, Justice Thompson's dissenting opinion, the Trade and Intercourse Act of 1802, which bound
the executive to remove all intruders from Indian land, and other
material which gave readers a more favorable view of the rights
of the Cherokees than did the earlier statements of Marshall, Baldwin, and Johnson. Marshall quickly joined dissenting Justices
Thompson and Story in supporting Peters's effort and in praising
the arguments of the counsel for the Indians.[21]

National Republicans took the hint from the Peters book and
quoted the law of 1802 in order to portray Jackson and his followers as "nullifiers." They reminded the public that the president
was "liable to impeachment" for refusing to enforce federal law.
State legislatures in New England and the Middle Atlantic states
controlled by the National Republicans passed resolutions condemning Georgia's actions, asserting that the Supreme Court had
jurisdiction in the case and emphasizing that the president's duty
was to enforce the federal laws.[22]

Such statements only strengthened the resolve of the Cherokees to pursue their legal struggle against "lawless intruders" in
Georgia and to pray for Clay's election in 1832. The tribe issued
a second "Appeal to the American People" in May, 1831, claiming
that the Supreme Court had clearly bound the federal government to protect its political and property rights. The Cherokees
absolutely refused to submit to Georgia or to Jackson. Events in
Georgia soon provided them with a second opportunity to appeal
to the Supreme Court.[23]

Late in December, 1830, the legislature of Georgia enacted a law prohibiting the presence of whites in Indian country after March 1, 1831, without a license from the state. Georgia officials wanted to exclude white missionaries who opposed removal from residing among the Cherokees, for they believed this step would expedite the seizure of Indian land containing rich gold deposits. The missionaries, however, proved stubborn. They decided to challenge Georgia's authority by remaining without the proper licenses. The state responded by sending its militia to arrest them on July 7. The Jackson administration was an accomplice to this act, since it had assured Georgia officials that the missionaries did not have federal immunity from arrest even though they dispensed the government's funds for civilizing the Indians. President Jackson even agreed to remove one of the missionaries from his position as United States postmaster in order to make him amenable to the laws of Georgia. Ironically, the arrest of the missionaries bolstered the morale of the Cherokees and opposition leaders because Georgia had finally become a party to a dispute over which the Supreme Court did have jurisdiction.[24]

Samuel A. Worcester and Elizur Butler, two of the missionaries arrested by Georgia, refused to accept pardons or licenses from the governor. The antiremoval American Board in Boston retained William Wirt to plead their case before the Supreme Court. The resulting litigation against the state of Georgia played an interesting role in the 1832 presidential election.[25]

The National Republicans convened in Baltimore on December 12, 1831, to name candidates for the 1832 election. James Barbour, former secretary of war under Adams, served as the presiding officer. In his keynote address, Barbour vilified nearly every act of the Jackson administration. The last issue he discussed, but "perhaps the most important of all," as he put it, was the president's Indian policy. Barbour condemned Georgia's treatment of the Indians and the incarcerated missionaries; he charged that Georgia's actions had "the countenance and approbation of the general executive." Barbour also accused the administration of refusing to enforce the 1802 law requiring the president to remove intruders from the Indian country and warned that nullification of federal law would disrupt the Union. He urged the election of Henry Clay to the presidency, for "he will, on all occasions, assert the suprem-

acy of the laws." Such rhetoric was only one indication that the
Indian question would play a significant role in the campaign.[26]

Both of the attorneys hired by the American Board to defend
the missionaries in Georgia were candidates for national office.
John Sergeant, former congressman from Pennsylvania and chief
counsel for the Bank of the United States, received the vice-presidential nomination of the National Republican party and, in his
acceptance statement on December 14, pledged that the ticket
would "maintain the supremacy of the constitution and laws" of
the land at all times. William Wirt, who had also handled the
earlier case of the Cherokees, received the presidential nomination of the Anti-Masons. The ambitions of leading anti-Jackson
politicians were thus inextricably tied to the outcome of *Worcester
v. Georgia.*[27]

Between the winter of 1831–32 and the casting of the final
ballot in November, anti-Jacksonites increasingly used the deteriorating position of the Cherokees as a political football. National
Republican and Anti-Mason leaders did not view it as the major
issue, but they were anxious to drain every ounce of propaganda
possible out of it. The harsh treatment accorded Worcester and
Butler received considerable attention in the opposition press.
Some leaders in Congress worked to bring the question of criminal
proceedings in Georgia courts against the Indians before the Supreme Court. At the same time, a delegation of Cherokees toured
eastern cities seeking monetary aid, encouraging the presentation
of memorials to Congress, and providing antiadministration editors with ample materials to write glowing accounts of the tribe's
progress toward civilization. National Republicans in Congress
introduced memorials in favor of the missionaries and the Cherokees as soon as they received them. Thomas McKenney, recently
dismissed as head of the Indian Bureau and a convert to the opposition, was busy trying to convince leaders of the New York Indian
Board and others that Jackson had betrayed their humanitarian
cause. Meanwhile, the case of the Georgia missionaries came before the Supreme Court.[28]

The Court took up the case after the attorneys for the missionaries had accepted their nominations for national office. This time no
legal technicalities blocked Chief Justice Marshall from rendering

a decision in favor of the plaintiffs. In his lengthy majority opinion delivered on March 3, 1832, Marshall declared Georgia's extension of state law over the Indians unconstitutional and ordered the immediate release of the missionaries. The Court issued a special mandate ordering the state court that convicted Worcester and Butler to reverse its decision and release them. Justice Joseph Story sighed with relief when the chief justice issued the majority opinion and observed that "the Court can wash their hands clean of the iniquity of oppressing the Indians, and disregarding their rights."[29]

Unfortunately for the missionaries and the Cherokees, federal law contained enough loopholes to make the Court's decision meaningless. The law stated that the government could not send United States marshals to free the prisoners until the state judge refused in writing to comply with the Court's order. Since the state of Georgia had boycotted the Supreme Court proceedings, its intentions were unmistakably clear. To make matters worse, the Supreme Court adjourned before there was any opportunity to report Georgia's intransigence.[30]

President Jackson did not have legal authority to use military force to execute the Supreme Court's order. Until the Court issued a writ of habeas corpus or summoned state officials before it for contempt, the president was legally powerless to act. Even then, however, the Court had no way to enforce its decree. The existing habeas corpus law did not apply in this particular case since the missionaries were not being held under federal authority. Moreover, there was no provision in existing legislation for a writ of error in case the state court declined to acknowledge in writing its refusal to obey the order. Since the Georgia court did exactly that, enforcement of the decision in *Worcester* v. *Georgia* was impossible under existing law. As President Jackson himself observed, "the decision of the supreme court has fell still born, and they find that they cannot coerce Georgia to yield to its mandate." The president hoped that the Court's inability to enforce its mandate would prompt the Cherokees to emigrate in exasperation, and in order to exert additional pressure on them, Secretary of War Lewis Cass asked Baptist missionary Isaac McCoy to "reason" with some of the leading supporters of the Indians in Congress. McCoy visited several opposition leaders and tried unsuccessfully to convince them that the voluntary removal of the Cherokees was the only sensible solution to "the perplexing question arising out of the late decision of the Supreme Court." Jacksonians generally agreed that the removal of the Indians was the only way to alleviate the ominous prospect of federal-state or Indian-white conflict in Georgia, and the president was confident that their removal would ease the tense situation without drawing Georgia into the ranks of the South Carolina nullifiers and without endangering his popularity in the southern states that were anxious to expel their Indian residents.[31]

A number of prominent anti-Jackson leaders, including William Wirt, knew that the Court and the president were powerless to act. Yet they saw the situation as a perfect opportunity to impugn the administration's integrity. They charged Jackson with willful nonenforcement of a Supreme Court decree and took great pains to familiarize the public with Marshall's opinion and to portray Jackson as a subverter of the Constitution who left the missionaries to languish in prison. National Republicans spread rumors that Jackson had promised Georgia officials that he would refuse to carry out any Court order favoring the Indians. Ambrose Spencer, who was working frantically in New York to unite all anti-Jacksonites under one unified banner, assured Daniel Webster that "the effect of fastening upon him such declarations, would be incalculably great." Both Spencer and Webster encouraged widespread publication of Jackson's alleged promise to Georgia. The *Boston Daily Advertiser* summed up the anti-Jackson position:

> Will the Christian people of the United States give their sanction, by placing him again in office, to the conduct of a President who treats the ministers of the christian religion with open outrage; loads them with chains; drags them from their peaceful homes to prison; commits them in defiance of law like common criminals to the Penitentiary, and violently keeps them there, against the decision of the highest law authority affirming their innocence? For throughout this whole business we are to recollect that the real difficulty lies not in the perversity of Georgia, who would not dare to act unless she felt herself supported at head quarters, but in the contumacy of the President, who tacitly and openly bears her out in all her violence.

Opposition leaders made shrewd use of the widespread concern in the North for the plight of the imprisoned missionaries and the Cherokees.[32]

This line of attack reinforced Henry Clay's arguments during the campaign. According to the Kentuckian, Jackson's alleged refusal to enforce the Court's order was just another example of his increasing usurpation of power and his refusal to recognize the supremacy of the Constitution as interpreted by the Court. Following Clay's strategy, the National Republican party platform issued on May 11, 1832, specifically defended the Court's authority, and the party press frequently linked Jackson's veto of the recharter of the Second Bank of the United States with his "nullification" of the Supreme Court's mandate in the Worcester case. The staunchest defenders of the Second Bank were also the most avid critics of Jackson's Indian policy. National Republican newspapers called the president "the persecutor of the missionaries— and the Indians—and the destroyer of the independence and authority of the judicial branch of the Government."[33]

In addition to these scathing attacks from his political adversaries, Jackson also received criticism from many church groups and from diverse humanitarian organizations. The American Peace Society, for example, lamented the plight of the "Oppressed Cherokees" and referred to the tribe as "an American Poland" hopelessly seeking "a refuge from the perfidy of a nation, which, to the cruelty of the Russian despotism, adds the hypocrisy of a claim to republicanism." Abolitionists such as William Lloyd Garrison and Arthur Tappan also rallied to the cause by defending the Indians and the imprisoned missionaries and holding public meetings in their behalf.[34]

The Jackson administration's first direct response to this criticism came in a reply to a memorial from the missionary society underwriting the legal defense of Worcester and Butler. Keenly aware of the publicity that his opponents were getting out of the continued imprisonment of the missionaries in Georgia, Jackson declared that he had no authority to intervene in behalf of Worcester and Butler. Administration spokesmen promptly upheld this statement with lengthy legal arguments demonstrating that the fate of the missionaries was purely a "Judicial question" out of the sphere of the executive branch of the government. Democrats bitterly condemned the "malignant fury" of the "political managers" who were willing to sacrifice "the best interests" of the Indians to embarrass the present administration. There was general agreement in the Democratic camp that "the coalition against Jackson and the fanaticism of his opponents is the key to their affected sympathy with the Indians."[35]

The Jackson administration tried vigorously to portray the Removal Act as a benevolent solution to a serious constitutional problem and to persuade the electorate that the executive had absolutely no authority to interfere in behalf of the missionaries in Georgia. Democratic editors also reminded their readers that Henry Clay and William Wirt, Jackson's two rivals for the presidency, had supported Indian removal while members of Adams's cabinet. In the meantime, Jackson cautioned Georgia Governor Wilson Lumpkin not to undertake any actions that might "give the Federal court a legal jurisdiction over a case that might arise with the Cherokees." Lumpkin heeded the president's advice and agreed to act in "concert" with the administration in order to prevent anti-Jacksonites from reaping additional political gains before the November election.[36]

The Removal Act and the trumped-up charge that he nullified the Supreme Court decree in the Worcester case probably cost Jackson a considerable number of votes in critical states like New York and Pennsylvania. The president's running mate, Martin Van Buren, for example, estimated that the Democratic ticket lost between eight and ten thousand votes in New York alone because of sympathy for the Cherokees and the missionaries. In any event, the issue was not the only concern of the American people and it did not defeat Jackson; he won a clear majority of the popular vote and carried states from every section of the Union.[37]

The winter of 1832–33 brought a temporary respite to the controversy over the Cherokee Indians and the imprisoned missionaries. Some National Republican editors continued their invective, but the ominous prospect of Georgia uniting with South Carolina to nullify the Tariff of 1832 led many opposition leaders to the realization that the bitter partisanship of earlier months had to subside, for the Union itself was now in danger of disruption. Jackson's forthright condemnation of nullification impressed influential opposition leader Daniel Webster as well as others who were momentarily, at least, assuaged by the administration's conciliatory statements concerning the southern Indians. In addition, the president asked Georgia officials to grant pardons to Worcester and Butler, and grateful opposition leaders persuaded the missionaries to accept them. The administration and many of its leading critics had apparently come to a gentlemen's agreement to put aside the Indian question for the moment in order to present a united front against the South Carolina fire-eaters. Jacksonians, National Republicans, and Anti-Masons loved the Union more than the Cherokees.[38]

When the prospect of nullification subsided, however, opposition leaders quickly renewed their attacks on the administration's Indian policy. Members of the nascent Whig party, which absorbed the National Republicans and Anti-Masons, as well as other dissidents, again championed the cause of the southern tribes. Under the leadership of Henry Clay in the Senate, they secured the adoption of resolutions censuring Jackson for, among other things, his alleged disregard of the Supreme Court's decision in the Worcester case. Clay, Webster, and John C. Calhoun became vigorous opponents of removal treaties submitted to the Senate for its advice and consent. Yet the Democrats and the Whigs did not necessarily divide into polar opposites on the handling of Indian affairs.[39]

While Whigs continually accused Democratic administrations of disregarding Indian rights, their party found ample room in its ranks for the authors of the Removal Act—Tennesseans Hugh L. White and John Bell—when they parted political company with Old Hickory. Moreover, William Henry Harrison, the only Whig elected to the presidency prior to 1848, favored Indian removal and selected John Bell as his secretary of war. Some Whigs undoubtedly opposed Indian removal on humanitarian grounds, but most merely treated it as a policy of their opponents. In office under Harrison and John Tyler, the Whigs did not alter the policy by allowing Indians still east of the Mississippi River to remain there. The Whigs found it expedient to condemn the Jacksonian removal policy when they were struggling to gain political control of the government but equally expedient to continue that policy when they themselves were in power.[40]

The United States in the Jacksonian era increasingly became a market-focused society dominated by "expectant capitalists" eager to remove all impediments to rapid exploitation of its natural resources. The federal government was under unremitting pressure to open new lands to settlement and purchase. The presence of Indian title in states and territories of the Union only frustrated the aspirations of settlers and speculators, while posing constitutional questions of a disruptive nature. Whether they were Democrats or Whigs in politics, expectant capitalists viewed allodial ownership of land as superior to Indian title and could little afford to sympathize with Indian claims to an *imperium in imperio*. Men of all political persuasions sought the immense tracts of valuable top soil, virgin lumber, and mineral reserves located in Indian country within the United States.[41]

The presence of Indian title within states and territories of the Union frequently acted as a brake on the economic and political development of adjacent areas. Many settlers were reluctant to farm or make improvements on land near Indian country for they feared depredations as well as the uncertainty of their claims. Some state and territorial legislatures were hesitant to organize new county governments and provide land surveys near Indian areas for similar reasons. Residents of states and territories containing Indian title continuously petitioned their representatives in Congress for its extinguishment, and congressmen worked hard for such measures. The propinquity of frontier settlements to hostile tribes meant continual expenditures by both the state and the federal government to protect the lives of American citizens. For all of these reasons, Indian removal became an acceptable and desirable policy evoking little opposition from large sectors of the American people during the Jacksonian era.

Another important reason for growing acceptance of the removal policy was the lack of any suitable alternatives. The American Board, Jackson's political adversaries, and numerous other supporters of the southern Indians argued that the tribes were independent nations with the sole and exclusive right to the property and government of the territories they occupied under treaty stipulations. The board and its allies agreed with Chief Justice Marshall that a degree of independence within the context of the surrounding white society was legally and politically possible as well as morally desirable. Advocates of removal, on the other hand, maintained that the presence of Indian enclaves within the United States would necessitate the presence of sizable military forces to protect Indians from white intruders and whites from Indian depredations. They warned that such conditions would impede economic development, increase the possibility of federal-state conflict, and endanger the existence of the Union.[42]

As Americans became increasingly anxious to justify their dispossession of the Indians, they quickly discovered that Jackson's removal policy, like the civilization program of earlier decades, provided them with a convenient humanitarian rationale. By equating removal with the preservation and civilization of the Indians, as Jackson did, they could stand on high moral ground while relieving the Indians of their land east of the Mississippi River. No presidential administration in the 1830s or '40s refuted Jackson's logic or Indian policy. Francis Scott Key, author of "The Star-Spangled Banner" and a Democrat from Maryland, succinctly stated the Jacksonian position when he remarked that the only way to save the Indians from the vices of white society while holding out to them its benefits was to "buy their lands & send them off." Many of the strongest opponents of removal, like the Reverend Samuel A. Worcester, resigned themselves to the policy after they witnessed the demoralization of the stragglers as emigration began in the early 1830s and continued throughout the ensuing decade. The opposition of missionary groups like the American Board also weakened when, amid fierce competition for educational annuities for emigrant tribes, the government assured the societies that it would help them reestablish their missions and schools in the trans-Mississippi West.[43]

During the 1830s and especially in the 1840s, schoolbook authors and writers in leading literary magazines and political journals argued that Providence or Progress demanded the removal of the Indians who were "disagreeable neighbors," blocking their vision of "cities, lifting their spires and turrets" over the country. Researchers in the nascent field of ethnology declared the Indians to be an "inferior race," thus providing additional justification for removal. A few individuals, such as abolitionists William Lloyd Garrison and Lydia Maria Child, saw removal, like African colonization, as a racist policy, but they were in the minority. Historians such as Francis Parkman and William H. Prescott, scientists like Henry Rowe Schoolcraft and Samuel G. Morton, and literary figures of the stature of Henry Wadsworth Longfellow and James Fenimore Cooper pitied the plight of the Indians but acknowledged that they had to make way for the American dream. Indian removal, especially when presented in humanitarian terms, seemed a logical and even enlightened policy to many Americans during the Jacksonian era.[44]

NOTES

1. *Debates in Congress,* 21st Cong., 1st sess., pp. 1141–46; Daniel Webster to Henry Clay, May 29, 1830, in Colton, *Private Correspondence of Henry Clay,* pp. 274–76; Clay to Edward Everett, June 16, 1830, in Calvin Colton, ed., *The Life, Correspondence, and Speeches of Henry Clay,* 6 vols. (New York: A. S. Barnes & Co., 1857), 4: 273–74; *Knoxville Register,* July 21, 1830; *New-York Observer,* October 30, 1830; Glyndon G. Van Deusen, *The Jacksonian Era, 1828–1848* (New York: Harper Torchbooks, 1963), pp. 48, 50; E. Malcolm Carroll's *Origins of the Whig Party* (Durham, N.C.: Duke University Press, 1925), pp. 55–66, completely omits the opposition's use of the Removal Act to build a substantial anti-Jackson following for the 1832 election.

2. Clay to J. S. Johnston, June 14, 1830, in Colton, *Private Correspondence of Henry Clay,* p. 278; Clay to Everett, June 16, 1830, in Colton, *Speeches of Henry Clay,* 4: 273; Clement Eaton, *Henry Clay and the Art of American Politics* (Boston: Little, Brown & Co., 1957), pp. 116–17. For the petitions opposing the Removal Act, see the indexes to the *House Journal,* 21st Cong., 2d sess. and the *Senate Journal,* 21st Cong., 2d sess.

3. Spencer to Evarts, June 21, 1830, Evarts Papers, Library of Congress; Wirt to Carr, June 21, 1830, same to [William Pope], June 25, 1830, same to [Madison], October 5, 1830, same to Judge Randall, October 7, 1830, William Wirt Papers, Maryland Historical Society, Annapolis, Md.; E. C. Tracy, *Memoir of the Life of Jeremiah Evarts* (Boston: Crocker & Brewster, 1845), pp. 432, 442–48; Anson Phelps Stokes, *Church and State in the United States,* 3 vols. (New York: Harper & Brothers, 1950), 1: 711.

4. Samuel Flagg Bemis, *John Quincy Adams and the Foundations of American Foreign Policy* (New York: Alfred A. Knopf, 1949), pp. 201, 208; Adams, *Memoirs,* 7: 90; Carl Schurz, *Life of Henry Clay,* 2 vols. (Boston: Houghton Mifflin Co., 1887), 2: 59; Eaton, *Henry Clay,* pp. 115–17.

5. Maurice G. Baxter, *Daniel Webster & the Supreme Court* (Amherst: University of Massachusetts Press, 1966), p. 143; Paul W. Gates, "The

Frontier Land Business in Wisconsin," *Wisconsin Magazine of History* 52 (Summer 1969): 308.

6. Spencer to Evarts, June 21, 1830, Evarts Papers, Library of Congress; [Evarts] to Greene, March 31, 1830, Papers of the American Board; Joseph C. Burke, "The Cherokee Cases: A Study in Law, Politics, and Morality," *Stanford Law Review* 21 (February 1969): 506. It is interesting to note that Spencer subsequently served as a commissioner for removing the New York Indians. See T. Hartley Crawford to Spencer, February 17, 1842, IA, LS, 31: 468–70, RG 75, NA; Spencer to [Crawford], February 23, 1842, IA, LR, Seneca Agency, RG 75, NA.

7. Erdman, "Theodore Frelinghuysen," p. 16; Frelinghuysen to Evarts, February 1, 1830, Evarts Papers, Library of Congress; Frelinghuysen to Evarts, January 11, March 7, 1830, Evarts Family Papers, Yale University; Clifford S. Griffin, "Religious Benevolence as Social Control, 1815–1860," *Mississippi Valley Historical Review* 44 (December 1957): 430.

8. Wirt to Carr, June 21, 1830, same to Thomas Swann, October 4, 1830, same to [Madison], October 5, 1830, same to Randall, October 7, 1830, Wirt Papers.

9. Wirt to Carr, June 21, 1830, same to [Pope], June 25, 1830, same to Swann, September 13, 30, October 4, December 6, 1830, same to [Madison], October 5, 1830, same to Randall, October 7, November 19, 1830, Marshall to Carr, June 28, 1830, Wirt Papers; *Niles' Register* 34 (September 4, 1830): 19; *Knoxville Register,* July 21, August 18, 1830; *Nashville Republican and State Gazette,* October 6, 1830, January 4, 1831; Marvin R. Cain, "William Wirt against Andrew Jackson: Reflection on an Era," *Mid-America* 47 (April 1965): 125. Cf. Kenneth W. Treacy, "Another View on Wirt in *Cherokee Nation,*" *American Journal of Legal History* 5 (October 1961): 385–88.

10. Spencer to Evarts, June 21, 1830, Webster to [Evarts], June 28, 1830, Everett to same, July 29, 1830, Clay to same, August 23, 1830, Evarts Papers, Library of Congress; Tracy, *Life of Jeremiah Evarts,* p. 432. Also see Jeremiah Evarts, ed., *Speeches on the Passage of the Bill for the Removal of the Indians, Delivered in Congress of the United States, April and May, 1830* (Boston: Perkins & Marvin, 1830); *North American Review* 31 (October 1830): 396–442.

11. *Georgian* (Savannah), September 9, 1830, quoting the *National Intelligencer;* Clay to Ascher Robbins, August 23, 1830, Miscellaneous MSS., New-York Historical Society, New York, N.Y. (hereafter cited as Misc. MSS., N.Y.). For the events surrounding McKenney's dismissal, see chapter 6. McKenney's reasons for converting to the opposition are detailed in McKenney to Reverend [Philip] Milledoler, August 22, 1831,

Milledoler Papers, New-York Historical Society, New York (microfilm edition in possession of Herman J. Viola).

12. Frelinghuysen to Evarts, January 24, 1831, Clay to Evarts, August 23, 1830, Evarts Papers, Library of Congress; [Evarts] to Everett, February 14, 1831, Papers of the American Board; *New-York Observer,* October 30, 1830; Wirt to Carr, June 21, October 9, 1830, same to Swann, December 6, 1830, same to Mrs. Wirt, February 10, 1831, Wirt Papers.

13. Wirt to Carr, September 29, 1830, same to Swann, December 6, 1830, same to Governor George R. Gilmore, June 4, 1830, same to Mrs. Wirt, February 10, 1831, J[oh]n Ross to Wirt, October 30, 1830, Wirt Papers; Frelinghuysen to Evarts, January 24, 1831, Evarts Papers, Library of Congress; Carroll, *Origins of the Whig Party,* pp. 31–32. For the anti-Jacksonite attack on the first treaty negotiated by the administration under the terms of the Removal Act, see *New-York Observer,* October 30, 1830.

14. *National Banner and Nashville Whig,* June 17, 1830; Gilmer to Wirt, June 19, 1830, in *Niles' Register* 39 (September 18, 1830): 70; Secretary of War, *Annual Report* (1830), pp. 32–34; Gilmer to Eaton, January 1831, in *Senate Document 512,* 23rd Cong., 1st sess., 2: 396; Archibald Yell to James K. Polk, January 10, 1831, in Herbert Weaver and Paul H. Bergeron, eds., *Correspondence of James K. Polk, 1817–1832* (Nashville: Vanderbilt University Press, 1969), pp. 380–81; *Nashville Republican and State Gazette,* December 18, 1830, April 14, 1831; Jackson to William B. Lewis, August 25, 1830, same to Secretary of War [1831], in Bassett, *Correspondence of Andrew Jackson,* 4: 177, 220.

15. Richardson, *Papers of the Presidents,* 2: 519–23. Also see ibid., pp. 512–13.

16. *Cherokee Nation v. State of Georgia,* 5 Peters 1 (1831): 1–15; *American Spectator and Washington City Chronicle,* March 19, 1831; *Niles' Register* 40 (March 26, 1831): 61; Burke, "Cherokee Cases," pp. 512–14.

17. *Cherokee Nation v. State of Georgia,* 5 Peters 1 (1831): 15–20.

18. Ibid. Marshall's contribution to the development of the theory of wardship administration is discussed in Esther B. Strong, "Wardship in American Indian Administration: A Political Instrumentality for Social Adjustment" (Ph.D. diss., Yale University, 1941), pp. 165–70. For Marshall's criticism of the removal policy, see Marshall to Carr, June 28, 1830, Wirt Papers.

19. *Cherokee Nation v. State of Georgia,* 5 Peters 1 (1831): 20–50; *Richmond Enquirer,* March 24, 29, April 29, June 14, 1831; *National Intelligencer,* March 29, April 5, 1831; *Niles' Register* 40 (April 2, 1831): 82; Burke, "Cherokee Cases," pp. 515–16; Eaton to Coffee, March 31, 1831, IA, LS, 7: 168, RG 75, NA.

20. *Cherokee Nation* v. *State of Georgia*, 5 Peters 1 (1831), 50–80; Story to Richard Peters, May 17, September 2, 1831, Marshall to same, May 19, 1831, Peters Papers, Historical Society of Pennsylvania, Philadelphia, Pa.; Burke, "Cherokee Cases," 516–18. For Story's personal opinion of the situation in Georgia, see Story to Professor Ashmun, January 30, 1831, in William W. Story, ed., *Life and Letters of Joseph Story*, 2 vols. (Boston: Charles C. Little and James Brown, 1851), 2: 47–48.

21. J. W. A. Sanford to Gilmer, May 5, 1831, *Senate Document 512*, 23rd Cong., 1st sess., 2: 452; Ross to Wirt, May 10, 1831, Wirt Papers; *Niles' Register* 40 (June 25, 1831): 298; Richard Peters, *The Case of the Cherokee Nation against the State of Georgia, with an Appendix* (Philadelphia: J. Grigg, 1831), pp. 1–286; *American Quarterly Review* 11 (March 1832): 1–30; Fitzpatrick, *Autobiography of Martin Van Buren*, p. 292; Marshall to Peters, May 19, 1831, Peters Papers; Story to Peters, June 24, 1831, in Story, *Life and Letters*, 2: 46. Both Marshall and Story favored Clay's election in 1832. See Charles Warren, ed., *The Story-Marshall Correspondence (1819–1831)*, Anglo-American Legal History Series, vol. 1, no. 7 (1942), pp. 23, 26–27.

22. *North American Review* 33 (July 1831): 136–53; *Boston Courier*, May 19, 1831; McKenney to Milledoler, August 22, 1831, Milledoler Papers; Herman V. Ames, ed., *Reserved Rights of the States and the Jurisdiction of the Federal Courts, 1819–1832* (Philadelphia: University of Pennsylvania, Department of History, 1901), pp. 42–44.

23. Ross to Wirt, May 10, 1831, Wirt Papers; D. A. Reese to Gilmer, June 8, 1831, Alex[ander] Y. McGill to same, June 8, 1831, *Senate Document 512*, 23rd Cong., 1st sess., 2: 484, 3: 490; *Niles' Register* 40 (June 25, 1831): 298; Rachel C. Eaton, *John Ross and the Cherokee Indians* (Chicago: Private Edition, 1921), pp. 54–55.

24. Gilmer to [Jackson], June 17, 1830, *Senate Document 512*, 23rd Cong., 1st sess., 2: 230; *Nashville Republican and State Gazette*, January 1, 1831; Ames, *Reserved Rights of the States*, pp. 40–41; W. S. Coody to Wirt, February 26, 1831, Gilmer to Worcester, May 16, 1831, Wirt Papers; *Missionary Herald* 27 (March 1831): 80–84; Eaton to Gilmer, May 4, 1831, IA, LS, 7: 208, RG 75, NA; Jack F. Kilpatrick and Anna G. Kilpatrick, *New Echota Letters: Contributions of Samuel A. Worcester to the Cherokee Phoenix* (Dallas: Southern Methodist University Press, 1968), pp. 95–114. Also see E[aton] to [Jackson], February 21, 1831, Records of the Office of the Secretary of War, Letters to the President (hereafter cited as SW, LS, President), 2: 226, RG 107, NA.

25. Greene to Wirt, July 12, 1831, Wirt Papers; *Arkansas Gazette* (Little Rock), November 2, 1831.

26. *Niles' Register* 41 (December 24, 1831): 311–12. Baptist missionary Isaac McCoy noted in early 1832 that "the friends of the present

administration are almost universally favorable to the policy of locating all the Indians in the west, while the opposite party in politics advocates the opposite course. It is impossible to suppose that the lines could be so accurately drawn to divide the two political parties upon the Indian question, were they uninfluenced by political considerations." McCoy's Journal, March 28, 1832, McCoy Papers, Kansas State Historical Society, Topeka, Kansas.

27. *Niles' Register* 41 (December 24, 1831): 305; Richard P. Longaker, "Andrew Jackson and the Judiciary," *Political Science Quarterly* 71 (September 1956): 347 n; National Anti-Masonic Convention Resolutions, September 28, 1831, William Wirt Papers and Letterbooks, Library of Congress, Washington, D.C.; Wirt to Swann, October 3, 1831, Wirt Papers, Maryland Historical Society; Burke, "Cherokee Cases," p. 520; Erik M. Eriksson, "Official Newspaper Organs and Jackson's Re-Election, 1832," *Tennessee Historical Magazine* 9 (April 1925): 50.

28. *Niles' Register* 41 (November 19, 1831): 227, 41 (December 24, 1831): 313; *New-York Evening Post,* January 6, 1832; *New-York Daily Advertiser,* January 27, 1832; *National Intelligencer,* March 27, 1832; John Ridge to Roberts Vaux, January 18, 1832, Frelinghuysen to same, February 4, 1832, G. M. Dallas to same, February 12, 1832, Vaux Papers, Historical Society of Pennsylvania, Philadelphia, Pa.; *Debates in Congress,* 22d Cong., 1st sess., pp. 3105, 3117–119; *American Spectator and Washington City Chronicle,* December 31, 1831; McKenney to John McLean, January 29, 1831, McLean Papers, Library of Congress, Washington, D.C.; McKenney to Milledoler, August 21, 1831, Milledoler Papers; McKenney to George W. Strong, October 4, 1831, Misc. MSS., N.Y. (microfilm copy in possession of Herman J. Viola); McKenney to Adams, January 23, 1832, Adams Family Papers, Massachusetts Historical Society, Boston, Mass. (typescript copy in possession of Herman J. Viola); *Poulson's American Daily Advertiser* (Philadelphia), January 17–25, 1832; Adams, *Memoirs,* 8: 477.

29. *Worcester* v. *Georgia,* 6 Peters 515 (1832): 536–63; Story to Mrs. Story, March 4, 1832, in Story, *Life and Letters,* 2: 87.

30. Charles Warren, *The Supreme Court in United States History,* 3 vols. (Boston: Little, Brown & Co., 1923), 2: 224; Burke, "Cherokee Cases," pp. 525–26; *Niles' Register* 42 (March 31, 1832): 78; *North-Carolina Free Press* (Tarborough), April 10, 1832.

31. Warren, *Supreme Court,* 2: 224; Albert Somit, "The Political and Administrative Ideas of Andrew Jackson" (Ph.D. diss., University of Chicago, 1947), pp. 88–90; Burke, "Cherokee Cases," pp. 525–26; *Niles' Register* 42 (March 31, 1832): 78; *North-Carolina Free Press,* April 10, 1832; Jackson to Coffee, April 7, 1832, in Bassett, *Correspondence of*

Andrew Jackson, 4: 430; McCoy's Journal, March 28, 1832, McCoy Papers; Longaker, "Jackson and the Judiciary," pp. 348–50, 364. Many scholars continue to charge Jackson with willful nonenforcement of the Supreme Court decree. The evidence usually cited to support this position is Horace Greeley's *The American Conflict,* 2 vols. (Hartford: O. D. Case & Co., 1864–66), 1: 106, which attributed the following statement to Jackson: "Well: John Marshall has made his decision: *now let him enforce it!*" For some examples of statements following this approach, see Van Deusen, *Jacksonian Era,* 49; Young, *Redskins, Ruffleshirts and Rednecks,* p. 17; Prucha, *American Indian Policy,* p. 245; Edward Pessen, *Jacksonian America: Society, Personality, and Politics* (Homewood, Ill.: Dorsey Press, 1969), p. 320. Richard P. Longaker asserts, in "Andrew Jackson and the Judiciary," p. 350, that "considering the prospect of active resistance in Georgia and the explosive situation in South Carolina at the time, one is left to wonder whether Jackson should not be praised for prudence instead of being condemned for inaction."

32. Frelinghuysen to Vaux, March 6, 1832, Vaux Papers; Story to Ticknor, March 8, 1832, in Story, *Life and Letters,* 2: 83; Spencer to Webster, March 14, 1832, Webster Papers, Library of Congress, Washington, D.C.; Clay to Brooke, March 28, 1832, in Colton, *Private Correspondence of Henry Clay,* p. 331; Wirt to Lewis Williams, April 28, 1832, Wirt Papers, Maryland Historical Society; *Niles' Register* 42 (March 31, 1832): 78, 42 (April 14, 1832): 112, 43 (October 27, 1832): 140; *National Intelligencer,* March 27, April 5, 1832; *House Journal,* 22d Cong., 1st sess., pp. 808, 869; *New Bern Spectator* (North Carolina), April 13, 1832; *Pittsburgh Gazette,* August 28, October 30, 1832; ibid., October 26, 1832, quoting the *Boston Daily Advertiser.*

33. Van Deusen, *Jacksonian Era,* pp. 48, 50; Thomas H. McKee, comp., *The National Conventions and Platforms of All Political Parties, 1789–1900,* 3rd ed. rev. (Baltimore: Friedenwald Co., 1900), p. 29; *Pittsburgh Gazette,* August 28, 1832; *Niles' Register* 43 (September 15, 1832): 47; *Globe* (Washington), October 24, 1832; Harriet A. Weed, ed., *Autobiography of Thurlow Weed* (Boston: Houghton, Mifflin & Co., 1883), pp. 371–72. For a short time in at least one state, the Indian issue received more attention in the partisan press than the debates over the tariff and the Bank. See Donald B. Cole, *Jacksonian Democracy in New Hampshire, 1800–1851* (Cambridge: Harvard University Press, 1970), p. 99.

34. *Calumet* 1 (September–October 1832): 263; Ridge to Vaux, January 18, 1832, Vaux Papers; Lindsay Swift, *William Lloyd Garrison* (Philadelphia: George W. Jacobs & Co., 1911), p. 90.

35. Bernard C. Steiner, ed., "Notes: Jackson and the Missionaries," *American Historical Review* 29 (July 1924): 722–23; Jackson to Anthony

Butler, March 6, 1832, in Bassett, *Correspondence of Andrew Jackson*, 4: 415; *Morning Courier and New-York Enquirer*, March 20, 1832, May 7, 8, 1832; *Baltimore Republican and Commercial Advertiser*, March 21, 1832; *North-Carolina Free Press*, April 10, 1832; *Niles' Register* 42 (April 14, 1832): 112; *Globe*, May 22, October 24, 1832; *Warrenton Reporter*, November 1, 1832; *Richmond Enquirer*, November 2, 6, 9, 1832.

36. Cass to Newnan, July 12, 1832, IA, LS, 9: 24, RG 75, NA; *Globe*, October 24, 1832; Jackson to Lumpkin, June 22, 1832, in Bassett, *Correspondence of Andrew Jackson*, 4: 451; Lumpkin to Cass, September 15, 1832, *Senate Document 512*, 23rd Cong., 1st sess., 3: 452.

37. Fitzpatrick, *Autobiography of Martin Van Buren*, pp. 293–95; Samuel R. Gammon, Jr., *The Presidential Campaign of 1832* (Baltimore: Johns Hopkins University Press, 1922), pp. 136–38; Svend Petersen, *A Statistical History of the American Presidential Elections* (New York: Ungar, 1963), p. 21.

38. *Boston Courier*, November 20, December 3, 4, 15, 1832; *Pittsburgh Gazette*, December 21, 1832; *National Intelligencer*, January 2, 1833; *Morning Courier and New-York Enquirer*, January 21, 1833; Richardson, *Papers of the Presidents*, 2: 597, 599, 604, 610–32; Martin Van Buren to Forsyth, December 18, 1832, Van Buren Papers, Library of Congress, Washington, D.C.; Lumpkin to Cass, January 2, 19, 1833, same to Silas Wright, Jr., et al., January 5, 1833, same to Forsyth, January 4, 19, 1833, in Lumpkin, *Removal of the Cherokee Indians*, 1: 196–208; Story to Judge Fay, February 10, 1833, same to Mrs. Story, January 27, 1833, in Story, *Life and Letters*, 2: 122, 219; *Niles' Register* 43 (February 16, 1833): 419; Wirt to John Williams, February 26, 1833, Wirt Papers, Maryland Historical Society; Webster to Perry, April 10, 1833, in Fletcher Webster, ed., *The Private Correspondence of Daniel Webster*, 2 vols. (Boston: Little, Brown & Co., 1857), 1: 534–35; *Missionary Herald* 29 (March 1833): 111–13; Kilpatrick and Kilpatrick, *New Echota Letters*, pp. 116–28; Carroll, *Origins of the Whig Party*, pp. 71–75, 78–81; Warren, *Supreme Court*, 2: 236–38; Burke, "Cherokee Cases," pp. 530–31. For an analysis of the effects of the nullification crisis on emerging party alignments, see Norman D. Brown, *Daniel Webster and the Politics of Availability* (Athens: University of Georgia Press, 1969).

39. Pessen, *Jacksonian America*, p. 341; Eaton, *Henry Clay*, pp. 107, 117, 152; Phillips, *Georgia and States' Rights*, p. 86.

40. *Nashville Daily Republican Banner*, April 27, 1839; Nancy N. Scott, ed., *A Memoir of Hugh Lawson White* (Philadelphia: J. B. Lippincott & Co., 1856), pp. 167, 169; Dale Van Every, *Disinherited: The Lost Birthright of the American Indian* (New York: Avon Books, 1966), pp. 279–80. For the reception given White and Bell by the Whigs when these

Tennesseans refused to support Van Buren for the presidency in 1836, see Joseph Howard Parks, *John Bell of Tennessee* (Baton Rouge: Louisiana State University Press, 1950), pp. 84–132.

41. The interpretation presented here and in the following paragraph is based on contemporary accounts and on a large number of works dealing with the Jacksonian era. For a complete listing of these sources, see Satz, "Federal Indian Policy," pp. 68 n–70 n.

42. Prucha, "Andrew Jackson's Indian Policy," pp. 534–36; James W. Silver, "A Counter-Proposal to the Indian Removal Policy of Andrew Jackson," *Journal of Mississippi History* 4 (October 1942): 207–15. Also see Jack D. Forbes, "Frontiers in American History and the Role of the Frontier Historian," *Ethnohistory* 15 (Spring 1968): 231.

43. *Globe*, May 22, 1833; Van Every, *Disinherited*, pp. 279–84; Key to Roger B. Taney, November 6, 1833, in "Letters of Francis Scott Key to Roger Brooke Taney, and Other Correspondence," *Maryland Historical Magazine* 5 (March 1910): 28; Worcester to [Samuel Chandler], July 7, 1835, in George H. Shirk, ed., "Some Letters from the Reverend Samuel A. Worcester at Park Hill," *Chronicles of Oklahoma* 26 (Winter 1948–49): 471; Everett to Evarts, February 21, 1831, Evarts Papers, Library of Congress; Isaac McCoy to Lewis Cass, April 10, 1832, McCoy Papers. Also see chapter 9, note 15.

44. Ruth Miller Elson, *Guardians of Tradition: American Schoolbooks of the Nineteenth Century* (Lincoln: University of Nebraska Press, 1964), pp. 71–81; *North American Review* 38 (April 1834): 466, 40 (January 1835): 75, 46 (January 1838): 116–18, 52 (January 1841): 77–79; *United States Magazine and Democratic Review* 14 (February 1844): 184; *Southern Quarterly Review* 8 (October 1845): 444; Morton to E. George Squier, December 8, 1846, Squier Papers, Library of Congress, Washington, D.C.; Samuel George Morton, *Crania Americana; or, A Comparative View of the Skulls of Various Aboriginal Nations* (Philadelphia: J. Dobson, 1839), pp. 6, 63, 81–82, 260; Henry R. Schoolcraft, *Personal Memoirs of a Residence of Thirty Years with the Indian Tribes on the American Frontiers* (Philadelphia: Lippincott, Grambo & Co., 1851); Robert W. Mardock, *The Reformers and the American Indian* (Columbia: University of Missouri Press, 1971), pp. 8–9; Horsman, "American Indian Policy," pp. 137–40; Roy Harvey Pearce, *Savagism and Civilization: A Study of the Indian and the American Mind*, rev. ed. (Baltimore: Johns Hopkins Press, 1967), p. 64; David Bidney, "The Idea of the Savage in North American Ethnohistory," *Journal of the History of Ideas* 15 (April 1954): 325–27.

3 /

The Test Case of the Removal Policy

THE REMOVAL ACT of 1830 provided the Jackson administration with congressional sanction and the necessary funds to begin relocating eastern tribes in the trans-Mississippi West. Although the measure failed to offer a blueprint for achieving that goal, President Jackson quickly established the guidelines and procedures for Indian removal that he and his four immediate successors followed.

Jackson's basic Indian policy was to promote removal without doing anything that would alienate public support by appearing blatantly immoral. Old Hickory wanted to accomplish Indian removal quickly, cheaply, and humanely, but his emphasis on speed and economy often undermined efforts to provide adequate care for Indian emigrants.

The president's eagerness to promote removal discouraged any long-range planning by the War Department, which demonstrated an overwhelming willingness to allow the exigencies of the moment to determine the components of the removal process. This lack of planning and cohesiveness resulted in much bungling and an extraordinary diffusion of power that shifted decision making from Washington to local areas. Jackson and, later, Martin Van Buren, John Tyler, and James K. Polk were willing to allow subordinates a considerable amount of decision-making power, including authority to exploit the economic naiveté of the Indians and tribal rivalries in order to expedite Indian removal. The presidential administrations of the Jacksonian era recognized that the success or failure of the goal of relieving the states and territories of their Indian population depended on events taking place hundreds of miles away from Washington. And while the voluntary emigration of small groups of Indians was taking place even during the debates on the Removal Bill as a result of provisions of older treaties, the new measure meant that the federal government had assumed responsibility for operations of a far greater magnitude.[1]

Officials in the Indian Bureau knew that some sort of planning was necessary to guide the large-scale movements of Indians called for by the new legislation. As early as 1829, Indian Bureau head Thomas McKenney had asked Secretary of War John H. Eaton and President Jackson to formulate "one regular and systematic plan" for this tremendous undertaking. McKenney thought that "the country on which it is proposed to place these people at rest, and forever, should be clearly defined, and nothing left unprovided for by the Government, that concerns either their security, preservation, or improvement." Such systematic planning, however, never occurred. The Jackson administration indicated during the debates on the Removal Bill that it opposed any delays in removing Indians to the West which were intended to allow Congress time to define explicitly the "mode and manner" of Indian removal. Later President Jackson and his successors spent so much time trying to convince the Indians to emigrate and trying to counteract the opposition of their opponents that they paid scant attention to systematizing the removal process. While some notable attempts at rationalization occurred during the Jacksonian era, the object of most of them was merely to reduce expenditures or to appease public opinion.[2]

The economy-minded Jackson administration was particularly eager to demonstrate that Indian removal would not be an excessive burden on the federal government. During the debates on the Removal Bill, antiadministration congressmen had warned that tremendous federal spending would result from the passage of the measure. Henry Clay, for example, argued that Indian removal would cost more than forty million dollars. Thomas McKenney and second auditor William B. Lewis, however, assured the president and the press that the total cost would be closer to three or four million dollars. In order to guarantee this comparatively low figure, McKenney and Lewis secured the adoption of the system of accepting bids from contractors for removing the Indians. This procedure, however, was particularly reprehensible to anti-Jacksonites, who argued that only harsh, inhuman treatment would result from its implementation. Ironically, these men were at least partially responsible for the adoption of the bidding system and the economy-mindedness that characterized federal Indian policy during the Jacksonian era.[3]

Although the Jackson administration spent considerable effort reassuring congressmen that Indian removal was economically feasible, it lost little time in coaxing the southern tribes to emigrate. The New York Indian Board and the president's special emissaries to the southern Indians were already working to break down tribal resistance to removal. The southern tribes received the president's special attention. He told congressmen from the Old Northwest and officials in New York that they would have to wait before funds for removing the Indians in their states would be available because the administration was giving top priority to putting into motion "a great tide of Southern Indian emigration." Jackson was evidently quite eager to pay off his election debt to the southern states which had helped to propel him into the presidency.[4]

Shortly after the passage of the Removal Act in May, 1830, Jackson and Secretary of War Eaton urged the Choctaws, Cherokees, Creeks, and Chickasaws—four of the largest Southern tribes —to send delegates to meet them in Tennessee to discuss their future. The Cherokees and the Creeks, looking to the Supreme Court as their savior, refused Jackson's invitation. The president and his entourage, however, met with the Chickasaws at the Masonic Hall in Franklin, Tennessee, in the summer. Little came from this meeting except a provisional agreement with Jackson's "Chickasaw friends," but the president's personal diplomacy demonstrated that he meant business. Opposition leaders eagerly attacked the machinations of the "travelling cabinet" and asked whether Jackson was acting as the president or as an Indian commissioner. Such criticism had little effect on Old Hickory, who soon concentrated his efforts on the Choctaws, the neighbors of the Chickasaws, who had refused to travel to Tennessee.[5]

The Choctaws comprised a powerful tribe which had played a significant role in the diplomacy of the lower Mississippi Valley for generations. Jackson had always considered them a tremendous obstruction to American development in the Southwest. Together with the removal of the Chickasaws, the emigration of the Choctaws would relieve Mississippi of its Indian population and tighten America's grip on the lower Mississippi Valley.[6]

Some Choctaws were not entirely unreceptive to the idea of removal. For a number of years the Choctaw mixed-blood leader Greenwood LeFlore had listened attentively to offers from the War Department to shower him with special favors if he encouraged his tribe to leave Mississippi. During the Adams administration, Thomas McKenney had urged LeFlore to *"rise up"* like Moses and Aaron and point his people to *"a goodly land"* across the Mississippi River. McKenney promised to do "great things" for LeFlore if he would persuade his kinsmen to emigrate. Such pressure on LeFlore and other Choctaw leaders increased with the advent of the Jackson administration. Pamphlets urging Choctaw leaders to be the Joshuas of their nation flooded the tribal council at the time that the extension of Mississippi laws over the Indians in early 1830 had thrown them into great confusion.[7]

LeFlore saw the chaos resulting from the extension of state laws over his tribe as an excellent opportunity to consolidate his power while reaping some of the benefits promised him by the United States. In April, 1830, the shrewd mixed-blood decided upon the novel idea of drafting a removal "treaty" with generous provisions and submitting it to President Jackson as a fait accompli. He believed that this unprecedented action would galvanize the Choctaws, thereby strengthening his political position as well as making the Jackson administration indebted to him. LeFlore received encouragement and aid from Alexander Talley, a resident Methodist missionary, who feared that the abrogation of tribal law by the state legislature would lead to the demoralization of the Choctaws and the wholesale introduction of liquor among them by avaricious whites.[8]

President Jackson responded promptly to LeFlore's move. Keeping firmly in mind the fact that the Choctaws constituted

"one of the most numerous and powerful tribes within our borders" and that the conclusion of a treaty with them might thereby
have "a controlling effect" upon other tribes, he gave serious consideration to LeFlore's "treaty." While Jackson personally
doubted the necessity and wisdom of all the provisions in that
unique document, he concurred with other administration officials who viewed it as "the basis" of a formal agreement.[9]

The president was so anxious to take advantage of LeFlore's
initiative that on May 6 he broke precedent by transmitting the
treaty to the Senate for its advice before formally asking that body
to ratify the document. Jackson admitted to the members of the
Senate that the pecuniary stipulations in the treaty were extrava-
gant, but he urged them not to be parsimonious in this important
matter. He suggested that the total amount of money paid to the
Choctaws for their land in Mississippi was of "minor importance,"
for the sale of Indian land to white settlers would adequately cover
the cost of removal. The president cautioned the Senate to give
the treaty serious consideration, since it involved "a question in
which several of the States of this Union have the deepest interest,
and which, if left undecided much longer, may eventuate in serious injury to the Indians."[10]

Jackson openly admitted that his request for advice without
asking for ratification of the treaty was an extraordinary step. He
defended this unusual action by saying that he wanted the Senate
to consider some amendments he had drawn up and that he
needed its opinion since the United States had not actually taken
part in drafting the document. The president advised the Senate
that he would "most cheerfully adopt any modifications which on
a frank interchange of opinions my constitutional advisers may
suggest and which I shall be satisfied are reconcilable with my
official duties." Most senators, however, found the terms of the
treaty unreasonable, and some questioned whether it represented
the will of the entire tribe. For these reasons the Senate returned
the treaty to Jackson without taking any action. The entire episode, however, demonstrated the president's willingness to take
unprecedented action to remove the southern Indians.[11]

Jackson moved quickly after the Senate refused to consider
LeFlore's treaty. He sent Secretary Eaton and his close friend John
Coffee to Mississippi to secure a formal treaty with the Choctaws.

The successful negotiations in Mississippi and the ensuing removal of these Indians deserves extended analysis for two important reasons. First, the Choctaws were the first tribe to sign a removal treaty under the stipulations of the Removal Act of 1830. Secondly, both the Jacksonians and their political opponents viewed the Choctaws as a crucial test case for the administration's Indian policy.[12]

Approximately five to six thousand Choctaws met the United States negotiating team at Dancing Rabbit Creek in Noxubee County, Mississippi, during mid-September, 1830. Secretary Eaton relied on the army to handle the enormous problem of provisioning the Indians during the parley. Every Indian attending the treaty council received rations of beef, corn, and salt each day the negotiations continued. After taking care of the immediate needs of the Indians, Eaton took additional measures to assure the successful completion of the negotiations.[13]

The secretary of war ordered all the missionaries who had accompanied the Choctaws to the treaty grounds to leave the area during the meeting. Eaton feared they would impede the negotiations, and he refused to listen to their criticism of his orders. Following their exclusion, the secretary of war distributed generous presents of calico, quilts, soap, razors, and similar items to the Indians. At the same time he and Coffee continually warned the Choctaws that the only alternative to removal and self-government in the West was submission to state laws and disruption of tribal life. Some final inducements included the promise of land grants and other privileges to tribal leaders, land allotments to those preferring to remain behind, annuities for the support of education and tribal government, transportation to the West, subsistence for one year, and reimbursement for any property or livestock left behind. All of these provisions formed the basis of the removal treaty dictated by the commissioners and signed by Choctaw "chiefs, captains, and head men" on September 27 and 28, 1830.[14]

According to the Treaty of Dancing Rabbit Creek, the United States pledged to make the westward trek of the Choctaws as comfortable and orderly as humanly possible. The treaty called for three groups of emigrants to the new Choctaw area lying west of Arkansas Territory in what is now Oklahoma. One group was to leave in the fall of 1831, another in 1832, and the last in 1833. The federal government accepted full responsibility for transporting and providing subsistence for these emigrants, and the War Department began making preparations for the first group before the Senate ratified the treaty. The Jackson administration was particularly anxious to have the Choctaw removal proceed quickly but also amicably and without problems, since its opponents would win a moral victory if it was anything but humane and successful.[15]

The task of providing for the emigrants fell to Commissary General of Subsistence George Gibson, who had capably provided the army with rations since 1818. Gibson was fully cognizant of the tremendous administrative burden and moral responsibility he was undertaking. The general's instructions to his subordinates also reflected the administration's desire to use the Choctaw removal as a model to impress other tribes and its political opponents with the fact that removal was a beneficent policy. At the same time, however, Gibson was under strict orders to economize as much as possible in order to disprove charges that removal would financially overburden the government. The responsibilities on the general's shoulders were tremendous; as he put it, "every care and economy are to be practiced."[16]

During the long interval between the signing of the treaty and the departure of the first group of emigrants in 1831, the War Department was busy preparing the Choctaws for removal. At the outset, the department found it necessary to reconcile dissident tribesmen to emigration.

One of the immediate results of the signing of the removal treaty was the outbreak of intertribal conflict in Mississippi. Opposition to the treaty became a pawn in the factional strife between mixed-bloods who espoused emigration and received support from Baptist and Methodist missionaries who wanted to remove the Choctaws from the contaminating influence of white frontiersmen, and full-bloods who opposed emigration and had the sympathy of Presbyterian missionaries who had been at work among the Choctaws longer than the Baptists and Methodists and wanted to continue their operations in Mississippi. One district voted to replace LeFlore as chief, while others threatened to depose all those who had signed the treaty. Apparently not all members of the tribe believed that removal was the only alternative open to them;

many thought that Eaton and Coffee had deceived them. Mushulatubba, a full-blood chief and a famous warrior who had signed the treaty, argued that his people had a right to remain on their ancient lands even though the state had extended its laws over them; he had already announced his candidacy for election to the United States Congress. Some dissident Choctaws even made threats against the lives of the chiefs who, they alleged, had signed the Treaty of Dancing Rabbit Creek in exchange for bribes from Secretary of War Eaton. Growing opposition to the treaty and rumors that discontented full-bloods might take up arms against the government led Secretary Eaton to take immediate action.[17]

Eaton undertook several steps, including intimidation and interference in tribal government, to bind the Choctaws to the treaty. First, he warned the Choctaws that murder and violence would only result in their confinement in Mississippi prisons. "Keep at peace and be happy," he advised, "for otherwise you will soon become wretched and miserable indeed." Eaton dispatched a cavalry company to the Choctaw country to maintain peace and assure the tribe's allegiance to the treaty. He also warned the Indians that "no other Chiefs will be acknowledged by the Government where they now are, and where the laws of the State of Mississippi govern, but those with whom the late treaty was made." The secretary also advised the Indian agent in Mississippi to tell the Choctaws that "when they move and settle in their new country west, . . . then they will be at a liberty to make their own laws, elect their own Chiefs, and live under their own Government." Until the Choctaws actually arrived in the West, however, Eaton refused to countenance any changes in tribal government or leaders. Meanwhile, he stated for public consumption in his annual report for 1830 that the "unhappiness" of the Choctaw full-bloods was merely "the work of persons who have sought, through the channels of their ignorance, to persuade them to the belief that great injustice has been practised."[18]

In order to placate the dissident Choctaws, Eaton offered George S. Gaines of Demopolis, Mississippi, the position of chief removal agent west of the Mississippi River. George Gaines, the brother of General Edmund Pendleton Gaines, an old army comrade of the president, was highly respected by the Indians because of his long and honest record of dealings with them as a merchant.

Other steps taken to assure support for the treaty included the granting of special privileges to tribal leaders. Chief David Folsom, for example, received federal assistance to send his two sons to a private academy in Georgia in return for his support of the treaty. By such actions, the War Department quieted much of the tribal dissension.[19]

Although the administration intimidated or appeased most Choctaw opponents of the treaty, it still had to secure the Senate's ratification of the document. President Jackson undertook an extensive lobbying effort, but the Senate dallied five months before ratifying it. The administration, however, did not wait that long before preparing the Indians for removal. Although some Choctaws refused to get ready until the Senate ratified the treaty, the War Department and Greenwood LeFlore immediately began preparations to put the document into effect.[20]

While the Senate was discussing the fate of the Choctaw treaty, agent Gaines conducted an exploring party of Choctaws to the area assigned to them in the West by the government. The War Department hoped that this expedition would allay rumors fostered by administration opponents and antitreaty Indians that the area was unfit for human habitation. The journey had the desired effect. The exploring party happily reported that the land was suitable for farming and well wooded and contained sufficient water courses. By the beginning of 1831, Gaines had reconciled a majority of the tribe to removal and adherence to the treaty.[21]

The War Department's initial arrangements for removing the Choctaws were extensive. Government estimates indicated that approximately five to six thousand Choctaws and their slaves would leave in the first group. Commissary General of Subsistence Gibson worked closely with Gaines and other agents to assure the "comfort and happiness" of the emigrants. To guarantee sufficient supplies of food for the Choctaws, General Gibson ordered a census of the tribe. Meanwhile, Gaines and his subordinates encouraged Arkansas farmers to plant corn instead of cotton. In order to prepare for unexpected emergencies, however, field agents ordered corn on a standby basis from merchants in New Orleans and Saint Louis. They prepared wagons, blankets, guns, axes, hoes, and plows for the emigrants. The agents also ascertained the availability of drinking water along the proposed routes, advertised for cattle in Arkansas and Missouri, and erected depots at various stopping places and stocked them with corn and animals that could be slaughtered as the need arose. To lessen the chance that a "defalcation" by a contractor might place the Indians in a "distressed" state, General Gibson ordered the agents to award the contracts for food supplies to several contractors. The editor of the *Arkansas Gazette* praised these efforts to make the westward trek of the Choctaws as comfortable as possible and also happily noted that Indian removal would provide "profitable employment" for the people of his territory.[22]

In spite of the initial efforts of the War Department and the smaller-than-anticipated number of Choctaw emigrants in the first party, the Indians left Mississippi later in the fall than planned and encountered many needless ordeals. Indeed, the Choctaw removal of 1831 provides an excellent case study of the confusion, bureaucratic inefficiency, and unnecessary, albeit unintentioned, hardships that typified the westward emigration of the American Indians during the Jacksonian era.

Events in Washington in mid-1831 seriously handicapped the preparations for the first removal party. Secretary of War Eaton resigned in April in order to "put on the agreeable garb of a private citizen" following the Peggy O'Neill affair. Lewis Cass, Eaton's successor, found it necessary to allow Indian removal agents extensive discretionary powers in order to cope with the multitude of new problems confronting him in his early months in office. In addition, Cass tried to use the patronage of the Choctaw removal operation to strengthen his own political position. Although Eaton had previously promised George Gaines the appointment as removal superintendent, Cass awarded the responsibility of removing the Choctaws to the Mississippi River to Tennessean Francis W. Armstrong. This appointment was clearly politically motivated. Armstrong, the brother of a confidant of President Jackson, had "talked loudly" for Jackson in the 1828 canvass and was now looking for a good sinecure. At the same time, George Gaines's brother, General Edmund Pendleton Gaines, had stirred the wrath of the president. The general's pronouncements against Indian removal and his failure to side with the president to protect the honor of Peggy O'Neill had caused a misunderstanding that was ripening into actual enmity. The selection of Armstrong, therefore, was a shrewd political move by Cass, who harbored thoughts of winning Old Hickory's support for a try at the presidency. Unfortunately for Cass, however, Armstrong's appointment actually impeded the removal process.[23]

Although Gaines soon resigned himself to accepting the fact that Cass would not honor Eaton's promise to him, the Choctaws were unwilling to submit to the patronage-dispensing whims of the new secretary of war. The Indians adamantly refused to prepare for emigration until their friend Gaines was at their side. "When Mr. Gaines is ready," they said, "we will be ready." The Choctaws knew and trusted Gaines. He had taken them to inspect their new country in the West, and now they wanted him to lead them there. Secretary Cass responded to the Choctaw demands and the slackening off of removal preparations by assigning Commissary General Gibson to overall control of the field operations, including authority to nominate agents.[24]

Anxious to placate the Choctaws and to commence emigration as soon as possible, Cass had Gibson transfer Armstrong to the important position of Choctaw agent in the West and then placed Gaines in control of all removal operations to the west bank of the Mississippi River. Gibson agreed with the secretary of war that the appointment of Gaines was a necessary step to *"break the ice & pave the way for future removals."* He ordered Gaines, who reluctantly accepted this limited position, to deliver the Indians to Captain John B. Clark of the U.S. Third Infantry, who would escort them from the western bank of the Mississippi River to their new home. Situated in Washington, far removed from Mississippi, Gibson found it necessary to delegate to Gaines and Clark a considerable amount of discretionary authority. Gibson informed both men that "the nature of the service requires that you should be allowed a discretion as to all matters that may incidentally arise." He also instructed them to "employ as many assistants [as necessary] and at such compensation as may be deemed fair for the services performed." The general concluded his instructions by directing the new superintendents to "apprise the department, at the instant, of every thing that concerns your duties."[25]

The result of such demanding orders was that the War Department received a flood of correspondence from field officials. Supervisory personnel in the field were extremely reluctant to undertake any activities without prior sanction from Washington. Agents, who were mostly military men on leave for service with the Indian department or civilians seeking to amass some capital to commence a career in politics or business, feared that any action taken without prior approval from the War Department might tarnish their military record or provide political opponents with ammunition at a later date. Field officials continually awaited approval of their plans by the War Department and constantly complained about the irregularity of the mails.[26]

At the same time, the extensive authority delegated to the removal agents caused other problems. Captain Clark in particular reacted caustically to the wide latitude which Gibson seemed to give his inexperienced field representatives. When first appointed as removal superintendent west of the Mississippi River, Clark was under the impression that Gibson would name subordinate agents to purchase and issue rations. To his astonishment, however, he soon received orders requiring him to select the points of issue for rations and to appoint persons to these posts, for whom he would be "strictly responsible." Dumbfounded by these instructions, Clark immediately protested to Gibson that he could not understand why he was asked to assume such a great degree of responsibility for a matter he knew so little about. "I hope the instructions," Clark wrote, "are not intended to mean all that they seem to convey, viz, that I will select agents from persons with whose integrity or qualifications I am entirely unacquainted, to be placed on duty beyond my immediate control, and to be responsible to the United States for the faithful performance of their duty." The captain also reminded Gibson that "agents selected for these stations must of necessity have supplies placed in their hands, and probably money for contingencies." Clark was anxious to know the exact extent of his responsibility for their actions. "Should any prove faithless and abuse the confidence reposed in them," he asked, "is it intended that I am to be accountable for their default?"[27]

Captain Clark had raised some extremely important questions. Officials in Washington recognized that it was impossible for them to direct all the multifarious aspects of Indian removal, but in their eagerness to allow agents in the field a good deal of discretionary authority they had placed very heavy burdens on the shoulders of men in lower echelons of the government service. Army personnel assigned to Indian duty especially resented this. Career officers like Clark had good reason to fear the possibility of frauds committed by civilian subordinates who were mostly politicians or expectant capitalists looking for temporary sinecures in the removal business. Wharton Rector, for example, resigned his higher-paying position as Quapaw subagent in order to become a "Special Agent" for removing the Choctaws. Rector was so eager to obtain this lower-paying job that he had his friend Ambrose H. Sevier, the Arkansas territorial delegate to Congress, pressure the administration into giving "our friend Rector" this new "berth." Doctor John T. Fulton, the brother of a close friend of President Jackson, gave up his medical practice, his office as postmaster, and his drug store in Little Rock in order to serve as a removal agent. With such men as Rector and Fulton seeking to turn the Choctaw removal into a profit-making business, it is easy to understand Captain Clark's reluctance to be responsible for unknown civilian subordinates.[28]

The response of the commissary general to Clark's inquiry was equivocal. Gibson assured the captain that "the department is willing to trust to your zeal and devotion in the duties assigned to you, without requiring a responsibility which neither could make you secure in assuming." In spite of this assurance, however, Gibson refused to relieve Clark of responsibility for "the whole operation of removal and subsistence from the Mississippi westward," and he also failed to provide the frustrated captain with any guidelines for his operations. As a result, Clark was left in doubt as to the exact place or time the Choctaws would cross the river, the route he should use to bring them to their new home, and the method he should adopt in supplying them with food. Thoroughly disgusted with Gibson's refusal to come to his aid, Clark requested an immediate transfer of duty. The captain's frustration ended when his transfer arrived, but the problems he complained about continued to plague other removal officers.[29]

The wide latitude of discretionary authority delegated to field officials led to many unforeseen problems, as did the fact that the entire removal operation was divided up among numerous field personnel. Bickering among the agents was widespread. Disagreements as to the best routes to take or the proper places or mode for distributing goods and rations caused unnecessary delays for the emigrants while field agents waited for Washington approval of their pet projects. The late arrival of the money appropriated by Congress for removing the Choctaws further complicated the already tense situation.[30]

Great delays resulted from the necessity of transferring funds from Washington to the field. Captain Jacob Brown, who replaced Clark as superintendent, reported that his men were "begging for funds. They tell me it will be impossible to sustain themselves and parties much longer." Brown advised the War Department to deposit funds in New Orleans immediately so he could draw on them. "I shall do every thing that is within the scope of human possibility," he told Gibson, adding that "three days ago, I parted with the last *five* dollars of my own money to start an express to the post. God grant the speedy arrival of funds."[31]

In response to the urgent need for funds by field officials, Commissary General Gibson sent newly appointed Choctaw agent Francis Armstrong from Washington to Little Rock, Arkansas, in November, 1831, with fifty thousand dollars. Armstrong did not arrive at Little Rock until late January because he stopped in Nashville to spend part of the winter at his home. He took this unusual step because of the severity of the weather. "There has never been any thing like the season thus far," he complained. On his journey from Nashville to Little Rock, which he began on January 1, he took along his brother William as an unofficial escort. "The truth is," Armstrong later confided to General Gibson, "I preferred confidential company, because the small sized notes . . . makes the money quite a bundle, and the rapidity of the Mississippi *settling about the swamps* makes me feel the risk greater than I thought it was when at Washington." Armstrong had good reason to be cautious. As he told Gibson, "a few days ago a set of villains boarded, while aground, the steamboat Favorite, and plundered and burnt her."[32]

Armstrong, his brother, and the fifty thousand dollars got to Little Rock safely in late January. But even with the arrival of the badly needed funds, there were other serious problems to tackle that the War Department had not previously considered. At a time when Jacksonians were seeking to undermine the "monstrous" Bank of the United States, Indian removal agents were discovering that the bank's notes were extremely handy items because there was "no safe place of deposit" in the field.[33]

Despite the shortcomings of the system of delegated power adopted by the War Department, it did have some merits. It allowed removal agents to feed hungry emigrants and provide clothing or medicine in emergency situations without waiting for authorization from Washington. Although the House of Representatives and the administration kept sharp vigilance over federal expenditures for removal, most agents placed the welfare of their charges as their first priority. Generally, the agents ignored budgets and authorized prices for rations when the Indians needed immediate assistance. The Choctaw emigrants of 1831 encountered a great deal of misery en route to the West as a result of their late departure, which exposed them to the severe winter storm blanketing the Missouri-Arkansas area. The conscientious efforts of the superintendents and many of the removal agents, however, saved thousands of them from what one writer calls the "living hell"of the winter of 1831–32.[34]

As the Choctaws made the trek to their new homeland, the French visitor Alexis de Tocqueville observed their arrival at Memphis, Tennessee. Tocqueville noted the presence of "the sick, newborn babies, and the old men on the point of death" among the emigrants during this "exceptionally severe" winter. "They had neither tents nor wagons, but only some provisions and weapons," he reported. As the Indians finally boarded the boat hired to transport them across the Mississippi River, the French visitor noted that "neither sob nor complaint rose from that silent assembly" and vowed that the sight of "afflictions beyond my powers to portray" would "never fade from my memory."[35]

The experiences of the first Choctaw removal party led the Jackson administration to rethink the entire problem of Indian removal and to propose some guidelines for the future. The initial step along these lines was an order from Secretary Cass in April, 1832, relieving all civilians from their posts and turning the entire problem over to the military. The secretary then issued regulations in May placing Commissary General of Subsistence Gibson in charge of all operations and systematizing the removal process. Cass claimed that these steps would alleviate the inefficiency and civilian-military conflict which had marred the first removal experience. He also convinced Congress to establish the office of commissioner of Indian affairs, which would serve as a nerve center for Indian matters under the War Department. Although Cass hoped all of these measures would contribute to greater administrative efficiency, another of the secretary's actions had even more significance for Indian emigrants.[36]

On July 14, 1832, Cass appointed a commission to "visit and examine the country set apart for the emigrating Indians west of the Mississippi." One purpose of this commission was to reconcile the southern Indians to removal by locating for them permanent districts "sufficiently fertile, salubrious, and extensive, and with boundaries, either natural or artificial, so clearly defined, as to preclude the possibility of dispute." President Jackson asserted there was enough good land across the river to provide for all the tribes, and he publicly urged the commissioners to be certain that "full justice should be done to each, and every measure adopted to be as much to their satisfaction as is compatible with the nature of such an arrangement."[37]

The establishment of this commission along the lines which had been suggested by Congressman Joseph Hemphill in 1830 indicated that the administration was willing to learn from its mistakes, but it also represented an attempt to shift public attention and criticism away from the difficulties of the Choctaw emigrants. Jackson was particularly anxious to silence his political opponents, who were riding the waves of sympathy for the beleaguered southern Indians and making it difficult for the administration to secure Senate ratification of additional removal treaties. Jackson and Secretary of War Cass made several unsuccessful attempts to convince William Jay, the son of Revolutionary War leader John Jay and himself a well-known humanitarian, and Roberts Vaux, a Philadelphia Quaker known as one of the most public-spirited men in the country, to serve on the commission. By the summer of 1832, the Jackson administration had recognized the necessity of improving the removal process in order to avoid the problems encountered with the first emigrants and to appease public opinion.[38]

The second and third Choctaw removals in 1832 and 1833 demonstrated that officials had learned some valuable lessons from their earlier experiences. The agents assembled the Indians early to vaccinate them and saw to it that they started their journey before winter in order that "much human suffering will be avoided." In spite of such efforts, however, the removal process still suffered from earlier problems. Jurisdictional disputes continued. The cholera took its toll. Field officials continued to look to Washington for approval of their intended actions, and they continued to complain about the slowness of the mail and the late arrival of funds. To make matters worse, the administration demanded that agents follow "a strictly economical course" in order to compensate for the large unplanned expenditures of the first removal party. The War Department ordered agents to justify in writing every single expense not lowered from earlier removals and reminded them that "there can be . . . no allowance, in addition for any purposes whatever." Consequently, field agents took economy measures that undermined their humanitarian improvements.[39]

One way to cut expenses was to reduce the cost of rations, but the government was already accepting only the lowest bids from contractors. The problem was that citizens of Arkansas and other adjoining areas saw that they were in a good position to make a handsome profit by compelling the government to accept their prices. The cost of rations averaged about seven cents a day for each Indian. In one effort to lower removal expenses, in 1832, military disbursing agent Lieutenant Gabriel J. Rains tried to supply destitute Choctaw arrivals in the West with old pork from the army storehouse at Fort Gibson in the Indian country. Rains admitted that the military had condemned the pork four or five years earlier, but he assured General Gibson that it was "not putrid nor spoiled, except by age and salt." Gibson agreed with Rains that the government could do little for emigrants who had consumed their allotted provisions except issue them the condemned meat. A year later, when some Choctaw emigrants were still suffering from lack of food, Gibson told Rains that "they will, no doubt, willingly accept, under present circumstances, what they formerly rejected."[40]

Needless to say, the Choctaws did not appreciate such federal efforts to economize at their expense. Comparatively, however, emigration under military control went well, for the Choctaws were basically content with the rations provided by the army officers. The independent contractor usually caused the most problems by inflating the prices of rations while providing skimpy or spoiled portions in order to reap a sizable profit. As one eyewitness wrote about the contractors supplying the Choctaws in the first removal contigent, "their object is to make money without the least feeling for the suffering of this unfortunate people." The Jackson administration might have alleviated this problem by enforcing strict quality control of the goods it purchased, but its emphasis on economy and speed in removal precluded this.[41]

A second possible way to reduce removal expenses was to cut the cost of transporting the Indians to the West. Mixed-blood leader Greenwood LeFlore, who had no intention of leaving Mississippi, suggested that the government pay a "commutation fee" of ten dollars to Indians willing to emigrate on their own. LeFlore assured administration leaders that this scheme would reduce the cost of removal to "a trifling" figure. Commissary General Gibson approved the plan and recommended it to President Jackson. Attorney General Roger B. Taney assured Jackson that the commutation method would not violate the Treaty of Dancing Rabbit Creek. Impressed with the possibility of cutting transportation expenses and Taney's assurance of the legality of the measure, Jackson personally approved the adoption of the commutation plan. In order to encourage the Choctaws to enroll for removal under this arrangement, the president increased the fee to thirteen dollars. Approximately thirty-two hundred Indians chose the commutation method because they feared the steamboats used by the government. The commutation system brought substantial savings while legally—if not morally—cancelling the government's obligation to bring the Indians safely to their new homes.[42]

This effort to economize had several unfortunate results. Agents Francis and William Armstrong soon discovered that the commutation idea was merely "a matter of speculation with some of the half-breeds to take the Indians over, and subsist them by hunting" along the way. They found it advisable to discourage the idea in order to "protect the common Indians from speculations upon them by leaders of their own party," but the scheme was extensively practiced by the mixed-bloods. Traders also favored this method of removal since the full-bloods made easy prey and because their commutation money would bring specie to areas where it was a scarce commodity. The commutation system saved the government money in the short run, but it also did much to wreck tribal harmony and engender disputes that would later cause the United States great frustration.[43]

Tribal harmony and confidence in the United States government also suffered as a result of another proposal by the administration. While the Choctaw emigrants were en route to the West in 1831, President Jackson decided that a portion of the land assigned to them was needed for the Chickasaws. This tribe had earlier signed a provisional removal treaty, but its emigration depended on the selection of a suitable site across the Mississippi River. Jackson believed he could easily induce the Choctaws to sell the Chickasaws a modest portion of the seventeen million acres they had recently received from the government in exchange for their eastern lands. The president reasoned that the Choctaws were "ancient friends" of the Chickasaws and should be willing to surrender a portion of their vast Western lands to them. He was also confident that the Chickasaws would react favorably to a location near their "elder brethren." Jackson sent Eaton and Coffee, the negotiators of the Choctaw treaty, to "effect an arrangement with the Choctaws."[44]

Eaton and Coffee attempted bribery. They promised tribal leaders they would become the heads of a new "federative government" in the West. The Chickasaws, however, were not pleased with the scheme. They were only one-third as numerous as the Choctaws and did not want to become politically submerged in any new Indian territory. Not until 1837 did these two tribes finally reach a mutual agreement along the lines suggested by the government. In the meantime, however, many Choctaws and their white friends found new reasons to doubt the sincerity of the government's pledge that they would have a permanent title to their trans-Mississippi lands.[45]

When the third party of Choctaw emigrants arrived in the West in 1833, General Gibson discharged the large force of removal agents that had supervised the entire operation. Secretary Cass promptly announced that the United States had fulfilled its legal obligations and that no more Choctaws could emigrate at government expense. Between thirteen and fifteen thousand Choctaws had left Mississippi, but about half that number still remained. Under the provisions of the treaty of 1830, those remaining were to submit to state laws and receive title to land allotments. Throughout the Jacksonian era and as late as the early 1900s, however, groups of full-bloods left Mississippi and traveled to the new Choctaw country in the West. Their hegira was largely a reaction to the treatment they received from the citizens of Mississippi.[46]

Three groups of Choctaws received allotments under the treaty of 1830 in addition to tribal leaders. These included heads of families desiring to remain in Mississippi, Indians who had cultivated the soil, and those whose debts prevented them from emigrating. The allotment provisions were largely specious efforts to silence the administration's opponents by demonstrating that the government would not coerce Indians to emigrate against their will and that the government acknowledged the right of Indian tillers of the soil to retain title to their improvements. The allotment system was also an attempt to alleviate the pecuniary embarrassments that prevented some Indians from emigrating and to provide white merchants with an opportunity to collect their debts. George S. Gaines, for example, directly benefited from the Choctaw removal which he helped to promote by securing allotments in return for debts owed his trading firm by the Indians. Indeed, the administration was willing to distribute large numbers of reserves because it believed only a few mixed-bloods would remain in the state. Jacksonian officials viewed the allotment provisions of the Choctaw treaty as an inducement to emigration, and they expected that the full-bloods would be eager to sell their land and join their brethren in the West rather than submit to white laws. President Jackson and his advisers were caught off guard, therefore, when thousands of Choctaws decided to take advantage of the allotment provisions and become homesteaders and American citizens in Mississippi.[47]

The Choctaws remaining in Mississippi were victims of one of the most flagrant cases of fraud, intimidation, and speculation ever recorded in American history. Shortly after the signing of the treaty but before the Senate ratified it, white squatters began inundating the Choctaw country. The War Department sent armed soldiers to remove the intruders, but they kept returning.

Speculators also came. While the army was attempting to keep unlawful squatters off the land, the speculators defrauded the Indians.[48]

The War Department issued strict orders to its field personnel that the government would not permit the Indians to sell their land unless they received a "fair" price. At the same time, however, the Jackson administration was anxious to guarantee the Indians their "right" to sell their land and to emigrate to the West. While the War Department was anxious to "avoid every thing of fraud and imposition" in the demarcation of allotments, its overwhelming purpose was to promote the speedy sale of allotments to white southerners. Secretary of War Eaton voiced concern that the "just demands" of the Indians claiming allotments be taken into account but also urged that "actual surveys to ascertain the quantity of land will not be necessary. The mere stepping over a field, and often the eye alone, will be enough to determine the quantity with sufficient accuracy." Field officials dutifully carried out these instructions. Some actively encouraged the Indians to make use of their freedom to sell their allotments, while others found more forceful ways to encourage removal.[49]

Indian agent William Ward, a southerner and avid supporter of removal, blatantly refused to register the names of heads of families seeking allotments during the six-month registration period provided by the treaty. Astonished by the large number of Choctaws willing to become American citizens in order to remain in Mississippi, Ward repeatedly turned them away. To make matters worse, local law enforcement officials refused to provide the Indians with redress for their grievances against white speculators and squatters.[50]

Increasing political pressure caused the Jackson administration to back away from its initial attempts to keep intruders off Indian lands. U.S. Marshal Anthony Campbell cautioned the administration that any interference with white intruders would be "very objectionable, as a measure of the administration" to southerners. Congressman Franklin E. Plummer of Mississippi warned that his state would not countenance the eviction of the "numerous families of the first respectability from Kentucky, Tennessee, Alabama, Georgia, the Carolinas, and the older settlements of Mississippi, who have, by the tacit consent of the United States' agent . . .

settled in the [Choctaw] nation, and pitched their crops for the year."[51]

Both Campbell's advice and Plummer's warning were unnecessary, since the administration had no intention of alienating public opinion in the South in order to enforce the treaty rights of Choctaws seeking land allotments. When agent Ward assured the War Department that the Indians did not really want the intruders removed, Secretary Cass ordered the recall of the troops sent to evict them. Cass wrote Congressman Plummer that "the President is happy to find that their residence there is acceptable and useful to the Indians; and that he is not called upon to execute those provisions of the treaty of 1830, which require their exclusion from the country."[52]

Abandoned by the government and left to the mercy of Mississippians and other Southern land-grabbers, many embittered Choctaws decided to sell their land as quickly as possible and to emigrate. A large number sold their property rights to the government for fifty cents an acre in order to avoid bickering with avaricious land speculators. Since the Indians did this of their own volition, the administration saw nothing immoral or illegal in it. Other Choctaws secured the services of white attorneys to plead their cases to the government. Some of the attorneys turned out to be speculators whose manipulations only increased the number of Choctaw complainants.[53]

The administration's reaction to the orgy of speculation and fraud in Mississippi was inconsistent with the image that it sought to portray as the benefactor of the southern Indians. The War Department ordered its field representatives to guarantee that all transactions between Indians and whites were "fair & equitable," but since the full-bloods had little notion of the exact meaning of an acre or the probable monetary value of their allotments, this task was too formidable for the small field staff in Mississippi. The administration, moreover, upheld the Indian land-owner's "right" to freedom of contract. To make matters worse, President Jackson refused to rebuke agent Ward. Jackson merely insisted that the Indians not on Ward's register would have to seek redress from Congress. Such petitions were a slow and cumbersome process. The administration was already speeding up the sale of the land ceded by the Choctaws in order to cover the cost of removal and rations for the emigrants, and Mississippi politicians were encouraging "noble pioneers" to settle in the old Choctaw country. But neither the white settlers, whom the Jacksonians alleged they were serving by removing the Indians, nor the Choctaws, who were legally entitled to their land, benefited from the speculation which followed the signing of the treaty of 1830. The immediate beneficiaries were land speculators, who included in their number Jacksonian politicians, federal marshals, and relatives and friends of agents of the General Land Office, among others.[54]

Some Choctaw mixed-bloods, like Greenwood LeFlore, remained unmolested in Mississippi and became prominent citizens and politicians. The majority of the full-bloods remaining in the state comprised a pitiful population of "stragglers" whose presence caused great "annoyance" to the people of Mississippi.[55]

During the latter part of Jackson's second administration, a congressional investigation promoted by prominent Whigs focused attention on the beleaguered Choctaws in Mississippi. John Bell of Tennessee, a convert to the anti-Jackson forces, charged that all the "embarrassments" suffered by these Indians resulted from the malfeasance of agent Ward and the administration's overzealousness in bringing Indian land to market. This criticism stirred the president to action. The administration offered to remiburse all Choctaw heads of families who could submit *"any credible evidence, documentary or oral, coming from any disinterested source"* that Ward had refused to register them. On Old Hickory's last day in office, Congress passed legislation providing for the appointment of a committee to adjust the Choctaw land claims.[56]

Investigations of the Choctaw claims during the administration of Martin Van Buren uncovered the extensive frauds perpetrated against Indian holders of reserves. Similar investigations took place under Presidents John Tyler and James K. Polk, but pressure from the Mississippi delegation in Congress led all three administrations to stress removal and reimbursement of the Indians rather than the relocation of allotments for those defrauded of their land. Some Choctaw stragglers made their way to the new western Indian country during the 1830s and '40s but the majority of these Indians remained in Mississippi as impoverished itinerant agricultural laborers. Their precarious position in the state became clear in 1833 when a new constitution was ratified by the people of

Mississippi. The new frame of government limited the suffrage to free white males and stipulated that the "legislature shall have power to admit to all the rights and privileges of free white citizens of this State all such ... Indians as shall choose to remain in this State, upon such terms as the legislature may from time to time deem proper." The vision of Choctaw homesteaders becoming American citizens residing in Mississippi had faded into obscurity.[57]

Andrew Jackson had hoped that the Choctaw removal of 1831–1833 would set into motion a great tide of Indian emigration to the trans-Mississippi West and simultaneously pacify domestic opposition to his removal policy. The fate of the emigrating Choctaws and their brethren remaining in Mississippi, however, demonstrated that noble rhetoric was insufficient to protect the Indians from poor planning and the vicissitudes of bureaucratic inefficiency or inclement weather, the incompetence or greed of removal personnel and contractors, and the land hunger of white speculators and squatters. The total expenditure incurred by the United States government under the Treaty of Dancing Rabbit Creek came to $5,097,367.50, or about two million dollars more than the amount the Jackson administration had assured Congress would be needed to remove *all* eastern tribes to lands west of the Mississippi River. Yet with respect to Jackson's original intentions, the Choctaw removal was only a partial failure. While it was not the showcase Jacksonians had hoped for, it did not prevent the removal of other eastern tribes.[58]

NOTES

1. McKenney to Eaton, November 17, 1829, IA, LS, 6: 163, RG 75, NA; Bureau of Indian Affairs, Annual Report (1829), p. 172. For a discussion of emigration to the West before 1830, see Grant Foreman, *Indians & Pioneers: The Story of the American Southwest before 1830*, rev. ed. (Norman: University of Oklahoma Press, 1936); Abel, "Indian Consolidation West of the Mississippi," pp. 241–369.

2. Bureau of Indian Affairs, *Annual Report* (1829), p. 166; *Debates in Congress*, 21st Cong., 1st sess., p. 1,132; Abel, "Indian Consolidation West of the Mississippi," p. 412.

3. McKenney to Eaton, April 6, 1830, IA, LS, 6: 374–75, RG 75, NA; Lewis to Eaton, April 12, 1830, in *United States' Telegraph*, August 5,

1830; *Arkansas Gazette,* September 15, 1830; Bureau of Indian Affairs, *Annual Report* (1829), p. 166. Also see *Niles' Register* 39 (September 4, 1830): 19, citing *National Intelligencer.*

4. Sam[ue]l Milroy to Lewis, November 24, 1830, William Hendricks to Milroy, January 12, 1831, Samuel Milroy Papers, Indiana Historical Society, Indianapolis, Ind.; Bureau of Indian Affairs, *Annual Report* (1830), p. 161; S. S. Hamilton to James Stryker, May 20, 1831, IA, LS, 7: 244, RG 75, NA; *Nashville Republican and State Gazette,* January 4, 1831. Congress provided funds in 1832 to extinguish Indian title to land in Illinois, Indiana, Missouri, and the territory of Michigan, but the Jackson administration continued to place greatest emphasis on the removal of the southern tribes. See Commissioner of Indian Affairs, *Annual Report* (1832), p. 162.

5. Jackson to John Pitchlynn, August 5, 1830, same to Lewis, August 31, 1830, same to Polk, August 31, 1830, in Bassett, *Correspondence of Andrew Jackson,* 4: 169, 178–79; Jackson to Polk, August 15, 1830, in Weaver and Bergeron, *Correspondence of James K. Polk,* p. 325; *Niles' Register* 38 (August 21, 1830): 457, 38 (September 18, 1830): 67; *Nashville Republican and State Gazette,* October 6, 23, 1830; Abel, "Indian Consolidation West of the Mississippi," p. 382 and n.

6. Angie Debo, *The Rise and Fall of the Choctaw Republic,* 2d ed. (Norman: University of Oklahoma Press, 1961), pp. 24–57; DeRosier, *Removal of the Choctaw Indians,* pp. v–vi, 164; *National Banner and Nashville Whig,* May 27, 1830.

7. McKenney to LeFlore, January 15, 1828, same to James L. McDonald, February 9, 1830, IA, LS, 4: 252, 6: 259–60, RG 75, NA; *Niles' Register* 38 (March 20, 1830): 73; Debo, *Choctaw Republic,* p. 51.

8. McKenney to White and Bell, April 9, 1830, IA, LS, 6: 381, RG 75, NA; *National Banner and Nashville Whig,* May 27, 1830; *Niles' Register* 38 (May 15, 1830): 216, 38 (August 21, 1830): 457–58, 39 (September 4, 1830): 19; Debo, *Choctaw Republic,* p. 52; Arthur H. DeRosier, Jr., "Andrew Jackson and Negotiations for the Removal of the Choctaw Indians," *Historian* 29 (May 1967): 347–49.

9. Richardson, *Papers of the Presidents,* 2:478–79; McKenney to White and Bell, April 9, 1830, IA, LS, 6: 381, RG 75, NA.

10. Richardson, *Papers of the Presidents,* 2: 478–79.

11. Ibid.; *Niles' Register* 39 (September 4, 1830): 19; Debo, *Choctaw Republic,* p. 52; Abel, "Indian Consolidation West of the Mississippi," pp. 374–75. Arthur H. DeRosier, Jr., erroneously asserts in his *Removal of the Choctaw Indians,* p. 116, that Jackson urged the Senate to reject LeFlore's treaty because it would set a precedent in treaty making that would "bankrupt the government."

12. Margaret L. Eaton, *The Autobiography of Peggy Eaton* (New York: Charles Scribner's Sons, 1932), p. 162; *Niles' Register* 39 (November 6, 1830): 182–83; Bureau of Indian Affairs, *Annual Report* (1830), p. 161; Eaton to Armstrong, April 26, 1831, IA, LS, 7: 199–200, RG 75, NA; DeRosier, *Removal of the Choctaw Indians*, pp. v, 164.

13. Coffee to Jackson, September 29, 1830, in Bassett, *Correspondence of Andrew Jackson*, 4: 180; Journal of Proceedings at Treaty of Dancing Rabbit Creek, 1830, *Senate Document 512*, 23rd Cong., 1st sess., 2: 251–52; *Niles' Register* 38 (October 23, 1830): 140; DeRosier, "Andrew Jackson and Negotiations," p. 352.

14. Journal of Proceedings at Treaty of Dancing Rabbit Creek, 1830, *Senate Document 512*, 23rd Cong., 1st sess., 2: 251–63; Coffee to Jackson, September 29, 1830, in Bassett, *Correspondence of Andrew Jackson*, 4: 180; *Arkansas Advocate* (Little Rock), October 20, 1830; Kappler, *Indian Affairs*, 2:221–27; *Niles' Register* 39 (November 6, 1830): 182–83; DeRosier, "Andrew Jackson and Negotiations," pp. 353–59. The opposition press bitterly denounced Eaton's handling of the negotiations and made some strong charges of misconduct. For examples, see *New-York Observer*, October 30, 1830; *New-York Daily Advertiser*, quoted in *Nashville Republican and State Gazette*, November 13, 1830.

15. Kappler, *Indian Affairs*, 2: 221–27; Bureau of Indian Affairs, *Annual Report* (1831), p. 172; DeRosier, *Removal of the Choctaw Indians*, pp. 129–30.

16. Gibson to Lieutenant J. R. Stephenson, December 7, 1830, *House Executive Document 171*, 22d Cong., 1st sess., pp. 3–4; Russell F. Weigley, *History of the United States Army* (New York: MacMillan Co., 1967), pp. 134–35; Francis Paul Prucha, *Broadax and Bayonet: The Role of the United States Army in the Development of the Northwest, 1815–1860* (Lincoln: University of Nebraska Press, 1967), p. 33; Grant Foreman, *Indian Removal: The Emigration of the Five Civilized Tribes of Indians*, new ed. (Norman: University of Oklahoma Press, 1953), p. 42. Arthur H. DeRosier, Jr., mistakenly calls Gibson a "civilian expert" and the Choctaw removal of 1831 a "civilian effort." See "The Choctaw Removal of 1831: A Civilian Effort," *Journal of the West* 6 (April 1967): 234–47. Francis Paul Prucha points out that the removal of 1831 was "essentially a civilian undertaking," but observes that "it was taken for granted that much of the work and the responsibility in the area west of the Mississippi would fall to army officers. There were few others to whom General Gibson could turn for directing the movement of the tribes in that relatively unknown and unmarked area." See *The Sword of the Republic: The United States Army on the Frontier, 1783–1846* (New York: Macmillan Co., 1969), p. 257.

17. Mushulatubbe to Voters of Mississippi, April 1, 1830, in *National Banner and Nashville Whig*, June 17, 1830; Eaton to Choctaws, November 24, 1830, IA, LS, 7: 94–96, RG 75, NA; Muriel H. Wright, "The Removal of the Choctaws to the Indian Territory, 1830–1833," *Chronicles of Oklahoma* 6 (June 1928): 105–6, 107 n; Debo, *Choctaw Republic*, pp. 51–52, 55; DeRosier, *Removal of the Choctaw Indians*, pp. 132–33; Foreman, *Indian Removal*, p. 29. For information concerning the rivalry between the mixed-bloods and full-bloods, see *Niles' Register* 38 (August 21, 1830): 457–58; *Arkansas Gazette*, September 8, 1830; Young, *Redskins, Ruffleshirts and Rednecks*, pp. 22–31.

18. Eaton to Choctaws, November 24, 1830, Hamilton to Ward, April 11, 1831, IA, LS, 7: 94–96, 184, RG 75, NA; Eaton to Jackson, December 1, 1830, SW, LS, President, 2: 263, RG 107, NA; Secretary of War, *Annual Report* (1830), p. 33.

19. [George S. Gaines], "Removal of the Choctaws," Alabama State Department of Archives and History, *Historical and Patriotic Series* 10 (1928): 14–15; Anthony W. Dillard, "The Treaty of Dancing Rabbit Creek between the United States and the Choctaw Indians in 1830," Alabama State Department of Archives and History, *Historical and Patriotic Series* 10 (1928): 29; Foreman, *Indian Removal*, pp. 27–28; DeRosier, "Choctaw Removal of 1831," p. 238; Eaton to Folsom, December 2, 1830, IA, LS, 7: 101, RG 75, NA. For information on Gaines and his relationship with the Choctaws, see: Reminiscences of Early Times in the Mississippi Territory, 1801–1815, clipping from the *Mobile Register*, J. F. H. Claiborne Collection, Mississippi Department of Archives and History, Jackson, Miss.; Gaines to Coffee, W[illia]m Clark & T[homa]s Hinds, August 13, 1826, John Coffee Papers, Tennessee Historical Society, Nashville, Tenn.; *Niles' Register* 38 (August 21, 1830): 458; Debo, *Choctaw Republic*, pp. 37, 54.

20. Kappler, *Indian Affairs*, 2: 221; *Niles' Register* 39 (February 26, 1831): 460; D. W. Haley to [Talley], November 3, 1830, in Wright, "Removal of the Choctaws," appendix, p. 125; *Arkansas Gazette*, December 8, 1830; Foreman, *Indian Removal*, pp. 31, 44; DeRosier, "Choctaw Removal of 1831," p. 238.

21. *Arkansas Gazette*, February 9, 1831; [Gaines], "Removal of the Choctaws," pp. 11–14; Dillard, "Treaty of Dancing Rabbit Creek," p. 30; DeRosier, "Choctaw Removal of 1831," p. 238.

22. Gibson to Lieutenant L. F. Carter, November 30, 1830, Carter to Gibson, February 17, 1831, in *Arkansas Gazette*, February 23, 1831; Eaton to Armstrong, April 26, 1831, same to LeFlore, May 7, 1831, IA, LS, 7: 199–200, 214, RG 75, NA; Captain J. B. Clark to Gibson, May 24, June 3, 4, 5, 1831, Rains to Gibson, June 5, October 26, 1831, Stephenson

to same, June 1, 1831, IA, Records of the Commissary General of Subsistence (hereafter cited as CGS), LR, Choctaw, RG 75, NA; Gibson to Clark, June 21, August 18, 1831, IA, CGS, LS, A, pp. 13–14, 40–44, RG 75, NA; Secretary of War, *Annual Report* (1831), p. 172; DeRosier, "Choctaw Removal of 1831," pp. 238–40; *Arkansas Gazette,* February 23, 1831. For the census roll of 1831, see IA, Choctaw Removal Records, RG 75, NA.

23. Eaton to Coffee, May 16, 1831, IA, LS, 7: 229, RG 75, NA; Coffee to Cass, August 21, 1831, IA, LR, Choctaw Agency Emigration, RG 75, NA; DeRosier, "Choctaw Removal of 1831," pp. 239–41; [Gaines], "Removal of the Choctaws," pp. 14–16; Carolyn T. Foreman, "The Armstrongs of Indian Territory," *Chronicles of Oklahoma* 30 (Autumn 1952): 294–95; James W. Silver, "Edmund Pendleton Gaines and Frontier Problems, 1801–1849," *Journal of Southern History* 1 (August 1935): 332. The degree of confusion in Washington concerning juridsictional matters relating to the removal of the Choctaws after Eaton's departure is evident in J. H. Hook to P. G. Randolph, July 2, 1831, *Senate Document 512,* 23rd Cong., 1st sess., 1: 21–22. For evidence that Cass had a national following as early as 1832 and was being mentioned as a potential presidential candidate for 1836, see *Pittsburgh Gazette,* December 21, 1832. Francis Armstrong's eagerness to find employment in the Indian removal operation is apparent in Armstrong to Eaton, December 9, 1829, IA, LR, Misc., RG 75, NA.

24. [Gaines], "Removal of the Choctaws," pp. 16–17; Foreman, *Indian Removal,* pp. 45–46; Gibson to Gaines, August 13, 1831, same to Clark, August 18, 1831, IA, CGS, LS, A, pp. 36–38, 40–41, RG 75, NA; Gibson to Colquhoun, August 13, 1831, *Senate Document 512,* 23rd Cong., 1st sess., 1: 33.

25. [Gaines], "Removal of the Choctaws," pp. 16–17; Gibson to Gaines, August 13, 1831, same to Clark, August 18, 1831, IA, CGS, LS, A, pp. 36–38, 40–41, RG 75, NA; Coffee to Cass, August 21, 1831, IA, LR, Choctaw Agency Emigration, RG 75, NA; Cass to Armstrong, September 7, 1831, Cass to Coffee, September 8, 1831, IA, LS, 7: 382, 384, RG 75, NA; [Gibson] to Clark, June 12, 1831, *House Executive Document 171,* 22nd Cong., 1st sess., p. 12. For an account of Gaines's efforts to prepare the Choctaws for emigration and his own views on the need for their removal, see *Mobile Commercial Register for the Country* (Alabama), November 12, 1831.

26. Clark to Gibson, April 13, 23, 27, May 24, June 5, 1831, IA, CGS, LR, Choctaw, RG 75, NA; Statement Showing the Names of Agents Employed . . . in the Removal and Subsistence of the Choctaw Indians, February 20, 1832, *House Executive Document 171,* 22d Cong., 1st sess., pp. 28–29.

27. Clark to Gibson, July 24, 1831, IA, CGS, LR, Choctaw, RG 75, NA.

28. Clark to Gibson, July 30, 1831, Taney to Rector, July 20, 1831, Rector to Gibson; August 23, 1831, Sevier to Gibson, August 21, 1831, Rector to Sevier, November 17, 1831, enclosed in Sevier to Gibson, December 11, 1831, IA, CGS, LR, Choctaw, RG 75, NA; G[ibson] to Rector, July 26, 1831, IA, CGS, LS, A, p. 32, RG 75, NA; Rector to Secretary of War, August 23, 1831, *Senate Document 512*, 23rd Cong., 1st sess., 2: 573–74; Foreman, *Indian Removal*, pp. 46–47, 51.

29. Clark to Gibson, July 24, 30, August 5, 11, 1831, IA, CGS, LR, Choctaw, RG 75, NA; G[ibson] to Clark, August 18, 1831, same to Captain Jacob Brown, September 9, 1831, IA, CGS, LS, A, pp. 40–42, 48, RG 75, NA.

30. [Gaines], "Removal of the Choctaws," p. 18; Clark to Gibson, August 11, 1831, Colquhoun to same, August 11, 1831, IA, CGS, LR, Choctaw, RG 75, NA; DeRosier, "Choctaw Removal of 1831," p. 240.

31. Brown to Gibson, January 11, 12, 1832, *Senate Document 512*, 23rd Cong., 1st sess., 1: 429–30.

32. Armstrong to Gibson, January 3, 26, 1832, *Senate Document 512*, 23rd Cong., 1st sess., 1: 368; Foreman, "Armstrongs of Indian Territory," p. 296.

33. Armstrong to Gibson, January 26, 1832, *Senate Document 512*, 23rd Cong., 1st sess., 1: 368; Clark to Gibson, July 30, 1831, IA, CGS, LR, Choctaw, RG 75, NA.

34. Stephenson to Gibson, December 12, 1831, Brown to same, December 15, 1831, Resolution of the House of Representatives, January 26, 1832, IA, CGS, LR, Choctaw, RG 75, NA; Gibson to Cass, February 20, 1832, *House Executive Document 171*, 22d Cong., 1st sess., p. 2; DeRosier, "Choctaw Removal of 1831," pp. 242–45.

35. Alexis de Tocqueville, *Democracy in America*, ed. J. P. Mayer, trans. George Lawrence (Garden City, N. Y.: Anchor Books, 1969), p. 324.

36. G[ibson] to Gaines, April 27, 1832, IA, CGS, LS, A, p. 105, RG 75, NA; Regulations Concerning the Removal of the Indians, May 15, 1832, Gibson to Armstrong, July 20, 1832, *Senate Document 512*, 23rd Cong., 1st sess., 1: 124–25, 343–49, 2: 825–31; Cass to W. Armstrong, July 2, 1832, IA, CGS, LR, Choctaw, RG 75, NA; U.S., *Stat.*, 4: 564. The most thorough account of the army's participation in Indian affairs before the Mexican War appears in Prucha, *Sword of the Republic*. For the events leading to the creation of the office of commissioner of Indian affairs, see chapter 6.

37. Cass to Wm. Carroll, Montfort Stokes, and Roberts Vaux, July 14, 1832, IA, LS, 9: 33–40, RG 75, NA. For the activities of the commission, see chapter 5.

38. Cass to Major J. W. Flowers, May 24, 1832, *Senate Document 512*, 23rd Cong., 1st sess., 2: 839; John Francis McDermott, ed., *The Western*

Journals of Washington Irving (Norman: University of Oklahoma Press, 1944), p. 9; McCoy's Journal, August 27, 1832, McCoy Papers; *Warrenton Reporter*, November 1, 1832; Jackson to Coffee, November 6, 1832, in Bassett, *Correspondence of Andrew Jackson*, 4: 483. For Hemphill's proposal, see chapter 1.

39. Brown to Gibson, March 8, 1832, February 7, 1833, W. Armstrong to Gibson, October 13, 1832, IA, CGS, LR, Choctaw, RG 75, NA; Cass to W. Armstrong, July 2, 1832, IA, LS, 8: 512, RG 75, NA; G[ibson] to Brown, April 12, 1832, J. H. H. to W. Armstrong, September 5, 1832, IA, LS, CGS, A, pp. 101–2, 230–31, RG 75, NA; F. Armstrong to Cass, April 20, 1832, W. Armstrong to Gibson, August 21, 1832, F. Armstrong to Gibson, December 2, 1832, J. P. Simonton to Gibson, May 2, 1833, *Senate Document 512*, 23rd Cong., 1st sess., 1: 372, 401, 886, 3: 303. Foreman, *Indian Removal*, pp. 74–75, 79; Wright, "Removal of the Choctaws," pp. 119–23. On January 26, 1832, the House of Representatives adopted a resolution calling for information from the executive department on the subject of expenditures involved in removal. For the administration's reply, see: Message from the President . . . in Relation to the Expenditures of the Removal of the Indians West of the Mississippi, March 15, 1832, *House Executive Document 171*, 22d Cong., 1st sess., pp. 1–2. President Jackson boasted to Congress on December 4, 1832, that he had made great strides in reducing the national debt. "That this has been accomplished without stinting the expenditures for all other proper objects will be seen," he contended, "by referring to the liberal provision made during the same period . . . for the removal and preservation of the Indians." Richardson, *Papers of the Presidents*, 2: 597.

40. Brown to Gibson, October 20, 1832, Rains to Gibson, November 20, 1832, April 5, 19, 1833, *Senate Document 512*, 23rd Cong., 1st sess., 1: 481, 837, 842–43; *Arkansas Gazette*, July 3, September 11, 1833; Lonnie J. White, "Arkansas Territorial Indian Affairs," *Arkansas Historical Quarterly* 21 (Autumn 1962): 208; Rains to Gibson, June 10, 1832, IA, CGS, LR, RG 75, NA; G[ibson] to Brown, April 11, 1833, IA, CGS, LS, A, p. 390, RG 75, NA; J. H. H. to Rains, May 6, 1833, IA, CGS, LS, B, p. 1, RG 75, NA.

41. Prucha, *Sword of the Republic*, pp. 257–58; DeRosier, "Choctaw Removal of 1831," p. 245; Captain John Page to Gibson, February 14, 1833, *Senate Document 512*, 23rd Cong., 1st sess., 1: 796; Joseph Kerr to Cass, June 14, 1832, in Wright, "Removal of the Choctaws," pp. 117–18.

42. G[ibson] to Taney, July 25, 1831, same to Gaines, August 13, 1831, Circular from G[ibson], August 12, 1831, J. H. H. to W. Armstrong, September 5, 1832, IA, CGS, LS, A, pp. 30–31, 35, 38, 230–31, RG 75, NA; F. Armstrong to Eaton, July 1, 1831, Colquhoun to Gibson, November 29, 1831, *Senate Document 512*, 23rd Cong., 1st sess., 1: 369, 592; *Arkansas*

Gazette, January 18, November 16, 1832; Wright, "Removal of the Choctaws," p. 123 n. According to War Department estimates in 1845, the actual cost of removing the Choctaws under government supervision in the early 1830s had amounted to $69.64 per Indian plus an additional $27.37 for subsistence in the West. See Secretary of War William Wilkins to W. P. Mangum, February 6, 1845, *Senate Document 86*, 28th Cong., 2d sess., p. 5.

43. F. Armstrong to Eaton, July 9, 1831, F. Armstrong to Gibson, September 17, 1832, W. Armstrong to Gibson, September 17, 1832, *Senate Document 512*, 23rd Cong., 1st sess., 1: 369–70, 379–80. Foreman, *Indian Removal*, pp. 49, 81, 100.

44. Coffee to Cass, August 21, 1831, IA, LR, Choctaw Agency Emigration, RG 75, NA; Jackson to Secretary of War, October 18, 1831, Woodbury to Eaton and Coffee, October 20, 1831, Robb to F. Armstrong, July 19, 1832, Eaton and Coffee to Chiefs and Headmen of the Chickasaw Nation, December 6, 1831, *Senate Document 512*, 23rd Cong., 1st sess., 2: 360–61, 624, 882, 3: 17. Also see Benjamin Reynolds to Eaton, March 27, 1831, Eaton to Coffee, May 16, 1831, same to LeFlore, June 1, 1831, *Senate Document 512*, 23rd Cong., 1st sess.; 2: 291–92, 301, 419–21; Eaton to Coffee, March 31, 1831, IA, LS, 7: 169–70, RG 75, NA.

45. Bureau of Indian Affairs, *Annual Report* (1831), p. 172; Commissioner of Indian Affairs, *Annual Report* (1832), p. 161; Chickasaw Nation to Coffee and Eaton, January 15, 1832, Cass to Charles A. Wicklife, March 1, 1832, *Senate Document 512*, 23rd Cong., 1st sess., 2: 291–92, 787; Eaton to Coffee, May 16, 1831, IA, LS, 7: 228, RG 75, NA; *New-York Advertiser*, January 21, 1832; Correspondence and Agreement between the Choctaws and Chickasaws, January 11–16, 1837, enclosed in W. Armstrong to Harris, January 27, 1837, IA, LR, Choctaw Agency Emigration, RG 75, NA; Kappler, *Indian Affairs*, 2: 361–62; Foreman, *Indian Removal*, pp. 195–203. Also see chapter 4.

46. Gibson to Rector, November 22, 1833, *Senate Document 512*, 23rd Cong., 1st sess., 1: 324; Memorial of the Choctaw Nation, 1873, *House Miscellaneous Document 94*, 42d Cong., 3rd sess., pp. 7–8; White, "Arkansas Territorial Indian Affairs," p. 207; DeRosier, *Removal of the Choctaw Indians*, p. 162; Wright, "Removal of the Choctaws," p. 123.

47. Kappler, *Indian Affairs*, 2: 221–27; Eaton to F. Armstrong, April 26, 1831, Hamilton to Gaines & Co., July 5, August 2, 1831, IA, LS, 7: 200, 293, 315, RG 75, NA; General Disposition of Moon Tubbu, January 30, 1838, IA, Choctaw Claims Journal of Commissioners Murray and Vroom, 1837–38, RG 75, NA; Young, *Redskins, Ruffleshirts and Rednecks*, pp. 3, 11–13, 19–20, 32, 44–45, 47–58.

48. Eaton to Ward, November 13, 1830, *Senate Document 512*, 23rd

Cong., 1st sess., 2: 42–43; Foreman, *Indian Removal*, p. 31; Young, *Redskins, Ruffleshirts and Rednecks*, p. 47.

49. Eaton to F. Armstrong, April 26, 1831, Hamilton to Ward, June 16, 1831, IA, LS, 7: 198–99, 277–78, RG 75, NA; Hamilton to Ward, October 29, 1831, IA, LR, Choctaw Agency Emigration, RG 75, NA; Taney to President, November 1, 1831, *Senate Document 25*, 25th Cong., 2d sess., p. 16.

50. Ward to Hamilton, June 21, 1831, A. Campbell to Cass, August 5, 1832, W. Armstrong to Gibson, October 13, 1832, *Senate Document 512*, 23rd Cong., 1st sess., 1: 386, 2: 493, 3: 416–18; Ward to Hamilton, October 29, 1831, IA, LR, Choctaw Agency Emigration, RG 75, NA; Application for Indemnity, for being Deprived by Settlers of Reservations of the Choctaw Indians, February 1, 1836, *American State Papers: Public Lands*, 8: 432; General Disposition of Jesse M. Field, January 5, 1838, IA, Choctaw Claims Journal, RG 75, NA; Memorial of the Choctaw Nation, 1873, *House Miscellaneous Document 94*, 42d Cong., 3rd sess., pp. 11–12. For evidence that Ward was both an intemperate and an incompetent agent, see General Disposition of Colonel McKinney Holderness, November 30, 1837, General Disposition of Field, January 5, 1838, General Disposition of Calvin Cushman, January 13, 1838, IA, Choctaw Claims Journal, RG 75, NA.

51. Robb to Campbell, July 19, August 29, 1832, IA, LS, 9: 68–69, 196, RG 75, NA; Cass to Plummer, May 23, 1832, Plummer to Cass, May 28, 1832, Campbell to same, August 5, 1832, *Senate Document 512*, 23rd Cong., 1st sess., 2: 837–38, 3: 361–63, 416–18.

52. Cass to Plummer, May 23, 1832, *Senate Document 512*, 23rd Cong., 1st sess., 2: 837–38. Also see Robb to Ward, July 18, 1832, Robb to Campbell, August 29, 1832, IA, LS, 9: 62–63, 196, RG 75, NA.

53. Taney to President, November 1, 1831, *Senate Document 25*, 25th Cong., 2d sess., p. 17; Oklarba to Cass, May 21, 1832, *Senate Document 512*, 23rd Cong., 1st sess., 3: 360; Young, *Redskins, Ruffleshirts and Rednecks*, pp. 49, 53–54.

54. Robb to Armstrong, July 19, 1832, Robb to Campbell, August 29, 1832, IA, LS, 9: 67–68, 196–97, RG 75, NA; Petition Adverse to the Location of Choctaw Reservations, February 1, 1836, *American State Papers: Public Lands*, 8: 430–31; Report on Pre-Emption Rights Defeated by Indian Reservations, April 22, 1836, *House Report 606*, 24th Cong., 1st sess., pp. 1–2; Commissioner of Indian Affairs, *Annual Report* (1848), p. 404; Colquhoun to Gibson, April 20, May 10, 1832, Colquhoun to Cass, August 15, 1833, *Senate Document 512*, 23rd Cong., 1st sess., 1: 605, 607–8, 4: 504; *Debates in Congress*, 23rd Cong., 1st sess., pp. 4475–76; Young, *Redskins, Ruffleshirts and Rednecks*, pp. 45–47, 49, 53–54. The War Department dismissed Ward in early November, but only because

the number of Indians, according to the administration, was too small to warrant a continuation of the agency there. See D. Kurtz to Ward, November 5, 1832, D. Kurtz to W. Armstrong, IA, LS, 9: 346–47, RG 75, NA.

55. Florence Rebecca Ray, *Greenwood LeFlore: Last Chief of the Choctaws East of the Mississippi River* (Memphis: Davis Printing Co., 1930), p. 29; Gaines to Gibson, June 30, 1832, Mayor J. Stocking, Jr., to Gaines, February 3, 1832, City Clerk Benjamin Wilkins to Gaines, February 1, 1832, *Senate Document 512*, 23rd Cong., 1st sess., 1: 944–46.

56. Bell's Report on Land Claims, &c. under the 14th Article [of the] Choctaw Treaty, May 11, 1836, *House Report 663*, 24th Cong., 1st sess., pp. 1–2; Butler to Cass, June 27, 1836, C. A. Harris to J. R. Poinsett, December 16, 1837, *Senate Document 25*, 25th Cong., 2d sess., pp. 2, 17–18.

57. David Dickson et al. to Cass, May 7, 1836, J. Thompson et al. to Jno. C. Spencer, December 22, 1842, Wilkins to J. J. McKay, January 21, 1845, *House Document 107*, 28th Cong., 2d sess., pp. 1–7; Commissioner of Indian Affairs, *Annual Report* (1838), p. 449, (1847), pp. 735–38; Wilkins to W. P. Mangum, February 6, 1845, *Senate Document 86*, 28th Cong., 2d sess., pp. 1, 6; *Arkansas Intelligencer* (Van Buren), April 19, December 27, 1845; Chs. Fischer to William Medill, November 14, 1845, Private & Unofficial, William Medill Papers, Library of Congress, Washington, D.C.; Memorial of the Choctaw Nation, 1873, *House Miscellaneous Document 94*, 42d Cong., 3d sess., pp. 2, 29; DeRosier, *Removal of the Choctaw Indians*, p. 136; Foreman, *Indian Removal*, pp. 102–4; Francis Newton Thorpe, *The Federal and State Constitutions*, 7 vols. (Washington, D.C.: GPO, 1909), 4: 2062. Secretary of War William Wilkins prepared a lengthy summary of the history of the Choctaw claims case for President Tyler in 1844. See Wilkins to [Tyler], December [7], 1844, SW, LS, President, 4: 210–30, RG 107, NA. For the subsequent history of the Mississippi Choctaw community, see John H. Peterson, Jr., "The Mississippi Band of Choctaw Indians: Their Recent History and Current Social Relations" (Ph.D. diss., University of Georgia, 1970).

58. For a precise breakdown of all expenditures under the Treaty of Dancing Rabbit Creek, see Wright, "Removal of the Choctaws," p. 124. The government received $8,095,614.89 for the sale of Choctaw land in Mississippi, but it had pledged not to make any profit from the sale of land under the treaty. Nearly sixty years after the signing of the treaty, the Choctaws finally received a rebate of $2,981,247.39, or the amount left after the government deducted all expenditures stemming from the treaty and ensuing litigation. See Memorial of the Choctaw Nation, 1873, *House Miscellaneous Document 94*, 42d Cong., 3rd sess., p. 5; Wright, "Removal of the Choctaws," p. 124.

4 /

Indian Removal

EVEN BEFORE the first party of Choctaws left Mississippi in 1831, the Jackson administration was busy negotiating removal treaties with other tribes. By the end of the president's second term in office, the United States had ratified nearly seventy treaties—a record unequaled by any other administration. During the years of Jackson's presidency, the United States acquired about one hundred million acres of Indian land for approximately sixty-eight million dollars and thirty-two million acres of land across the Mississippi River. Nearly forty-six thousand Indians emigrated to the West, while a little more than that number had treaty stipulations calling for removal. Only about nine thousand Indians, mostly in New York and the Great Lakes region, were without treaty stipulations requiring removal. During the decade following Jackson's presidency, the government relocated most of the tribes under obligation to emigrate and negotiated treaties with others to do the same. The removal experiences of all of these Indians closely paralleled that of the Choctaws.[1]

Treaty negotiations throughout the Jacksonian era generally resembled the procedures used with the Choctaws. Contrary to charges by many scholars, treaty making was not merely the equivalent of plying the Indians with "ample quantities of whiskey." Alexis de Tocqueville, the famous French visitor to the

United States in the early 1830s, presented a more accurate description of the process in his *Democracy in America*. Tocqueville assured his readers that "nowadays the dispossession of the Indians is accomplished in a regular and, so to say, quite legal manner." First, a team of American negotiators assembled them on the treaty ground and fed them. Then the commissioners advised them that the land in the West was far superior to their own. After many forceful speeches, the government officials gave the Indians generous presents. Usually the women and children, impressed by the merchandise distributed or anxious to improve their family's condition, urged the men to emigrate. If further encouragement seemed necessary, the negotiators warned the Indians that the extension of state law over the tribe or the nearness of white settlements would be disastrous for them. "In this way," Tocqueville noted, "the Americans cheaply acquire whole provinces which the richest sovereigns in Europe could not afford to buy."[2]

Even Tocqueville, as keen an observer as he was, missed some of the subtleties involved in negotiating removal treaties during the Jacksonian era. Henry R. Schoolcraft drew upon his many years of experience in the Indian service when he offered Commissioner William Medill the following advice concerning an upcoming treaty council in 1848:

> An Indian council is a test of diplomacy. The Indians are so *fickle*, that they will change there minds twice a day. It requires some of the qualities of Job to get along with them, and their friends, the halfbreeds. But perseverance in right views, will ultimately prevail. They have, after all, very little confidence in themselves, and a great deal in the United States.

As was the case with the Choctaws, the question of removal engendered factionalism among most tribes and split them into pro- and antiremoval groups. In order to assure the ascendancy of the proremoval faction, War Department officials frequently relied on influential half-bloods like Greenwood LeFlore who were amply rewarded for their services. Attempts were also made to win over leading full-blood chiefs by giving them goods, promising them land reserves, or perhaps giving them special medals with the portrait of the president on them. The latter were often viewed as "badges of power" by the Indians since they represented an important status symbol among the proremoval group. Indian medals together with land allotments and the various goods offered the Indians helped to promote "right views" at treaty negotiations, even though some Indians never fully understood the provisions of the documents that they signed.[3]

Another method used to obtain land cessions and the signing of removal treaties was the selection of a particular chief or faction to represent an entire tribe. President Jackson, for example, exploited growing tribal divisions among the Cherokee Indians in the 1830s in order to force their removal.

In the winter of 1832 the Cherokees jubilantly celebrated their apparent triumph over Georgia in the case of *Worcester* v. *Georgia*. Chief Justice Marshall's contention that the Indians were entitled to federal protection against intrusions by whites convinced most Cherokee leaders that they would not have to share the fate of the Choctaws and sign a removal treaty. Georgia state officials, however, soon made a mockery of Marshall's decision. Their harassment of the Cherokees together with continuing pressure from the Jackson administration for the negotiation of a removal treaty brought disunity to the tribe.[4]

Two rival factions emerged in Cherokee politics in the mid-1830s. The minority "Treaty party" feared the consequences of resisting Georgia and the Jackson administration. The Treaty party leaders included Major Ridge, who had served with Andrew Jackson against the Creek Indians during the War of 1812, his educated and politically ambitious son, John Ridge, and Major Ridge's nephews Elias Boudinot, the former editor of the influential *Cherokee Phoenix*, and Stand Watie, Boudinot's brother. Concluding that removal was inevitable, these men wanted to act quickly in order to avoid the wrath of Georgia and federal officials. They were also motivated, in part, by a desire to control tribal politics and the expectation of favors from the state and federal governments. The majority "National party," led by the charismatic John Ross, the son of a Scottish immigrant and mixed-blood mother, exerted every effort to thwart removal and, should it become a necessity, to exact the most favorable terms possible for the Cherokees so that they might be able to purchase a new home, perhaps somewhere beyond the territorial limits of the United States.[5]

After carefully scrutinizing the situation among the Cherokees, the Jackson administration decided to deal solely with the Treaty party. On December 29, 1835, representatives of the War Department and about one hundred members of the Treaty party signed a removal treaty. In spite of the fact that delegates of the National party, representing nearly sixteen thousand of the seventeen thousand Cherokees in the South, refused to be bound by this "treaty," the Senate ratified the document by the extremely narrow margin of one vote. Georgia Governor Wilson Lumpkin warmly applauded the Senate's action and declared that the treaty was valid for the tribe since "nineteen-twentieths of the Cherokees are too ignorant and depraved to entitle their opinion to any weight or consideration" in any important matter.[6]

Following Senate ratification of the treaty, the Jackson administration refused to permit leaders of the majority National party to hold meetings to discuss the treaty and their next course of action. The War Department also warned John Ross that it refused to recognize any established government among the Cherokees until their arrival in the trans-Mississippi West and that it would suppress with arms any efforts to thwart the implementation of the treaty provision calling for the removal of all Cherokees by mid-1838. Brigadier General John E. Wool cautioned the Cherokees that any delay in emigrating would result in reprisals. "You will be hunted up and dragged from your lurking places and hurried to the West," he warned. Meanwhile, in order to assure Cherokee fulfillment of the treaty stipulation, government field agents made "prudent advances" of funds to influential tribal leaders.[7]

In the two-year period provided by the treaty for the preparation of removal, the National party sought to expose the fraud committed upon the Cherokees by the government and the Treaty party. In the meantime, white Georgia "*vultures*" cheated the Indians out of their money and stole their land. The Cherokees, one of the most advanced tribes in the South, soon faced the prospect of moving to the West "*penniless*" as "*beggars.*" In spite of continued protest by the National party and petitions signed by a majority of the Cherokee Nation, the Jackson administration upheld the treaty as binding for the entire tribe.[8]

When the date for the removal of the Cherokee Indians passed in 1838, only two thousand had emigrated. Nearly fifteen thousand men, women, and children remained behind. Martin Van Buren, Jackson's hand-picked successor to the presidency, assigned General Winfield Scott the task of forcing the removal of those who had stayed in the South past the deadline. As part of the military operation to evict the Indians, the army built temporary stockades to house the Cherokees, who were rounded up as fugitives. Confronted with soldiers armed with rifles and bayonets, the Indians had to abandon their homes and leave their property, crops, and livestock behind. The Van Buren administration's emphasis on a speedy operation meant the Cherokees had to embark for the West without sufficient bedding, cooking utensils, or clothes and without their ponies or livestock. Perhaps the most brutal aspect of the internment of the Cherokees preceding their removal, however, were the acts of rape, bestiality, and murder committed by the "lawless rabble" and some soldiers who grossly exceeded their orders and the intentions of government officials in Washington. One Georgia volunteer engaged in removing the Cherokees remarked years later, "I fought through the civil war and have seen men shot to pieces and slaughtered by thousands, but the Cherokee removal was the cruelest work I ever knew." Using what John Ross and the leaders of the National party referred to as the "pretended treaty" of 1835 as a pretext, the Van Buren administration set into motion the Cherokee exodus to the site of present-day Oklahoma—the "Trail of Tears" along which several thousand men, women and children died as a result of malnutrition, exposure, cholera, and the physical hardships of the journey.[9]

The Seminoles in Florida Territory also suffered from the government's policy of selecting the group supposedly representative of a tribe. Following the passage of the Removal Act in 1830, the Jackson administration, anxious to appease Florida settlers who complained of Indian depredations and Georgia plantation owners who protested that runaway slaves were finding a haven with the Indians in Florida, negotiated a removal treaty with the Seminoles. Under increasing pressure from white settlers, government officials, and the devastating effects of the severe drought of 1831, Seminole leaders signed a provisional removal treaty on May 9,

1832. The document stipulated that removal was conditional, pending tribal approval of the site selected by the War Department for the Indians in the West. An exploring party of seven Seminoles reached the proposed trans-Mississippi location in the winter of 1833. Before the Indians returned home, they came under unremitting pressure from agent John Phagan, who finally coerced them to sign a final "treaty" binding the Seminoles to leave Florida by 1837 and to unite with the Creeks as one nation in the West. This so-called treaty, which included a "request" that Phagan be made the removal agent, was signed under extreme duress by the members of the exploring party, who feared for their safety should they refuse to put their marks on the paper.[10]

In spite of subsequent protests by the members of the exploring party and Seminole leaders in Florida and despite the fact that agent Phagan was soon dismissed from office for committing gross fraud against the Indians, President Jackson refused to question the legitimacy of the removal treaty signed in the West. Following Senate ratification of the document, the administration began an all-out effort to coax the Seminoles toward an early departure.[11]

Seminole leaders steadfastly refused to be intimidated into accepting the "fraudulent treaty" of 1833. In addition to their denial of the legitimacy of the document, they opposed removal for at least four other reasons. First, they felt a strong attachment to their native land. According to one black interpreter, a Seminole chief asserted that, "bress God, dis berry fine country. Fader, mudder, live here an chil'n—he no wanto go nowhere [else] 't all." Secondly, traders exerted tremendous influence over the Indians and, fearful of losing their easy prey, urged them to remain in Florida. More important, however, was the dismal prospect of being submerged politically by being forced to unite with the Creeks in the West. Secretary of War Lewis Cass deemed it desirable to unite all kindred tribes in the West as one people, but the Seminoles did not look forward to merging with the Creeks, who had long demanded that runaway slaves living with the Seminoles be turned over to them. This demand was based on the fact that the government had previously forced the Creeks to compensate Georgia planters for runaway slaves because the Seminoles were alleged to be a branch of the Creeks. Now that the Jackson administration was trying to force the Seminoles to unite with the

Creeks, they feared that the Creeks would seize their blacks. Finally, the slaves living with the Seminoles enjoyed an almost luxurious life compared to their counterparts elsewhere in the South and understandably refused to leave Florida. Since many of these blacks had great influence with the Seminole leaders, the Indians proved intransigent. Continuing threats from government officials that the Seminoles would be forced to surrender runaway slave "property" and to emigrate to the West led the Indians to take action. Near the end of December, 1835, Seminole and black warriors under the leadership of Micanopy ambushed and annihilated a contingent of about one hundred men under the command of Major Francis L. Dade.[12]

The destruction of Dade's command by Indian and black warriors spread alarm and hysteria throughout Florida and adjacent states. The ambush marked the beginning of a bloody seven-year war which took the lives of large numbers of Indians and whites and cost the United States ten times the Jackson administration's estimate of the total expenditure for removing all eastern Indians. As soldiers tried to flush the Indians and their black allies out of their hiding places, there was a tremendous outpouring of public sympathy for the Seminoles in the North. The war became a cause célèbre for the nascent peace movement, which argued that the Indians were merely fighting a "defensive" war. Other humanitarian reformers of the day also protested the alleged harsh treatment of the Indians at the hands of the army. An abortive attempt by Florida territorial officials to end the war in 1840 by using Cuban bloodhounds to track down the Indians brought instant rebuke from northern religious leaders, abolitionists, and politicians. Although the army leashed and muzzled the hounds when it used them, the episode provided critics of the war with a highly emotional issue. Even some military leaders privately sympathized with the Indians. Major Ethan Allen Hitchcock, for example, found service in Florida "dispicable" and wrote a friend, "I can hardly help wishing the 'right' to prevail which is, in this case, . . . praying for the Indians." Despite such protests, however, the public response to calls for volunteers to force the Seminoles to obey the "solemn treaty" of 1833 demonstrated that there was general sympathy in the country for the removal policy, although the tactics used in negotiating the Seminole removal treaty as well as the Cherokee treaty indicated that Indian sovereignty meant little to federal negotiators. The fact that there was written, therefore "legal," confirmation of the Seminole land cession seemed to be the important thing for administration leaders and the majority of Americans.[13]

The government also used the threat of economic sanctions to coerce tribal chiefs into signing removal treaties. Since the 1790s the War Department had invested the money appropriated by Congress for purchasing Indian land in state banks or stock and had paid the Indians only the annual interest on the amount owed them under treaty stipulations. This trust fund system, as it came to be known, gave the administration in Washington virtual control over the purse strings of many tribes. The withholding of annuities as a means of social control dates back to the early years of the republic and especially the administration of Thomas Jefferson, but it became a standard practice during the Jacksonian era.[14]

Field officials found they could often induce reluctant Indians to emigrate and hostile tribesmen to lay down their arms by threatening to cut off their annuities. Indian Commissioner T. Hartley Crawford observed in 1839, for example, that "there is wisdom in this most benevolent feature of our Indian policy, for, while it serves them and meets their wants, it must have a powerful effect in binding them to the performance of their duty to us." Commissary General George Gibson had earlier noted that "without some determined effort on the part of the United States [like withholding the annuities], it cannot be disguised that the Indians will perseveringly linger in their old haunts." Gibson even suggested, "Let the annuities be paid west of the Mississippi, and there is no reason to doubt that the scheme of emigration would meet with little future opposition."[15]

War Department officials during the 1830s and '40s were able to maintain considerable influence over tribal affairs by determining exactly whom the government would allow to receive the annuities for the tribes. Jackson, for example, altered the practice of paying annuities to recognized tribal chieftains or treasurers and divided the money equally among all members of the various tribes. The Jacksonians maintained that this was a more democratic procedure, but it conveniently allowed them to make it extremely difficult for the southern tribes to finance litigation against states declaring their jurisdiction over them. Congressional supporters of these beleaguered Indians managed to secure legislation in 1834 providing that annuities be paid only to tribal leaders or persons specifically designated by them. This measure, however, failed to prevent War Department officials from using the annuities as a form of economic pressure to secure the signing of removal treaties.[16]

In some instances the government did not even bother to obtain a formal removal treaty before relocating Indians. The Creek treaty of March 24, 1832, which opened approximately five million acres of eastern Alabama land to white settlement and ultimately led to the eviction of the Creeks, was not a removal treaty. Unable to convince Creek leaders of the virtues of its Indian removal policy, the Jackson administration finally persuaded them in 1832 to relinquish a large portion of their holdings in return for a pledge that the remainder of their land would be alloted to the chiefs, headmen, and heads of families. In order to secure the signature of the Creek leaders, the government also promised to protect the Indians against all intrusions on their allotments and against forcible eviction from Alabama. Considering President Jackson's repeated contention that he was helpless to protect Indians living within state boundaries when a state extended its laws over them, the Creek treaty of 1832 and its pledges must be viewed as a clever administration ploy to expedite Indian removal by opening the door to white speculation in Creek lands. By converting Creek tribal holdings into private allotments, the president was following the old policy of divide-and-rule.[17]

Using techniques perfected during the sale of the Choctaw allotments in Mississippi, white speculators quickly began defrauding the Creeks, driving them from their homes and forcing them to wander about the countryside in Alabama in search of food and shelter. By the summer of 1835, the starving and demoralized Creeks who had steadfastly refused to emigrate began stealing the crops and livestock of white settlers. Arson and murder soon followed as some Indians decided to retaliate against the injustices perpetrated upon them and condoned by the War Department under the guise of protecting their right to "freedom of contract." Such acts of desperation resulted in government intervention. Secretary of War Lewis Cass finally ordered the removal of the Creeks in 1836 as a military measure without the formality of a removal treaty. Thus the Jackson administration used the Indian-white conflict in Alabama resulting from the frauds in the "purchases" of Creek allotments as a pretext for accomplishing by force what it could not negotiate by diplomacy. By the spring of 1837, approximately fifteen thousand Creeks had emigrated across the Mississippi River without ever having signed a removal treaty.[18]

The Chickasaws in neighboring Mississippi also emigrated westward after signing an allotment treaty. Unlike the Creeks, however, the Chickasaws had early accepted the inevitability of removal. Even before the Choctaw exodus of 1831, the Chickasaws had agreed to emigrate if the United States would provide them with a suitable trans-Mississippi location. Although the Jackson administration had little luck in persuading the Chickasaws to merge with the Choctaws in their new western country, War Department officials persuaded the Chickasaws to sign an allotment treaty in 1832. The alleged purpose of this treaty was to provide the Indians with revenue in preparation for their ultimate relocation. The United States pledged that it would sell their land at a fair price, hold the funds in trust for them, and protect the Chickasaws from intruders while searching for a new home for them.[19]

Following the signing of the treaty, whites quickly settled in the Chickasaw domain. Washington officials initially sought to remove all of the intruders, but the task proved so formidable that the War Department generally evaded its obligation to evict them. Continuing pressure from white settlers and speculators and the death of Levi Colbert, the most formidable opponent to emigration, finally led the Chickasaws to agree to pay the Choctaws for the right to settle on a portion of their domain. The Chickasaw emigration to the new Choctaw country during the winter of 1837–38 was a direct result of the allotment treaty of 1832.[20]

Throughout the Jacksonian era there were some problems inherent in the treaty-making process itself that never received adequate attention. While presidents were well aware that the Senate could reject treaties, they were not always respectful of the fact that a chief might return with a treaty only to have his council or people reject it. The Senate jealously guarded its right to amend

or to delete treaty provisions, and Indians frequently found themselves bound to treaties which did not reflect their understanding
of prior agreements. Indians often could not comprehend why the
"Great White Father" and his "Council" had changed their minds.
Moreover, treaty stipulations were provisional until formally ratified by the Senate, and this caused hardships and delays for Indians
awaiting promised rations, goods, or specie. Settlers rarely waited,
however, for formal ratification of treaties before inundating Indian land. Treaties thereby served as an opening wedge for white
encroachment, regardless of the Senate's final decision.[21]

(The removal treaties negotiated during the 1830s and '40s were
remarkably similar. They all contained liberal provisions for Indians emigrating to the West and those remaining behind. The
government promised rations and transportation to the new country in the West, protection en route, medicine and physicians,
reimbursement for abandoned property, funds for the erection of
new buildings, mills, and schools, and maintenance of poor and
orphaned children.) Administration officials considered these provisions essential in order to placate public opinion, secure Senate
ratification of treaties, obtain future Indian appropriations from
the House of Representatives, and induce tribes to emigrate.[22]

(But in spite of the favorable terms promised in the removal
treaties, most emigrants faced unnecessary hardships.) The government stubbornly refused to abandon the system of furnishing
rations and transportation to the Indians by issuing contracts to
the lowest bidders. This policy, more than anything else, contributed to the sorrowful plight of the emigrants which writers
have immortalized in portraying the Trail of Tears. Contractors
were businessmen out to make a profit and the quality of rations
and transportation vehicles reflected this. As Commissioner T.
Hartley Crawford warned in 1839, "The rivalry of bidding, experience everywhere has shown, induces men, in the heat of the
moment, to offer to furnish articles of a given quality lower than
they can buy them; and, to make amends for this false step, resort
is had to an effort to impose upon the department inferior articles,
which sometimes may succeed." Benjamin Marshall, the Creek
interpreter, reported that contractors had cheated the Creek emigrants by providing them with beef from "some very bad cattle,
such as old bulls, and old oxen that were broken down, and not fit

either to work or to kill." Chickasaw agent A. M. Upshaw charged that the corn provided Chickasaw emigrants by contractors was so rotten that even their horses refused to eat it. The pork issued the Chickasaws was so putrid that many suffered from diarrhea and even died from eating it. Despite these disclosures and Commissioner Crawford's condemnation of the bidding policy, it continued in operation throughout the period. Even when the rations and method of transportation were the best possible, the haphazard planning of Indian removals took its toll in human lives. As one removal agent observed, "All that the contract granted them was secured to them. But all this could not shield them from the severity of the weather, cold sleeting storms, and hard frozen ground."[23]

The government's perpetual concern for economy also militated against safe and healthy trips. The commutation scheme of removal, for example, remained in use throughout the Jacksonian era in spite of its consequences during the Choctaw removal. While removal treaties promised medicine and physicians to emigrants, the War Department ruled that "*medicines* will only be procured when actually required, or danger from sickness is apprehended. In no instance will full medicine chests or surgical instruments be purchased." Such orders may have saved the government money, but they were disastrous for the Indians. The Creek Indians who were forced to emigrate from Alabama under military escort especially resented the mode of transportation and poor medical attention provided them by the contractors and protested that "we are men—we have woman and Children . . . why should we come like horses?" Even some frontiersmen lamented that avaricious contractors were driving "*the Poor Indians*" westward like "*a Drove of Wild Beasts.*"[24]

There is evidence to indicate that the War Department conducted inspections of the goods and transportation vehicles provided emigrants during this period. The continual emphasis on speedy removals, the tremendous strain on manpower necessitated by such inspections, and political pressure exerted by friends of the contractors, however, often resulted in shortcuts and careless or infrequent examinations. As opposition leaders and newspapers pointed out that Indian removal was costing far more than President Jackson's original estimate, administration officials became keenly sensitive of the need for retrenchment. While federal officials in Washington apparently did not purposely intend to make westward emigration a hazard to the lives of Indians, their eagerness to follow the path of political expediency and their continual efforts to economize in carrying out removal operations often had such an effect.[25]

Many of the measures taken to speed up the emigration of Indians led to strained Indian-white relations. The continued use of the allotment policy after the scandalous treatment of the Choctaws and Creeks is an excellent example. War Department officials viewed the allotment policy as a necessary evil to promote removal. There were some notable attempts to improve the procedures used in distributing reserves and some efforts to guarantee the Indian a "fair" price for his allotment, but the presidential administrations of the Jacksonian era maintained that once Indians entered into contracts to sell their land without coercion they were bound by them. Officials paid little attention to the fact that full-blood Indians were not imbued with the Lockian values of the American society and were unable to deal on equal terms with white speculators.[26]

The real beneficiaries of the allotment system were speculators, who obtained between eighty and ninety percent of the Indian title during these years. Thousands of acres of Indian land in the Old Southwest and the Old Northwest passed directly into the hands of speculators who used the allotments as a convenient device for taking tribal land away from the Indians, out of the public land system, and away from those white squatters seeking to put the preemption laws to work for themselves. To make matters worse, political considerations made it necessary to temporize on the issue of Indian claims resulting from frauds in the purchasing of allotments. Democratic presidents were especially sensitive to pressure from southern congressional delegations to tone down investigations of fraud in order to avoid any possible political embarrassment. Some Indian reserves, moreover, were never surveyed or located, and many Indians and their heirs had to wait generations before receiving their promised allotments. In 1848 Commissioner William Medill admitted to Secretary of War William Marcy that the adjudication of disputes over the ownership of Indian land allotments was an "embarrassing class of business" stemming from "the evil and corrupt policy of granting reservations in Indian treaties."²⁷

Just as the government continued to view the allotment system as a necessary evil to speed up Indian emigration, it countenanced the inclusion of provisions for the payment of traders' debts in removal treaties. The support of the traders was crucial to the successful negotiation of removal treaties because the Indians looked to them for advice and subsistence. Since the presidency of Thomas Jefferson, treaty negotiators had found the inclusion of traders' debts in removal treaties an excellent means of coaxing the tribes to emigrate, and the government adopted this practice on a large scale during the 1830s. The effect of such action was to substitute individual Indian debts for a tribal debt which could easily be paid off by making a land cession.²⁸

The inclusion of traders' debts helped to encourage removal, but it also defrauded the Indians out of the money that the government paid them for their land. Traders grossly inflated the prices of goods they sold and falsified their account books. One treaty commissioner reported that the traders stuck to the Indians and their money "like buzzards to a dead carcass," but he also admitted that "if they were kept off, the Indians would refuse to act without their secret council." The government found it necessary to placate these men, who were not among the most avid proponents of removal. The presence of the Indians in their state or territory meant prosperity to the traders, who included among their number leading businessmen and political figures. Henry R. Schoolcraft, one of America's early ethnologists and a government Indian agent, observed that "the trader, ever[y]where, takes hold of the Indian with a desperate grasp" because Indians served as his "props." Some traders arrogantly warned the War Department that they would not only prevent the emigration of Indians but would incite them to "wars of extermination" if the government refused to acknowledge their claims.²⁹

The necessity of appeasing the traders proved an embarrassment to presidential administrations during the Jacksonian era. A sizable and articulate segment of the American people voiced concern throughout this period over the plight of the Indians resulting from fraudulent claims by traders. There was a growing fear, as agent Lawrence Taliaferro put it, that the traders were trying to "*enslave* the poor Indian *body* and *mind* to their *dic-*

tatorial will." The Jackson, Van Buren, and Tyler administrations responded to this pressure by occasionally invoking secrecy about impending negotiations and by tightening up the procedures for examining traders' claims. The factors militating against the success of such efforts, however, were overwhelming. Tribal leaders found it convenient and rewarding to acknowledge the traders' debts, and the traders had important allies in the Indian service, Congress, and the executive departments who lobbied for their interests. More importantly, perhaps, Washington officials succumbed to the traders' demands because they deemed it "absolutely necessary" to accommodate their claims in order to secure the signing of removal treaties.[30]

Although the War Department directed field agents to scrutinize traders' claims in order to safeguard the Indians from gross frauds, it insisted that the Indians had a "moral duty" to pay every "just claim" against them. Since the full-bloods were not good judges of the prices of the merchandise that they bought, the traders saw to it that "legal" debts were enormous ones. Dr. Henry Van der Bogart, a physician who observed a claims investigation in Chicago during Jackson's presidency, remarked, "I often thought the cry of the inequity of this place was greater than the sin of Sodom." The tremendous pressures exerted by the traders on government officials during the depression years between 1837 and 1843 prevented any significant curtailment of the practice of acknowledging traders' debts.[31]

By March, 1843, the abuses of the practice had grown so widespread and opposition to it so vocal that the Senate, after conferring in secret session, refused to ratify any treaties attaching traders' claims. This decision and the rhetoric of officials in the Tyler and Polk administrations suggested that the practice had finally come to an end, but this was far from the truth. In 1847, for example, the Senate found it necessary to condemn the practice of paying unratified private debt claims from money provided the Indians, and traders continued to receive payments for their claims well into the 1850s. While the War Department and personnel assigned to the Indian Office made some notable efforts to end this practice during the Polk administration, political reality demanded the acknowledgement of additional claims. Licensed traders included many leading business and political figures, and the executive branch found it necessary to "avoid doing injustice in any case to persons who are bona fide and in good faith . . . creditors." In this case, as in many others, expediency frequently dictated that the rhetoric of Indian policy differed from the reality.[32]

By the end of the 1840s the United States had virtually accomplished Andrew Jackson's goal of removing the eastern Indians to the trans-Mississippi West. As early as 1842 the War Department informed President Tyler that although there were still some Indians residing East of the Mississippi River, "*there is no more land east of the Mississippi, remaining unceded, to be desired by us.*" This statement, however, did not adequately reflect the condition of the Indians of the Old Northwest and New York who, after making initial cessions of their land, faced the agony and vicissitudes of removal more than once.[33]

Defenders of the removal policy had long argued against the continuance of an *imperium in imperio* and asserted that Indians emigrating from states and territories of the Union would receive permanent locations in exchange. Neither the Jackson nor the Van Buren adminstration, however, set aside a specific region for the permanent residence of the northern tribes. While the southern tribes· received a new "country" outside the boundaries of any state or territory, the New York Indians settled in the Old Northwest, where the government had merely reshuffled indigenous tribes or coaxed them to move across the Mississippi River in order to make room for the growing pressures of white settlement, as well as to permit the opening and exploitation of rich mineral and timber land.[34]

As early as 1831 the French travelers Alexis de Tocqueville and Gustave de Beaumont noted the disparity in the treatment of the northern and southern Indians. They asked Sam Houston, a personal friend of Andrew Jackson, if the government intended to provide the northern Indians with a permanent reserve comparable to that provided the southern tribes. Houston's reply typified the position of the Jackson and Van Buren administrations. He asserted that the situation in the North and Old Northwest was not as critical as in the South and that the Indians in the former areas would be "pushed back as [white] advance is made."[35]

The checker-board type of settlement of tribes in the Old Northwest and the lack of any long-range planning for their future location led to great uneasiness among the Indians and white settlers. The indigenous tribes were frequently close enough to their old domiciles to return whenever the hunting or crops in their new location proved insufficient for their needs. The result was often Indian-white or intertribal hostilities.[36]

War broke out in Illinois in the spring of 1832, for example, when a hungry band of a thousand Sac and Fox Indians and their allies left their new home in Iowa Territory and crossed the Mississippi River in order to return to their ancient capital on the Rock River. Although the Indians entered Illinois in search of corn, they also returned as a means of protesting against the arrogance, brutality, and contempt shown them by frontiersmen whose claims that the Indians had no right whatsoever to visit their ancient burial grounds or to harvest their old cornfields did not exactly coincide with their interpretation of previous treaties. Black Hawk, an old, stubborn, and proud warrior who had supported Tecumseh and the English in the War of 1812, sought food, honor, and security for his people without aggressive warfare.[37]

Despite the fact that Black Hawk's band contained large numbers of women and children, who would never accompany a war party, the return of the Indians sent a wave of panic across the Illinois frontier. Governor John Reynolds promptly called out the state militia to repel the "invasion" and requested immediate aid from President Jackson. The result was a short but bloody war largely instigated by drunken militia troops who left Black Hawk no honorable alternative but the tomahawk. As one contemporary observed, the war was "the result of a border feeling, which permits the destruction of an Indian upon the same principle that it does the wolf."[38]

The ruthless suppression of "Indian hostilities" during the Black Hawk War broke the spirit of other tribes in the Old Northwest and led to new demands by frontiersmen for their removal. A newspaper in Galena, Illinois, near the Wisconsin border, for example, complained that the presence of Indians was a great impediment to progress. "Our country," lamented the *Galenian* after the conclusion of the hostilities, "instead of realizing the brilliant prospects of wealth and plenty, presents the melancholy spectacle of deserted cabins, of wasted uncultivated fields." The War Department responded quickly to such rhetoric from residents of an area that was reputed to possess one of the richest mineral deposits in the country.[39]

At the conclusion of the conflict with Black Hawk's band, the War Department persuaded the Winnebago Indians of present-day Wisconsin to sign a removal treaty. The Winnebagos, who received a tract of land in Iowa, underwent numerous changes in residence in the ensuing years as the War Department responded to pressure from white settlers and sought to use these Indians as a buffer zone between the Sac and Fox and their enemies the Sioux. The continual dislocation of the Winnebagos and their precarious situation between hostile tribes led to their deterioration as a society.[40]

The social and psychological strain induced by the constant uprooting and relocation of the Winnebagos, together with disease and dissipation, brought about a tremendous population decline approaching nearly the fifty percent mark. Suffering from the culture shock of repeated dislocations and the resultant tribal deterioration, many Winnebagos frequently returned to the security of their old hunting grounds in violation of the treaties that they had earlier signed. Winnebagos returning to the sites of their old villages to fish once more in their beloved waters and to stand again near their sacred clan burial grounds found that the Oneida Indians of New York, among others, had received title to the land from the United States government. In turn, the Oneidas, who had ceded their land in New York for the Wisconsin location, soon discovered that their new position was even more precarious than it had been in New York.[41]

While the Jackson administration was pushing the Winnebagos and other tribes of the Old Northwest farther west, it was fulfilling old treaty stipulations and seeking new treaties to settle the New York Indians in the region. The Winnebagos were told that they had to emigrate to free themselves from contact with white frontiersmen; at the same time, the administration was relocating New York Indians on their old land so that they could be "free from the destructive evils of their present near connexion with the whites [in New York]." The Winnebagos and other tribes relocated in Iowa Territory soon became "a source of great annoyance and dissatisfaction" to white settlers, who complained that the area was "inhabited by savages and wild beasts," and the New York

Indians resettled in the Old Northwest quickly became the victims of the great land boom that swept the area in the 1830s. Both groups faced the prospect of future removals.[42]

The Jackson and Van Buren administrations never undertook any long-range planning concerning the location of a permanent home for the Indians of the Old Northwest. The result was a makeshift arrangement that often resulted in great intertribal hostility.

The condition of the Indians in the Old Northwest and the eastern tribes relocated there underscores the fact that the creation of the southern Indian country was largely a response to the tremendous outpouring of public sympathy for the Cherokees and their neighbors. The deteriorating situation among the Winnebagos and other tribes in the Old Northwest that underwent continuous relocation never elicited the eloquent pleas or the countless petitions to Congress that were penned in behalf of the so-called civilized tribes of the South. Members of the peace movement, which was but one small manifestation of the reform spirit that permeated Jacksonian America, lamented the plight of the Indians of the Old Northwest and defended Black Hawk's actions in Illinois as a "defensive war" and "a resistance of evil," but such rhetoric was no match for the tremendous volume of petitions, letters, and resolutions presented to Congress in behalf of the Cherokees and their southern neighbors during the same period of time. Not until a large segment of the American people became concerned about the position of the northern tribes in the 1840s was serious attention focused on the need for constructing a northern counterpart to the southern Indian country. This situation is a further indication that the exigencies of the moment determined the components of the removal policy throughout the Jacksonian era.[43]

NOTES

1. Kappler, *Indian Affairs*, 2: 213–362; Commissioner of Indian Affairs, *Annual Report* (1836), p. 420; Statement of the General Land Office, August 8, 1836, Statement Showing the Number of Indians, December 1, 1836, Statement Showing the Quantity of Lands Ceded by the Indian Tribes to the United States, December 1, 1836, IA, Miscellaneous Records, 1: 300–1, 2: 6–8, 90–92, 98–100, RG 75, NA.

2. Tocqueville, *Democracy in America,* pp. 324–25, 325 n. For examples of contemporary scholars who suggest that treaty negotiations consisted of drowning the Indians with whiskey, see Foreman, *Indian Removal,* preface; Paul W. Gates, Introduction to *The John Tipton Papers (1809–1839),* comp. Glen A. Blackburn, ed. Nellie A. Robertson and Dorothy Riker, 3 vols. (Indianapolis: Indiana Historical Bureau, 1942), 1: 13–14; Pessen, *Jacksonian America,* p. 320. For an account of federal efforts to suppress the whiskey traffic among the Indians, see Prucha, *American Indian Policy,* pp. 102–38.

3. Schoolcraft to Medill, September 30, 1848, Medill Papers; McKenney to Eaton, December 21, 1829, IA, LS, 6: 199, RG 75, NA; Stockbridge Sachem and Counsellors to Henry R. Schoolcraft, January 4, 1838, enclosed in Schoolcraft to Harris, February 2, 1838, Thomas T. Hendrick et al. to Commissioner of Indian Affairs, December 10, 1838, in Carter and Bloom, *Territorial Papers,* 27: 913–14, 1107–8; Robert F. Berkhofer, Jr., "Faith and Factionalism among the Senecas: Theory and Ethnohistory," *Ethonohistory* 12 (Spring 1956): 110; Schoolcraft, *Memoirs,* p. 594. The above comments concerning the War Department's tactics in negotiating treaties are based on these sources: Kappler, *Indian Affairs,* 2: 213–425; *Senate Records,* Executive Messages Relating to Indian Relations, 1829–49, RG 46, NA; IA, Documents Relating to the Negotiation of Ratified Indian Treaties (hereafter cited as Treaty Negotiations), 1829–49, RG 75, NA; IA, Registers, vols. 2–36, LR, RG 75, NA. For a thorough study of the use of peace medals to promote federal Indian policy, see Francis Paul Prucha, *Indian Peace Medals in American History* (Madison: State Historical Society of Wisconsin, 1971).

4. Elijah Hicks to Cherokee Delegation in Washington, March 24, 1832, in *Niles' Register* 42 (May 12, 1832): 201; John Ross to Citizens of Amahee District, April 28, 1832, Wm. M. Davis to Cass, June 24, 1832, Cherokee Council to Cass, August 6, 1832, *Senate Document 512,* 23rd Cong., 1st sess., 3: 381, 418–19, 512; *Pittsburgh Gazette,* October 23, 1832; Commissioner of Indian Affairs, *Annual Report* (1832), p. 161; Cass to Cherokees, East, April 17, 1832, in Secretary of War, *Annual Report* (1832), p. 39; Grace S. Woodward, *The Cherokees* (Norman: University of Oklahoma Press, 1963), pp. 170–74, 176–77; Foreman, *Indian Removal,* pp. 244–49.

5. Edward Everett Dale and Gaston Litton, eds., *Cherokee Cavaliers: Forty Years of Cherokee History as Told in the Correspondence of the Ridge-Watie-Boudinot Family* (Norman: University of Oklahoma Press, 1939), pp. xvi–xvii; Foreman, *Indian Removal,* pp. 265–66; Woodward, *Cherokees,* pp. 171–82. For a sympathetic account of the Treaty party which views John Ridge as a realist and John Ross as an impractical leader,

see Thurman Wilkins, *Cherokee Tragedy: The Story of the Ridge Family and of the Decimation of a People* (New York: Macmillan Co., 1970).

6. Elias Boudinot to Stand Watie, February 28, 1835, John Ridge to Major Ridge et al., March 10, 1835, in Dale and Litton, *Cherokee Cavaliers*, pp. 10–14; Woodward, *Cherokees*, pp. 174–75, 190, 192; Foreman, *Indian Removal*, p. 269; Wilson Lumpkin to Jackson, September 24, 1836, in Lumpkin, *Removal of the Cherokee Indians*, 2: 45. The Cherokee population figure cited above is based on J. F. Schermerhorn to Cass, March 3, 1836, *Senate Document 120*, 25th Cong., 2d sess., p. 535. Following the ratification of the treaty by the Senate, congressional supporters of Ross and the National party made an unsuccessful attempt to defeat the Appropriations Bill for carrying the treaty into effect. See *Nashville Republican*, July 12, 1836, for the heated exchange between supporters and opponents of the treaty.

7. Foreman, *Indian Removal*, pp. 269, 273; Wool to Cherokees, March 22, 1837, Gunther Broadside Collection, Chicago Historical Society, Chicago, Ill.; Lumpkin and John Kennedy to Harris, March 23, 1837, *Senate Document 120*, 25th Cong., 2d sess., p. 816.

8. Woodward, *Cherokees*, pp. 192–95, 198–202; Foreman, *Indian Removal*, p. 272; Decree of Cherokee Council, August 1, 1838, in Commissioner of Indian Affairs, *Annual Report* (1839), pp. 417–18.

9. *New-York Observer*, July 14, 1838; Major H. M. Routledge to J[oel] R. Poinsett, August 8, 1838, Poinsett Papers, Historical Society of Pennsylvania, Philadelphia, Pa.; Decree of Cherokee Council, August 1, 1838, in Commissioner of Indian Affairs, *Annual Report* (1839), pp. 417–18; Eaton, *John Ross*, p. 64; Foreman, *Indian Removal*, pp. 284–312; Woodward, *Cherokees*, pp. 194–218; James Mooney, *Myths of the Cherokee and Sacred Formulas of the Cherokees* (1900; reprint ed., Nashville: Charles Elder, 1972), pp. 130–31; *Army and Navy Chronicle* 8 (January 3, 1839): 12, citing *New Orleans Bee*. For the quotation of the Georgia volunteer, see Mooney, *Myths of the Cherokee*, p. 130. James Mooney estimated that approximately four thousand of the eighteen thousand Cherokees removed under the Treaty of 1835 died as a result of the trek west or the circumstances surrounding their capture and detention before the emigration commenced. It is interesting to note that the mortality rate of the Indians who removed under military supervision was far greater than the rate of those who emigrated after John Ross convinced the army to allow the Cherokees to handle their own emigration. See Mooney, *Myths of the Cherokee*, p. 133; Foreman, *Indian Removal*, p. 312 n; Woodward, *Cherokees*, p. 218.

10. Cass to White, January 30, 1832, IA, LS, 8: 46–48, RG 75, NA; Memorial to Congress by the [Florida] Legislative Council, [February

1832], Memorial to Congress by Inhabitants of the [Florida] Territory, [March 26, 1832], in Carter and Bloom, *Territorial Papers*, 24: 667–69, 678–79; James Gadsen to Cass, May 21, 1832, *Senate Document 512*, 23rd Cong., 1st sess., 3: 360; Commissioner of Indian Affairs, *Annual Report* (1832), p. 161; Secretary of War, *Annual Report* (1832), p. 28; Proceedings of a Council held with a Delegation of Florida Indians at Fort Gibson, 1833, Senate Records, 23B-C1, RG 46, NA; Kappler, *Indian Affairs*, 2: 249–51, 290; Foreman, *Indian Removal*, pp. 315–21; John K. Mahon, *History of the Second Seminole War, 1835–1842* (Gainesville: University of Florida Press, 1967), pp. 73–86.

11. Mahon, *Second Seminole War*, pp. 83–86. For evidence of Phagan's misconduct in office, see James B. Thornton to Cass, August 29, 1833, Daniel Kurtz to Phagan, August 30, 1833, in Carter and Bloom, *Territorial Papers*, 24: 873, 876; James D. Wescott, Jr., to E. Herring, November 5, 1833, *House Document 271*, 24th Cong., 1st sess., p. 96; Edwin C. McReynolds, *The Seminoles* (Norman: University of Oklahoma Press, 1957), pp. 126–29.

12. W. A. Croffut, ed., *Fifty Years in Camp and Field: Diary of Major-General Ethan Allen Hitchcock, U.S.A.* (New York: G. P. Putnam's Sons, 1909), pp. 78–85, 111; Wiley Thompson to William P. Du Val, January 1, 1834, *House Document 271*, 24th Cong., 1st sess., pp. 8–9; Residents of Alachua County, Florida Territory, to Jackson, January 1834, Thompson to Cass, April 27, 1835, Thompson to Harris, June 17, 1835, *American State Papers: Military Affairs*, 4: 465–66, 470–71, 533–34; Commissioner of Indian Affairs, *Annual Report* (1835), p. 276. Also see Kenneth W. Porter, "Negroes and the Seminole War, 1835–1842," *Journal of Southern History* 30 (November 1964): 427–50. The Jackson administration's effort to unite "kindred tribes" in the West is discussed in chapter 5.

13. Kenneth W. Porter, "Florida Slaves and Free Negroes in the Seminole War, 1835–1842," *Journal of Negro History* 28 (October 1943): 395–98; Major General Th. S. Jessup to B. F. Butler, December 9, 1836, *House Document 78*, 25th Cong., 2d sess., p. 52; Winfield Scott, *Memoirs Of Lieut.-General Scott*, 2 vols. (New York: Sheldon & Company, 1864), 1: 260–61; Joseph Story to William W. Story, February 21, 1836, in Story, *Life and Letters*, 2: 229; *Nashville Republican*, July 14, 1836; *Arkansas Gazette*, March 15, 1836; *Charleston Courier* (South Carolina), April 30, 1836; Wm. Lloyd Garrison to George Thompson, May 24, 1836, in Walter M. Merrill and Louis Ruchames, eds., *The Letters of William Lloyd Garrison*, 2 vols. (Cambridge: Harvard University Press, Belknap Press, 1971), 1: 105–6; American Peace Society, *Eighth Annual Report* (Hartford: William Watson, 1836), p. 5; *Advocate of Peace* 2 (October 1838): 113; Peters to Poinsett, April 8, 1840, Poinsett Papers; Mahon, *Second Seminole War*,

pp. 265–67; James W. Covington, "Cuban Bloodhounds and the Seminoles," *Florida Historical Quarterly* 33 (October 1954): 111–19; *The Liberator* (Boston), March 19, April 9, August 20, 1841; *Congressional Globe*, 26th Cong., 1st sess., pp. 183, 259, 26th Cong., 2d sess., appendix, pp. 346–52; [Major Ethan Allen Hitchcock] to Rev. Wm. G. Eliot, Jr., March 1, 1841, Hitchcock Papers, Library of Congress, Washington, D.C.; *Nashville Daily Republican Banner*, April 22, 1841; Herbert E. Putnam, *Joel Roberts Poinsett, A Political Biography* (Washington, D.C.: Mimeoform Press, 1935), p. 160.

14. U.S., *Stat.*, 1: 460, 4: 730; McKenney to Johnson, June 13, 1829, IA, LS, 6: 13, RG 75, NA; Prucha, *American Indian Policy*, p. 192, 206–7; Strong, "Wardship," p. 93. For a brief account of the development and administration of the trust funds which ignores their role in social control, see George Dewey Harmon, "The Indian Trust Funds, 1797–1865," *Mississippi Valley Historical Review* 21 (June 1934): 23–30.

15. Commissioner of Indian Affairs, *Annual Report* (1839), p. 342; Report of Commissary General of Subsistence, November 12, 1835, in Commissioner of Indian Affairs, *Annual Report* (1835), pp. 290–91.

16. Circular to Superintendents and Agents, June 18, 1830, Randolph to Montgomery, June 18, 1830, Cass to Creek Delegation, February 10, 1832, IA, LS, 6: 486–87, 8: 88–89, RG 75, NA; Wirt to Carr, September 29, 1830, Ross to Wirt, January 1, 1831, Wirt Papers, Maryland Historical Society; McKenney to McLean, January 29, 1831, McLean Papers; Hamilton to Cherokee Delegation, January 14, 1831, D. A. Reese to Gilmore, June 8, 1831, Montgomery to Cass, October 28, 1831, Cass to Creek Delegation, February 19, 1832, *Senate Document 512*, 23rd Cong., 1st sess., 2: 265–66, 484, 632, 8: 88–89; *Niles' Register* 40 (August 13, 1831): 422, 40 (August 27, 1831): 454; Thomas L. McKenney, *Memoirs, Official and Personal*, 2 vols. (New York: Paine & Burgess, 1846), 1: 260–61; Eaton, *John Ross*, pp. 53–54; Abel, "Indian Consolidation West of the Mississippi," pp. 387–88; U.S., *Stat.*, 4: 737; Angie Debo, *The Road to Disappearance* (Norman: University of Oklahoma Press, 1941), p. 123; Arrel M. Gibson, *The Kickapoos: Lords of the Middle Border* (Norman: University of Oklahoma Press, 1963), p. 116.

17. Mary E. Young, "The Creek Frauds: A Study in Conscience and Corruption," *Mississippi Valley Historical Review* 42 (December 1955): 412–14. Also see Commissioner of Indian Affairs, *Annual Report* (1832), pp. 160–61; Herring to George W. Elliot, January 23, 1833, IA, LS, 9: 516, RG 75, NA.

18. Young, "Creek Frauds," pp. 414–37; Debo, *Road to Disappearance*, pp. 100–2; Peter A. Brannon, "Removal of Indians from Alabama," *Alabama Historical Quarterly* 12 (1950): 96–98; *Nashville Republican*,

July 5, 8, 12, 14, 23, 1836; *American Beacon and Norfolk and Portsmouth Daily Advertiser* (Virginia), July 9, 1836; *Congressional Globe,* 24th Cong., 2d sess., p. 146; Secretary of War, *Annual Report* (1836), pp. 121–22; T. Hartley Crawford to Poinsett, October 25, 1837, Poinsett Papers; George Dewey Harmon, *Sixty Years of Indian Affairs: Political, Economic and Diplomatic, 1789–1850* (Chapel Hill: University of North Carolina Press, 1941), pp. 201–25. A number of Creeks remained in Alabama in a rather "degraded" position. See C[rawford] to Governor Arthur P. Bagby, February 19, 1841, IA, LS, 30: 119–20, RG 75, NA; Grant Foreman, *The Five Civilized Tribes* (Norman: University of Oklahoma Press, 1934), p. 175.

19. Young, "Indian Removal and Land Allotment," p. 39; Arrell M. Gibson, *The Chickasaws* (Norman: University of Oklahoma Press, 1971), pp. 175–76. For the efforts to merge the Choctaws and the Chickasaws, see chapter 3.

20. Foreman, *Indian Removal,* p. 199; Gibson, *Chickasaws,* pp. 176–82; *Niles' Register* 53 (December 2, 1837): 211. For details of the Chicksaw emigration to the West, see Gibson, *Chickasaws,* pp. 179–215.

21. See *Arkansas Gazette,* October 13, 1830; Eaton to Ward, November 13, 1830, *Senate Document 512,* 23rd Cong., 1st sess., 2: 42–43; Joseph M. Street to Colonel J. Taylor, December 1, 1832, IA, LR, Sac and Fox Agency, RG 75, NA; T. J. V. Owen to [Elias Kent Kane], Confidential, December 25, 1833, Kane Papers, Chicago Historical Society, Chicago, Ill.; *Journal of the Executive Proceedings of the Senate,* 5: 138–39; Senate Resolution of February 24, 1841, Milroy Papers; B[ell] to Webster, June 3, 1841, same to John Chambers, James D. Doty, and T. Hartley Crawford, September 3, 1841, IA, LS, 30: 328, 31: 84–86, RG 75, NA. Following Greenwood LeFlore's attempt to submit treaty proposals to President Jackson in 1830, the executive branch generally sought congressional approval before entering into treaty negotiations with Indians. See George W. Lawe to Crawford, August 21, 1843, Doty to Lawe, October 19, 1843, Lawe Papers, Chicago Historical Society, Chicago, Ill.; Commissioner of Indian Affairs, *Annual Report* (1846), p. 220.

22. Kappler, *Indian Affairs,* 2: 213–425. Also see Jackson to Coffee, November 6, 1832, in Bassett, *Correspondence of Andrew Jackson,* 4: 483; Lieutenant L. Van Horne to Gibson, October 7, 1835, in Commissioner of Indian Affairs, *Annual Report* (1834), pp. 263–64; Report of the Commissary General of Subsistence, November 12, 1835, in Commissioner of Indian Affairs, *Annual Report* (1835), pp. 287–88.

23. Revised Regulations No. 5, May 13, 1837, IA, Misc. Records, 2: 296, RG 75, NA; Crawford to Poinsett, December 30, 1839, *House Document 103,* 26th Cong., 1st sess., p. 7; Marshall's statement, January 25,

1842, *House Executive Document 219,* 27th Cong., 3rd sess., pp. 88–89; Gibson, *Chickasaws,* p. 193; Lieutenant J. T. Sprague to Alabama Emigrating Co., October 2, 1836, Sprague to Harris, April 1, 1837, IA, LR, Creek Agency Emigration, RG 75, NA. Also see chapter 7 for information on profiteering in supplying emigrants with goods or transportation. Additional references to problems stemming from the policy of issuing contracts for rations and transportation to the lowest bidders appear in Satz, "Federal Indian Policy," p. 122 n.

24. Benj. F. Curry to Herring, August 4, 1832, *Senate Document 512,* 23rd Cong., 1st sess., 3: 416; Revised Regulations No. 5, May 13, 1837, IA, Misc. Records, 2: 292–93, 302–3, RG 75, NA; Emigrating Creeks to Sprague, December 21, 1836, IA, LR, Creek Agency Emigration, RG 75, NA; Gibson to Tyler, August 10, 1841, Records of the Department of State (hereafter cited as DS), LR, Misc., RG 59, NA.

25. Revised Regulations No. 5, May 13, 1837, IA, Misc. Records, 2: 298, RG 75, NA; Elbert Herring to William Clark, June 3, 1833, C[rawford] to Henry Toland, December 21, 1841, IA, LS, 10: 398–99, 31: 303–4, RG 75, NA; Sam. J. Potts to Medill, Private and Unofficial, May 27, 1847, Medill Papers; also see footnote 23. For evidence that the large expenditures for Indian removal were attracting considerable attention, see Message from the President . . . in Relation to the Expenditures of the Removal of the Indians West of the Mississippi, March 15, 1832, *House Executive Document 171,* 22d Cong., 1st sess., pp. 1–2; Senate Resolution of December 23, 1833, Gibson to Cass, October 31, 1834, *Senate Document 512,* 23rd Cong., 1st sess., 1: 3–4; *American Beacon and Norfolk and Portsmouth Daily Advertiser,* July 11, 1836, citing *National Intelligencer.*

26. Regulations of February 5, 1836, IA, Chickasaw Removal Records, LS, A, pp. 76–78, RG 75, NA; Crawford to Poinsett, April 18, 1840, K[urtz] to A. Lea, October 1, 1841, IA, Report Books, 2: 65–67, 3: 17–18, RG 75, NA; Circular from Medill, October 2, 1846, in Commissioner of Indian Affairs, *Annual Report* (1846), p. 228; Morton, *Crania Americana,* p. 83; Young, *Redskins, Ruffleshirts and Rednecks,* pp. 3–4, 13, 192–93; Paul W. Gates and Robert W. Swenson, *History of Public Land Law Development* (Washington, D.C.: GPO, 1968), pp. 203, 452, 463.

27. Paul W. Gates, "The Role of the Land Speculator in Western Development," *Pennsylvania Magazine of History and Biography* 66 (July 1942): 330–31; Young, *Redskins, Ruffleshirts and Rednecks,* pp. 47–193; Roy M. Robbins, "Preemption—A Frontier Triumph," *Mississippi Valley Historical Review* 18 (December 1931): 333, 343–44; Petition Adverse to the Location of Choctaw Reserves, February 1, 1836, *American State Papers: Public Lands,* 8: 430–31; Report on Pre-Emption Rights Defeated by Indian Reservations, April 22, 1836, *House Report 606,* 24th Cong., 1st

sess., pp. 1–2; Herbert A. Kellar, ed., *Solon Robinson, Pioneer and Agriculturalist: Selected Writings (1832–1851)*, 2 vols. (Indianapolis: Indiana Historical Bureau, 1936), 1: 11–15, 66–76, 80–84, 186–88, 192–93, 197–201, 406, 2: 447–48; Kappler, *Indian Affairs*, 2: 273–77, 367–70, 372–75; Cass to John T. Douglas, June 25, 1836, H[arris] to Poinsett, March 21, 1838, Crawford to Dougherty, July 1, 1839, Chas. E. Mix to Parks and Elwood, August 9, 1851, IA, LS, 19: 80–82, 23: 484, 27: 2, 45: 53–54, RG 75, NA; Albert S. White to Poinsett, October 16, 1837, Parks and Elwood to Luke Lea, July 29, 1851, IA, Registers, LR, 10: W339, 39: P415, RG 75, NA; U.S., *Stat.*, 10: 20; Commissioner of Indian Affairs, *Annual Report* (1848), p. 405.

28. Clark and Cass to Benton, December 27, 1828, *House Document 117*, 20th Cong., 2d sess., pp. 110–11; "Documents: Thomas Forsyth to Lewis Cass, St. Louis, October 24, 1831: Draper MSS., 6T152–164," *Ethnohistory* 4 (Spring 1957): 200; Reginald Horsman, *Expansion and American Indian Policy, 1783–1812* (East Lansing: Michigan State University Press, 1967), pp. 112, 145; James L. Clayton, "The Impact of Traders' Claims on the American Fur Trade," in *The Frontier in American Development: Essays in Honor of Paul Wallace Gates*, ed. David M. Ellis (Ithaca: Cornell University Press, 1969), pp. 300–5; G. E. E. Lindquist, "Indian Treaty Making," *Chronicles of Oklahoma* 26 (Winter 1948–49): 445.

29. Schoolcraft, *Memoirs*, pp. 627, 685; John Chambers to Orlando Brown, October 6, 1849, Brown Papers, Filson History Club, Louisville, Ky.; John Caldwell to Cass, March 13, 1833, Caldwell MSS., Illinois State Historical Society, Springfield, Ill.; Jos[eph] M. Street to Hitchcock, January 8, 1839, Crawford to Poinsett, January 28, 1839, *House Document 229*, 25th Cong., 3rd sess., pp. 51–54, 60; Crawford to Poinsett, September 17, 1839, Poinsett Papers; Thomas Dowling to Dr. N. U. Miller, Private, February 20, 1845, T. P. Andrews to Medill, December 24, 1846, Schoolcraft to Medill, September 30, 1848, Medill Papers; Clayton, "Impact of Traders' Claims," pp. 311–15.

30. *Executive Proceedings of the Senate*, 4: 383–84; Clayton, "Impact of Traders' Claims," pp. 304–14; Lawrence Taliaferro to Governor Dodge, July 24, 1837, IA, LR, St. Peters Agency, RG 75, NA; Robb to Armstrong, July 19, 1832, Crawford to W. W. Wick, March 2, 1841, Crawford to Ramsey Crooks, March 2, 1841, IA, LS, 9: 67, 30: 149, 151, RG 75, NA; G[eorge] B. Porter to Jackson, December 15, 1833, Porter Papers, Chicago Historical Society, Chicago, Ill.; Joseph M. Street to Henry Dodge, April 8, 1837, enclosed in Dodge to Harris, April 21, 1837, IA, LR, Prairie du Chien Agency, RG 75, NA; Harris to Poinsett, February 12, 1838, *Senate Document 198*, 25th Cong., 2d sess., pp. 1–2; H. S. Dousman

to William Aitken, March 4, 1838, Henry Hastings Sibley Papers, Minnesota Historical Society, Minneapolis, Minn.; Crawford to Poinsett, January 28, 1839, *House Document 229*, 25th Cong., 3rd sess., pp. 51–54; Crawford to John Fleming, Jr., May 31, 1839, in Carter and Bloom, *Territorial Papers*, 27: 1,237–38; Crawford to Poinsett, September 17, 1839, Poinsett Papers; Lawe to James D. Doty, March 11, 1843, Lawe Papers; Geo. W. Ewing to Medill, December 24, 1845, Medill Papers; Bell to President, August 31, 1841, in Richardson, *Papers of the Presidents*, 4: 62.

31. C[rawford] to John Johnston, March 26, 1841, same to Ewing, Walker & Co., August 19, 1841, IA, LS, 30: 189–90, 31: 29, RG 75, NA; Van der Bogart to Walter Monteith, October 14, 1832, Van der Bogart Papers, Chicago Historical Society, Chicago, Ill.; Street to Hitchcock, January 8, 1839, *House Document 229*, 25th Cong., 3rd sess., p. 60; Dodge to Fleming, May 31, 1839, in Carter and Bloom, *Territorial Papers*, 27: 1,238; Ramsey Crooks to Lawe, April 4, 1839, Memorandum of an Agreement between Joseph Bryan and John T. Cochrane with Robert Grignon, 1842, Lawe Papers; Clayton, "Impact of Traders' Claims," pp. 316–17. During the depression years of the late 1830s and early 1840s, claims against Indians served as bills of credit on the frontier. See Agreement between J. François Charett and Charles and Alexander Grignon, July 28, 1843, Lawe Papers.

32. *Executive Proceedings of the Senate*, 6: 170; Doty to Lawe, March 31, May 24, 1843, Lawe Papers; Horatio Hill to [Jas. Shields], December 1, 1845, Hill Papers, Chicago Historical Society, Chicago, Ill.; Ewing to Medill, December 24, 1845, Joseph Sinclair to Medill, April 5, 8, 12, 29, May 11, August 21, 1848, Medill Papers; Commissioner of Indian Affairs, *Annual Report* (1846), pp. 214–15, 220, (1847), p. 741, (1854), p. 227; Albert G. Ellis to Dodge, September 10, 1846, Dodge to Medill, September 26, 1846, in Commissioner of Indian Affairs, *Annual Report* (1846), pp. 253–55; Petition of P. Chouteau, Jr., W. G. and G. W. Ewing and S. Philips to William L. Marcy, enclosed in Chouteau, W. G. and G. W. Ewing to Medill, May 10, 1847, Medill to Chouteau & Co., W. G. and G. W. Ewing, May 19, 1847, *House Report 489*, 31st Cong., 1st sess., pp. 62–66, 69; U.S., *Stat.*, 9: 203; Kappler, *Indian Affairs*, 2: 633; Clayton, "Impact of Traders' Claims," pp. 303, 316–19.

33. Secretary of War, *Annual Report* (1842), p. 190; U.S. Office of Indian Affairs, *Indian Land Tenure: Economic Status and Population Trends* (Washington, D.C.: GPO, 1935), p. 5.

34. The Northern Indians and their removal experiences in the Jacksonian era have not received the same amount of careful study that scholars have given the southern tribes. For the separate histories of many of the northern Indians, see Muriel H. Wright, *A Guide to the Indian*

Tribes of Oklahoma (Norman: University of Oklahoma Press, 1951); Grant Foreman, The Last Trek of the Indians (Chicago: University of Chicago Press, 1946).

35. Quoted in George Wilson Pierson, Tocqueville and Beaumont in America (New York: Oxford University Press, 1938), p. 615.

36. For the physical arrangement of the tribes during the Jacksonian era, see Charles C. Royce, Indian Land Cessions in the United States, Bureau of American Ethnology, Eighteenth Annual Report, 1896–1897, vol. 2 (Washington, D.C., 1899).

37. For a brilliant analysis of the events leading up to the conflict, see Anthony F. C. Wallace, Prelude to Disaster: The Course of Indian-White Relations Which Led to the Black Hawk War of 1832 (Springfield: Illinois State Historical Library, 1970). The most thorough account of the Sac and Fox Indians and the Black Hawk War is William T. Hagan's The Sac and Fox Indians (Norman: University of Oklahoma Press, 1958).

38. Wallace, Prelude to Disaster, pp. 39, 49, 50, 51; Reynolds to Clark, May 26, 1831, Clark to Eaton, May 30, 1831, Bureau of Indian Affairs, Annual Report (1831), pp. 180–81; Reynolds to Gaines, May 28, 1831, Black Hawk War Papers, Illinois State Historical Society, Springfield, Ill.; Jackson to Reynolds, July 16, 1831, Andrew Jackson Papers, Illinois State Historical Society, Springfield, Ill.; Major General Alex. Macomb to Brigadier General Henry Atkinson, May 5, 1832, Records of the Headquarters of the Army (hereafter cited as Army Headquarters), LS, 4/2: 80–82, RG 108, NA; Charles Whittlesey, "Recollections of a Tour through Wisconsin in 1832," State Historical Society of Wisconsin, Collections 1 (1854): 83. Cecil Eby's "That Disgraceful Affair," The Black Hawk War (New York: W. W. Norton & Co., Inc., 1973), describes the mass hysteria that swept the Illinois frontier when Black Hawk returned, the role of the militia in provoking the hostilities, and the tactics of American and Indian leaders. For brief but informative accounts of the military operations involved in the Black Hawk War, see Roger L. Nichols, General Henry Atkinson: A Western Military Career (Norman: University of Oklahoma Press, 1965), pp. 152–75; Prucha, Sword of the Republic, pp. 211–31.

39. Macomb to Secretary of War, August 23, 1832, Army Headquarters, LS, 4/2: 153–54, RG 108, NA; Cass to Major General [Winfield] Scott, September 4, 1832, Lewis Cass MSS., Illinois State Historical Library, Springfield, Ill.; Galenian, August 22, 1832, clipping in the Henry R. Schoolcraft Papers, Library of Congress, Washington, D.C. For further evidence of the War Department's interest in "metalliferous" lands in the Old Northwest, see Eaton to General John McNeil, March 30, 1829, Senate Records, 21B-C1, RG 46, NA.

40. Louise Phelps Kellogg, "The Removal of the Winnebago," Wisconsin Academy of Science, Arts, and Letters, *Transactions* 21 (1929): 23–29.

41. Ibid., pp. 28–29; William T. Hagan, *American Indians* (Chicago: University of Chicago Press, 1961), pp. 82–83; Dodge to Harris, February 15, 1837, August 16, 1838, Resolution by the Territorial Assembly [of Wisconsin], March 11, 1839, in Carter and Bloom, *Territorial Papers,* 27: 735–37, 1056–57, 1217; Commissioner of Indian Affairs, *Annual Report* (1840), p. 229, (1843), p. 263, (1846), p. 219, (1847), p. 739; Secretary of War, *Annual Report* (1838), p. 110, (1846), p. 60; Bell to Tyler, August 31, 1841, Richardson, *Papers of the Presidents,* 4: 59–60; *United States Magazine and Democratic Review* 18 (May 1846): 334; Petition of Oneida Nation to Dodge, March 15, 1839, Charles Caron to Lawe, May 16, 1843, Doty to Lawe, November 20, 1843, Lawe Papers; Crawford to John Chambers, May 5, 1843, in Commissioner of Indian Affairs, *Annual Report* (1843), p. 284; Dodge to Medill, October 8, 1846, in Commissioner of Indian Affairs, *Annual Report* (1846), p. 252; Alex F. Ricciardelli, "The Adoption of White Agriculture by the Oneida Indians," *Ethnohistory* 10 (Fall 1963): 309, 313; *North American Review* 143 (November 1886): 443.

42. McKenney to Justus Ingersoll, September 21, 1829, IA, LS, 6: 90–91, RG 75, NA; Commissioner of Indian Affairs, *Annual Report* (1842), p. 379, (1846), p. 219; *Prairie Farmer* 4 (May 1844): 117; Gates, "Frontier Land Business in Wisconsin," pp. 306, 313.

43. *Calumet* 1 (September–October 1832): 261–62; Beaver, *Church, State, and the American Indians,* p. 115. See chapter 8 for the attempt to create a northern Indian territory.

5 /

The Promise of Indian Self-Rule

in the West

PRESIDENT JACKSON had publicly assured Congress and the American people that his removal policy would help to ameliorate the condition of the "much-injured race" of Indians. He maintained that the policy would allow the government to "raise up an interesting commonwealth" of Indians across the Mississippi River. Indian emigrants would have "governments of their own choice, subject to no other control from the United States than such as may be necessary to preserve peace on the frontier and between the several tribes."[1]

Jackson had presented Indian removal as a means of safeguarding tribal integrity from white laws. Only by emigrating outside the limits of the states and territories of the United States, he argued, could the Indians be "perpetuated as Nations ... [and enjoy] the right of living under their own laws." He also promised that emigrants would receive permanent title to their new land, enjoy their old tribal government, and receive generous gifts from the federal government unfettered by the perplexing questions of sovereignty that had arisen in the East. Unfortunately for the Indians, however, federal Indian policy did not exactly coincide with Jackson's promises.[2]

From the arrival of the first groups of emigrants in the trans-Mississippi West, federal officials undermined tribal sovereignty in order to provide orderly supervision of the heterogeneous tribesmen congregating alongside America's exposed western frontier. Regardless of presidential rhetoric and treaty pledges, government efforts to promote tranquil Indian-white relations on the frontier often resulted in the emasculation of Indian sovereignty in the West.[3]

Jackson's promises that the Indians would be sovereign in the West were directed against the virulent critics of his removal policy. Privately, however, he admitted that complete self-rule for the Indians was unlikely for some time. In the draft of his first annual message to Congress he wrote that "the idea of exclusive self-government" for the Indians was "impracticable" because "no people were ever free, or capable of forming and carrying into execution a social compact for themselves until education and intelligence was first introduced." Although he omitted this passage in his final draft of the message, it adequately reflects his thinking. The adoption of the white man's ways by the Indians would have to precede "exclusive self government." Until then, the paternal hand of the United States would watch over the tribesmen. Although there were sincere efforts by some advocates of Jackson's removal policy to incorporate the emigrants into American society, constitutional arguments, sectional animosities, territorial expansionism, and the idea of white superiority left them at the mercy of American paternalism.[4]

As early as 1829 Secretary of War John Eaton urged Congress to establish a "Territory" outside the geographical limits of the western states and territories for Indian emigrants. Eaton wanted the United States to provide laws for the "general government" of this territory and to serve as a policeman among the transplanted tribes. The Indians would make their own "municipal regulations" in council as was their custom, but a "Governor" appointed by the president would have a military command at his disposal as well as a veto power over tribal declarations of war. Eaton believed that such a territorial government would prevent intertribal hostilities and provide adequate protection for the emigrants. "No better plan can be thought of," he told President Jackson, "than that the United States shall put in operation such a system of Indian protection and government, West of the Mississippi, as that a confidence may be reposed, that they are indeed our fostered children, and the Government not only so disposed to consider, but practically to evince their good feelings toward them."[5]

Secretary Eaton's proposals received the active support of Baptist missionary Isaac McCoy, an ardent proponent of Indian removal and the establishment of a permanent trans-Mississippi Indian territory. While employed as superintendent of surveys for the War Department in 1831, McCoy began surveying a district west of Missouri in the central portion of the new Indian country for a capital for the territory proposed by Eaton. Acting without specific orders from Eaton in this matter, McCoy found himself in an embarrassing position when the secretary left the War Department in mid-1831. McCoy assured Lewis Cass, the new secretary of war, that Eaton had intended to issue orders for the survey before his abrupt departure from office. The missionary told Cass, an old acquaintance from Michigan Territory, "I cannot too warmly express my predilection in favor of the scheme . . . of reserving a tract 30 or 40 miles square, in a central part of the territory, for a common ground, on which individuals of any tribe might settle; and within which, would eventually be located their seat of government."[6]

McCoy vigorously argued that the establishment of a "regular Territorial Government" for the Indian country was "essential" to the "future prosperity" of the transplanted Indians. Noting the likelihood of disputes among neighboring emigrant tribes and between the emigrants and the indigenous Indians, McCoy urged Cass to bring all of the Indians together in a council in order to "explain to them the nature of the relation which, hereafter, they would be required to sustain one to another, to elicit mutual pledges of peace, and to originate measures suited to their present condition, which would lead to the rudiments of a territorial compact and government." The missionary's plan was to unite all of the tribes into a single "body politic" which would become an integral part of the United States, governed by a superintendent appointed by the president. A territorial form of government for the new Indian country, McCoy argued, would provide a more efficient means of promoting the beneficent "designs of Government" than the existing system of having resident agents live among the tribes. The agency system only promoted "the distinct and independent interests of the tribes," whereas a single council would unite their interests and bring harmony and tranquility.[7]

McCoy's optimism about the future prospects of his proposed Indian territory was boundless. Indian merchants and mill owners, he observed, would be happy to have people of other tribes frequent their business places and would thereby serve as a source of intertribal harmony. "The better informed, and those in more comfortable condition," moreover, "would have the ascendancy among their less fortunate brethren, while the latter would profit by the talents and enterprize of the former." The establishment of schools and Christian churches in the territory would "promote their happiness in this world" as well as "prepare them for the next." Although McCoy agreed that President Jackson's removal policy was "the most judicious and humane policy ever conceived by a civilized power" for an aboriginal population, there was one additional step that he thought the government needed to take. The establishment of an Indian territory would be the logical culmination of the administration's Indian policy. "From conclusions rationally drawn," McCoy told Secretary Cass, "[I] believe, that, should the scheme now entered upon by our country be steadily followed up, the epoch will be calendared for posterity as the crisis of Indian degredation and decline, and as the date of their prosperity."[8]

Other advocates of Jackson's Indian removal policy also hoped that it would be the initial step toward the eventual assimilation of the Indians. Several leaders of the Dutch Reformed and Baptist churches, for example, argued that enlightened men would find excellent conditions in the West to transform the emigrants into industrious citizens. They would be able to Christianize and civilize the tribesmen before the tide of white population reached their new homeland. By the time the line of settlement approached the western Indian territory, the tribesmen would be ready for assimilation into American society and become "a new and interesting State of the Union." These enthusiastic advocates of removal asserted that emigration and civilization of the Indians would naturally lead to their future admission to full American citizenship.[9]

Leading critics of Jackson's removal policy strongly challenged this line of reasoning. Jeremiah Evarts, writing under the pseudonym William Penn for the national press, labeled the plan of a wilderness Indian commonwealth as "entirely visionary." Evarts reminded his readers that even the English philosopher John Locke had failed to construct a workable plan of government for a distant American colony. Yet the Jackson administration and its allies contemplated establishing a single territory for Indians with different languages and customs without giving sufficient thought to the manifold problems that might arise. Evarts doubted that the government could find "suitable administrators" for the proposed territory. He feared that the men selected for the positions would be "much more intent on the emoluments of office, than on promoting the happiness of the Indians." Finally, Evarts warned that American cupidity would undoubtedly make a mockery of Jackson's pledge that the territory would be a "permanent" Indian homeland. The New Englander predicted:

> Twenty years hence, Texas . . . will have been settled by the descendants of Anglo-Americans. The State of Missouri will be populous. There will be great roads through the new Indian country, and caravans will be passing and repassing in many directions. The emigrant Indians will be *denationalized*, and will have no common bond of union.

Like many opponents of removal, Evarts also believed that congressional legislation was an inadequate guarantee of Indian sovereignty since Congress could always take away what it had previously granted.[10]

The passage of the Removal Bill on May 28, 1830, was a bitter defeat for Evarts and others who hoped that the Indians would remain on their ancient lands. The new act provided the chief executive with power to divide any unorganized area west of the Mississippi River into "a suitable number of districts" for Indian emigrants who would receive permanent title to their new land. According to this legislation, the entire area claimed by the United States west of the Mississippi River in 1830, excluding Louisiana, Arkansas, and Missouri, was potentially available for Indian settlement.[11]

The Removal Act contained several provisions relating to the governance of this new "Indian country." All existing regulations

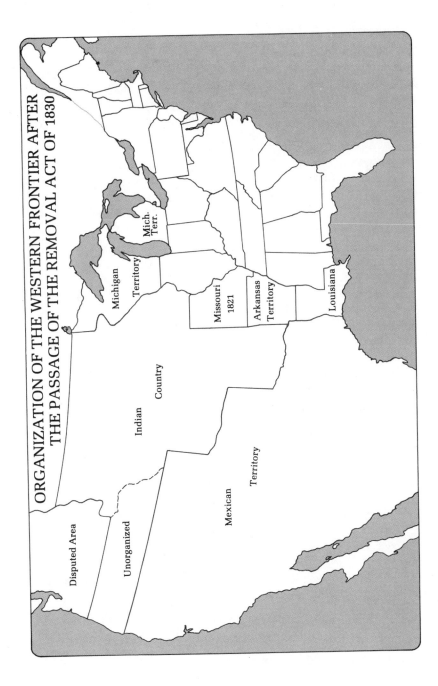

ORGANIZATION OF THE WESTERN FRONTIER AFTER
THE PASSAGE OF THE REMOVAL ACT OF 1830

Disputed Area

Unorganized

Indian Country

Mexican Territory

Michigan Territory

Mich. Terr.

Missouri 1821

Arkansas Territory

Louisiana

relating to the supervision of trade and intercourse with the Indians remained in effect. In addition, the president was to guarantee the protection of the emigrants against "all interruption or disturbance from any other tribe or nation of Indians, or from any other person or persons whatever." It was under the provisions of this act that the Jackson administration negotiated removal treaties with the southern and eastern Indians and started relocating them west of Missouri and Arkansas in the 1830s.[12]

The Treaty of Dancing Rabbit Creek with the Choctaws, the first tribe to emigrate under the Removal Act, reflected President Jackson's thinking about the future status of the Indian tribes in the West and also demonstrated the kind of promises that were necessary to effect Indian emigration. The treaty acknowledged the right of the Choctaws to self-government in the West but prohibited them from making any laws inconsistent with those of the United States. The federal government, moreover, would provide the Indians with a resident agent to guide their actions. The Jackson administration showed its willingness to interfere directly with the existing system of tribal government by offering to pay a five-hundred-dollar salary for twenty years should the Choctaws decide to elect "an additional principal Chief of the whole [tribe] to superintend and govern upon republican principles." While the treaty declared that the Choctaws recognized the right of Congress to "exercise a legislation over Indian affairs," it also held out the prospect of allowing the tribe to send a delegate to Congress at a later date.[13]

When the Choctaws began arriving in their new country west of Arkansas in the early 1830s, the first contingents attempted to reestablish their tribal government and enact laws suited to their new position. Choctaw agent Francis W. Armstrong, however, refused to permit them to take any immediate steps until more emigrants arrived. Armstrong pointed out that only one-fourth of the tribe was present and advised the Indians that a minority could not legislate for the majority. When emigrant Peter Pitchlynn, a Choctaw district chief, applied to the Indian Bureau in 1832 for the annual stipend promised men of his rank in the Treaty of Dancing Rabbit Creek, he received the curt reply that he was not entitled to it because his election had occurred east of the Mississippi River. Although the Choctaws succeeded in setting up a new legal code in the mid-1830s, agent Armstrong's continual interference in tribal affairs was a clear indication that the Indians were far from being completely sovereign in their new land. Captain John Stuart, who was stationed at Fort Coffee in the new Choctaw country, maintained in 1836 that the Choctaws and the Cherokees undoubtedly preferred American supervision of their affairs to the "interference of [the] Individual States" from which they had emigrated. Removal had freed the Choctaws from the tyranny of Mississippi state laws but not from federal supervision.[14]

As Indian removal commenced in earnest in the early 1830s, the Jackson administration discovered that the legislation governing Indian-white relations was little suited to the exigencies of the trans-Mississippi frontier. Existing legislation dating back to 1802 prohibited the sale of liquor to Indians, required the president to remove intruders from Indian land, and called for the extension of federal jurisdiction in all crimes committed on Indian land except those by Indians against Indians. The Removal Act, however, neither specified how these acts were to be made applicable in areas without federal courts nor provided the president with any new authority to regulate tribal affairs.[15]

Another serious problem that the Jackson administration had to face was the prospect of having to settle clashing boundary disputes between tribes in the new Indian country. Although Isaac McCoy received a commission in mid-1831 to survey boundary lines for the emigrants, the administration's concern for providing specific borders for the various tribes was rather tardy. Emigrants were already arriving in the West while the surveys were in progress, and serious disputes resulted. Even before 1830, contingents of southern Indians and tribesmen from the Old Northwest had moved to the area west of the Mississippi in search of isolation from white society. In addition, the Pawnees and other fierce tribes that roamed the western "prairies" were a source of "great annoyance" to the new emigrant Indians. The poor planning for the permanent settlement of the relocated tribes and their protection from indigenous hostile tribes or boundary disputes with earlier emigrants was a further indication that an overhauling of existing legislation was urgently needed if the government was to maintain order in the new Indian country.[16]

Tennessee Democrat John Bell, an architect of the Removal Act, sought to provide the administration with the necessary legislation. Early in 1832 he introduced a bill in the House of Representatives calling for the War Department to submit "a plan for the government of the Indians who have removed, or may remove . . . so far as it may be proper for the United States, and necessary for the Indians, that such authority should be exercised over them." Bell suggested that the plan contain proposals for civilizing the Indians and regulating commerce with them. He especially urged that Secretary of War Cass consider excluding all whites from the "Indian country" except those granted special licenses by federal agents. In order to discourage the Indians from committing depredations against their neighbors, Bell asked Congress to grant President Jackson authority to reimburse injured parties with funds deducted from Indian annuities. Finally, he recommended that the president receive "such temporary authority . . . as may be necessary to preserve the peace" among the emigrants until Congress provided them with a form of government. Bell also introduced a second bill, calling for the creation of a commission to travel to the Indian country and report to the War Department on existing conditions as well as to recommend permanent boundaries for future emigrants.[17]

Bell's proposals came long after the first emigrants had arrived in the West, and they were a tacit admission that haste and poor planning had characterized the execution of the Indian removal policy. When Congressman Joseph Hemphill of Pennsylvania had urged a delay in voting on the Removal Bill in 1830 in order to allow time for a commission to make a report similar to the one Bell now proposed, the Tennessean and other administration supporters opposed the idea. Bell had contended at that time that "no three living men could perform the duties" required in less than two years, but now, two years later, he was admitting that the Jackson administration had insufficient knowledge of the conditions in the Indian country.[18]

Despite the tardiness of Bell's proposals for a survey of conditions in the West, his suggestions apparently reflected the administration's thinking about the permanency of the Indian country. President Jackson told his closest friends that he wanted to unite the major southern tribes into a "confederacy" which might admit other tribes as they became sufficiently advanced along the path of civilization. He was also willing to hold out the prospect of allowing the most "civilized" Indians, like the Choctaws and Cherokees, the right to send delegates to Congress and even suggested to the latter that they might receive separate territorial status.[19]

While Bell's proposals reflected the thinking of President Jackson and the earlier plans of Secretary of War Eaton, they also represented the hopes and aspirations of Baptist missionary Isaac McCoy, who believed that political activism and moral suasion were both useful tactics. McCoy had arrived in Washington from the West early in March, and he helped Bell work for the passage of his bills. The missionary also lobbied for support for the removal policy and published, at his personal expense, an "Address to the Philanthropists in the United States . . . on the Condition and Prospects of the American Indians" which enthusiastically endorsed the plan of congregating the Indians in a western territory. McCoy's actions were an attempt to secure official and public support for the establishment of a permanent Indian territory along the lines described earlier by former secretary of war Eaton.[20]

The missionary's arrival in Washington was timed to promote the adoption of the territorial plan he had already suggested to Secretary Cass. On March 16, the same day Bell introduced his proposals, McCoy's letter to Cass was read by one of the missionary's friends in the House of Representatives and then published as a public document. McCoy had seven hundred extra copies printed at his own expense, and he sent them, together with copies of his "Address," to government officials and private citizens throughout the country. Such efforts undoubtedly helped to secure the passage of Bell's proposals.[21]

On July 14, 1832, the House passed an act calling for the establishment of a commission to visit the new Indian country and to make recommendations for "a plan for the improvement, government, and security of the Indians" to the War Department. The Jackson administration, in an effort to appease public opinion and silence its critics who were bemoaning the inhumanity of the removal policy, attempted to appoint several nationally known humanitarians, including an anti-Jacksonian, to the commission. When these individuals refused to serve, Secretary of War Cass appointed Montfort Stokes, the former Democratic governor of North Carolina, who served as chairman; the Reverend John F. Schermerhorn of New York, an ardent Jacksonian and member of the proremoval Dutch Reformed church; and Henry I. Ellsworth, a prominent Connecticut businessman. Although Isaac McCoy had eagerly sought an appointment to the commission, Cass had bypassed the missionary in order to make appointments that would strengthen his own political position.[22]

Cass told the commissioners that the Removal Act was a "solemn national declaration, containing pledges, which neither the Government nor the country will suffer to be violated" and instructed them to take adequate steps to assure the Indians of the permanency of their new possessions. The basic tasks of the Stokes commission included the settlement of existing disputes among the emigrants, the arrangement of tribal boundaries, the reconciliation of the hostile plains tribes to the emigrants, and, generally, "the examination and suggestion of any topics calculated to improve their condition, and to enable the Government the better to discharge the great moral debt, which circumstances, and the situation of this hapless race, have imposed upon them."[23]

The secretary of war particularly stressed the need to guarantee the tribesmen "permanent" establishment by reuniting all Indians connected by "consanguinity & manners" in adjacent locations. "It is important," Cass said, "that the tribes should not be broken into fragments, but that portions of each should be brought together." He argued, for example, that the Creeks in Alabama were closely related to the Seminoles in Florida and should form "but one people," as was the case with the Cherokees scattered in Alabama, Georgia, North Carolina, and Tennessee, whom he hoped to "unite together" in the West. In effect Cass wanted to strengthen the bonds of Indian groups, clans, or towns that had functioned as independent units for generations or longer. Since large, easily manipulated political-social units did not already exist among many of the Indians east of the Mississippi River, the Jackson administration was going to promote their establishment in the new Indian country. Developing the concept of monolithic tribes was the government's way of simplifying treaty negotiations and making it easier for agents to administer federal policy and control Indian society.[24]

Cass urged the commissioners to be extremely careful in their handling of affairs in the Indian country. "In the great change we are now urging them to make," he said, "it is desirable that all of their political relations, as well among themselves as with us, should be established upon a permanent basis, beyond the necessity of any future alteration." He also cautioned them to consider carefully all alternatives before reporting proposals for Indian betterment, since he intended to submit their report to Congress as the "foundation of a system of legislation" for these emigrants.[25]

While the Stokes commission was en route to the West with a strong military escort, administration leaders discussed the question of providing the emigrants with a system of government. Indian commissioner Elbert Herring told Secretary Cass that he personally disliked the "rude civil regulations" of the tribesmen and distrusted the tremendous power of the chiefs. Cass agreed that the rudimentary political and social institutions of the emigrants needed "modifications." Herring urged the adoption of a "code of laws" to provide "cement" to bind together the various independent Indian groups lacking strong internal principles of amalgamation. Such a code would have to be simple, suited to their wants, and adapted to "the first dawnings of the social compact" among them. The general consensus of the War Department was that Indians did not have any cohesive system of basic laws to hold them together. No one suggested that the Indians had their own socio-legal systems and that attempts to dictate principles of government to them were contrary to the administration's assurance that the tribesmen could pursue their own way of life in the trans-Mississippi West. The ethnocentrism of federal officials prevented them from realizing that the Indians did not necessarily view the white man's concept of government as superior to their own.[26]

While Washington officials discussed the basic needs of the emigrants and the Stokes commission was traveling to the Indian country, Isaac McCoy continued his efforts to secure the establishment of an Indian territory. McCoy had received instructions from Secretary Cass ordering him to acquaint the commissioners with his surveys of the Indian country. The missionary, however, took full advantage of this order and prepared a detailed series of proposals for the future welfare of the Indians for the commissioners to consider.[27]

McCoy urged the Stokes commission to recommend the establishment of an Indian territory, which he suggested be named

Aboriginia. His proposals for this territory were an elaboration of the earlier scheme he had recommended to Secretary Cass. The missionary wanted to replace resident agents among the various tribes with a complete array of territorial officials. There would be a governor appointed by the president, and other territorial and district officers who might be Indians. In the central portion of the territory, there should be "a central council fire, where the tribes may meet and smoke the pipe of peace, to mingle gratitude to God with the ascending fumes, and to cast the recollections of past injuries done by others with the ashes, to the earth." McCoy also suggested a revamping of the trade regulations to protect the Indians from the introduction of "ardent spirits" and strongly recommended federal expenditures to promote the education of Indian youth. The "cap-stone of your edifice" for the territory which will be "the last experiment of Indian reform," he told the commissioners, will be providing for the representation of the Indian territory in Congress. "You go from us," he told Stokes and his colleagues, "the almoners of mercy, to these despairing poor, charged with the choicest blessings that we have to send."[28]

After receiving McCoy's suggestions and spending a year in the West reconciling the emigrants to their new homes, settling boundary disputes, and working with the United States Dragoons to pacify the indigenous tribes, the Stokes commission sent a lengthy report to Secretary Cass and made numerous suggestions for future policy.[29] The commissioners urged immediate action by Congress to prevent Indian-white conflict in the West. They warned that white traders charged exorbitant prices for goods and suggested that the government furnish the Indians with supplies at "first cost" instead of cash annuities. They also asked for the removal of all whiskey vendors from the Indian country and advised Congress to prohibit contact between Indians and whites. Only agents and those engaged in educating the Indians should have free admission to the area. In order to prevent "collisions" between Indians and whites, the Stokes commission favored the establishment of a five-mile-wide neutral strip of land to separate the Indian country from the Arkansas-Missouri line. Finally, the commission recommended the establishment of a territorial government for the emigrants.[30]

Stokes and his associates forwarded a detailed proposal for an Indian territory to Secretary Cass. They agreed that the United

States could maintain a "constitutional supervision over all her red children" without impairing "in the least", the sovereignty of the individual tribes within their allotted boundaries. While the government should encourage the Indians to adopt "municipal laws" for their own tribes, a territorial legislature or council could regulate intertribal affairs and provide a common system of justice for the emigrants. The commissioners warned that the Indians would never receive adequate justice in the neighboring courts of Arkansas and Missouri, and they urged the creation of a territorial government to guarantee that avaricious frontiersmen would not violate federal trade and intercourse acts with impunity. The Stokes commission also noted that some recent emigrants were openly violating federal law by running distilleries in the Indian country. These tribesmen jealously guarded their "fancied rights" and refused to recognize the applicability of American laws in their new homeland. For all of these reasons, the commissioners strongly urged the immediate creation of a territorial government for the Indian country.[31]

The proposed Indian territory was to consist of a governor, a secretary, agents residing with the various tribes, a marshal, a prosecuting attorney, and a judiciary with an adequate number of clerks. All of these officials were to be presidential appointees. The governor, situated at Fort Leavenworth, only seventeen or eighteen days distant from Washington, was to superintend the affairs of all western tribes and receive weekly reports from agents. Each tribe would send delegates to an annual council at Forth Leavenworth. This "council of the red men" would meet in a large amphitheater constructed by the government, and the delegates would receive a stipend from Congress. The commissioners believed that the council would serve as a stabilizing force in the Indian country. "Here distant tribes may meet to settle difficulties, make peace, renew their friendship, and propose salutary regulations for their respective tribes," they suggested. The Indians would also exhibit their improvement in civilization and permit the more "savage" tribes to see and taste "the fruits of civilization." The assemblage would also provide the federal government with a useful means of simultaneously informing all of its "red children" of its wishes and policies. The Stokes commission hoped that the formation of an Indian territory would promote peace among the tribesmen and perhaps "ere long, [they might] adopt some general articles of confederation for their own republic, not inconsistent with the wishes of [the United States] Government."[32]

Secretary Cass sent the commission's report to Congress, where it underwent close scrutiny. Together with earlier recommendations from Cass, Isaac McCoy, Thomas McKenney, and other government officials, it received the support of the House Committee on Indian Affairs. The committee introduced three bills on May 20, 1834, which represented an attempt to provide an integrated system of Indian policy along the lines suggested by the Stokes commission. The first bill called for the formal organization of the Indian Office in the War Department. The second measure provided for a new and more vigorous trade and intercourse law, and the third authorized the establishment of a territorial government for the Indian country. The House committee report was a nonpartisan effort to provide a comprehensive system of Indian policy. As the *National Intelligencer* observed, "The report seems, with a view to secure a real reform, to have avoided all topics of a culpatory character, or [those] that could be used to excite party considerations." The first two proposals received sufficient bipartisan support in both houses of Congress to become law, but heated debate ensued over the Territorial Bill.[33]

The proposal for the establishment of the "Western Territory" closely resembled the suggestions of the Stokes commission but contained several important innovations. It established permanent territorial boundaries for the Indian country west of Arkansas and Missouri and called for the issuance of land patents to the Indians. The new territory was to comprise all the land stretching from the Mexican possessions on the south and west to the western boundaries of Arkansas and Missouri on the east and the Platte River in the north. The House bill specifically granted the governor, who was to be appointed by the president, the power to veto legislation proposed by the Indian council, as well as the right to convene or dissolve that assembly at his will. A judicial system consisting of tribal chiefs, however, could render decisions concerning intertribal affairs, subject to presidential intervention in specific cases. The bill also allowed the confederated tribes to elect a delegate to Congress who would receive the same powers, privileges, and compensation as delegates from other territories. Finally, the bill stipulated that the proposed confederation of tribes

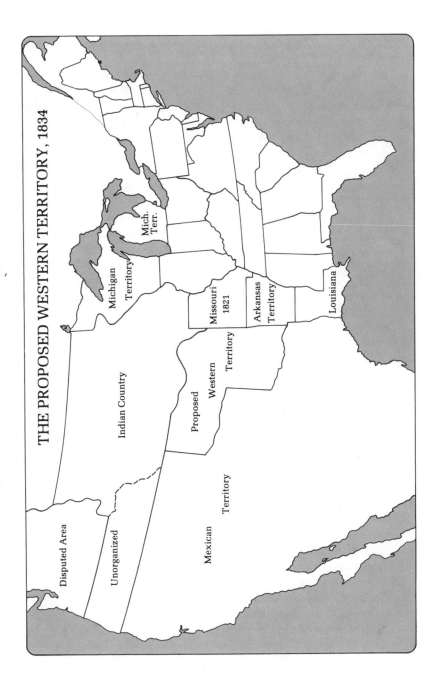

THE PROPOSED WESTERN TERRITORY, 1834

would not be binding unless the Cherokees, Choctaws, and Creeks agreed to join it.[34]

The House bill was ably defended by Democratic members of the Georgia delegation and by Horace Everett of Vermont, an anti-Jacksonian. They argued that the measure would fulfull the government's deep obligations to the emigrants and urged its immediate enactment. A number of anti-Jackson congressmen, however, opposed the creation of an Indian territory and worked to defeat or indefinitely postpone the proposal.[35]

Former president John Quincy Adams, now representing Massachusetts, claimed that Congress did not have sufficient authority to establish a government for Indians. He feared that supporters of the bill intended to make the proposed territory an integral part of the Union and warned that the admission of a state composed entirely of Indians was unconstitutional as well as a dangerous precedent. Adams also spoke in behalf of those easterners who argued that rapid settlement of the West and the admission of new territories would create an imbalance in the Union and mean the loss of Eastern power and prestige.[36]

Other anti-Jacksonites blasted the proposal for different reasons. Ohio Congressman Samuel F. Vinton protested the creation of a territorial government placing excessive power in the hands of the executive branch of the government and the military. New York Congressman Millard Fillmore charged that the administration was trying to rush the legislation through too hastily and recommended further deliberations. Even Democrat William S. Archer of Virginia, who had supported Indian removal, joined anti-Jacksonites in opposing the bill and warned that the proposed legislation would destroy the "sacred" pledge of 1830 by subjugating the Indians to a "proconsular" form of government instead of providing them with self-rule in the West. Archer also cautioned his southern colleagues that once they admitted "Indian legislators" into the halls of Congress they would be confronted with bills seeking to extend the same privilege to the "deeper colored race." The Virginia Democrat, together with anti-Jacksonites Adams, Vinton, and Fillmore, secured the postponement of the measure, which proved to be its death knell.[37]

Congressional failure to enact the Territorial Bill meant that the newly enacted Trade and Intercourse Act of 1834 became the sole organic statute for the area designated Indian country by the Removal Act of 1830. This act might justifiably be called federal segregation legislation. It excluded all whites from the trans-Mississippi Indian country except those with licenses or passports certified by government agents. In spite of the fact that President Jackson disagreed with Chief Justice Marshall's contention that the tribes were "domestic dependent nations," the law of 1834 extended America's "paternalistic guardianship" over all of the emigrants in the West. It prohibited them from bartering with whites, provided for the use of military force to expel intruders, forbade the sale or conveyance of Indian land without prior approval from the Indian Office, and permitted the federal government to make deductions from annuities for depredations committed by the Indians or for property stolen by them. The act was an attempt to control Indian-white relations in the West by drastically limiting the possibilities of contact between the two groups. Only federal officials, teachers, and missionaries would have easy access to the Indian country.[38]

The Trade and Intercourse Act of 1834 placed Indian emigrants at the mercy of the white man's conception of justice. Although President Jackson had promised the emigrants self-rule and sovereignty in the West, the 1834 act stated that American laws would take precedence over Indian laws and customs in all cases involving Indians and whites. Moreover, the location of courts in Arkansas and Missouri for violators of federal laws in the Indian country often precluded a fair trial for the Indians, as the Stokes commission had warned. White juries were not prone to finding Indians innocent of alleged attacks on white communities or whites guilty of fraudulent practices. The local judicial officers in white communities adjoining the Indian country reflected the dominant attitudes of their respective communities and, in many instances, were not very effective administrators of federal laws designed to protect the Indians from avaricious whites.[39]

The Cherokees who survived the Trail of Tears set up their own law-enforcement machinery upon arriving in the Indian country in the late 1830s, but they found themselves constantly harrassed by officials of the U.S. District Court at Van Buren, Arkansas. For at least twenty years following their settlement in present-day Oklahoma, the Cherokees and their defenders lamented that "the course pursued by the district court places the Cherokees in a degraded position, that no free people can bear patiently." Cherokee agent George Butler reported as late as 1855 that "it has been the case, too frequently, of an Indian having been arrested for some trivial offense, taken to Van Buren, put into jail, and left to linger there until trial day; perhaps then they could find nothing against him, and the poor fellow would return home, injured in health and purse." The district court's ruling that the Indians were incompetent to serve as witnesses against whites, together with its practice of arresting tribesmen in the Indian country without notifying the chiefs or the local agent, led to "much disturbance and dissatisfaction" among the Indians. Arkansas Governor John Pope had warned as early as 1831 that prohibiting Indians from testifying against whites would mean that whites would commit crimes with impunity in the Indian country. Yet not until 1847 did Indians become "competent witnesses" in the white courts neighboring the Indian country. Even then, however, federal law did not provide them with a trial by a jury of peers in their own region. They still had to appear in white courts.[40]

Another source of difficulty was the fact that tribal customs conflicting with the white man's laws or prejudices were openly violated in the Indian country and in the district courts in Arkansas and Missouri. The Creeks, for example, had no aversion to intermarriage with Negroes. They readily accepted such unions and considered Negroes as bona fide members of their tribe. White officials, however, flatly ignored this custom when it came to the distribution of tribal annuities, and white juries in Arkansas and Missouri had little sympathy for the pleas of black Creeks. The district court in Arkansas, moreover, claimed that it had complete jurisdiction over all Negroes living with the Indians. Although the court would not allow the Indians to testify in court, it followed the extraordinary policy, for a southern court, of allowing black slaves held by the Indians to testify against their masters. The Cherokees particularly protested against such "aggravated oppressions" by a "foreign tribunal" which would not even permit Indians to be tried by a jury of their peers.[41]

The laws of 1834 also seriously impaired tribal sovereignty in another way. The mere presence of federal agents and military detachments in the Indian country meant that the tribesmen were not completely sovereign. Agents and frontier post commanding officers found it easier to deal with a central tribal authority rather than a series of chiefs or headmen and encouraged the recognition of a specific figure as the leader of a particular group of Indians. The result was the evolution of a political-social organization which assumed functions hitherto the prerogative of independent Indian clans or towns. In the transformation from old Indian ways to patterns induced by federal pressure, many of the activities which had invigorated local Indian life and made the tribesmen self-reliant and resolute were taken away from them.[42]

Emigrant Indians increasingly looked to the leaders recognized by agents and military officers for guidance and direction. Frequently, government officials used the threat of withholding Indian annuities to force compliance with their wishes. When the Creeks who were forcibly removed from Alabama arrived in the West in late 1836, for example, Superintendent William Armstrong and General Matthew Arbuckle warned these destitute emigrants that their annuity would be withheld unless they accepted the leadership of the chief officially recognized by the United States government. The Creeks had little choice because, since the passage of the Trade and Intercourse Act of 1834, the Indian Office had proscribed visits to Washington by tribal delegations seeking redress for grievances unless they had the official assent of their agent. Although emigrants proceeded to develop their tribal governments and to manage their own affairs when the War Department did not find their actions undesirable, they always found themselves subject to the rather arbitrary and often makeshift rule of the War Department and its field representatives.[43]

NOTES

1. Richardson, *Presidential Papers*, 2: 458.

2. Ibid., pp. 458–59; Jackson to David Haley, October 15, 1829, Andrew Jackson Papers, Library of Congress, Washington, D.C.

3. Not all of the problems encountered by the emigrants in the West stemmed from United States interference in tribal affairs, however. Grant Foreman discusses other difficulties the emigrants had to face in adjusting to their new environment and establishing amicable relations with the indigenous Plains Indians in his *Advancing the Frontier, 1830–1860* (Nor-

man: University of Oklahoma Press, 1933) and describes the "rehabilitation and reconstruction" of the emigrants in his *Five Civilized Tribes.*

4. Draft of First Annual Message, December 8, 1829, in Bassett, *Correspondence of Andrew Jackson,* 4: 103–104.

5. Secretary of War, *Annual Report* (1829), p. 31. For a useful but incomplete survey of attempts to create an Indian territory, see Annie H. Abel, "Proposals for an Indian State, 1778–1878," *American Historical Association, Annual Report for the Year 1907* 1 (1908): 87–104.

6. McCoy, *Baptist Indian Missions,* pp. 414, 423–24; [McCoy] to Bolles, May 12, 1831, McCoy Papers; *McCoy's Annual Register of Indian Affairs within the Indian (or Western) Territory* 4 (1838): 18 (hereafter cited as *McCoy's Register*); McCoy to Cass, February 1, 1832, *House Document 172,* 22d Cong., 1st sess., p. 10.

7. McCoy to Cass, February 1, 1832, *House Document 172,* 22d Cong., 1st sess., pp. 10–11.

8. Ibid., pp. 11–12.

9. *Magazine of the Reformed Dutch Church* 4 (October 1829): 222; *American Baptist Magazine* 10 (April 1830): 126–27. Also see chapter 1 for a discussion of the New York Indian Board and other religious groups that supported Indian removal.

10. [Evarts], *Essays on the Present Crisis,* pp. 97–98.

11. U.S., *Stat.,* 4: 411–12. Also see the Appendix.

12. U.S., *Stat.,* 4: 412.

13. Kappler, *Indian Affairs,* 2: 221–27; Lindquist, "Indian Treaty Making," p. 447. Also see Thomas J. Farnham, *Travels in the Great Western Prairies, the Anahuac and Rocky Mountains, and in the Oregon Territory,* 2 vols. (London: Richard Bentley, 1843), 1: 117–18.

14. Foreman, *Indian Removal,* p. 66; W. David Baird, *Peter Pitchlynn: Chief of the Choctaws* (Norman: University of Oklahoma Press, 1972), p. 45; Oliver Knight, "Fifty Years of Choctaw Law, 1834–1884," *Chronicles of Oklahoma* 31 (Spring 1958): 82, 91, 94; Armstrong's Report for 1839, in Commissioner of Indian Affairs, *Annual Report* (1839), p. 468; Foreman, *Five Civilized Tribes,* p. 33; Stuart to Herring, January 28, 1836, in Carter and Bloom, *Territorial Papers,* 21: 1,158.

15. Felix S. Cohen, *Handbook of Federal Indian Law* (Washington, D.C.: GPO, 1942), pp. 71–72; Bureau of Indian Affairs, *Annual Report* (1830), p. 163, (1831), p. 175. For an authoritative account of the early legislation, see Prucha, *American Indian Policy,* pp. 41–212.

16. McCoy, *Baptist Indian Missions,* p. 393; McCoy to Eaton, March 6, 31, 1829, McCoy's Journal, March 22, 31, 1829, [McCoy] to Bolles, May 12, 1831, McCoy Papers; McCoy to Cass, February 1, 1832, *House Document 172,* 22d Cong., 1st sess., pp. 1, 9–10; Creeks, West, to Jackson,

October 29, 1831, *Senate Document 512,* 23rd Cong., 1st sess., 2: 637; Eaton to Coffee, May 16, 1831, IA, LS, 7: 227, RG 75, NA; Macomb's Report to Secretary of War, November 1832, Army Headquarters, LS, 4/2: 183, RG 108, NA. For an account of emigration to the West before the Removal Act, see Foreman, *Indians & Pioneers.*

17. HR 483, HR 484, *Original Bills,* 22d Cong., 1st sess.; *House Journal,* 22d Cong., 1st sess., p. 505.

18. Cass to Flowers, May 24, 1832, *Senate Document 512,* 23rd Cong., 1st sess., 2: 839; *Debates in Congress,* 21st Cong., 1st sess., p. 1,135. For Hemphill's alternative to the Removal Bill, see chapter 1. President Jackson admitted on December 3, 1833, that there were indeed many "unsettled questions" concerning the "condition and prospects" of the emigrants in the West for which the government did not have "ample means of information." See Richardson, *Papers of the Presidents,* 3: 33. Also see Secretary of War, *Annual Report* (1833), pp. 18–19.

19. Jackson to Coffee, February 19, 1832, in Bassett, *Correspondence of Andrew Jackson,* 4: 406; Cass to Cherokees, East, April 17, 1832, in Secretary of War, *Annual Report* (1832), p. 38; Cass to Flowers, May 24, 1832, *Senate Document 512,* 23rd Cong., 1st sess., 2: 839; Robb to Chester, July 20, 1832, IA, LS, 9: 75, RG 75, NA.

20. McCoy, *Baptist Indian Missions,* p. 430; McCoy's Journal, March 28, 1832, McCoy Papers. For McCoy's address, see McCoy, *Baptist Indian Missions,* pp. 431–38.

21. McCoy, *Baptist Indian Missions,* p. 439; Copy of a Report Made by Isaac McCoy, March 16, 1832, *House Document 172,* 22d Cong., 1st sess., p. 1. For further evidence that McCoy was working closely with Bell and other friends of the Jackson administration, see McCoy's Journal, March 28, 1832, McCoy papers.

22. U.S., *Stat.,* 4: 595–96; Cass to Flowers, May 24, 1832, *Senate Document 512,* 23rd Cong., 1st sess., 2: 839; McCoy's Journal, March 28, August 27, 1832, McCoy Papers; McDermott, *Western Journals of Washington Irving,* p. 9; *Warrenton Reporter,* November 1, 1832; Cass to Commissioners, July 14, 1832, IA, LS, 9: 33–40, RG 75, NA. For biographical information concerning the commissioners, see John B. Meserve, "Governor Montfort Stokes," *Chronicles of Oklahoma* 13 (September 1935): 338–40; William O. Foster, "The Career of Montfort Stokes in Oklahoma," *Chronicles of Oklahoma* 18 (March 1940): 35–52; James W. Van Hoeven, "Salvation and Indian Removal: The Career Biography of the Rev. John Freeman Schermerhorn, Indian Commissioner" (Ph.D. diss., Vanderbilt University, 1972); Claribel R. Barnett, "Henry Leavitt Ellsworth," in Johnson and Malone, *Dictionary of American Biography,* 6: 110–11.

23. Cass to Commissioners, July 14, 1832, IA, LS, 9: 33–40, RG 75, NA; Secretary of War, *Annual Report* (1832), pp. 25–26.

24. Cass to Commissioners, July 14, 1832, IA, LS, 9: 33–36, RG 75, NA. Also see Cass to Gadsen, January 20, 1832, Herring to Schermerhorn, June 4, 1833, Harris to Atkinson, July 21, 1837, IA, LS, 8: 48–49; 10: 404, 22: 141–43, RG 75, NA; *McCoy's Register* 1 (1835): 19–20; A. L. Kroeber, "Nature of the Land-Holding Group," *Ethnohistory* 2 (Fall 1955): 304, 313–14; Emily J. Blasingham, "The Depopulation of the Illinois Indians," *Ethnohistory* 3 (Summer 1956): 216. The administration's efforts to merge the Choctaw and Chickasaw Indians is discussed in chapter 3, and its efforts to merge the Seminoles and Creeks is treated in chapter 4.

25. Cass to Commissioners, July 14, 1832, IA, LS, 9: 32–41, RG 75, NA. Also see Jackson's Fifth Annual Message, December 3, 1833, in Richardson, *Papers of the Presidents*, 3: 33.

26. Macomb to Commanding Officer, Cantonment Gibson, November 5, 1832, Army Headquarters, LS, 4/2: 177–78, RG 108, NA; Commissioner of Indian Affairs, *Annual Report* (1832), p. 163, (1833), p. 173; Secretary of War, *Annual Report* (1832), p. 28. For a brief but enlightening discussion of the failure of government officials to recognize existing Indian patterns of law and order, see William T. Hagan, *Indian Police and Judges: Experiments in Acculturation and Control* (New Haven: Yale University Press, 1966), pp. 9–11.

27. Herring to McCoy, May 21, 1832, McCoy to Commissioners, West, October 15, 1832, *Senate Document 512*, 23rd Cong., 1st sess., 2: 836, 3: 486–98; McCoy, *Baptist Indian Missions*, p. 459.

28. McCoy to Commissioners, West, October 15, 1832, *Senate Document 512*, 23rd Cong., 1st sess., 3: 486–98.

29. Edwin C. McReynolds, *Oklahoma: A History of the Sooner State* (Norman: University of Oklahoma Press, 1954), pp. 141–43; Van Hoeven, "Salvation and Indian Removal," pp. 127–61; Commissioners to Secretary of War, February 10, 1834, *House Report 474*, 23rd Cong., 1st sess., pp. 78–131. For the operations of the dragoons in the trans-Mississippi Indian country, see Prucha, *Sword of the Republic*, pp. 245–48, 365–95; William B. Hughes, "The First Dragoons on the Western Frontier, 1834–1846," *Arizona and the West* 12 (Summer 1970): 115–38; Carl L. Davis and LeRoy H. Fischer, "Dragoon Life in Indian Territory, 1833–1846," *Chronicles of Oklahoma* 48 (Spring 1970): 2–24.

30. Commissioners to Secretary of War, February 10, 1834, *House Report 474*, 23rd Cong., 1st sess., pp. 95–97, 102.

31. Ibid., pp. 100, 103, 129.

32. Ibid., pp. 101–2.

33. Report of Horace Everett, May 20, 1834, *House Report 474*, 23rd Cong., 1st sess., pp. 1–37; *House Journal*, 23rd Cong., 1st sess., p. 833;

Congressional Globe, 23rd Cong., 1st sess., p. 396; McCoy to Christiana McCoy, March 16, 1834, McCoy Papers; Prucha, *American Indian Policy,* pp. 259–73; *National Intelligencer,* June 28, 1834, quoted in *Niles' Register* 46 (July 5, 1834): 317; U.S., *Stat.,* 4: 729–38.

34. HR 490, *Original Bills,* 23rd Cong., 1st sess.

35. *Congressional Globe,* 23rd Cong., 1st sess., p. 472; Debates in Congress, 23rd Cong., 1st sess., pp. 4763–79; *Niles' Register* 46 (June 28, 1834): 307, 46 (July 5, 1834): 317, quoting *National Intelligencer,* June 28, 1834.

36. *Congressional Globe,* 23rd Cong., 1st sess., p. 472; *Debates in Congress,* 23rd Cong., 1st sess., pp. 4763, 4769; *Niles' Register* 46 (June 28, 1834): 307; Major L. Wilson," 'Liberty and Union': An Analysis of Three Concepts Involved in the Nullification Controversy," *Journal of Southern History* 33 (August 1967): 342.

37. *Debates in Congress,* 23rd Cong., 1st sess., pp. 4764, 4775–77, 4779; *Congressional Globe,* 23rd Cong., 1st sess., p. 472; *Niles' Register* 46 (June 28, 1834): 307. For Georgia Congressman George C. Gilmer's unsuccessful efforts to bring up the bill at the next session of Congress, see *House Journal,* 23rd Cong., 2d sess., p. 65, 424–26, 430–33.

38. U.S., *Stat.,* 4: 729–35; Arnold J. Lien, "The Acquisition of Citizenship by the Native American Indians," *Washington University Studies* 13 (1925): 137; Strong, "Wardship," pp. 125–26. It is interesting to note that Francis Thorpe reprinted the 1834 Trade and Intercourse Act and included it as the organic statute relating to the government of the Indian country in his *Federal and State Constitutions,* 2: 1097–1104. The Indian Office named the area embraced in the defeated Territorial Bill of 1834 the "superintendency of the Western Territory." See Commissioner of Indian Affairs, *Annual Report* (1834), p. 269.

39. U.S., *Stat.,* 4: 733; Glen Shirley, *Law West of Fort Smith: A History of Frontier Justice in the Indian Territory, 1834–1896* (New York: Henry Holt & Co., 1957), pp. 9–11; George Butler to Dr. Charles W. Dean, August 11, 1855, in Commissioner of Indian Affairs, *Annual Report* (1855), pp. 125–27. Also see U.S., *Stat.,* 5: 147, 680; C[rawford] to Bell, May 29, 1841, IA, Report Books, 2: 417–18, RG 75, NA. For details concerning the development of a separate minor federal judiciary in the 1840s to enforce federal law, see Charles A. Lindquist, "The Origin and Development of the United States Commissioner System," *American Journal of Legal History* 14 (January 1970): 1–16.

40. Butler to Dean, August 11, 1855, in Commissioner of Indian Affairs, *Annual Report* (1855), pp. 125–27; Pope to Arkansas House of Representatives, October 27, 1831, in *Arkansas Gazette,* November 2, 1831; U.S., *Stat.,* 9: 203. Also see Foreman, *Five Civilized Tribes,* p. 360. The legislation of 1847 was part of the Polk administration's effort to

provide more effective enforcement of federal laws prohibiting the sale of liquor in the Indian country. See chapter 8.

41. Annie H. Abel, *The American Indian as Slaveholder and Secessionist: An Omitted Chapter in the Diplomatic History of the Southern Confederacy*, 3 vols. (Cleveland: Arthur H. Clark Co., 1915–25), 1: 23 n; Butler to Dean, August 11, 1855, in Commissioner of Indian Affairs, *Annual Report* (1855), pp. 125–27.

42. See Macomb to Atkinson, January 5, 1833, Army Headquarters, LS 4/2: 200, RG 108, NA; Foreman, *Five Civilized Tribes*, pp. 423–24; Spoehr, "Changing Kinship Systems," pp. 220, 224–25; Alexander Lesser, *The Pawnee Ghost Dance Hand Game: A Study of Culture Change* (New York: Columbia University Press, 1933), p. 44.

43. Spoehr, "Changing Kinship Systems," pp. 220, 224–25; Foreman, *Indian Removal*, p. 157; Herring to Stevens T. Mason, July 12, 1834, IA, Records of the Michigan Superintendency and Mackinac Agency (hereafter cited as Michigan Superintendency, Mackinac Agency) LR, RG 75, NA; Revised Regulations No. 3, June 1, 1837, IA, Misc. Records, 2: 263, RG 75, NA; Foreman, *Five Civilized Tribes*, p. 425; Eblen, *Governors and Territorial Government*, p. 251. Arrell Gibson points out in his study of the *Chickasaws*, pp. 251–54, that although these emigrants developed self-government in the West they nevertheless had to win "official support" from "every level of the federal hierarchy" before they were able to sever their ties with the Choctaws in 1855.

6 /

The Office of Indian Affairs

CONGRESSIONAL INACTION on the Stokes commission's proposal for the establishment of an Indian territory forced the transplanted tribesmen to deal with the United States government through the Office of Indian Affairs and its representatives. Although the Indian Office recognized its obligation to promote the social welfare of the tribesmen, the Indians did not represent a constituency that presidents or congressmen recognized and relied on for votes. This situation, together with the congressional parsimony that characterized the 1830s and '40s, seriously limited the funds available for Indian administration. At the same time, moreover, party leaders found that the Indian service offered numerous sinecures with which to build political machines that would enable them to exert influence at the local, state, or national level. All of these factors impeded the development of an effective administrative system.[1]

Congress had relegated all matters pertaining to Indian affairs to the War Department in 1789. It failed, however, to take any further initiative in establishing administrative machinery for Indian affairs. Consequently, George Washington permitted the ad-hoc development of an Indian section in the War Department consisting of several clerks working under the direction of the Secretary of War. Subordinates in the field included military men and civilians who had differing terms of office and salaries and lacked clearly defined duties. This lack of organization and direction frustrated numerous government officials. During the administration of James Monroe, Secretary of War John C. Calhoun became so overburdened with the handling of Indian affairs that he asked his friend Thomas L. McKenney to head an "Indian Bureau" under his command.[2]

The Bureau of Indian Affairs officially opened for business on March 16, 1824. Its entire staff consisted of McKenney, two experienced War Department clerks, and a messenger; they kept office hours from nine to three o'clock six days a week. Their primary task was to supervise the government's relations with the thousands of Indians residing within the territorial limits of the United States.[3]

From an administrative point of view, the Indian Bureau had become an enormous quagmire before Jackson took office in March, 1829. Every secretary of war following Calhoun had stressed the need to reorganize and give direction to the bureau. Peter B. Porter, head of the War Department during the last year of the John Quincy Adams administration, constantly complained that the bureau's operations were more "perplexing" to him than any other of his arduous duties. The major source of complaint and frustration for Porter was "the want of a well digested system of principles and rules for the administration of our Indian concerns."[4]

Four major weaknesses existed in the bureau's conduct of Indian affairs before Jackson came to power. First, there was no uniformity in the various laws and treaties governing American Indian relations. Secondly, regulations for field personnel were either "undefined" or "vacillating." Secretary Porter claimed that "there appears to have been scarcely any other rule to guide the Officers and agents in the discharge of their functions . . . than their own several notions of justice and policy." To compound the confusion, the bureau did not have uniform accounting procedures. Finally, the entire establishment lacked legitimacy. Prerogative-minded and economy-conscious congressmen continually questioned the legal basis for the bureau's operations and warned that it was an extralegal establishment operating only under "Executive arrangement." Thomas McKenney, who headed the bureau, poignantly summarized its problems by noting that it was "too powerless to be effective, and too responsible for its feebleness."[5]

The precarious position of the Indian Bureau and its personnel led to a virtual standstill in its operations immediately preceding Jackson's inaugural. McKenney and his clerks felt "officially incapacitated to act, except negatively and as Keepers of the records entrusted to us respectively." Deeply concerned about retaining his position as a result of his pro-Adams stand in the 1828 campaign, McKenney lost little time in convincing the new secretary of war of the importance of his bureau. John Eaton learned from McKenney that the bureau handled, among other things, an extensive amount of correspondence relating to the drafting of Indian treaties, trade and intercourse laws, funds for Indians under treaty stipulations, instructions to field personnel, and an "almost endless" number of congressional inquiries. Impressed with the onerous duties which the bureau would remove from his shoulders, Eaton convinced President Jackson to retain its staff in order to provide continuity and experience.[6]

John Eaton's tenure in the War Department helped to bring some order to the administration of Indian affairs. Eaton, Jackson's former campaign manager and his "private confidential friend," stressed the need to systematize the routine of the bureau, to update and coordinate the laws governing Indian-white relations, and to keep more accurate accounts of the operations of the field staff.[7]

The fiscal operations of the bureau especially received Eaton's careful scrutiny. Since the presidency of James Madison, the War Department had allowed field officials "discretionary authority" to use funds appropriated by Congress for a specific purpose for other needs deemed more "pressing" by agents. This so-called counterwarrant system continued in use during subsequent administrations and greatly complicated the accounting process. To make matters worse, the Treasury Department asked field officials to send their accounts directly to that department. This procedure meant that the Indian Bureau did not have an opportunity to audit the accounts of its own personnel. By the time Eaton took charge of the War Department, the "arrearages" in the Indian service were enormous. Before he left office in June, 1831, Eaton had

called attention to this problem and many other needs and inade-
quacies of the Indian Bureau.[8]

Eaton's departure from the cabinet as a result of the Peggy
O'Neill affair brought Lewis Cass to the War Department in the
summer of 1831. Cass had impressive credentials for his new position. He had served eighteen years as territorial governor and
superintendent of Indian affairs in Michigan, and he was the only
secretary of war during the Jacksonian era with prior experience
on the frontier in military matters and Indian affairs. Henry R.
Schoolcraft, an Indian agent who was also one of America's early
ethnologists, believed Cass was an excellent choice for this position and later praised him for his views on Indian affairs which
"resemble, very strikingly, those of William Penn." Many Americans agreed that Cass was the most informed man in the country
on Indian matters. As early as 1816 he had recognized the need
for reform in the Indian service. During the latter part of the
Adams administration, he worked closely with Thomas McKenney
and William Clark, the superintendent at Saint Louis, to formulate
a new code of regulations for the administration of Indian affairs.
Although Congress failed to act on their plan when it was submitted for consideration in early 1829, Cass lost little time as secretary
of war in pressing Congress to adopt it.[9]

Cass's early months in the War Department and the lessons
learned from the Choctaw removal strengthened his conviction
that a complete reorganization of the Indian service was necessary. Bureaucratic problems stemming from Jackson's removal
policy so overtaxed the secretary that he devoted nearly half of his
first annual report to them. In order to provide a central clearing
house for Indian affairs in the War Department, Cass urged Congress to create the position of commissioner of Indian affairs. He
convinced legislative leaders of the urgency for this office, and
they agreed to permit the president to name an Indian commissioner, with their advice and consent, who would have responsibility for "the direction and management of all Indian affairs, and of
all matters arising out of Indian relations." Congress officially recognized that this commissioner was not to be just another clerk in
the War Department by providing the new officer with a salary
exceeding that of the chief clerk in the department. After this
initial victory, Cass turned his attention to the vexing problems of
the Indian field service.[10]

The field service was an amorphous bureaucracy consisting of four superintendents, eighteen agents, twenty-seven subagents, thirty-four interpreters, and a miscellaneous group of officers. The combined income of all these employees amounted to nearly sixty thousand dollars. An examination of the field service by the House Committee on Indian Affairs which was considering the recommendations of the Stokes commission in 1834 failed to uncover "any lawful authority for the appointment of a majority of the agents and subagents of Indian affairs now in office. For years, usage, rendered colorably lawful only by reference to indirect and equivocal legislation, has been the only sanction for their appointment." The fact that presidents had determined the number of employees and their salaries without congressional approval dismayed the House committee. Together with Secretary Cass, members of the committee drafted legislation to provide for the legitimate organization of the Indian Bureau and its field service.[11]

This legislation, which became law on June 30, 1834, established the Office of Indian Affairs under the Indian commissioner. It also provided for more orderly arrangement of the field staff by recognizing in law what had evolved through years of custom. By the end of 1834 the Jackson administration had, on paper at least, restructured the heretofore amorphous Indian service into a more cohesive operation.[12]

The administrative machinery Cass helped create in the early 1830s remained in operation throughout the Jacksonian era and well into the twentieth century. In order to understand the problems facing administrators of federal policy as well as the Indians themselves during this period, it is necessary to look at the men involved in formulating and executing Indian policy and the operations of the administrative system to which they belonged. Perhaps the best starting place for such an examination is the focal point of the system created by the Jacksonians—the commissioner of Indian affairs.

The most logical choice for commissioner in 1832, based on experience, was Thomas McKenney. McKenney had served as superintendent of Indian trade between 1816 and 1822 before being named head of the Indian Bureau by Calhoun. With his wide experience in administration, he was generally acknowledged as a leading authority on Indian matters. In spite of McKenney's efforts to appease Jackson for his pro-Adams position in the 1828 campaign and his earlier support for Calhoun in 1824, Jackson was apparently only interested in retaining McKenney long enough to permit Eaton to familiarize himself with the operations of the Indian Bureau and to use McKenney's name to help secure the passage of the Removal Bill.[13]

McKenney's refusal to grant Jackson and Eaton's personal friend Sam Houston preferential treatment in his bid to supply rations to emigrants did not endear him to the administration. Shortly after the passage of the Removal Bill, the chief clerk of the War Department, Philip Randolph, Eaton's brother-in-law, warned McKenney that he was being lax in making his required weekly reports to the secretary. Hours later the bewildered official learned that his services were no longer required. Randolph told him that "this course is dictated by a sense of publick duty, and not from any consideration of private feeling." When McKenney asked for clarification of the grounds for his dismissal, the clerk remarked, "Why, Sir, every body knows your qualifications for the place; but General Jackson has long been satisfied that you are not in harmony with him in his views in regard to the Indians." McKenney's dismissal removed one of the few experienced contenders for the position of Indian commissioner.[14]

The man who replaced McKenney as head of the Indian Bureau in 1830 was Samuel S. Hamilton. Hamilton had served as a clerk in the bureau since the Adams administration. Little is known about his previous background, but he had edited a compilation of Indian treaties and had served as McKenney's chief clerk. Hamilton's appointment as head of the Indian Bureau indicated, as the *National Intelligencer* noted, that "the station, though an important one, was but a Clerkship, not requiring confirmation by the Senate." While Hamilton proved to be an able administrator, the Jackson administration returned him to his old position when Eaton left the War Department.[15]

Lewis Cass assumed the position of secretary of war during the second week of August, 1831. Several days later Elbert Herring of New York replaced Hamilton as head of the Indian Bureau. Herring, then fifty-four years of age, was a Princeton graduate who had become a prominent New York lawyer and judge. Unfortunately, he had no experience in Indian affairs. Just why Cass, who was a strong advocate of reform and reorganization of the Indian Bureau, chose such a man to head its operations is unclear. Anti-Jacksonites charged that Herring was a protégé of Van Buren, who was rapidly becoming the president's closest advisor. Jackson, however, correctly pointed out that Herring had close ties to the old Clintonian faction in New York which had little love for Van Buren. Jackson maintained throughout his life that Herring was Secretary Cass's "intimate personal friend." In any event, Herring did not bring any administrative expertise or knowledge of Indian affairs to the bureau.[16]

When Congress created the office of Indian commissioner in 1832, Herring received the position. Jackson, writing later in life, maintained that Cass had urged him to give Herring the job. According to Jackson, the request took him, members of the cabinet, and congressional leaders by surprise. Cass had previously complained that Herring was an inefficient and blundering administrator and was "entirely incapable of discharging his duties in such a manner as to give that aid which the public interest required." Jackson claimed he appointed Herring to the office only because Cass assured him that he had finally mastered the Indian Bureau's operations and had undertaken an intensive study of Indian society. Thus Herring became Indian commissioner on July 10, 1832, in spite of the fact that his incompetency had apparently played a role in creating the office.[17]

When Cass left the War Department in mid-1836 to become envoy to France, Jackson transferred Herring to a less prestigious position in the field service. A presidential election was approaching and it is possible that Jackson was sensitive to the fact that, as a New Yorker, Herring's continuance in office might embarrass Martin Van Buren. Jackson had already named Attorney General Benjamin F. Butler, Van Buren's close friend and associate in the Albany Regency, as acting secretary of war. Jackson may also have been aware that Van Buren would feel obligated to retain any appointee he named to this position. Since Jackson had shown considerable interest in Indian affairs, it is likely that he wanted someone he could trust to fill this important position. Whatever the actual motivation, however, Jackson named fellow Tennessean Carey Allen Harris as Indian commissioner on July 4, 1836.[18]

Harris was thirty years old when he accepted the Indian Office appointment. Before moving to Washington in the early 1830s, he had assisted in publishing the Nashville *Republican*. In Washington, Harris became a clerk in the War Department under Cass and occasionally served as acting secretary of war when Cass was away on business or vacationing. He held the positions of acting secretary and Indian commissioner simultaneously when Cass resigned until Butler took over the War Department in the fall of 1836. Harris was a member of Jackson's inner elite, and he had open access to the president. As Jackson probably predicted, Van Buren retained Harris when he entered office in 1837.[19]

The selection of Harris was unfortunate because he was too avaricious to resist the numerous opportunities which his position offered for peculation in issuing contracts for emigrants and in adjudicating disputes over Indian allotments. Former president Jackson learned from "a real friend" in mid-1838 that there was "treachery" in the Indian Office, and he sent President Van Buren a "confidential" message from the Hermitage warning him to "be vigilant" in examining accounts from that department. Meanwhile, Daniel Kurtz, an Indian Office clerk since 1827, had become suspicious of the commissioner's dealings and cautioned him that he was drawing too freely upon the large funds at his disposal. Harris reacted to Kurtz's criticism and his growing awareness that he was under close scrutiny by the administration by prohibiting Kurtz and other clerks from handling any incoming correspondence unless his wife had first checked the contents of the letters. In addition to this precaution, he contemplated leaving Washington. Early in June he asked Secretary of War Joel Poinsett for a transfer to a frontier post in Iowa Territory which paid a smaller salary and suggested that his written request be burned if the administration chose not to grant it. Later, while Harris was away on official business in early October, Kurtz picked up and read a private letter to the commissioner which a messenger had mistakenly opened. The contents of the document completely astonished Kurtz.[20]

The letter from Thomas J. Porter of Mississippi, according to a congressional investigating committee in 1842, "made propositions for securing certain [Indian] reservations for the benefit of the *writer* and *Mr. Harris,* who was regarded as *a partner* in the speculation, and was to profit by the lands" being set aside as allotments. Kurtz immediately informed President Van Buren of Porter's scheme. Van Buren promptly demanded an explanation from Harris for the alleged activities. Harris, badly shaken by the exposure of his actions, stalled and promised that a full explanation would soon be made. Shortly afterwards Harris sent a vague note to the president, who found the commissioner's defense of his actions *"Not Sufficient"* and accepted his resignation on October 19, 1838.[21]

Van Buren appointed Thomas Hartley Crawford of Pennsylvania to succeed Harris. Crawford was an "old and warm friend" of Andrew Jackson who happened to be out of political office at the time. The Pennsylvanian, fifty-two years of age when he became commissioner, was a Princeton graduate, lawyer, former United States congressman, and former state legislator. Crawford had defied public opinion in Pennsylvania in 1830 when he supported Jackson's Removal Bill in the House of Representatives. Later, in 1836, Jackson appointed him to investigate alleged frauds in the purchases of Creek allotments, and his report was a condemnation of the speculation and fraud committed against the Indians. Crawford was the only commissioner during the Jacksonian era who had some prior experience in actually dealing with Indians, but Henry R. Schoolcraft, an enlightened Indian agent and a good Jacksonian Democrat, feared that he was "personally unacquainted with the character of the Indians, and the geography of the western country, and not likely, therefore, to be very ready or practical in the administrative duties of the office." Crawford's nomination, however, met Jackson's wholehearted approval. Old Hickory wrote from the Hermitage that "Mr. Crawford is a man of talents, and with his late duties, must have become familiar with the Indian character and I have no doubt will fill the office to which you have assigned him *well*—'he is honest, & faithful to the constitution.' "[22]

T. Hartley Crawford had the longest tenure of any Indian commissioner during the Jacksonian era and made an indelible imprint on the office during his seven years as its head. The Pennsylvanian was a patient, careful, consistent, and devoted public servant. Although he served four chief executives—Van Buren, William Henry Harrison, John Tyler, and James K. Polk—his exceptionally long tenure was not the result of being apolitical. As commissioner he kept close watch on the changing political situation and always remained a fervent Jacksonian Democrat. He stayed in office under Harrison and Tyler only because they could not find a suitable replacement. The men these presidents considered for Crawford's position and the reasons they rejected them provide some insight into their conception of the role of the commissioner of Indian affairs.[23]

John Bell, a former Tennessee Democrat turned Whig and a coauthor of the Removal Act of 1830, took the helm of the War Department at the beginning of the Harrison-Tyler administration in 1841. Bell wanted an efficient man he could trust as commissioner, and he asked his friend Major Ethan Allen Hitchcock, the grandson of Revolutionary War hero Ethan Allen, to take charge of the Indian Office.[24] Hitchcock had previously served three years on Indian duty in the Old Northwest, where he performed his assignments with great dignity and honesty. He was a West Point graduate and had served as the commandant of cadets at the academy and as an instructor in infantry tactics. Hitchcock was on assignment in Florida fighting the intransigent Seminoles when the Whigs took office in 1841.[25]

In spite of his brilliant military record, Major Hitchcock was not a typical career soldier. He had an exceptionally inquisitive mind, and his voluminous writings on alchemy, religion, and the arts later earned him the nickname Pen of the Army. Hitchcock was widely known as a humanitarian, and the American Colonization Society had repeatedly urged him to accept the governorship of their colony in Liberia. He was also extremely sympathetic about the condition of the American Indians. Major General Edmund Pendleton Gaines believed Hitchcock was "the most highly qualified *soldier* or *citizen* . . . for the office of *Commissioner of Indian Affairs.*" Gaines, a persistent opponent of Jackson's Indian removal policy, observed that "by employing only such men as E. A. Hitchcock to treat with and hold Executive intercourse with them [the Indians], according to *Treaties*, the *law of the land,* and *Natural Equity,* and *common justice,* we should soon win their confidence."[26]

Major Hitchcock ultimately refused the position because he did not want to retire from the military. Bell persuaded him to remain in Washington, and he later conducted an inspection tour of the Indian country for the government. Meanwhile, Attorney General John J. Crittenden recommended James Harlan, father of Supreme Court Justice John Marshall Harlan, who was secretary of state in Kentucky and had served as a delegate to the 1840 Whig convention. Harlan, however, was "not just the man" that Bell wanted, and he continued his search. While Bell was looking for the proper man for the job, two Whigs eagerly lobbied for the position.[27]

Thomas McKenney, whose reputation had been enhanced in the 1830s by antiremoval speeches and publications on Indians, had never given up his dream of "a restoration" to the Indian Office. He viewed his tenure as chief of the original Indian Bureau as nothing less than Indian commissioner at "half pay." McKenney was an old acquaintance of President Harrison, and he went to Washington after the Whig victory in 1840 to lobby for his former job.[28]

When President Harrison died shortly after entering office, McKenney claimed that Old Tippecanoe had "assigned" him to the position of Indian commissioner before his death. McKenney had stumped vigorously for the Whig ticket in the eastern coast during the 1840 campaign, and letters supporting his pretensions poured into the executive mansion and the War Department from such members of the Whig "elite" as Nicholas Biddle, Daniel Webster, and George Poindexter. Petitions in support of McKenney's "reinstatement" also came from the Union Female Missionary Society of Philadelphia, leading Whig newspaper editors throughout the eastern coast, and members of the Moravian and Quaker churches. Even the American Board of Commissioners for Foreign Missions sympathized with McKenney's desire to return to his former position.[29]

McKenney's efforts, however, were in vain. Secretary Bell adamantly refused to permit him to "force himself in." The reasons for Bell's opposition to McKenney are unclear, but rumor had it that McKenney had embezzled funds while serving in the War Department. It is also possible that Bell, a coauthor of the Removal Act, disliked McKenney's duplicity concerning the question of Indian removal. In any event, the secretary "star-chambered" him.[30]

Robert Stuart, a fur trader and Whig politician in Michigan, was another man with experience in Indian affairs who coveted the position of commissioner. John Jacob Astor and Ramsey Crooks, two outstanding leaders in the American fur trade, lobbied in Washington for his appointment, as did the entire Michigan congressional delegation. Some Whig politicians, however, raised objections. First, they noted that Stuart had served as the head of the Michigan Anti-Slavery Society in 1837, and there was considerable opposition to appointing an "abolitionist" as commissioner. Secondly, they charged that his close ties with the American Fur Company caused his motives to be suspect. To the first charge, Stuart replied that while he believed slavery was a moral wrong, he was not an abolitionist. To the second accusation, he responded that "my former connexion & influence over both Traders & Indians, so far from being objectionable, is in my own opinion, a very strong argument in my favor, & might under some circumstances, be worth half a dozen Regiments of Troops." Stuart tried hard to convince "Messrs. Clay, Webster &c." that this was true.[31]

Robert Stuart's efforts to receive appointment as commissioner ultimately failed because of internal problems in the Tyler administration. During the fall of 1841, many Whigs, including Secretary of War Bell, resigned from the cabinet after the president broke with the party on its domestic program. Tyler's primary objective during the next three years was to fortify his political position in order to recapture the presidency in 1844. One result of this situation was that T. Hartley Crawford retained his position. Crawford had close ties with key Democratic politicians in Pennsylvania, and Tyler was especially eager to keep that state friendly to his political aspirations. At the same time, however, the president made an effort to appease Whigs by naming Stuart to an important field post in Michigan.[32]

When James K. Polk entered the White House in March, 1845, Crawford had served as Indian commissioner for seven years. Although Secretary of War William L. Marcy found his work "fully satisfactory," Polk decided to transfer his friend to a federal judgeship. The vacancy created by Crawford's "promotion" immediately became the bone of contention between the spoils-hungry factions of the victorious Democratic party. To replace Crawford, Polk chose a westerner with considerable political weight.[33]

The new commissioner was William Medill, a forty-three-year-old former congressman from Ohio. Medill had served three terms in the Ohio state legislature and two terms in the U.S. Congress before he lost his bid for reelection in 1842. After Polk's victory, he had rushed to Washington with other office-seekers to get the "hang" of the town. He went east with impressive credentials, including the backing of leading Van Buren Democrats in Ohio. Postmaster General Cave Johnson secured the position of second assistant postmaster general for Medill in March, 1845, and he quickly became the central figure in Washington for patronage seekers from his state. At the end of the year, Polk nominated him for commissioner of Indian affairs in a move to placate the Van Buren men in Ohio who, along with Van Buren followers elsewhere in the country, were seething with discontent over the president's tendency to bypass their wing of the party in distributing the patronage at his disposal.[34]

Medill's appointment marked a turning point in the nomination of men for the office of Indian commissioner. While his background was similar to that of his predecessors, none of them focused as much attention on the question of party patronage as did Medill. The Ohioan accepted the position of commissioner because he thought that it was a more "useful" job than assistant postmaster general and his associates agreed that it was also "worth more than any Law Practice."[35]

Medill's participation in the distribution of federal patronage under President Polk was extensive. He even had direct access to the president concerning appointments to numerous posts outside the Indian Office. Medill himself was no political lightweight. There was talk among some Democrats that he would make an excellent vice-presidential candidate in 1848. Attracted by such a possibility, he used the prerogatives of his office to enhance his own political standing. He served as "a friend at Court" for Democrats in the Old Northwest and handled applications for all kinds of patronage appointments, bids for mail routes and the public printing, applications for pensions, patents, and land warrants, appointments to West Point, and investments in U.S. Treasury notes. There seems little doubt that Medill's appointment had more to do with the handling of political patronage for the Polk administration than federal Indian affairs. By the end of Polk's term, the position of commissioner of Indian affairs was generally viewed by politicians as an important patronage office.[36]

The first commissioner appointed by the Whigs when they came to power in 1849, Orlando Brown, was little more than the liaison man between Kentucky "kingmaker" John J. Crittenden and President Zachary Taylor. Brown's appointment marked the culmination of the trend throughout the Jacksonian era of appointing politicians rather than administrators to the position of Indian commissioner. Men like McKenney and Hamilton who had experience in Indian affairs and administration were passed by, while political favorites like Herring or Harris and politicians from key states, like Crawford and Medill, who were out of office, secured the job in spite of their inadequate experience in Indian affairs. As one contemporary noted in 1841, "The head of the Indian Bureau is acknowledged by the country as one of the most important [political appointments] and approaches near[er] the Cabinet than any other." All of the men who held or aspired to the post during the Jacksonian era viewed it as a stepping-stone to higher office. Friends of Major Ethan Allen Hitchcock, for example, urged him to accept the job in 1841 and assured him, "cast your bread upon the waters and it shall be gathered in two-fold."[37]

Although the Indian commissioners were political appointees with important roles in the distribution of the federal patronage, they were generally capable men with broad experience in public life. More importantly, perhaps, they usually had a strong desire to leave behind a record of constructive accomplishment. This was fortunate for the government and the Indians, since the opportunities for speculation and graft in the Indian service were tremendous as a result of the contract system for supplying emigrants and the vexing question of title to Indian allotments. Andrew Jackson and virtually every president following him claimed that they spent more time worrying about the fiscal concerns of the Indian Office than any other department of the government. Yet only Carey A. Harris disgraced the office, and President Van Buren dismissed him as soon as his nefarious activities became known. Although William Medill's conduct as commissioner came under attack by Whig congressmen during the 1848 presidential campaign, a special congressional investigating committee exonerated him from the Whig charges of malfeasance in office. In spite of the political nature of their appointment, most of the Indian commissioners proved to be able, trustworthy, and efficient administrators. Their annual reports provided Congress and the executive departments with important information about Indian affairs and helped to guide and shape federal Indian policy by inviting proposals for policy changes and by calling attention to administrative needs. Yet, to illustrate the dual nature of their appointment, their reports also served as a handy means of promoting the incumbent and his party's political image and position.[38]

There was one notable effort to make the commissioner of Indian affairs a nonpolitical appointment during the Jacksonian period. Congressman Thomas W. Gilmer, a Virginia Democrat committed to economy and reform in the federal government, suggested in 1842 that the president select a commissioner from the ranks of the Indian Office. Gilmer believed that the clerks would work harder and more efficiently if they knew merit would receive such a reward. "The hope of promotion," he observed, "is the most powerful encouragement to official fidelity and skill." Gilmer especially warned that the practice of appointing commissioners for "mere political or personal considerations" only hampered the effective administration of Indian affairs. He believed that the merit system and promotion from the ranks of the clerks would increase the effectiveness of the office and cut down the needless proliferation of clerks. Gilmer's suggestion had many merits, but the federal government never put it to the test during the Jacksonian era.[39]

Although Indian commissioners were not selected for their experience, the persistence of trained personnel in the lower echelons of the Indian Office helped to bring badly needed continuity and expertise to the administration of Indian affairs. When Jackson entered the presidency in 1829, Thomas McKenney's old Indian Bureau occupied only one room of the commodious, two-story War Department building which stood two hundred feet west of the White House. The office, which contained what Nicholas Biddle once referred to as a gallery of "uncouth portraits of savages of both sexes," consisted of McKenney, the head of the bureau, a chief clerk, a recording clerk, a bookkeeper, and a messenger. By the last year of Jackson's presidency, the office employed six clerks, including two appointed by President John Quincy Adams. Daniel

Kurtz, a hold-over from the pre-Jackson period, was serving as chief clerk.[40]

As a result of the problems arising from the removal of Indians to the trans-Mississippi West, Secretary of War Benjamin F. Butler had the six clerks employed in the office of the commissary general of subsistence on business relating to Indian emigration join the six clerks in the Indian Office on November 11, 1836. During the remainder of the Jacksonian era, the clerical staff remained at about twelve—a larger number than served the secretary of war before the Mexican War—and occupied seven rooms in the War Department building. Many of these clerks had served under more than one president. Hezekiah Miller, the recording clerk during the Adams administration, was still in office under Polk. Samuel Potts, who received his appointment from Jackson, was also working when Polk came to office. Although a great variety of considerations, including political favoritism, played a role in the selection of Indian Office clerks, Commissioner T. Hartley Crawford claimed in 1842 that "fidelity, experience, general attention, weight of moral character, personal confidence [and] the having a family or not" were the criteria most often used. While there was a considerable amount of "rotation" during the 1830s and '40s, the office always had some experienced men on duty.[41]

The tendency toward politicization of the office of Indian commissioner was unfortunate in terms of the effectiveness of the Indian Office. While the department had always been a center of great activity, the progress of the Indian removal policy tremendously increased the work load of the clerks. Field agents inundated the office with correspondence at the same time that congressional inquiries, claims resulting from treaty provisions, and private petitions of citizens required extensive research by the clerks. The office was literally "afloat" with paperwork, and commissioners continually pleaded for additional clerical assistance. Commissioner Crawford, for example, complained in 1840 that the settlement of disputes over the ownership of land allotments was consuming too much of his clerks' time:

> The correspondence on this part of the public business intrusted to me, is very extensive and it is had with citizens of the following states, within which the reservations generally are situated—viz—

Georgia, N[orth] Carolina, Tennessee, Alabama, Mississippi, Louisiana, Arkansas, Missouri, Illinois, Indiana, Ohio, Michigan, New York —and the Territories of Wisconsin [and] Iowa—& indirectly with individuals resident of other States who are interested directly or remotely with claims of this character ... which have been the subject of contest for years and necessarily require much research & a laborious examination of conflicting testimony.

Yet while "constant attention, unceasing vigilance, and efficient and intelligent aids" were desperately needed to have the office function at maximum capacity, the political guillotine increasingly came into use, especially during the 1840s.[42]

The removal of Indian Office clerks for political reasons was particularly unfortunate since the trend throughout the late 1830s and the '40s was to assign a specific division of labor among the clerks in order to "facilitate the transaction of business, and relieve it from the disadvantage of fluctuation." Virginia Democrat Thomas W. Gilmore warned Congress in 1842 that the records of the Indian Office were "very imperfect" and treated with "unpardonable negligence" by the clerks. "Retrenchment Gilmer"—as his associates called him—maintained that the government would benefit more from rewarding competent clerks with tenure than from throwing open the Indian Office to the patronage seekers. Unfortunately, the economy-minded Virginian and many of his colleagues also believed that the department could increase its efficiency while reducing its staff. As a result, the already overburdened clerks found their job security threatened simultaneously by the mood for retrenchment in Congress and by the patronage-hungry "friends" of Congress and the administration. The removal of experienced clerks to satisfy Congressmen or accommodate patronage seekers during this period undoubtedly did little to increase the efficiency of the office. Clerks apparently knew little about the work of their associates, and the removal of one might thereby disrupt the activities of the entire office. The victorious Whigs in 1849 removed the Democratic clerk in charge of land reservations, only to find that "the current business is so much impeded as to cause dissatisfaction and even complaints." The politicization of the Indian Office during the Jacksonian era meant that Indian affairs were subordinated to political concerns.

Nowhere was this so apparent as in the administrative machinery of the Indian field service.[43]

NOTES

1. Laurence F. Schmeckebier has a brief, impressionistic sketch of the Indian Office and its operations during the Jacksonian era in his *The Office of Indian Affairs: Its History, Activities, and Organization* (Baltimore: Johns Hopkins Press, 1927), pp. 27–43. Leonard D. White's *The Jacksonians: A Study in Administrative History, 1829–1861* (New York: Macmillan Co., 1954), omits a discussion of the administrative machinery of federal Indian policy.

2. U.S., *Stat.*, 1: 49–50, 331; Calhoun to McKenney, March 11, 1824, *House Document 146*, 19th Cong., 1st sess., p. 6; *Niles' Register* 26 (March 27, 1824): 50; McKenney, *Memoirs*, 1: 53, 56; Viola, "McKenney and the Administration of Indian Affairs," pp. 33–34; McKenney to Forward, November 3, 1841, Gratz Collection. For a summary of constitutional grants of power concerning Indians, see Clara E. Leisure, "Governmental Organization and Administration of Indian Affairs in the United States" (M.A. thesis, Ohio University, 1948), pp. 6–7.

3. Calhoun to McKenney, March 11, 1824, *House Document 146*, 19th Cong., 1st sess., p. 6; Viola, "McKenney and the Administration of Indian Affairs," pp. 36–39.

4. McKenney to James C. Mitchel, August 23, 1828, McKenney to Eaton, November 17, 1829, IA, LS, 5: 94, 6: 167, RG 75, NA; Secretary of War, *Annual Report* (1828), pp. 20–21; Porter to Cass, July 28, 1828, in Carter and Bloom, *Territorial Papers*, 11:1194.

5. Porter to Cass, July 28, 1828, in Carter and Bloom, *Territorial Papers*, 11:1195; John Cocke to [James Barbour], March 21, 1826, Barbour to Cocke, March 24, 1826, *House Document 146*, 19th Cong., 1st sess., p. 5; Bureau of Indian Affairs, *Annual Report* (1829), p. 167; McKenney to Eaton, November 17, 1829, IA, LS, 6: 166, RG 75, NA. Also see Leonard D. White, *The Jeffersonians: A Study in Administrative History, 1801–1829* (New York: Macmillan Co., 1951), pp. 507–10.

6. McKenney to Major Charles J. Nourse, March 9, 1829, McKenney to Eaton, March 18, 1829, IA, LS, 5: 326, 357–59, RG 75, NA; *United States' Telegraph*, April 21, 1829; McKenney, *Memoirs*, 1: 195, 205–6, 223; Viola, "McKenney and the Administration of Indian Affairs," pp. 37–39; McKenney to McLean, January 29, 1831, McLean Papers.

7. Eaton to Indian Office, March 24, 1829, Eaton to McKenney, April 2, 1829, IA, LR, Misc., RG 75, NA; McKenney to Col. John Crowell, May 1, 1829, McKenney to Cass, June 9, 1829, IA, LS, 5: 431, 6: 3, RG 75, NA.

For Eaton's relation to Jackson, see Gabriel L. Lowe, Jr., "John H. Eaton, Jackson's Campaign Manager," *Tennessee Historical Quarterly* 11 (June 1952): 100–47; L. McLane to Martin Van Buren, February 19, 1829, Van Buren Papers; Jackson to Coffee, May 30, 1829, in Bassett, *Correspondence of Andrew Jackson,* 4: 38.

8. *Niles' Register* 26 (March 27, 1824): 50; McKenney to Cass and Clark, January 2, 1829, McKenney to Eaton, March 11, 18, 24, 1829, April 7, June 6, November 17, 1829, McKenney to Capt. Thomas Griffith, March 26, 1829, McKenney to DuVal, March 28, 1829, McKenney to Superintendents and Agents, May 29, 1829, McKenney to Indian Agents, June 9, 1829, Eaton to William Lee, March 16, 1829, IA, LS, 5: 249–51, 328–31, 345, 356–59, 368, 370, 379, 398–99, 452, 468–71, 6: 3, 167–68, RG 75, NA; *Georgian,* January 5, 1830; McKenney, *Memoirs,* 1: 212–13; Schoolcraft, *Personal Memoirs,* pp. 323–24; Commissioner of Indian Affairs, *Annual Report* (1841), pp. 258–59; Secretary of War, *Annual Report* (1830), pp. 32–33; U.S., *Stat.,* 4: 433.

9. Francis Paul Prucha, *Lewis Cass and American Indian Policy* (Detroit: Wayne State University Press, 1967), pp. 1–15; Schoolcraft to Cass, June 28, 1831, in Carter and Bloom, *Territorial Papers,* 12: 304–5; [Schoolcraft] to Isaac Collins, September 18, 1848, Schoolcraft Papers; Robert W. Unger, "Lewis Cass, Indian Superintendent of the Michigan Territory, 1813–1831: A Survey of Public Opinion as Reported by the Newspapers of the Old Northwest Territory" (Ph.D. diss., Ball State University, 1967), pp. 165–67, 176–79, 181, 190; *Morning Courier and New-York Enquirer,* January 25, 1832, *Pittsburgh Gazette,* December 21, 1832; Francis Paul Prucha and Donald F. Carmony, eds., "A Memorandum of Lewis Cass: Concerning a System for the Regulation of Indian Affairs," *Wisconsin Magazine of History* 51 (Autumn 1968): 35–50; Cass to Porter, September 8, 1828, IA, LR, Michigan Superintendency, RG 75, NA; Secretary of War, *Annual Reports* (1828), pp. 20–21; *House Journal,* 20th Cong., 1st sess., p. 105; McKenney to Cass and Clark, January 2, 1829, IA, LS, 5: 249–51, RG 75, NA; Report of Cass and Clark, February 9, 1829, *House Document 117,* 20th Cong., 2d sess., pp. 52–77. The *Senate Journal* does not mention the presentation of the Cass-Clark proposals. They were appended to the secretary of war's reply to requests made by the Senate for information concerning Indian affairs. See *Senate Journal,* 20th Cong., 2d sess., p. 114; *Senate Document 72,* 20th Cong., 2d sess., pp. 10–52.

10. Secretary of War, *Annual Report* (1831), pp. 27–34; *Senate Journal,* 22d Cong., 1st sess., pp. 155, 309–10, 313; *House Journal,* 22d Cong., 1st sess., pp. 819, 820, 823, 1029, 1092; U.S., *Stat.,* 4: 564; Testimony of Hugh L. White, February 13, 1837, in *Niles' Register* 32 (July 8, 1837): 295; U.S. Department of State, *Register of Officers and Agents, Civil,*

Military, and Naval in the Service of the United States (1831), p. 84, (1833), p. 77; Unger, "Lewis Cass," pp. 176–77; Ruth Gallaher, "The Indian Agent in the United States before 1850," *Iowa Journal of History and Politics* 14 (January 1916): 40–41. For the specific duties of the Indian commissioner, see Regulations of November 8, 1836, Revised Regulations, no. 1, November 11, 1836, IA, Misc. Records, 2: 3–6, RG 75, NA.

11. Lewis to Cass, February 24, 1834, IA, LR, Misc., RG 75, NA; Cass to Lewis, February 26, 1834, Secretary of War, Reports to Congress, 3: 249–50, RG 107, NA; Report on Regulating the Indian Department, May 20, 1834, *House Report 474*, 23d Cong., 1st sess., pp. 1–9, 23–27; Prucha, *American Indian Policy*, pp. 259-61. For an example of congressional legislation providing the president with authority to hire field personnel according to his discretion, see U.S., *Stat.*, 1: 331. The Indian field service is discussed in chapter 7.

12. U.S., *Stat.*, 4: 735–38.

13. For a sympathetic, scholarly examination of McKenney's career in Indian affairs, see Viola, "McKenney and the Administration of Indian Affairs." McKenney's political activities before 1829 and his precarious position when Jackson entered the White House are evident in Adams, *Memoirs*, 6: 47–48, 56, 66, 69, 291, 396, 400; William M. Meigs, *The Life of John Caldwell Calhoun*, 2 vols. (New York: G. E. Strechert & Co., 1917), 1: 293; *United States' Telegraph*, April 21, 1829; McKenney, *Memoirs*, 1: 195, 205–6, 223; McKenney to McLean, January 29, 1831, McLean Papers; McKenney to Forward, November 3, 1841, Gratz Collection; *North American Review* 63 (October 1846): 482.

14. McKenney, *Memoirs*, 1: 206–22, 262; McKenney to McLean, January 29, 1831, McLean Papers; McKenney to Forward, November 3, 1841, Gratz Collection; Philip G. Randolph to McKenney, August 16, 1830 (two letters of the same date), SW, Letters Sent Relating to Military Affairs (herafter cited as LS, Military Affairs), 13: 7, 9, RG 107, NA; *North American Review* 63 (October 1846): 482–83; *Niles' Register* 39 (September 4, 1830): 19. For additional information on the rations incident, see Report on Rations to Emigrants, July 5, 1832, *House Report 502*, 22d Cong., 1st sess., pp. 1–75.

15. Department of State, *Register of Officers* (1827), p. 70, (1831), p. 84; Hamilton to A. J. Donelson, April 20, 1829, Jackson Papers, Library of Congress; Schmeckebier, *Office of Indian Affairs*, pp. 577–78; McKenney to Porter, October 6, 1828, Hamilton to Cass, May 9, 1829, IA, LS, 5: 148, 432, RG 75, NA; *National Intelligencer*, quoted in *Georgian*, September 9, 1830; Eaton to [Jackson], December 17, 1830, Secretary of War, LS, President, 2: 264, RG 107, NA; Eaton to Red Men of the Muscogee Nation, May 16, 1831, *Senate Document 512*, 23d Cong., 1st sess.,

2: 290; Viola, "McKenney and the Administration of Indian Affairs," pp. 37–38. Hamilton began signing the Indian Bureau correspondence in early August; see Hamilton to Clark, August 9, 1830, IA, LS, 7: 7, RG 75, NA.

16. Secretary of State to Cass, August 8, 1831, Department of State, Domestic Letters Sent (hereafter cited as DS, LS, Domestic), 24: 192, RG 59, NA; Department of State, *Register of Officers* (1831), p. 84; David McAdam, ed., *History of the Bench and Bar of New York*, 2 vols. (New York: New York History Co., 1897–99), 1: 357; Testimony of White, February 13, 1837, in *Niles' Register* 32 (July 8, 1837): 295; Jackson to Francis P. Blair, April 2, 1837, in Bassett, *Correspondence of Andrew Jackson*, 5: 472–73; Jackson to the Public, June 13, 1837, in *Nashville Union*, June 13, 1837. Herring began signing the Indian Bureau correspondence in early August; see Herring to Montgomery, August 12, 1831, IA, LS, 7: 326, RG 75, NA.

17. *Executive Proceedings of the Senate*, 4: 280, 289; Testimony of White, February 13, 1837, in *Niles' Register* 32 (July 8, 1837): 295–96; Jackson to Blair, April 2, 1837, in Bassett, *Correspondence of Andrew Jackson*, 5: 472–73; Jackson to the Public, June 13, 1837, in *Nashville Union*, June 13, 1837.

18. Jackson to the Public, June 13, 1837, in *Nashville Union*, June 13, 1837; Jackson to Butler, October 4, 1836, Butler Papers, Princeton University Library (microfilm edition at University of Pennsylvania Library); William A. Butler, *A Retrospect of Forty Years, 1825–1865* ed. Harriet A. Butler (New York: Charles Scribner's Sons, 1911), pp. 33, 34, 99; Van Buren to Poinsett, February 4, 1837, Poinsett Papers; Commission of Harris, July 4, 1836, IA, Misc. Records, 2: 1, RG 75, NA.

19. Undated biographical statement concerning Harris, Harris to Cass, July 21, 1835, Carey Allen Harris Correspondence, Tennessee Historical Society, Nashville, Tenn.; *History of Tennessee from the Earliest Time to the Present* (Nashville: Goodspeed Publishing Co., 1886), p. 632; Department of State, *Register of Officers* (1833), p. 77, (1835), p. 80 (1837), p. 90; Harris to President, May 31, 1836, IA, LS, 18: 468, RG 75, NA; Jackson to Harris, August 7, 1836, Jackson Papers, Library of Congress; Jackson to Butler, October 4, 1836, Butler Papers; H[arris] to [Jackson], October 17, 1836, SW, LS, President, 3: 186–89, RG 107, NA; *Arkansas Gazette*, November 15, 1836; Sidney H. Aronson, *Status and Kinship in the Higher Civil Service: Standards of Selection in the Administrations of John Adams, Thomas Jefferson, and Andrew Jackson* (Cambridge: Harvard University Press, 1964), appendix C, p. 211.

20. Schoolcraft, *Personal Memoirs*, pp. 596–97, 615; Jackson to Van Buren, Confidential, June 1, 1838, Jackson Papers, Library of Congress;

Jackson to Blair, Confidential, June 4, 1838, in Bassett, *Correspondence of Andrew Jackson*, 5: 553; Van Buren to Jackson, June 17, 1838, Van Buren Papers; Harris to Poinsett, Confidential, June 9, 1838, Poinsett Papers; Sanford to Hitchcock, November 18, 1838, Hitchcock Papers; Testimony of David Kurtz, [1842], Poinsett to [Jno. T. Cochrane], March 16, 1842, *House Report 604*, 27th Cong., 2d sess. pp. 7–8, 9–10

21. Report of John T. Stuart, April 12, 1842, Harris to Poinsett, October 19, 1838, *House Report 604*, 27th Cong., 2d sess., pp. 4–5, 6; Sanford to Hitchcock, November 18, 1838, Hitchcock Papers. For details of the congressional investigation of the so-called Harris scandal, see C[rawford] to Stuart, March 8, 1842, IA, Chickasaw Removal Records, LS, B, pp. 204–5, RG 75, NA; *House Journal*, 27th Cong., 2d sess., pp. 687, 822; Report of Stuart, April 12, 1842, Appendix to Report of Stuart, May 16, 1842, *House Report 604*, 27th Cong., 2d sess., pp. 1–10, appendix, pp. 1–3; C[ave] Johnson to James K. Polk, Private, April 29, 1842, Polk Papers, Library of Congress, Washington, D.C. Mary E. Young has uncovered evidence that Harris was involved with speculators in Creek allotments in Alabama and received "loans" amounting to one-half share of their company stock. See *Redskins, Ruffleshirts and Rednecks*, pp. 91, 93. Leonard D. White claims in *The Jacksonians*, p. 419, that "no clerical or auditing scandal occurred in the Washington offices during the Jacksonian period."

22. Crawford to Jackson, May 29, 1843, Jackson Papers, Library of Congress; Charles Lanman, *Biographical Annals of the Civil Government of The United States during its First Century* (Washington, D.C.: James Anglim, Publisher, 1876), p. 100; *Debates in Congress*, 21st Cong., 1st sess., p. 1133; Cass to Crawford and Alfred Balch, July 12, 1836, IA, LS, 19: 182–88, RG 75, NA; Harmon, *Sixty Years of Indian Affairs*, p. 216; Schoolcraft, *Personal Memoirs*, p. 615; Jackson to Van Buren, November 19, 1838, Van Buren Papers. An early statement of Crawford's political views appears in *Pennsylvania Intelligencer* (Harrisburg), September 2, 1825. For Crawford's role in disclosing the frauds against the Creeks, see IA, Creek Removal Records, Docket Books of Crawford and Balch, vols. 1–5, Reports of Crawford and Balch, vols. 1–3, RG 75, NA.

23. See *Centennial History of the City of Washington, D.C.* (Dayton: W. J. Shuey, Publisher, 1892), p. 735; Putnam, *Joel Roberts Poinsett*, p. 153; Mahon, *Second Seminole War*, p. 271; Crawford to Poinsett, April 29, 1841, November 5, 1844, Poinsett Papers; Hamilton to Milroy, February 10, 1845, Milroy Papers.

24. Horace Everet[t] to Hitchcock, February 16, 1841 (two letters of the same date), Hitchcock to Captain W. W. S. Bliss, March 11, 1841,

Hitchcock Papers. For evidence of the close friendship between Bell and Hitchcock, see Bell to Hitchcock, December 7, 1838, Hitchcock Papers. Hitchcock's anti-Jackson sympathies are evident in Hitchcock to Mrs. Lucy C. Hitchcock, September 3, 1836, Hitchcock Papers.

25. I. Bernard Cohen, *Ethan Allen Hitchcock: Soldier-Humanitarian-Scholar, Discoverer of the "True Subject" of the Hermetic Art* (Worcester, Mass.: American Antiquarian Society, 1952), pp. 34–36; Ernest S. Bates, "Ethan Allen Hitchcock," in Johnson and Malone, *Dictionary of American Biography,* 5: 73–74.

26. Cohen, *Ethan Allen Hitchcock,* pp. 34–36; Gaines to Bell, March 4, 1841, Hitchcock Papers. Gaines's opposition to Jackson's policy is discussed in Silver, "Counter-Proposal to the Indian Removal Policy of Andrew Jackson," pp. 207–15.

27. Hitchcock to Mrs. Lucy Hitchcock, May 14, 1841, Hitchcock to Bliss, May 28, 1841, Hitchcock to John A. Hitchcock, July 21, 1841, Hitchcock Papers; Bell to [Robert P.] Letcher, May 2, 1841, John Jordan Crittenden Papers, Library of Congress, Washington, D.C.; Robert S. Cotterill, "James Harlan," in Johnson and Malone, *Dictionary of American Biography,* 8: 267–69.

28. McKenney to Bell, March 1, 1841, N[icholas] Biddle to Webster, March 2, 1841, SW, LR, Unregistered Series, 1841-M, RG 107, NA; McKenney to Forward, November 3, 1841, Gratz Collection. For McKenney's earlier ties with Harrison, see Harrison et al. to Adams, January 25, 1827, in McKenney, *Memoirs,* 1: appendix D, pp. 315–16. McKenney's anti-Jackson writings after his dismissal from the Indian Bureau in 1830 included a vitriolic attack against Jackson's position toward the Bank of the United States. See *Essays on the Spirit of Jacksonism as Exemplified in its Deadly Hostility to the Bank of the United States, and in the Odious Calumnies Employed for its Destruction* (Philadelphia: Jasper Harding, Printer, 1835). McKenney and James Hall coauthored a multivolume study of the American Indians entitled *History of the Indian Tribes of North America, with Biographical Sketches and Anecdotes of the Principal Chiefs,* 3 vols. (Philadelphia: E. C. Biddle, 1836–44).

29. McKenney to William D. Lewis, October 27, 1840, August 28, 1841, McKenney-Lewis Correspondence, Huntington Library, San Marino, California (microfilm edition in possession of Herman J. Viola); McKenney to Forward, November 3, 1841, Gratz Collection. For the voluminous petitions and letters favoring McKenney's appointment as commissioner, see SW, LR, Unregistered Series, 1841-M, RG 107, NA. For evidence that McKenney was not held in esteem by at least two of Harrison's confidants who were helping him screen the many candidates besieging Washington in the scramble for offices after the Whig victory,

see Dorothy B. Goebel, *William Henry Harrison: A Political Biography* (Indianapolis: Indiana Historical Bureau, 1926), p. 375.

30. Bell to Letcher, May 2, 1841, Crittenden Papers; McKenney, *Memoirs,* 1: 27–28, 30; McKenney to Forward, November 3, 1841, McKenney to J[ohn] C. Spencer, November 3, 1841, Gratz Collection. Also see note 29.

31. Stuart to W[illia]m Woodbridge, February 26, June 3, 29, 1841, Woodbridge Papers, Burton Historical Collection, Detroit Public Library, Detroit, Mich. For biographical information about Stuart, see W. J. Ghent, "Robert Stuart," in Johnson and Malone, *Dictionary of American Biography,* 18: 175–76; Lawton T. Hemans, *Life and Times of Stevens Thomson Mason: The Boy Governor of Michigan,* 2d ed. (Lansing: Michigan Historical Commission, 1930), p. 251.

32. Van Deusen, *Jacksonian Era,* pp. 158–59; Robert J. Morgan, *A Whig Embattled: The Presidency under John Tyler* (Lincoln: University of Nebraska Press, 1954), pp. 165–71; *Detroit Daily Advertiser,* March 28, 1843; Ghent, "Robert Stuart," pp. 175–76.

33. Crawford to Polk, July 22, 1832, Matthew St. Clair Drake to Polk, September 18, 1832, in Weaver and Bergeron, *Correspondence of James K. Polk,* pp. 488–90, 511; Marcy to President, October 2, 1845, SW, LS, President, 4: 242, RG 107, NA; *Executive Proceedings of the Senate,* 7: 21; F. Regis Noel, *The Court-House of the District of Columbia,* 2d ed. (Washington, D.C.: Law Reporter Printing Co., 1939), p. 80; Chs. Fischer to Medill, Private & Unofficial, November 14, 1845, Medill Papers.

34. Dwight L. Smith, "William Medill," in *The Governors of Ohio* (Columbus: Ohio Historical Society, 1954), pp. 68–69; W. Thomas to [Medill], February 6, 1845, Democrats of the Ohio Legislature to Polk, February 13, 1845, Casper Thull to Medill, March 2, 1845, James Carson to Medill, March 3, 1845, Israel Brown to Medill, June 27, 1845, Commission of Medill, October 28, 1845, Medill to Johnson, October 29, 1845, Medill Papers; *Arkansas Intelligencer,* April 19, May 3, 1845; *Executive Proceedings of the Senate,* 7: 21, 22, 24–25. Medill's affiliation with the Van Buren wing of the Democratic party in Ohio is documented in Edgar A. Holt, "Party Politics in Ohio, 1840–1850," *Ohio Historical Society Collections* 1 (1930): 173. For the position of Ohio Van Burenites concerning Polk's distribution of the patronage, see Francis P. Wiesenburger, *The History of the State of Ohio,* vol. 3, *The Passing of the Frontier, 1825–1850,* ed. Carl Wittke (Columbus: Ohio State Archaeological and Historical Society, 1941), pp. 441–43.

35. Sam Hood to Medill, March 4, 1846, G. W. Ewing to Medill, March 18, 1846, Polk to Medill, September 19, 1846, H. C. Whitmore to Medill, January 27, 1848, Medill Papers.

36. The Medill Papers at the Library of Congress contain numerous applications for appointments and Medill's replies. The quotation cited above is from J. S. Smith to Medill, January 31, 1848, Medill Papers. For the effort to promote Medill as a possible vice-presidential candidate in 1848, see M. I. Dougherty to Medill, February 25, 1848, Medill Papers; *Pennsylvanian* (Philadelphia), February 25, 1848.

37. Brown to Taylor, June 4, 1849, Brown Papers, Kentucky Historical Society, Frankfort, Ky.; Brown to Crittenden, July 10, 1849, Crittenden Papers; Holman Hamilton, *Zachary Taylor: Soldier in the White House* (Indianapolis: Bobbs-Merrill Co., Inc., 1951), p. 173; G. Glenn Clift, "The Governors of Kentucky [1792–1824] with Biographical Sketch and Notes: The Old Master, Colonel Orlando Brown, 1801–1867," *Register of the Kentucky Historical Society* 49 (January 1951): 15–17; George R. Poage, *Henry Clay and the Whig Party* (Chapel Hill: University of North Carolina Press, 1936), pp. 187–88; J. T. Sprague to Hitchcock, March 9, 1841, Hitchcock Papers; White, *The Jacksonians,* pp. 101, 347–48. The analysis of Brown in the above paragraph is also based on an examination of the Brown Papers at the Filson History Club.

38. *Niles' Register* 47 (December 13, 1834): 233; Jackson to Blair, Confidential, June 4, 1838, in Bassett, *Correspondence of Andrew Jackson,* 5: 553; Commissioner of Indian Affairs, *Annual Report* (1840), p. 390, (1841), p. 263; Whitman to Medill, January 2, 1847, Wm. Camp to Medill, February 20, 1848, Potts to Medill, September 26, 1848, Jn. Hough to Medill, December 26, 1848, Medill Papers; White, *The Jacksonians,* pp. 75, 87, 101, 327, 347–48, 436. For examples of the patronage at the disposal of the Indian commissioner, see List of All Printers Employed by the Indian Department, September 30, 1835–September 30, 1837, IA, Misc. Records, 3: 38–39, RG 75, NA; Statements concerning Dayton newspapers, June 8, 1848, Medill Papers. See notes 20 and 21 for references to the Harris episode. For the charges against Medill and the subsequent congressional investigation, see *Congressional Globe,* 30th Cong., 1st sess., pp. 904–5, 1055, 1058, 1068–70, 1071, 30th Cong., 2d sess., pp. 242–44, 552; Report of Geo[rge] Fries, February 17, 1849, plus enclosures, *House Report 104,* 30th Cong., 2d sess., pp. 1–71. Marshall E. Dimock erroneously contends in his study of *Congressional Investigating Commissions* (Baltimore: Johns Hopkins Press, 1929), p. 94, that "in 1848 a House Committee found the Commissioner of Indian Affairs guilty of marked inefficiencies."

39. Gilmer's Report on Retrenchment and Reorganization of Executive Departments, May 23, 1842, *House Report 741,* 27th Cong., 2d sess., pp. 19–20.

40. McKenney to Eaton, March 18, 1829, IA, LS, 5: 357–59, RG 75,

NA; Viola, "McKenney and the Administration of Indian Affairs," pp. 36–37, 149; Biddle to Webster, March 2, 1841, SW, LR, Unregistered Series, 1841-M, RG 107, NA; McKenney, *Memoirs,* 1: 205; Department of State, *Register of Officers* (1827), p. 70, (1829), p. 71, (1831), p. 84, (1833), p. 78, (1835), p. 80; Revised Regulations, No. 1, November 11, 1836, IA, Misc. Records, 2: 4–5, RG 75, NA; Erik M. Ericksson, "The Federal Civil Service under President Jackson," *Mississippi Valley Historical Review* 13 (March 1927): 529–30. The paintings in the Indian Bureau in 1829 constituted the first ethnological collection in the nation's capitol; see Herman J. Viola, "Washington's First Museum: The Indian Office Collection of Thomas L. McKenney," *Smithsonian Journal of History* 3 (Fall 1968): 1–18.

41. Revised Regulations, No. 1, November 11, 1836, IA, Misc. Records, 2: 4–5, RG 75, NA; Department of State, *Register of Officers* (1837), pp. 90–91, (1839), p. 81, (1841), p. 94, (1843), p. 163, (1845), pp. 15–16, (1847), p. 135, (1849), p. 132; Crawford's Testimony, March 12, 1842, Gilmore's Report, May 23, 1842, *House Report 741,* 27th Cong., 2d sess., pp. 9, 34; Robert Mills, *Guide to the National Executive Offices and the Capitol of the United States* (Washington, D.C.: P. Force, Printer, 1842), pp. 19, 21; Robert Mills, *Guide to the Capitol and National Executive Offices of the United States* (Washington, D.C.: Wm. Greer, Printer, 1847–48), pp. 51–52; Carl R. Fish, *The Civil Service and the Patronage* (New York: Longmans, Green, & Co., 1905), appendix B, pp. 248–49; White, *The Jacksonians,* pp. 329, 349, 355–56, 362.

42. McKenney to Eaton, March 18, 1829, Lea to Commissioner of Indian Affairs, October 8, 1841, IA, LS, 5: 357–58, 31: 200, RG 75, NA; Statement of Clerks Employed during 1836, IA, Misc. Records, 2: 120–21, RG 75, NA; Crawford to Poinsett, December 30, 1839, *House Document 103,* 26th Cong., 1st sess., pp. 9–11; Crawford to Poinsett, April 18, 1840, Crawford to Secretary of War, December 8, 1841, Crawford to Spencer, February 11, 1842, IA, Report Books, 2: 65–67, 3: 62, 98–99, RG 75, NA; Gilmore's Report, May 23, 1842, Testimony of Crawford, March 12, 1842, Testimony of Second Auditor, April 6, 1842, *House Report 741,* 27th Cong., 2d sess., pp. 19–20, 34, 55; *Congressional Globe,* 27th Cong., 2d sess., pp. 246, 479; U.S., *Stat.,* 5: 409, 583, 718; Trevitt to Medill, March 28, 1847, Tuthill to Medill, April 11, 1848, Medill Papers. For an idea of the operations of the Indian Office personnel, see Testimony of Crawford, March 12, 1841, *House Report 741,* 27th Cong., 2d sess., pp. 35–36. To gauge the extent of removals throughout the Jacksonian era, see the entries for the Indian Office in the issues of the Department of State, *Register of Officers,* listed in footnotes 40 and 41.

43. Crawford to Poinsett, December 30, 1839, *House Document 103,* 26th Cong., 1st sess., p. 9; Gilmore's Report, May 23, 1842, Testimony of Crawford, March 12, 1842, *House Report 741,* 27th Cong., 2d sess., pp. 25–26, 28, 34; White, *The Jacksonians,* pp. 155, 553; Brown to T. Ewing, February 28, 1850, Brown Papers, Kentucky Historical Society.

7 /

The Indian Field Service

WHILE THE INDIAN OFFICE was responsible for helping Congress and the executive branch formulate Indian policy and coordinate its administration, personnel in the field shouldered the burden of putting Indian policy into effect and supplying information to help Washington officials make their decisions. The lack of long-range planning which characterized Indian removal during the Jacksonian era resulted in a remarkable diffusion of power and decision making authority from Washington to the field. Decision making took place at various echelons in the bureaucracy because the very nature of the questions involved in Indian removal necessitated a sharing of power.

Nineteenth-century America was a nation of loosely connected communities, and government bureaucrats in their Washington offices had to rely heavily upon the initiative and judgment of their scattered subordinates. The implementation of decisions made in Washington often depended on the intelligence, character, integrity, and interests of scattered field officials. Numerous studies of nineteenth-century public administration and land policy indicate that the federal government was an incorrigible bungler, presiding weakly over its territories and the distribution of its public lands. The administration of Indian policy during the Jacksonian era displays a similar pattern of federal initiative.[1]

The Indian service, like other federal operations, suffered from what political scientist M. I. Ostrogorski once called "the weakened spring of government." The entrepreneurial impulse permeated Jacksonian America, and expectant capitalists wanted the government to encourage rather than impede the development of private enterprise and the exploitation of the nation's resources. Governmental neglect and irresolution in the area of Indian administration stemmed from the excesses of partisan politics and the prevailing belief that retrenchment and good government were synonymous. T. Hartley Crawford, one of the ablest Indian commissioners during this period, admitted that "system is the life of any well-conducted business, public or private." Yet system is exactly what Congress and the executive failed to provide in Indian administration during the Jacksonian era.[2]

In 1834 the Jackson administration, responding to some suggestions from the Stokes commission, secured the adoption of legislation to restructure and legitimize the far-flung Indian service bureaucracy that had evolved in an ad-hoc fashion during the early decades of the republic. Until 1834 the laws and regulations governing the Indian service consisted of a mixed assortment of congressional acts, treaty provisions, and executive orders dating back to the time of the Articles of Confederation. The duties of field officials had always been vague. When Lawrence Taliaferro became the agent to the Sioux in 1819, for example, he did not receive specific instructions, and even the exact limits of his jurisdiction remained a mystery for some time. The legislation of 1834 was an attempt to correct such ambiguities, and with some modifications it remained in force throughout the Jacksonian era.[3]

The laws of 1834 established two sets of authorities in the field, subordinate to the War Department, which had chief responsibility for Indian affairs. One set of officials consisted of civilian employees—superintendents, territorial governors acting as ex-officio superintendents, and agents, subagents, and other minor officials under their direction. The second group were the commandants of military posts and garrisons in the field.[4]

The position of superintendent of Indian affairs was the focal point of the field service just as the Indian commissioner was the nerve center of the entire administrative establishment in Washington. The superintendents, who received a salary of fifteen hundred dollars, had authority to "exercise a general supervision and control over the official conduct and accounts of all officers and persons" employed in the area under their jurisdiction. The laws of 1834 called for a superintendent at Saint Louis for all Indians west of the Mississippi River, including those outside the boundaries of the states and territories. The law also ordered the territorial governor of Michigan to serve simultaneously as ex-officio superintendent of Indian affairs.[5]

The superintendents had tremendous responsibilities. They were in charge of a large number of field officials and had to keep accurate accounts for all of the agencies and subagencies under their jurisdiction. They also maintained special records for migrating Indians, treaty negotiations, claims investigations, and other miscellaneous circumstances. The job was extremely exhausting, challenging, and frustrating. New appointees often found that they had to spend weeks clearing up old business left by their predecessors, and Congress was parsimonious when it came to requests for clerical assistance. Joshua Pilcher, a devoted superintendent at Saint Louis in the late 1830s, ruined his health by working days, nights, and weekends to fulfill all of his obligations and finally resorted to hiring slaves to help with his chores. The overworked superintendents formed an indispensable part of the administrative machinery of Indian policy, but Congress and the executive branch did little to ease their burdens or to regulate their activities.[6]

The law of 1834 neglected to specify qualifications for the position of superintendent and failed to prohibit other field officials from simultaneously holding this office. The result was that Indian agents frequently received orders to serve as acting superintendents in order to keep the administrative machinery in the field functioning when funds were especially tight. Commissioner William Medill warned in 1848 that this was "a very imperfect and objectionable arrangement," since the duties of the superintendents were "highly important and responsible, and in many ways entirely incompatible with the local duties of agent[s]." Congress had originally intended that the superintendent would serve as an important check on the work of agents. "By constant and active supervision," the commissioner pointed out, "they can materially aid in preventing or correcting abuses or errors." While Commissioner Medill fervently argued that "superintendents should be

Andrew Jackson

John H. Eaton, Jackson's
secretary of war

Thomas L. McKenney, head of
the original Indian Bureau (from
his *Memoirs,* 1846)

Isaac McCoy, Baptist missionary
and proponent of Indian removal

Major Ridge, Cherokee Treaty
party leader (from the McKenney
and Hall *Indian Tribes of North
America*, 1836–44)

Greenwood LeFlore, Choctaw
leader

John Ridge, Cherokee Treaty
party leader (from the McKenney
and Hall *Indian Tribes of North
America*, 1836–44)

John Ross, Cherokee National
party leader (from the McKenney
and Hall *Indian Tribes of North
America*, 1836–44)

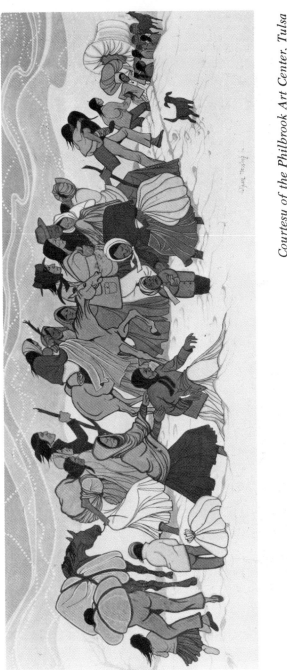

Choctaw Removal, by Valjean Hessing

Massacre of the Whites by the Indians and Blacks in Florida.

The above is intended to represent the horrid Massacre of the Whites in Florida, in December 1835, and January, February, March and April 1836, when near Four Hundred (including women and children) fell victims to the barbarity of the Negroes and Indians.

Courtesy of the Library of Congress

Anti-Indian propaganda from the Seminole War: a woodcut from *An Authentic Narrative of the Seminole War* (1836)

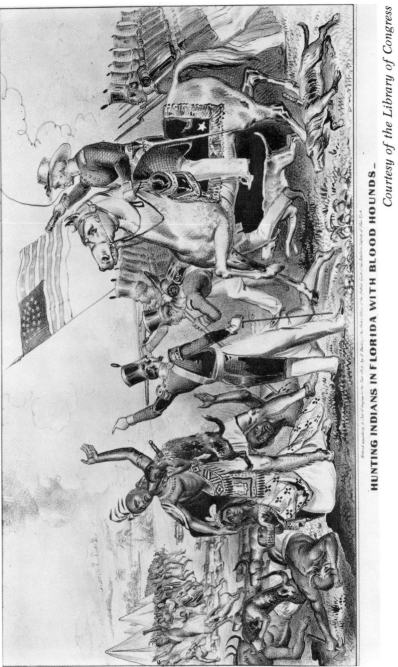

HUNTING INDIANS IN FLORIDA WITH BLOOD HOUNDS –

Pro-Indian propaganda from the Seminole War: a political cartoon by James C. Baillie

International Indian Council at Tahlequah, 1843

Courtesy of the Kansas State
Historical Society
Joseph N. Bourassa, Potawatomi
teacher

Courtesy of the Oklahoma
Historical Society
John Bemo, Seminole teacher

Courtesy of the Smithsonian
Institution, National
Anthropological Archives
Peter Pitchlynn, Choctaw leader

Indian school (from Thomas L. McKenney's *Memoirs*)

free from all local duties as [an] agent for a tribe," dual office holding among field officials was evidently a common practice throughout the Jacksonian period.[7]

The provision of the 1834 law which permitted the territorial governor of Michigan to continue serving as ex-officio Indian superintendent reflected the myopic vision of American legislators concerning Indian affairs. Since 1789 Congress had found it convenient to use the territory, as a readily definable geographical area, and the territorial governor, as a federal official with a salary provided by law, to dispose on paper of the problem of Indian administration on the frontier. While the law of 1834 continued this combination of offices only for Michigan, the organic laws of new territories in the Old Northwest and the Pacific Northwest later perpetuated the practice. The arrangement was an administrative blunder of significant dimensions. Territorial governors were responsible for advancing the interests of the white population in their territories. Indian superintendents, on the other hand, were to act as the guardians of Indian rights and welfare. As the representatives of white settlers, governors sought to promote rapid emigration of Indians from their territories, but as Indian superintendents they had an obligation to help the Indians become "civilized" by teaching them to farm and to master other sedentary trades. The combination of territorial governor and Indian superintendent may have made sense economically, but the resulting strains and role conflict were tremendous.[8]

A governor who showed too much concern for Indian rights or the sanctity of Indian treaties ran the risk of precipitating efforts to remove him from office. An attempt to evict squatters from Indian lands in Michigan Territory by Steven T. Mason in the mid-1830s, for example, had a deleterious effect on his political career. Yet governors had to serve, as Henry R. Schoolcraft pointed out, as "an umpire between the Indian tribes and the [white] citizens." While territorial governors generally sided with white settlers when such a choice was unavoidable, they did occasionally defy public opinion in order to protect Indians from gross frauds or bodily harm. The tendency, however, was to follow the path of expediency.[9]

After the superintendent in the bureaucratic hierarchy came the agent. The law of 1834 called for the appointment of a specified number of agents by the president with the advice and consent of the Senate. Agents were to "give bond, with two or more securities, in the penal sum of two thousand dollars . . . [and] receive the annual compensation of fifteen hundred dollars." Although Congress specifically denoted the location of the agencies, it permitted the president discretionary authority to discontinue or transfer any agencies as the need arose. The term for agents was fixed at four years. They were to reside "within or near" the territory of the tribe under their jurisdiction, and they needed prior permission to leave the area. Congress also ruled that the president could require military officers to execute the duties of Indian agents.[10]

The subagents were the next echelon in the bureaucracy. Congress authorized the president to name a "competent number" of subagents who would give bond for one thousand dollars, but it did not specify the exact nature of the work of the subagent and the difference between his duties and the agent's. The law of 1834 merely stated that "no sub-agent shall be appointed who shall reside within the limits of any agency where there is an agent appointed." Both agents and subagents were to "manage and superintend the intercourse with the Indians within their respective agencies, agreeably to law; to obey all legal instructions . . . and to carry into effect such regulations as may be prescribed by the President."[11]

Since Congress did not specifically outline all of the various duties of agents and subagents, tradition, the exigencies of the frontier, the immediate needs of the Indians, and instructions from the Office of Indian Affairs provided field personnel with guidelines. One commissioner ably summed up the duties of these officials in the following manner: "He is the Representative of the Government to attend to the complaints of the Indians [,] supply their wants, redress their grievances [,] soften their ruggedness, change their habits and ameliorate their condition." Agents had responsibilities to both the Indians and whites. They were to punish unruly Indians, settle disputes between tribes or between whites and Indians, oversee the expenditure of funds for improving the education and general condition of the Indians, disburse annuities and gifts, license Indian traders, and settle their claims.[12]

Congress and the executive displayed little foresight when they failed to distinguish the duties of agents from those of subagents.

Baptist missionary Isaac McCoy noted in 1835 that "the duties and responsibilities of the two are precisely the same. The only difference is that the compensation of an Agent is $1500 per ann. and the compensation of a Sub-Agent $750 per ann." The lack of any real difference in duties and the tremendous reduction in salaries for subagents caused ill feeling among these officials, who continually protested that they deserved equal pay with the agents. Many competent and experienced subagents resigned their positions because of the low pay. George Lawe at Green Bay, Wisconsin Territory, complained that he was "barely able to support" his family on a subagent's salary. Superintendent James D. Doty, a close friend of Lawe's father, helped out by securing additional pay for him as an interpreter but cautioned Lawe that "it is not worth while to mention to any one what salary you receive."[13]

Other subagents actively lobbied for the position of agent. Joshua Pilcher, subagent to the Sioux in 1835, worked with his political ally Senator Thomas Hart Benton to secure the position of agent and thereby double his salary. Samuel Milroy, a prominent Indiana Democrat, performed special favors for Vice-President Richard M. Johnson, who held out the hope of getting Congress to change Milroy's subagency into an agency. The net effect of the government's failure to make the pay of subagents commensurate with their duties was the politicization of the subagents as these officers found it necessary to align themselves with political forces opposed to their immediate superiors whose jobs they coveted or to deal with men who were in a position to return favors granted to them.[14]

An attempt to provide subagents with more adequate remuneration was made at the end of the Van Buren administration. Commissioner Crawford admitted late in 1839 that the duties of agents and subagents were "precisely the same" and suggested that all field officials should be paid a salary "graduated by the service required" of them. Congress was not receptive to this plan, since it would have meant the immediate doubling of the salary of most subagents. Instead, congressmen continued to take steps to economize which only added to the confusion already existing in the Indian service. In order to cut back all "unnecessary" expenditures, for example, Congress encouraged the reduction of agencies to subagencies without any corresponding reduction in the duties required by the field personnel in charge, although they would receive a fifty percent cut in pay. Such actions were not likely to bolster the morale of field officials. The Indian Office had to reassure Congress continually that the compensation received by its field staff was not excessive but only the minimum necessary to find "incumbents of proper qualifications," because of "the magnitude of the interests committed to them."[15]

In addition to agents and subagents, the law of 1834 made provisions for interpreters, blacksmiths, farmers, mechanics, and teachers. Congress specifically stipulated that "in all cases of the appointments of interpreters or other persons employed for the benefit of the Indians, a preference shall be given to persons of Indian descent, if such can be found, who are properly qualified for the execution of the duties." The Indians were to direct these officials themselves when the secretary of war deemed them "competent" to do so. By giving agents and subagents authority to name "suitable persons" to these positions, however, Congress had created an obstacle to its announced goal of turning over the direction of these individuals to the Indians.[16]

Throughout the Jacksonian era there was a tremendous proliferation of minor offices in the field service because of necessities imposed by the removal of the Indians and the government's obligations to them under treaties. These positions offered agents and subagents an excellent way of rewarding their friends and building up a sizable following to support their political ambitions.[17]

The law of 1834 provided ample opportunities for the Indian service to become an adjunct of partisan politics. In addition to the discretionary authority given field personnel to name minor officials, instructions for extra duties frequently carried the clause, "If from any cause, you decline executing this service, you will be pleased to appoint some person in whom you have confidence to perform it." The field service offered a large number of openings for patronage-hungry politicians, and the removal process was frequently retarded by officials who had a vested interest in maintaining the Indians in a given area in order to retain their patronage power. Men like John Tipton, agent to the Miami and Potawatomi Indians, built up powerful political machines upon the opportunities provided by treaties for blacksmiths, mechanics, farmers, and the like and upon their authority to grant or deny traders' licenses. During his career as an Indian agent between 1823 and 1831, Tipton played an important role in dispensing the federal patronage in northern Indiana. A shrewd man with political ambitions, he realized that the patronage at his disposal as well as his control over the licensing of traders meant that local office seekers and merchants would have to court his friendship and promote his political aspirations, since their fortunes were inextricably interwoven with his. Using his position as agent to build up a political base, Tipton, like many other agents, eventually sought political office. Tipton's political acumen during his years as Indian agent led to his election to the United States Senate in 1831.[18]

Since the positions of superintendent, agent, and subagent were choice patronage appointments, scheming politicians were always attempting to secure them for their own followers. Incumbents found it necessary to keep in the good graces of their state or territorial legislature and delegation in Congress as well as the traders, who had considerable influence on the frontier and in Washington. The result was that the officials' obligations to the Indians became subjugated to political considerations. Field officers were especially reluctant to reprimand or remove incompetent subordinates who might be aligned with men of political power.[19]

Although neither Congress nor the Jackson administration purposely designed the legislation of 1834 to lead to the establishment of political sinecures, both were well aware of the greed of office seekers. Jackson had complained to a confidant during his first month in office that he was "crowded with thousand[s] of applicants for office, and if I had a tit for every applicant to suck the Treasury pap, all would go away well satisfied, but as their are not office[s] for more than one out of five hundred who applies, many must go away dissatisfied." Some of the victorious Whigs in 1840 feared that the "wolves of the antechamber" and other "*spoil hunting* parasites" out "prowling for offices" might disgrace their party. President James K. Polk lamented in 1845 that "the office seekers have become so numerous that they hold the balance of power between the two great parties of the country."[20]

Rather than reforming the procedures for selecting field personnel and providing criteria for evaluating their effectiveness, the chief executives and congressmen continually thought in terms of how available patronage positions would benefit their party's interests. Presidents, moreover, were especially attentive to the requests for patronage positions from congressional leaders whose support was crucial for their legislative programs and from fur traders whose assistance they needed to secure the signing of removal treaties. Throughout the Jacksonian era, changes in political leadership usually meant the "release from *Indian captivity*" for a substantial number of field officials.[21]

The most active periods of political removals coincided with Jackson's first two years in office, Martin Van Buren's efforts to build solid support for his reelection, the Whig accession in 1841, Tyler's effort to "buy" support for the 1844 election, and the advent of the Polk administration. While many experienced field agents succumbed to the political guillotine during these years, a suprisingly large number managed to survive for relatively long periods of time. Some of the removals had little to do with partisan politics. Jackson could have dismissed John Quincy Adams's brother-in-law from the Indian service in 1829, but he did not avail himself of the opportunity. Many of Jackson's removals actually resulted from attempts to remove incompetent agents or to promote economy by consolidating agencies. The general trend, however, was unmistakable. A substantial number of men with long years of faithful service in Indian affairs, such as Henry R. Schoolcraft, were sacrificed on the altar of party politics. The result was detrimental to the development of anything approaching a career service based on merit and experience.[22]

The politicization of the Indian service during the mid-1830s had progressed so far that President Jackson found it necessary to prohibit field officials from intruding in local politics. Although Jackson ordered that "no officer of this general government will be permitted to interfere with local elections of the State[s]," there is evidence to indicate that many field officials spent a considerable amount of their time "out electioneering." As one observant Washington editor noted, presidents could readily employ "electioneering agents" at federal expense by issuing orders from the Indian Office to have an "agent" visit one of the tribes in the South, the Old Northwest, or perhaps the East. The agent would receive regular pay and traveling expenses while ostensibly on government business. It is impossible to calculate the exact extent of such maneuvers, but the political milieu of the period was certainly conducive to this type of activity.[23]

Throughout the Jacksonian era the gargantuan appetite of what one writer called "the office-seeking class" diminished the efficiency of the Indian service. Patronage seekers continually complained about the "d-d small *pickings* for the *small fry*" as they relentlessly besieged official Washington with thousands of written requests for positions. One unsuccessful applicant for Lawrence Taliaferro's position as agent to the Sioux pointedly reminded President Van Buren that the "old republican doctrine of rotation in Office" was a "leading principle of the party" that propelled him into the White House. Every day of the year applications for a superintendency, an agency, a subagency, a clerkship, or even the office of Indian commissioner poured into Washington.[24]

Unfortunately, the personnel employed by the Indian Office had to spend much of their time refuting charges made against them by traders and their allies or by political opponents and office seekers. Agent Henry R. Schoolcraft noted in 1838 that the partisan press frequently carried items relating to Indian affairs in which "facts are distorted, opinions misapprehended, and the acts and policy of the government and its agents greatly misconceived in some things, and wholly misrepresented in others." Such editorials, he suggested, were usually the work of "some ambitious man who wishes to get on the backs of the Indians to ride into office, or to promote, in some other way, selfish and concealed ends." Robert Stuart, Schoolcraft's successor in 1841, once warned a subordinate to be cautious in executing his duties because "there are always jealous people, ready to surmise and report evil." Superintendents always had to be on their guard against agents who coveted their position and were quick to report anything that might tarnish their record, while subagents did much the same in their attempt to secure the higher-paying position of agent. Political factionalism in many states and territories turned the Indian service into a sordid battleground, with superintendencies, agencies, and subagencies being little more than pawns in the game of political patronage and power.[25]

It is difficult to generalize about the character and integrity of the men in the Indian field service during the Jacksonian period. The available biographical information on many of these individuals is exceedingly scanty. While partisan politics did have a great deal to do with Indian appointments, officials usually stressed the need to find members of their political party who were men of *"sober, steady habits."*[26]

There were some capable agents who managed to survive the changes in administrations. Lawrence Taliaferro, the agent at Saint Peters in present-day Minnesota, for example, served every president from Monroe to Van Buren before he resigned. He spoke over a dozen Indian dialects, opposed the influence of traders over the Indians, and used his own funds when necessary to prevent the Indians under his jurisdiction from going hungry. Joseph M. Street, agent to the Sac and Fox, was so beloved by these Indians that Chief Wapello asked to be buried next to him when he died. Agent and ethnologist Henry R. Schoolcraft married an Indian and served ably in the Indian service between 1822 and 1841 and again during the Polk administration. William Clark of the famous Lewis and Clark expedition had a distinguished career in Indian affairs, beginning in 1807 and lasting until his death in 1838. Clark was universally respected by the Indians and was a model administrator.[27]

The agents who discharged their duties faithfully and had deep sympathy for the welfare of the Indians during this period are largely forgotten individuals who deserve a better fate. Even Grant Foreman, one of the severest critics of Jacksonian Indian policy in recent times, admitted that the emigrant Indians owed many of their accomplishments in the trans-Mississippi Indian country to enlightened agents. Many of these men made serious efforts to understand Indian society, and their correspondence with Washington superiors deserves recognition as early treatises in American ethnology.[28]

But there were also agents who were callous toward the Indians or viewed the Indian service as a purely "muney maickin" business. A frontier correspondent of Secretary of War John Eaton frankly admitted in 1829 that an appointment to a field post in the Indian service had a "corrupting nature." Cherokee agent Pierce M. Butler, who waged an unsuccessful campaign in 1843 to become superintendent of the western Indian country, told a confidant that "the ap[poin]t[ment] carries on its face no mor[e] pay than an ordinary agent. The contingencies . . . treaties . . . *(pay well)*, let them give it to me. They told a friend of mine at Washington that . . . there was no increase of pay & c, not so." Butler maintained that "the appointment is a pretty one." Although Butler enjoyed the confidence of the Cherokees, emphasis on profiteering and politics by field personnel generally meant that they had little time for the welfare of the Indians. In 1848 Henry R. Schoolcraft, who was conducting a statistical study of the Indians for the government, urged Commissioner William Medill to visit some of the agencies in order to "wake up the drowsy" field officials. Schoolcraft complained that Indian agents were too often preoccupied with "possessing sinecures" to undertake "researches & inquiries" for the benefit of their charges.[29]

In addition to the increasing politicization of the Indian service, there were other factors which militated against effective administration of Indian affairs. There was, for example, a tremendous lack of coordination between the various echelons of the bureaucracy. The chain of command was often vague, as were the exact jurisdictions of field officials. When the United States began to expand its operations during the late 1830s and especially the 1840s, the situation grew worse. Communications between Washington and the far-flung agencies in the West sometimes took weeks or even months, and field personnel often found it impossible or inexpedient to comply with Indian Office regulations.[30]

Sometimes the commissioner of Indian affairs learned important news through unofficial channels before the reports of field agents arrived. Early in 1842, for example, Commissioner Crawford charged Cherokee agent Pierce Butler with "neglect of official duty" for not promptly reporting the murder of an Arkansas resident by a Cherokee. Butler responded to this censure by informing the commissioner that "in twenty four hours after the murder, I repaired to the spot, in thirty six after [it] I wrote you fully explaining all the facts connected with the unfortunate affair." Butler suggested that the reason the commissioner had first heard of the incident from unofficial sources was that there was no direct mail route from the Indian country and as a result, "the mail often miscarries from two to three consecutive weeks." The irregularity of the mails was a constant source of complaint. The situation was further complicated by the fact that many field agents did not have copies of the treaties they were to enforce or the regulations with which they were to comply in the discharge of their duties.[31]

The publication date of the earliest composite copy of Indian Office regulations was 1850. Before then many new agents came to their jobs with virtually no knowledge of their duties. Correspondence files which might have helped new agents were usually missing or left in shambles by the disgruntled former occupant of an agency. Frequently, however, the rules and regulations of the Indian service appeared in newspapers receiving the War Department's patronage. Thoughtful supervisors aided their new subordinates, but the field service generally suffered from the lack of any compilation of instructions, regulations, and treaties. Even when orders and regulations were available to agents, they were sometimes "liable to double construction," and even honest agents might become subject to censure "entirely through ignorance for the want of [specific] instructions." What regulations did exist, moreover, were notoriously "blind" to the duties and needs of the field personnel because they were drafted by Washington bureaucrats who had little knowledge of frontier conditions. The Indian Office might have alleviated many of the problems facing its field personnel if it had maintained more effective liaison with them and had taken into account conditions in the Indian country when drafting regulations.[32]

The Van Buren administration made some notable efforts to provide the "supervisory power at Washington" with more information about the field service. Secretary of War Joel R. Poinsett, a South Carolina Unionist with great administrative talent, worked closely with Indian Commissioner Crawford to improve communications between Washington and the field and to secure more information about the activities of field personnel. Secretary Poinsett and Commissioner Crawford asked Congress to provide for an "Inspector of Indian affairs" who would visit the field personnel and "inspect their books, examine into their proceedings, view the condition of the different tribes, and furnish such a report as will enable the department to correct abuses, to understand and provide for the wants of the Indians, and generally, to extend over the whole matter a more complete supervision than has heretofore been found practical." The establishment of the office of Indian inspector might have led to tighter control by Washington officials and greater uniformity in administrative practices in the field, but Congress was not in the mood to expand the Indian service bureaucracy during the depression years of the late 1830s.[33]

Although Congress failed to provide for an Indian inspector, it did take notice of at least one aspect of the Indian service which needed reform. The law of 1834 allowed the president to assign military officers to serve as Indian agents. This was undoubtedly intended as an economy move, since military personnel assigned to Indian duty received no additional pay except traveling expenses. Under this provision, commanding officers at military posts on the frontier frequently received orders to serve as Indian agents, removal agents, or disbursing agents. Army officers like Colonel Zachary Taylor, who served a tour of duty in the Indian service in the mid-1830s, generally found the assignments dull, routine, time-consuming, and more onerous than their military assignments. They were especially reluctant to perform such duties without extra pay, since they always ran the risk of having Treasury Department auditors disallow expenses which were not provided by regulation but were necessary to effect good Indian-white relations. Although the Indian Office encouraged army officers to arrest traders selling whiskey to the Indians and to confiscate their merchandise, the military men often received little support from Washington officials when sly traders filed suit against them for false arrest and the illegal seizure of private property. Colonel Taylor, who found himself besieged with law suits for property damages stemming from direct orders he carried out while serving as an Indian agent, became intensely irate when Washington officials failed to reimburse him for his legal expenses. Taylor caustically informed the Indian Office that he was not a candidate for "martyrdom."[34]

As early as 1829, military commanders complained about the drain on army officers caused by assignment to Indian duty. Major General Alexander Macomb, the commanding general of the army, warned that "the requisitions for officers for the performance of various duties not connected with Regimental affairs, are so numerous, that it is seldom as many as two officers are present for duty with each company." Macomb cautioned that the continued assignment of army personnel to the Indian service would seriously impair the efficiency of the artillery and infantry battalions from which the secretary of war took them. Commanding officers at frontier posts heartily agreed. Not until Martin Van Buren's administration, however, did Congress seek to relieve the military of part of this burden.[35]

An act of July 5, 1838, placed severe restrictions on the assignment of army officers as acting paymasters or disbursing agents for the Indian Office. These positions were the most troublesome assigned to military men. Congress, however, had removed an important check on the financial operations of the Indian field service, since army officers had done much to uncover and prevent peculation. Congress had also complicated the fiscal operations of the department by failing to specify who would perform the duties previously assigned to military personnel. The result was that Commissioner Crawford had to "resort to such expedients as would best carry me through the year." Superintendents, agents, and subagents, already overburdened with their own duties, received instructions to take over the jobs of paymasters and disbursing agents. The law of 1838, moreover, failed to relieve the strain on the army caused by assignments to Indian duty, because the War Department continued to use military men to perform other tasks for the Indian Office whenever expedient.[36]

Just as Congress failed to provide the Indian service with paymasters and disbursing agents in 1838, it neglected to deal with many other pressing problems of Indian administration. Congress bypassed its opportunity to play a role in regulating the bureaucracy needed to remove the Indians to the West and did nothing to establish criteria for the necessary personnel. The law of 1834 failed to provide guidelines for supplying rations, medicine, and other items to emigrants and neglected to provide for close scrutiny of the actual removal operations. The need for such supervision was clearly evident as early as the first Choctaw removal in 1831–32, but Congress did not intercede to share in the regulation of Indian removal.[37]

One result of congressional inactivity in this area was that profiteering in contracts for Indian rations became an easy means for expectant capitalists to make their fortunes. When the Whigs took office in 1841, Secretary of War John Bell decided to launch an investigation of what were rumored to be "extraordinary proceedings" in the Indian country, and he sent Ethan Allen Hitchcock, recently promoted to lieutenant colonel, to the West with orders to ascertain the validity of the rumors. Hitchcock arrived in the West in early December and returned to Washington in mid-April of 1842, long after Bell and other Whigs had left President Tyler's cabinet in disgust over his opposition to their domestic programs. He brought with him a "bushel of documents" containing the testimony of Indians, agents, contractors, and others.[38]

Hitchcock's documents directly implicated government agents and citizens of the states adjoining the Indian country in frauds against the Indians. "It is certain," he claimed, "that no man can travel through the Indian country and leave it without being painfully convinced that the Indians were deeply and unmercifully wronged." What particularly angered Hitchcock was testimony revealing that "the agents of the Government were also the agents of the contractors and hence when the Indians complained to the Government agent the contractor's agent would give them no satisfaction." Hitchcock advised the War Department that "written contracts in this section of the country rarely show the persons interested." While "one or two names" appeared on the contract itself, there were always "more well selected partners" lurking in the background. Indeed, bidding for contracts had reached the state of an "art" or "science." Honest officials had to be careful, for "if you touch a contractor violently, you are in danger of galvanizing a whole community producing denunciations in quarters from which they might be least expected." To make matters worse for the Indians, the courts in neighboring states refused to permit them to testify in their own behalf against scheming contractors.[39]

In spite of the serious implications of the testimony Hitchcock compiled and congressional resolutions passed in May and August of 1842 calling for his documents, the Tyler administration decided not to permit a full disclosure of the findings. President Tyler later defended this action by observing that Hitchcock had obtained the testimony by "*ex parte* inquiries of various persons whose statements were necessarily without sanction of an oath, and which the persons implicated had had no opportunity to contradict or explain." In addition, he cautioned that there was little likelihood that the testimony could ever be verified, since the economy-minded Congress had passed a statute prohibiting the financing of any commissions or courts of inquiry except in cases of military court-martials. "The institution of [further] inquiries into the conduct of public agents, however urgent the necessity for such inquiry may be," Tyler charged, "is thereby virtually denied to the Executive." In asserting that he would invoke executive privilege and withhold Hitchcock's unsubstantiated findings from Congress, the president brushed aside rumors that he might be impeached for his action. He subsequently warned Congress that "if evils of magnitude shall arise in consequence of the law [prohibiting executive inquiries], I take to myself no portion of the responsibility." Tyler apparently agreed with Secretary of War John C. Spencer, who argued that "Indians can be made to say anything," and he steadfastly refused for almost nine months to release any of the testimony compiled by Hitchcock. Finally, on January 31, 1843, Tyler bowed to increasing Congressional pressure by sending the House of Representatives a copy of Hitchcock's material on alleged frauds along with a detailed statement defending the right of executive privilege and urging that numerous portions of the documents be kept "confidential."[40]

Tyler's reluctance to have Hitchcock's full report made public was undoubtedly partly political in nature. Influential traders, businessmen, and politicians continually flooded the Office of Indian Affairs with requests for special attention for their bids for contracts. Tyler, a president without a party after his break with Whig leaders, used the contracts for rations as political pawns to help promote his candidacy for election in 1844. Thomas Dowling, a former Harrison Whig from Terre Haute, Indiana, for example, received a contract for nearly sixty thousand dollars to remove six hundred Miami Indians from his state. Dowling told his brother that "the President was my friend in the whole matter, and no man ever acted more like a friend to another than he has. He would listen to no postponement, and gave the Indian Commissioner to understand that it was his *will.*" The Indiana contractor also boasted, "I will make at least ten thousand dollars, which will, with prudence, enable me to rear the superstructure of an independence for myself, family, and relations." Funds appropriated by Congress for Indian removal in the Jacksonian era were sufficient to provide healthy and safe emigration to the West, but legislators failed to take steps to guarantee that the money would be used in the intended manner, and the executive branch was too involved in partisan intrigues to check the avarice of the contractors.[41]

Another unfortunate oversight of Congress was its failure to provide regulations for the appointment of treaty commissioners. While the Senate had the right to refuse to ratify a treaty, the selection of treaty commissioners might have served as one method by which opponents of the removal policy and advocates of Indian rights could have monitored executive activities in Indian affairs. Negotiations in the field usually determined the future location of tribes and federal financial obligations to them. Careful vigilance over the nomination of treaty commissioners would have provided Congress with additional leverage in the treaty-making process. Throughout this period, however, presidents used their own standards in choosing commissioners.[42]

President Jackson's criteria for selecting treaty negotiators reflected his attitude toward Indian removal in general. He appointed men who had the greatest influence over the tribe, since his object was to secure the signing of removal treaties as quickly as possible. Jackson also paid attention to petitions from state or territorial legislators and congressmen. His appointees included secretaries of war, commissioners of Indian affairs, superintendents, agents, army officers, Democrats temporarily out of office, state officials, merchants, fur traders, planters, close personal friends, and even a Protestant minister. Jackson's successors continued the practice of choosing men with considerable influence over the tribes. The emphasis was clearly on the rapid negotiation of removal treaties.[43]

Friends of the Indians frequently urged that only "able men—men of sound judgment, capable of patient investigation and deliberation—of dignified personal deportment, tempered with conciliatory manners" should receive appointment as treaty commissioners. Some of the men selected to negotiate treaties undoubtedly met these qualifications, but the political nature of the position and the tremendous emphasis on speedy removal was not conducive to such appointments. A Whig critic of the treaty-making process observed in 1851 that "the business of negotiating treaties with the Indian tribes has heretofore been attended with manifold abuses and an incalculable waste of public money."[44]

Congress also failed to provide adequate checks for another influential class of field employees, the interpreters. According to the law of 1834, agents had the authority to appoint Indian interpreters who had the critical task of putting "every important transaction between Government agents and Indians" into a language the native could understand. Their linguistic ability influenced events in the field far beyond what their actual position in the Indian service hierarchy suggested. As one Indian commissioner recognized, "Everything depends on their capacity and fidelity." Working without adequate supervision or for their own ends, they could seriously prejudice Indian understanding of federal policy. There was growing recognition in the field service during the Jacksonian era that the government needed "men of firmness and integrity of character to act as Indian interpreters" and also men "firmly attached to the cause of emigration." Some interpreters were men of "unexceptionable character," but agent Henry R. Schoolcraft warned in 1839 that "we often suffer from the blunders of interpreters, who are not only illiterate, but not trustworthy." Schoolcraft, who argued that even "trifling mistakes [by an interpreter] may be injurious" in the long run, tried to convince the Indian Office to publish "a compendious dictionary, and general grammar of the Indian languages." He even suggested the establishment of an academy to train "moral men" in the "principles of Indian grammar," but his plans succumbed to the cry for retrenchment in government expenditures.[45]

One of the major difficulties in obtaining men of good character to serve as interpreters was the meager salary of three hundred dollars provided by the act of 1834. Field officials had to compete with fur traders for competent interpreters, and they quickly discovered that the salary set by law was insufficient to obtain the best men. Commissioner Crawford warned in 1839 that three hundred dollars was "a sum utterly inadequate to the support of a family, scarcely equal to the maintenance of an individual, and altogether disproportionate to the services he ought to render." Congress occasionally responded to individual requests for higher wages for interpreters, but it did not raise the salary of these officials as a whole. Even when Congress acted favorably on individual petitions, a year or more often passed by before an interpreter received his extra pay. Indian commissioners warned that "true policy demands that the compensation . . . [provided interpreters] be sufficient to remunerate capable men, and place them beyond the reach of temptation to do wrong," but they remained at the bottom of the pay scale.[46]

The question of salaries in general caused problems throughout the period. Commissioner T. Hartley Crawford advised the War Department in 1839 that members of the field service were grossly underpaid. "The magnitude of the interests committed to them, and the responsible duties expected of them," he maintained, "entitle them to that measure of compensation, which will probably enable the department to select incumbents of proper qualifications." The House of Representatives, however, continually stressed the need to economize and placed strict limits on the number of field employees, in spite of the Indian Office's responsibility for a large number of tribes scattered across a wide frontier. Throughout this period, government compensation rates remained close to the subsistence level, and the House vigorously opposed Indian Office attempts to provide "extra allowances" to field personnel for additional duties performed by them. Congressmen reasoned that federal employees should perform all tasks assigned them at their regular wages.[47]

In spite of congressional decrees prohibiting extra pay, Indian Office clerks and field personnel expected and demanded additional remuneration for "special duties." Oftentimes such activities actually saved the administrative machinery of Indian affairs from falling apart. William Armstrong, the Choctaw agent, for example, assumed the extra duties of disbursing agent in 1839 because Congress had failed to provide any replacement for the army disbursing agents it removed from Indian duty. Armstrong had to increase his bond from two hundred to forty thousand dollars, yet as late as 1851 his heirs still had not received the extra allowance promised him by the Indian Office. When Superintendent William Clark at Saint Louis died in 1838, his chief clerk, George Maguire, who had served under him for nearly a decade, took full command of the office pending instructions from Washington, which arrived seven months later. The Indian Office refused to pay Maguire for his extra services because the commissioner had not officially asked him to perform them. The fact that Maguire and Armstrong had provided badly needed continuity and assistance did not interest economy-minded bureaucrats and congressmen in Washington.[48]

Congressional emphasis on economy had a deleterious impact on many other aspects of Indian administration. In order to reduce expenses of the Indian Office "as far and as fast as practicable," for example, Congress encouraged the discontinuance of agencies where only small numbers of Indians remained. The law which created the position of Indian commissioner in 1832 specifically granted the president authority to discontinue agencies as soon as the Indians emigrated westward. Under this legislation, the Choctaw Agency in Mississippi closed its doors in November, 1832, before the last group of emigrants departed because President Jackson believed that the six thousand Indians remaining in the state were an insufficient number to warrant an agent. Other agencies were consolidated or discontinued as removal progressed. This policy had unfortunate consequences for, as one army officer observed, "Indians do not recognize any government officer between their immediate agent and the President."[49]

Congress failed to realize that the ratification of an Indian treaty did not immediately end the problem of Indian-white relations in states or territories where Indians refused to emigrate in spite of a few scratches on a piece of parchment. Indeed, the closing of the Choctaw Agency in Mississippi left the Indians in an extremely precarious position. Landless because they were cheated out of their allotments provided by the treaty of 1830, the Choctaws were an outcast group in a society based on rather clear-cut and mutually exclusive social relations between whites and blacks. Until the Bureau of Indian Affairs "rediscovered" the Choctaw presence in Mississippi in 1918, the Indians lived an existence worse than that of the average black in that state. Closing agencies to promote economy in government did not foster tranquil Indian-white relations in areas where Indians stayed behind, nor did it assure the faithful performance of treaty obligations to the Indians choosing to emigrate.[50]

Congressional parsimony and executive efforts to trim expenses had other serious consequences for the administration of Indian affairs. President Jackson had discovered the evils of the counter-warrant system of spending money appropriated for one purpose for another during his first days in office, and his administration officially condemned the practice. Democrats and Whigs in Congress expended tremendous energy to simplify the system of public accounts and promote efficiency in fiscal operations, but the needs of the field personnel often dictated the continuation of the counterwarrant system in order to comply with treaty stipulations and to promote better Indian-white relations when money promised by the government for a specific purpose failed to arrive in time. Sometimes counterrequisitions were used for nefarious purposes. Agents might draw upon unexpended balances accredited to their accounts and deposit them in banks of their own choosing or loan the money to individuals or other departments of the government. The result was that the Indian Office could not readily ascertain the status of funds appropriated for Indian affairs, and its fiscal records were in a state of "inextricable confusion." The accounting procedures of the department at times caused more problems than the Indians. While all presidential administrations sought to correct these difficulties, the counterwarrant system remained in use because it often provided the only available source of funds to execute federal Indian policy.[51]

Much of the blame for the ineffectiveness of the Indian service during the Jacksonian era rests with the limited vision of the chief executives. These leaders were too concerned with partisan politics and removing the Indians as cheaply and as quickly as possible to provide adequate administrative machinery and safeguards against corruption. Congress and the American public, however, must also share a considerable portion of the blame. Congress was more interested in reducing expenditures and guarding its own prerogatives than in facilitating the administration of Indian affairs. Legislative leaders were too involved with other issues deemed important by their constituents and too busy with political fence-mending to devote time to the development of a competent Indian service. Proposals to reform field operations often failed to win congressional approval because legislators feared that "unnecessary increases" in federal expenditures might endanger pet projects of influential constituents. Congressional parsimony even hampered efforts to investigate alleged abuses and frauds in the Indian service. Opposition leaders were always eager to find fault with the administration of Indian affairs, but they offered few alternatives to correct abuses. Whigs as well as Democrats failed to save the Indian service from the vicissitudes of partisanship.[52]

Another important reason why government officials failed to take remedial action to provide cohesiveness and direction to the administrative machinery of Indian affairs was that the Indians did not play a meaningful role in the American political system. Congressional inaction on the Territorial Bill of 1834 left the Indians outside the American political process, but treaties and federal laws nevertheless subjected them to American supervision. As early as election day in 1828, agent Henry R. Schoolcraft noted that one of the principal defects in American Indian policy was that the Indians were "politically a nonentity." Because of this, he argued, "the whole Indian race is not, in the political scales, worth one white man's vote." The solution to the problem was apparent to Schoolcraft: "If the Indian were raised to the right of giving his suffrage, a plenty of politicians, on the frontiers, would enter into plans to better him." As long as the Indians remained outside the political process, Schoolcraft warned, congressmen would only sponsor legislation promoting Indian interests "on a pinch" whenever it would be expedient to do so and the legislation would be "dropped in a hurry" once public apathy returned.[53]

Schoolcraft's predictions were farsighted. The defeat of the Territorial Bill of 1834 left the Indians subject to American wardship but unable to participate in the decision-making process responsible for that supervision. An optimistic frontier newspaper editor expressed the belief in 1845 that "the American press" would act as a "great lever of public opinion" and aid in preventing "abuses in the management of Indian Affairs" from escaping with "greater impunity than other branches of the public service." Yet throughout the Jacksonian era there was no constituency with sufficient voting power to influence Congress or the president that protested against the maladministration of Indian affairs or the gross profiteering at the expense of the health and safety of Indian emigrants. The Indians remained, as the compiler of the Seventh Census noted, merely an "unrepresented" population group under American stewardship.[54]

NOTES

1. See Wallace D. Farnham, " 'The Weakened Spring of Government': A Study in Nineteenth-Century American History," *American Historical Review* 68 (April 1963): 676, 679; M. I. Ostrogorski, *Democracy and the Organization of Political Parties,* Trans. Frederick Clarke, 2 vols. (London: Macmillan & Co., Ltd., 1902), 2: 550; Malcolm Rohrbough, *The Land Office Business: The Settlement and Administration of American Public Lands, 1789–1837* (New York: Oxford University Press, 1968); Young, *Redskins, Ruffleshirts and Rednecks,* pp. 172–93; Eblen, *Governors and Territorial Government,* pp. 237–70, 317–18.

2. Ostrogorski, *Democracy,* 2: 550; Crawford to Poinsett, December 30, 1839, *House Document 103,* 26th Cong., 1st sess., p. 10. For references to works dealing with the entrepreneurial spirit in the Jacksonian era, see chapter 2, note 41.

3. U.S., *Stat.,* 1: 331, 4: 735–38; Roy W. Meyer, *History of the Santee Sioux: United States Indian Policy on Trial* (Lincoln: University of Nebraska Press, 1967): 54; Herring to Mason, July 12, 1834, in Carter and Bloom, *Territorial Papers,* 13: 178. For evidence that Taliaferro's predicament was not unique, see Chester L. Guthrie and Leo L. Gerald, "Upper Missouri Agency: An Account of Indian Administration on the Frontier," *Pacific Historical Review* 10 (March 1941): 49–52. The standard account of the congressional legislation of 1834 is Prucha, *American Indian Policy,* pp. 250–73.

4. U.S., *Stat.,* 4: 735–37.

5. Ibid., 4: 735.

6. Herring to Porter, July 2, 1834, Herring to Dodge, June 22, 1836, Harris to Dodge, July 26, 1838, in Carter and Bloom, *Territorial Papers,* 12: 780–81, 27: 63–67, 1045; Revised Regulations No. 3, June 1, 1837, IA, Misc. Records, 2: 242, RG 75, NA; Brown to Harris, April 3, 1838, IA, LR, Misc., RG75, NA; Crawford to Poinsett, December 30, 1839, *House Document 103,* 26th Cong., 1st sess., pp. 3, 6; Testimony of Crawford, March 12, 1842, *House Report 741,* 27th Cong., 2d sess., p. 37; M[edill] to Governor Joseph Lane, August 31, 1848, IA, LS, 41: 207–8, RG 75, NA; Commissioner of Indian Affairs, *Annual Report* (1849), p. 955; John E. Sunder, *Joshua Pilcher: Fur Trader and Indian Agent* (Norman: University of Oklahoma Press, 1968), pp. 145–48. Also see Eblen, *Governors and Territorial Government,* pp. 268–69.

7. U.S., *Stat.,* 4: 735; Commissioner of Indian Affairs, *Annual Report* (1848), p. 391, (1849), pp. 952–53; Gallaher, "Indian Agent," p. 51.

8. U.S., *Stat.,* 1: 68, 4: 735; Cha[rles] Thomson to [Winthrop] Sargent, March 11, 1789, Herring to Porter, July 2, 1834, Herring to Dodge, June

22, 1836, in Carter and Bloom, *Territorial Papers*, 2: 189; 12: 780, 27: 63; Crawford to Poinsett, December 30, 1839, *House Document 103*, 26th Cong., 1st sess., p. 3; *Congressional Globe*, 28th Cong., 2d sess., appendix, p. 44; M[edill] to Lane, August 31, 1848, IA, LS, 41: 207–8, RG 75, NA; Eblen, *Governors and Territorial Government*, pp. 241–42, 257, 268–70, 299–300. William M. Neil's study of "The Territorial Governor as Indian Superintendent in the Trans-Mississippi West," *Mississippi Valley Historical Review* 43 (September 1956): 213–37, is an excellent survey of the problems stemming from combining the two offices.

9. Hemans, *Stevens Thomson Mason*, pp. 252–54; Schoolcraft, *Memoirs*, p. 396; Eblen, *Governors and Territorial Government*, pp. 265, 267, 269, 299; Henry P. Beers, *The Western Military Frontier, 1815–1846* (Philadelphia: University of Pennsylvania Press, 1935), p. 144.

10. U.S., *Stat.*, 4: 735–38. Subsequent legislation provided for additional agencies; ibid., 5: 163. See John E. Sunder's biography of *Joshua Pilcher* for one of the best accounts of an Indian agent yet published.

11. U.S., *Stat.*, pp. 736–38.

12. Revised Regulations No. 3, June 1, 1837, IA, Misc. Records, 2: 243–67, RG 75, NA; Brown to Harris, April 3, 1838, IA, LR, Misc., RG 75, NA; Testimony of Crawford, March 12, 1842, *House Report 741*, 27th Cong., 2d sess., p. 37; C[rawford] to Secretary of War, December 8, 1841, Crawford to James M. Porter, July 26, 1843, IA, Report Books, 3: 62, 472, RG 75, NA; Gallaher, "Indian Agent," pp. 37, 50.

13. *McCoy's Register* 1 (1835): 4; J. L. Bean to Cass, February 15, 1835, IA, LR, Upper Missouri Agency, RG 75, NA; Sunder, *Joshua Pilcher*, pp. 110, 136; Doty to Lawe, June 12, 15, August 7, 1842, Lawe to N & H Weed Co., August 1, 1842, Lawe to Lewis, February 13, 1844, Lawe Papers.

14. Sunder, *Joshua Pilcher*, p. 122; Johnson to Milroy, March 8, 19, 1840, Milroy Papers.

15. Crawford to Poinsett, December 30, 1839, *House Document 103*, 26th Cong., 1st sess., pp. 4–5; U.S., *Stat.* 4: 564. Also see Reduction in Agencies under Act of July 9, 1832, IA, Misc. Records, 1: 55, RG 75, NA.

16. U.S., *Stat.*, 4: 737. Also see Revised Regulations No. 3, June 1, 1837, IA, Misc. Records, 2: 248, RG 75, NA; Testimony of Crawford, March 12, 1842, *House Report 741*, 27th Cong., 2d sess., pp. 38–39.

17. See Department of State *Register of Officers* (1829), pp. 82–89, (1831), pp. 95–102, (1833), pp. 88–93, (1835), pp. 80–85, (1837), pp. 91–99, (1839), pp. 82–89, (1841), pp. 95–101, (1843), pp. 163–71, (1845), pp. 16–18, (1847), pp. 135–37, (1849), pp. 133–35.

18. Herring to Mason, July 12, 1834, H[arris] to Crawford & Balch, October 7, 1836, IA, LS, 13: 177–78, 20: 14, RG 75, NA; T. A. Howard to Milroy, April 6, 1835, Milroy Papers; Revised Regulations No. 3 and No.

5, May 13, 1837, June 1, 1837, IA, Misc. Records, 2: 243, 285–91, RG 75, NA; Harris to Dodge, September 13, 1838, in Carter and Bloom, *Territorial Papers*, 27: 1066; Wm. Gra[y]son to Poinsett, April 14, 1840, Poinsett Papers; Doty to Lawe, June 29, July 23, 1842, Lawe to David Jones, August 6, 1842, Lawe to Doty, November 28, 1842, Lawe Papers. Also see note 19. For a biographical sketch of Tipton, see Paul W. Gates, Introduction to Blackburn, *John Tipton Papers*, 1: 3–53.

19. See Jos[eph] M. Street to Hitchcock, January 18, 1839, *House Document 229*, 25th Cong., 3rd sess., p. 60; Gra[y]son to Poinsett, April 14, 1840, Poinsett Papers; C[rawford] to Stuart, February 12, 1842, IA, LS, 31: 456–57, RG 75, NA; Lawe to Doty, November 28, 1842, Lawe Papers; G. W. Ewing to Milroy, March 6, 1845, Milroy Papers; G. B. Flood to Medill, March 9, 1846, M. H. Harvey to Andrews, December 14, 1846, Andrews to Medill, December 24, 1846, Medill Papers. Also see note 18; Sunder, *Joshua Pilcher*, pp. 141–43, 162–66; Meyers, *Santee Sioux*, p. 63.

20. Jackson to Coffee, March 22, 1829, in Bassett, *Correspondence of Andrew Jackson*, 4: 14; Adams, *Memoirs*, 11: 156; Fillmore to T. Childs, December 20, 1840, in Frank H. Severance, ed., *Millard Fillmore Papers*, 2 vols. (Buffalo, N.Y.: Buffalo Historical Society, 1907), 2: 215; Milo M. Quaife, ed., *The Diary of James K. Polk during His Presidency, 1845 to 1849*, 4 vols. (Chicago: McClurg & Co., 1910), 2: 314.

21. The above paragraph is based on an examination of the incoming and outgoing correspondence of the Indian Office. See IA, Records of the Employees Section, Registers of Applications and Recommendations for Appointments (hereafter cited as Registers), RG 75, NA; IA, Registers, LR, vols. 2–36, RG 75, NA; IA, LS, vols. 5–41, RG 75, NA. The quotation is from H. H. Robinson to Medill, November 14, 1848, Medill Papers.

22. The above paragraph is based on an examination of the outgoing correspondence of the Indian Office. See IA, LS, vols. 5–41, RG 75, NA. Also see *United States' Telegraph*, September 27, 1830; Reduction in Agencies under Act of July 9, 1832, IA, Misc. Records, 1: 55, RG 75, NA; Statement of removals from office in Indian Department since 1789, enclosed in Crawford to Poinsett, March 6, 1840, *House Document 132*, 26th Cong., 1st sess., p. 16; William G. Brownlow to [Thomas A. R.] Nelson, March 8, 1841, Thomas A. R. Nelson Papers, McClung Historical Collection, Lawson McGhee Library, Knoxville, Tenn.; *Madisonian* (Washington, D.C.), April 12, 1841, *Richmond Enquirer*, May 21, 1841; B[ell] to [Tyler], July 28, 1841, plus enclosure, S[pencer] to same, April 1, 1842, plus enclosure, SW, LS, President, 4: 60–61, 105–9, RG 107, NA; *Detroit Daily Advertiser*, March 28, 1843; W. L. Marcy to J. M. Porter, May 19, 1845, Marcy Papers, Library of Congress, Washington, D.C.; *United States Magazine and Democratic Review* 27 (November 1850):

388; Fish, *Civil Service*, pp. 147–48, 152–53, 158, appendix C, p. 252; Robert J. Morgan, *A Whig Embattled: The Presidency under John Tyler* (Lincoln: University of Nebraska Press, 1954), pp. 83–86, 165–71; White, *The Jacksonians*, pp. 20–21, 309, 348–49.

23. Unsigned letter, June 10, 1835, Notes and endorsement by Jackson, June 29, 1835, enclosed in Geo[rge] L. Kinnard to Jackson, June 15, 29, 1835, IA, LR, Misc., RG 75, NA; *United States' Telegraph*, April 21, 1829; Sunder, *Joshua Pilcher*, pp. 150–51, 162. For an example of an agent who used the "*patronage*, & *money* of the Government" to influence public opinion, see the charges made against John Phagan in Jos-[eph] M. White to [Jackson], January 19, 1832, plus enclosures, in Carter and Bloom, *Territorial Papers*, 24: 633–35.

24. White, *The Jacksonians*, p. 329; O. G. Catis to Brown, August 14, 1849, Brown Papers, Filson History Club; William L. D. Ewing to [Van Buren], October 7, 1838, IA, LR, St. Peters Agency, RG 75, NA. For the applications for appointments, see IA, Registers, LR, vols. 2–36, RG 75, NA; IA, Records of the Employees Sections, Registers, RG 75, NA.

25. The above paragraph is based on an examination of the correspondence of the field agents. See IA, Registers, LR, vols. 2–36, RG 75, NA. The quotations are from Schoolcraft, *Personal Memoirs*, pp. 592, 675; Stuart to Lawe, September 2, 1842, Lawe Papers.

26. Wiley Thompson to Gibson, April 27, 1835, in *American State Papers: Military Affairs*, 6: 553. Also see Crawford to Poinsett, Unofficial, September 4, 1839, Poinsett Papers; White, *The Jacksonians*, p. 327. LeRoy H. Fischer has edited a series of articles by his graduate students on the agents to the major southern tribes relocated in the West. The biographical profiles contain useful information, but they must be used with care since they are of uneven quality. See "United States Indian Agents to the Five Civilized Tribes," *Chronicles of Oklahoma* 50 (Winter 1972–73): 410–57, and 51 (Spring 1973): 34–84. The National Archives has prepared historical sketches for each jurisdiction in the field for which the Indian Office maintained a correspondence file. The sketches include a description of the boundaries and tribes for each jurisdiction and the names and dates of appointment of the field officials. See Edward E. Hill, comp., *Historical Sketches for Jurisdictional and Subject Headings Used for the Letters Received by the Office of Indian Affairs, 1824–1880*, IA, Microfilm edition, T1105, RG 75, NA. Useful information on field officials also appears in Department of State, *Register of Officers* (1829–49).

27. See Willoughby M. Babcock, Jr., "Major Lawrence Taliaferro, Indian Agent," *Mississippi Valley Historical Review* 11 (December 1924): 358–75; Gallaher, "Indian Agent," p. 48; Walter Hough, "Henry Rowe Schoolcraft," in Johnson and Malone, *Dictionary of American Biography*,

16: 456–57; Harlow Lindley, "William Clark—the Indian Agent," *Proceedings of the Mississippi Valley Historical Association* 2 (1908–1909): 63–75; Clipping from *The Globe*, September 15, 1838, Schoolcraft Papers; Schoolcraft, *Personal Memoirs*, p. 608; John L. Loos, "William Clark: Indian Agent," *Kansas Quarterly* 3 (Fall 1971): 29–37.

28. See Foreman, *Five Civilized Tribes*, p. 424. Not all Washington bureaucrats appreciated the lengthy reports of the field agents. See Lea to Commissioner of Indian Affairs, October 4, 1841, IA, LR, Misc., RG 75, NA.

29. Abigail Houston to Henry B. Milroy, May 3, 1840, Milroy Papers; J. T. Canbey to Eaton, November 9, 1829, IA, LR, Misc., RG 75, NA; Butler to Franklin H. Elmore, May 9, 1843, Elmore Papers, Library of Congress, Washington, D.C.; Schoolcraft to Medill, September 30, 1848, Medill Papers. For a biographical sketch of Butler's career, see Carolyn T. Foreman, "Pierce Mason Butler," *Chronicles of Oklahoma* 30 (Spring 1952): 6–28. One Indian agent became a fugitive from justice after "barbarously" murdering a trader in the Creek Nation. See *Northern Standard* (Clarksville, Texas), September 4, 1844.

30. See notes 31 and 32. The problems mentioned above remained unresolved after the Jacksonian era. See Alban W. Hoopes, *Indian Affairs and their Administration with Special Reference to the Far West, 1849–1860* (Philadelphia: University of Pennsylvania Press, 1932), p. 238.

31. Butler to Crawford, February 23, 1842, in Foreman, "Pierce Mason Butler," p. 11. Also see Sunder, *Joshua Pilcher*, p. 113; note 32.

32. Stokes to Harris, August 20, 1836, in Foster, "Career of Montfort Stokes," p. 44; Schoolcraft to Harris, October 30, 1837, IA, Michigan Superintendency, Mackinac Agency, LS, RG 75, NA; Department of State, *Register of Officers* (1837), p. 90 n; Polke to Milroy, January 28, 1840, Milroy Papers; C[rawford] to Schoolcraft, August 28, 1841, same to Johnston, January 8, 1842, IA, LS, 21: 63, 31: 357, RG 75, NA; Stuart to Lawe, August 10, September 2, 1842, May 16, 1843, Lawe to Doty, August 21, 1842, September 7, 30, October 22, 1842, March 17, April 10, June 10, October 16, 1843, Doty to Lawe, October 14, 1842, Lawe Papers; *United States Magazine and Democratic Review* 18 (May 1846): 333–34; Philander Prescott to Medill, September 15, 1848, Medill Papers; Clippings on Indian Affairs, Schoolcraft Papers. For the first published compilation of Indian Office regulations, see U.S., Office of Indian Affairs, *Office Copy of the Laws, Regulations, Etc. of the Indian Bureau, 1850* (Washington, D.C.: Gideon & Co., Printers, 1850).

33. H. M. Rutledge to Poinsett, December 22, 1837, D. Levy to Poinsett, January 19, 1839, Poinsett Papers; Sanford to Hitchcock, November 18, 1838, Hitchcock Papers; Secretary of War, *Annual Report* (1838), p

113; Crawford to Poinsett, December 30, 1839, *House Document 103,* 26th Cong., 1st sess., p. 8. For additional information on Poinsett, see Putnam, *Joel Roberts Poinsett;* J. Fred Rippy, *Joel R. Poinsett: Versatile American* (Durham: Duke University Press, 1935).

34. U.S., *Stat.,* 4: 736; Herring to Lt. Colonel Whiting, July 19, 1834, Herring to Zachary Taylor, July 22, 1834, Harris to Taylor, October 7, 1836, IA, LS, 13: 223–25, 238–42, 20: 16, RG 75, NA; Cass to Schoolcraft, Private, October 20, 1834, Schoolcraft Papers; Report of the Commissary General of Subsistence, November 12, 1835, in Secretary of War, *Annual Report* (1835), p. 293; General Order No. 43, June 28, 1836, Records of the Adjutant General's Office (hereafter cited as AGO), General Order Books, 7: 231–32, RG 94, NA; Taylor to Harris, September 4, 1836, LR, Prairie du Chien Agency, RG 75, NA; Harris to G. W. Jones, February 4, 1837, Brig. Genl. Geo. M. Brooke to Harris, February 19, 1837, Harris to Dodge, October 6, 1837, in Carter and Bloom, *Territorial Papers,* 27: 725, 738, 860–61; Revised Regulations No. 3 and 5, May 13, 1837, June 1, 1837, IA, Misc. Records, 2: 248–50, 291–92, RG 75, NA; Brown to Harris, April 3, 1838, IA, LR, Misc., RG 75, NA; H[itchcock] to Col. W. J. Worth, April 18, 1841, Hitchcock Papers; Robert P. Fogerty, "An Institutional Study of the Territorial Courts in the Old Northwest, 1788–1848" (Ph.D. diss., University of Minnesota, 1942), pp. 383–85. In 1843 Taylor, then a brigadier general, ransomed two American boys from the Comanche Indians for four hundred and fifty dollars, only to be told that the Indian Office lacked sufficient funds to reimburse him. See C[rawford] to Spencer, January 6, 1843, IA, Report Books, 3: 352, RG 75, NA.

35. Secretary of War, *Annual Report* (1829), p. 28; Report of Macomb, November 1832, Army Headquarters, LS, 4/2: 185, RG 108, NA; Taylor to Harris, September 4, 1836, LR, Prairie du Chien Agency, RG 75, NA; Harris to Jones, February 4, 1837, in Carter and Bloom, *Territorial Papers,* 27: 725.

36. U.S., *Stat.,* 5: 260; Croffut, *Diary of Major-General Ethan Allen Hitchcock,* pp. 114–17; C. S. to Hitchcock, July 7, 1838, Hitchcock to Harris, July 20, 1838, Sandford to Hitchcock, November 18, 1838, E. A. Hitchcock to Judge Hitchcock, March 18, 1839, E. A. H[itchcock] to Worth, April 18, 1841, Hitchcock Papers; Harris to Brown, July 13, 1838, Crawford to Dodge and Lucas, June 17, 1839, IA, LS, 24: 494, 26: 371, RG 75, NA; Crawford to McKissack, June 15, 1839, in Carter and Bloom, *Territorial Papers,* 27: 1246; Special Orders No. 48, July 5, 1839, AGO, Special Orders Books, 3: 391, RG 94, NA; Crawford to Poinsett, December 30, 1839, *House Document 103,* 26th Cong., 1st sess., pp. 6, 10–11; Tipton to Gales and Seaton, [January 15, 1839], in Blackburn, *John Tipton Papers,* 3: 797; Sunder, *Joshua Pilcher,* pp. 148–49. Cf. Beers, *Western Military Frontier,* p. 109.

37. The law of 1834 merely specified that "the President . . . is hereby, authorized to prescribe such rules and regulations as he may think fit, for carrying into effect the various provisions of this act, and of any other act relating to Indian affairs, and for the settlement of the accounts of the Indian department." See U.S., *Stat.*, 4: 738.

38. B[ell] to [Tyler], May 31, 1841, SW, LS, President, 4: 48–49, RG 107, NA; Resolution . . . in relation to certain malpractices in the Indian Department, June 12, 1841, *Senate Document 18*, 27th Cong., 1st sess., p. 1; Bell to Abraham Martin, Confidential, August 7, 1841, Extract of Special Orders No. 68, September 28, 1841, Lea to Hitchcock, September 28, 1841, Hitchcock Papers; Croffut, *Diary of Major-General Ethan Allen Hitchcock*, p. 157. For information concerning Hitchcock's investigations and his final report to the War Department, see Grant Foreman, ed., *A Traveler in Indian Territory: The Journal of Ethan Allen Hitchcock* (Cedar Rapids: Torch Press, 1930); Report of Hitchcock, April 28, 1842, plus enclosures, *House Report 271*, 27th Cong., 3d sess., pp. 23–155.

39. Hitchcock to Spencer, April 28, 1842, *House Report 271*, 27th Cong., 3d sess., pp. 32, 38; Foreman, *Journal of Ethan Allen Hitchcock*, p. 69; Hitchcock to Spencer, February 4, 1842, IA, LR, Creek Agency, RG 75, NA. See chapter 5 for a discussion of the legal jurisdiction in the Indian country.

40. Tyler to the House of Representatives, January 31, 1843, *House Report 271*, 27th Cong., 3d sess., pp. 19–23; Croffut, *Diary of Major-General Ethan Allen Hitchcock*, p. 157. For details of the ensuing conflict between the House of Representatives and President Tyler over the disclosure of Hitchcock's findings, see ibid., pp. 156–58; *House Journal*, 27th Cong., 2d sess., pp. 465–69, 831–32, 1183, 1284–91; *Congressional Globe*, 27th Cong., 2d sess., pp. 579–81; Report of James Cooper, February 25, 1843, Tyler to the House of Representatives, January 31, 1843, *House Report 271*, 27th Cong., 3d sess., pp. 1–23. Herman Wolkinson, in his study of the "Demands of Congressional Committees for Executive Papers," *Federal Bar Journal* 10 (April 1949): pp. 115–19, 150, contends that Tyler's position was a justified reiteration of a principle of executive privilege first established by Thomas Jefferson. For Hitchcock's report, see note 38.

41. Report of Cooper, February 25, 1843, *House Report 271*, 27th Cong., 3d sess., p. 2; Thomas Dowling to John Dowling, April 11, 24, 1844, John Dowling Papers, Indiana State Historical Society, Indianapolis, Indiana; Dowling to Crawford, May 6, 27, 1844, IA, LR, Miami Agency Emigration, RG 75, NA. For Dowling's political affiliation, see table showing the names of Indiana legislators, 1837–38, Milroy Papers; Dowling to Miller, Private, February 20, 1845, Medill Papers.

42. See *Congressional Globe*, 27th Cong., 2d sess., p. 664; Lea to A. H. H. Stuart, February 10, 1851, *House Executive Document 26*, 31st Cong., 2d sess., p. 4. For the salary of the treaty commissioners and Indian Office regulations governing them, see U.S., *Stat.*, 1: 54; Revised Regulations No. 3, June 1, 1837, IA, Misc. Records, 2: 258–60, RG 75, NA. Cf. White, *The Jacksonians*, pp. 117–18.

43. The above paragraph is based on an examination of a wide variety of biographical sources relating to the commissioners who negotiated Indian treaties. For a list of commissioners who negotiated and signed treaties that were later ratified by the Senate, see John M. Martin, *List of Documents Concerning the Negotiation of Ratified Indian Treaties, 1801–1869* (Washington, D.C.: National Archives, 1949), appendix, pp. 169–71.

44. [Hitchcock] to Spencer, December 21, 1841, Hitchcock Papers; Lea to Stuart, February 10, 1851, *House Executive Document 26*, 31st Cong., 2d sess., p. 4.

45. U.S., *Stat.*, 4: 737; Crawford to Poinsett, December 30, 1839, *House Document 103*, 26th Cong., 1st sess., p. 5; Peter S. Du Ponceau to Schoolcraft, October 11, 1834, Schoolcraft Papers; D. L. Clinch to Brigadier General R. Jones, April 20, 1835, *American State Papers: Military Affairs*, 6: 533; Revised Regulations No. 3, June 1, 1837, IA, Misc. Records, 2: 247–48; Commissioner of Indian Affairs, *Annual Report* (1837), p. 528; James Logan to Medill, January 22, 1848, Medill Papers; George Combe, *Notes on the United States of North America during a Phrenological Visit in 1838–9–40*, 3 vols. (Edinburgh: McLachlan, Stewart & Company, 1841), 2: 348; Report of Schoolcraft, September 30, 1839, in Commissioner of Indian Affairs, *Annual Report* (1839), p. 481; Schoolcraft, *Personal Memoirs*, pp. 583, 626, 636, 637. Cf. White, *The Jacksonians*, pp. 117–18.

46. U.S., *Stat.*, 4: 737, 6: 661; Sunder, *Joshua Pilcher*, pp. 113–14; Herring to Pilcher, September 17, 1835, IA, LS, 17: 101–2, RG 75, NA; Crawford to Poinsett, December 30, 1839, *House Document 103*, 26th Cong., 1st sess., p. 5; Commissioner of Indian Affairs, *Annual Report* (1837), p. 528; Report of Schoolcraft, September 30, 1839, in Commissioner of Indian Affairs, *Annual Report* (1839), p. 481.

47. Crawford to Poinsett, December 30, 1839, *House Document 103*, 26th Cong., 1st sess., p. 4; Report of Gilmer, May 23, 1842, *House Report 741*, 27th Cong., 2d sess., pp. 25–26; White, *The Jacksonians*, p. 376. For an excellent summary of the major decisions concerning "extra pay" allowances for governmental officials between 1832 and 1844, see W. L. Devereaux to Pierce Mason Butler, July 1, 1844, Butler Papers, South Carolinian Library, University of South Carolina, Columbia, S.C.

48. Chiefs of the First Christian Party of Oneida [Indians] to George
Boyd, November 19, 1838, Doty to Nathan Goodell, June 29, 1842, Doty
to Lawe, August 9, 1842, Lawe Papers; Spencer to [Tyler], February 4,
March 10, 1842, SW, LS, President, 4: 96–97, 103–5, RG 107, NA; Testi-
mony of Devereaux, April 20, 1842, *House Report 741*, 27th Cong., 2d
sess., pp. 57–59; C[rawford] to Butler, February 20, 1843, IA, LS, 33:
302–3, RG 75, NA; Devereaux to Butler, July 1, 1844, P. M. Butler Papers;
John Luce to Poinsett, October 16, 1847, Poinsett Papers; Report of John
Crowell, January 29, 1851, *House Report 17*, 31st Cong., 2d sess., pp. 1–6;
Sunder, *Joshua Pilcher*, p. 144.

49. *Arkansas Gazette*, October 13, 1829, U.S., *Stat.*, 4: 564; Reduction
in Agencies under Act of July 9, 1832, IA, Misc. Records, 1: 55, RG 75, NA;
Governor Pope to Matthew Arbuckle, August 10, 1830, IA, LR, Cherokee
Agency West, RG 75, NA; Herring to Peter Menard, Jr., February 7, 1832,
Kurtz to Ward, November 5, 1832, IA, LS, 7: 79, 9: 346–47, RG 75, NA;
Commissioner of Indian Affairs, *Annual Report* (1832), p. 159; Hitchcock
to Spencer, April 7, 1842, IA, LR, Creek Agency, RG 75, NA.

50. The history of the Choctaws remaining in Mississippi is brilliantly
told in Peterson, "Mississippi Band of Choctaw Indians."

51. McKenney to Cass, May 26, 1830, Circular from Crawford, March
16, 1841, Resolution of the Senate, June 8, 1841, enclosed in C[rawford]
to Pilcher, August 19, 1841, Crawford to Butler, February 20, 1843, IA,
LS, 6: 433, 30: 172, 31: 29, 33: 302–3, RG 75, NA; Commissioner of Indian
Affairs, *Annual Report* (1838), p. 453, (1841), pp. 258–60, (1846), pp.
223–24, (1848), p. 404; Crawford to Bell, May 15, 1841, Crawford to
White, December 30, 1842, IA, Report Books, 2: 413–14, 3: 357, RG 75,
NA; Special Message from Bell to Tyler, May 31, 1841, *Senate Executive
Document 1*, 27th Cong., 1st sess., pp. 40–41; U.S., *Stat.*, 5: 553; Secretary
of War, *Annual Report* (1843), p. 59; Circular from Medill, April 9, 1847,
in Office of Indian Affairs, *Office Copy of the Laws*, p. 76. The origins of
the counterwarrant system and the Jackson administration's initial response to the practice are detailed in chapter 6. For efforts to overhaul
the public accounting system during this period, see Fred Wilbur Powell,
comp., *Control of Federal Expenditures: A Documentary History, 1775–
1894* (Washington, D.C.: Brookings Institution, 1939), pp. 512–606.

52. Crawford to Poinsett, December 30, 1839, *House Document 103*,
26th Cong., 1st sess., p. 10. C[rawford] to White, August 20, 1841, IA, LS,
31: 38, RG 75, NA; Crawford to Spencer, April 1, 1842, IA, Report Books,
3: 131, RG 75, NA; Poinsett to Gouv[erne]r Kemble, January 2, 1843,
Poinsett Papers; *Congressional Globe*, 23rd Cong., 2d sess., pp. 118–19,
143, 152–56; Bell's Report on Abuses in Indian Affairs, July 2, 1836, *House
Report 853*, 24th Cong., 1st sess., p. 1; *United States Magazine and Demo-*

cratic Review 18 (May 1846): 333–34; White, *The Jacksonians,* pp. 155, 161–62. Leonard D. White asserts that "the record of Congress in the field of administration [in the Jacksonian period] was a record characterized by delay, indifference, partisanship, and reluctance to provide the resources for effective work." See ibid., p. 162.

53. Schoolcraft, *Personal Memoirs,* pp. 318–19. For a discussion of the Territorial Bill of 1834, see chapter 5. Additional efforts to organize an Indian territory are detailed in chapter 8.

54. *Arkansas Intelligencer,* July 26, 1845; J. D. B. DeBow, comp., *Statistical View of the United States ... being a Compendium of the Seventh Census* (Washington, D.C.: Beverely Tucker, Senate Printer, 1854), p. 41.

8 /

Protecting the Frontiers

AS THE INDIAN REMOVAL POLICY brought thousands of emigrants to the trans-Mississippi West in the 1830s, the residents of the frontier states became alarmed about the "red menace" on their flank. Many westerners viewed the tribesmen as undesirable neighbors. Some Americans, on the other hand, made sincere efforts to revive the defeated Territorial Bill of 1834 and to incorporate the relocated Indians into American society, but their attempts failed because of constitutional arguments, sectional animosities, the desire for territorial expansion, and the idea of white superiority, as well as the nationalistic opposition of the large southern tribes. The result was that the emigrant tribesmen remained subject to American control without having a voice in the decision-making process concerning their affairs. Indian policy increasingly became associated with frontier defense as the United States entered upon an unprecedented era of western expansion.[1]

Even before the Jackson administration sent the Stokes commission to the new Indian country to investigate conditions in 1832, it had recognized that the far-flung nature of the proposed area would necessitate the organization of a mobile military force to police the Indian-white line of settlement and to protect America's growing trade with the Southwest. In March, 1833, Congress authorized the organization of the First Regiment of United States Dragoons, which received orders to help garrison forts in the Indian country and to patrol the extensive area in order to prevent depredations by the indigenous tribes upon the emigrants or by either group of tribesmen upon white settlers in adjoining states and territories.[2]

The organization and deployment of the dragoons in the Indian country failed to relieve the anxiety of Missouri and Arkansas frontiersmen, who protested vigorously against treaty stipulations which provided emigrant Indians with rifles for protection against the "wild nations" of the plains. As a result of such provisions, there were over twenty thousand armed emigrant warriors west of the Arkansas-Missouri line in the mid-1830s. The western portion of the land assigned to the southern tribes was on the hunting grounds of the fierce Comanches, Kiowas, Katakas, and Wichitas, who pillaged trade caravans between Missouri and Santa Fe. Many frontiersmen feared that the emigrants might join hands with these depredators to make bloody raids on their common foe, the Americans. Residents of Arkansas and Missouri especially became alarmed when the outbreak of hostilities in Florida in 1835, the controversy over the Cherokee treaty of 1835, and the Creek controversy in Alabama in the mid-1830s led to the reduction of troops stationed in the West at the same time that the government was forcibly relocating these Indians there. The presence of captured Seminole warriors together with other Indians removed under duress from the East meant that a large number of hostile Indians were within "striking distance" of the American frontier. Kentuckian Herman Bowman warned Vice-President Martin Van Buren in 1836 that the areas adjoining the Indian country constituted "a more expos'd frontier, than at present is a part of any Civilized nation."[3]

The Jackson administration sought to alleviate the growing anxiety among residents of the southwestern frontier by assuring them that it was encouraging the recent emigrants to substitute "moral" law for the use of "physical force." In his annual message to Congress at the close of 1835, President Jackson urged the adoption of legislation to provide closer "regulation" of the transplanted tribes. He also suggested that "some principles of intercommunication" would help to put an end to "those bloody wars whose prosecution seems to have made part of their social system."[4]

Early in 1836 Democratic Senator John Tipton of Indiana and
Whig Congressman Horace Everett of Vermont introduced bills
calling for the organization of an Indian confederacy in the trans-
Mississippi West under federal supervision. Both proposals were
similar to the defeated Territorial Bill of 1834. They called for the
granting of land patents to the Indians to assuage their fear that
the government might renege on its promises to give them permanent title to their land; the establishment of an annual intertribal council, with ultimate veto power in the hands of a
superintendent appointed by the president; and a delegate of
Indian descent to represent the territory in Congress. Both Tipton
and Everett maintained that a territorial government for the Indian country would redeem the government's pledges to the emigrants and provide for better protection on the frontier, and their
bills had the active support of the Jackson administration.[5]

Indian Commissioner Carey A. Harris believed that the organization of an Indian territory with "supervisory power" in the
hands of a government official was necessary to bind the tribesmen
closer to the federal government. He pointed out that while
American citizens would undoubtedly have closer commercial
relations with the Indians in the future, the United States pres-
ently had no way of supervising the laws of the separate tribes. A
confederation of the tribes would create laws and regulations of
"an international character" in the Indian country and make
American supervision of Indian affairs less cumbersome.[6]

Secretary of War Benjamin F. Butler shared the commissioner's
enthusiasm for the proposed legislation, but he urged its adoption
on much broader principles. Butler called the existing agency
system an inadequate form of wardship that was "imprudent" to
Americans and "unjust" to the Indians. "We must institute a comprehensive system of guardianship, adapted to the circumstances
and wants of the [Indian] people, and calculated to lead them,
gradually and safely, to the exercise of self-government," he advised President Jackson.[7]

Butler was a man of deep religious convictions who believed
that the United States had a moral debt to the Indians. He particularly favored the idea of allowing the proposed Indian confederacy
to send a delegate to Congress. "The daily presence of a native
Delegate on the floor of the House of Representatives of the
United States," he assured Jackson, "would, more than any other

single act, attest to the world and to the Indian tribes the sincerity of our endeavors for their preservation and happiness." Butler was certain that the creation of a territorial government for the "red man" would bring "more precious and durable accession to the glory of our country, than . . . any triumph we can achieve in arts or in arms." At the same time, however, he cautioned that it was necessary to establish military posts at "convenient" locations in the Indian country in order to fulfill the "sacred" treaty pledges that the emigrants would be protected from encroachments in their new country and to prevent the "savage passions" of the congregated Indians from unleashing "terrible and disastrous" attacks against white settlements.[8]

President Jackson publicly endorsed the views of Harris and Butler. He asked Congress to adopt "a well-digested and comprehensive system for the protection, supervision, and improvement" of the emigrant Indians. He also stressed the urgency of establishing a sufficient number of military posts throughout the Indian country. "Both measures are necessary," he advised Congress, "for the double purpose of protecting the Indians from intestine war, and in other respects complying with our engagements to them, and of securing our western frontier against incursions which otherwise will assuredly be made on it."[9]

Although Congress failed to act on either the House or Senate bill, Tipton and Everett were encouraged by the administration's support and reintroduced their proposals during the winter of 1836–37. President Jackson gave the proposals an added boost by reaffirming the government's commitments to the emigrants in his farewell address in March.[10]

Meanwhile the continual flow of emigrants to the Indian country was causing serious strains on the field service. At the same time, reports of Indian unrest and rumors about possible depredations against white frontier communities abounded. A western correspondent of a Chicago newspaper estimated in 1838 that there were fifty thousand "restive" warriors in the Indian country, adjacent to America's western settlements. "Unless the Government keeps a strong force in that quarter," he warned, "the tomahawk and scalping knife will . . . be reeking with the blood of our citizens, and the fair and cultivated fields, where now reigns prosperity and contentment, will be the grave yard of the innocent and unprotected." Such prospects, coupled with pressure from western congressmen and military advisors, led the Van Buren administration to vigorously support the organization of the Indian country into a more manageable political unit. Administration leaders had already taken an initial step in this direction upon entering office in 1837 when they persuaded Congress to solicit the feelings of the emigrants toward the creation of a trans-Mississippi Indian confederacy under American supervision.[11]

Reverend Isaac McCoy, a staunch defender of Indian removal and isolation in the West as a civilizing device, received instructions in mid-1837 to survey the opinion of the various tribes concerning the legislation pending in Congress. While many of the smaller tribes, including the northern Indians relocated west of Missouri, supported the plan of territorial organization, the Cherokees, Choctaws, and Creeks vehemently opposed it. These large tribes especially resented the provision for a territorial council based on equal representation that would allow the smaller tribes to outvote them. McCoy, who had hopes of becoming the superintendent of the proposed Indian territory, suggested that their reluctance to accept the arrangement might have also resulted from undue pressure from federal agents. According to the missionary, field officials uniformly opposed the Territorial Bill because "they suppose the tendency of the measure will be to render agencies unnecessary." McCoy's observation was basically correct. As early as the debates on the Removal Bill in 1830 and the establishment of the Stokes commission in 1832, some agents had voiced their concern that any innovations in the management of Indian affairs in the field might jeopardize their jobs. The agents' fears were well founded. McCoy, anxious to place all of the emigrants under his benevolent protection and guidance, combined his lobbying for an Indian territory with attacks on the agency system. Since the agents were the local representatives of the United States government and the dispensers of annuities and treaty goods, their opposition to the formation of an Indian territory impressed many tribesmen.[12]

In spite of the formidable Indian opposition to the Territorial Bill, McCoy urged Congress to pass the measure. "Due reflection," he suggested, would lead the reluctant tribes to put aside "national pride" and become a part of the new experiment. To counter any opposition to the proposed legislation on constitutional grounds, he advised Congress that "we have already introduced precisely such regulations as *we* chose [for the Indian country], and have required their submission to them." McCoy argued that territorial organization would at least permit the Indians some voice in the adoption of further regulations for their homeland, and the missionary headed for Washington to lobby for the bill.[13]

Congressional advocates of an Indian territory welcomed McCoy's report. Although the Removal Act of 1830 had guaranteed the emigrants permanent title to their trans-Mississippi land, they had never actually received land patents. To make matters worse, trade routes to the Southwest and the Pacific Coast cut through the Indian country and the westward flow of white emigrants along these paths during the depression years of the late 1830s made a mockery of Indian sovereignty. Secretary of War Joel R. Poinsett, moreover, was urging the extinguishment of the Indian title to the land between the Mississippi and Missouri Rivers in order to establish a line of frontier states. These conditions led some congressmen to believe that the organization of an Indian territory was the only way to guarantee the Indians permanent title to their land and to fulfill the government's promise of self-rule. Other congressional proponents of the measure thought that it would provide more adequate supervision of the tribes and protection for the frontier. The latter were particularly concerned about reports that recent Seminole, Creek, and Cherokee emigrants to the Indian country were in a "surly mood" and had sufficient arms and ammunition to devastate the frontier settlements. Both groups of legislators supported McCoy's call for the creation of an Indian confederacy. Neither group believed that the existing system of resident agents among the tribes was a sufficient guarantee for the kind of protection they sought.[14]

The Senate began serious debate on the proposal for an Indian territory in mid-April, 1838. The leading defenders of the legislation were Democrats John Tipton of Indiana, Wilson Lumpkin of Georgia, and Lewis F. Linn of Missouri, and anti–Van Burenite Hugh L. White of Tennessee. Tipton, a former Indian agent from Indiana who had speculated in Indian lands, was a personal friend of Isaac McCoy; he had apparently converted to the missionary's views as early as 1836 when he had supported a similar territorial bill. Lumpkin had served as governor of Georgia during the controversy with the Cherokees in the early 1830s, and White was a coauthor of the Removal Act. All three argued that, together with educational programs, the introduction of a representative form of government for the Indians under federal supervision would fulfill the pledges made to them when they left their ancient homes. Tipton, Lumpkin, and White favored the eventual assimilation of the Indians into American society and saw the creation of an Indian territory as a necessary step to that goal. Linn joined them in supporting the bill simply because it was "the most effectual measure that could be devised for the protection of Missouri, Arkansas and Wisconsin." He especially favored the proposal for allowing the Indians to send a delegate to Congress, since it would provide "a means of holding them the more strongly to the United States."[15]

Democrat Clement C. Clay of Alabama, however, pointed out that the leaders of the largest tribes, including the Choctaws and Creeks, opposed the bill. He introduced a memorial from an intertribal delegation in Washington protesting the organization of a territory. "We have removed and settled in the West, under the firm pledge of the Government of the United States to protect us, and that we should be permitted to remain free from the operation of any State or Territorial laws," the memorialists reminded Congress. The defense of Indian rights, however, was merely a tactic employed by Clay and other opponents of the bill. Opposition to the measure actually centered on its implications for the future status of the free Negro and the balance of power between the slave South and the free North.[16]

Democrat John Norvell of Michigan vehemently opposed the attempt to provide the Indians with a delegate in Congress in order to bind them closer to the federal government. Norvell, a Kentuckian by birth, feared that the proposal might be "the entering wedge to something more." He specifically warned that it might establish a precedent whereby abolitionists would later demand representation for free Negroes. Norvell told his colleagues that he never wished to see the day when either Indians or blacks held seats in Congress. On April 27 he offered an amendment to the bill which sought to provide the tribesmen with an "agent" in Washington instead of a delegate to Congress. Norvell's amendment came only a few months after the Senate had passed resolutions by John C. Calhoun defending the South's "peculiar institution," and it reopened the sectional debate.[17]

Calhoun and several other leading states' rights southerners joined Norvell in opposing the provision for an Indian delegate to Congress. The vote on Norvell's amendment, however, was not along strictly sectional lines. Democrats from every section of the Union split on the issue. Only the Whigs overwhelmingly opposed it. "We cannot recall the past," lamented Whig Oliver H. Smith of Indiana, "but let us atone as far as possible for our past policy, by carrying out in good faith the provisions of this bill." The amendment failed by a vote of twenty-four to sixteen, but Calhoun and his allies had just begun their assault.[18]

William R. King of Alabama warned his southern colleagues that the proposed Territorial Bill would restrict the westward expansion of slavery into the Southwest while simultaneously freeing the North of "wild Indians" and opening new areas for northern settlement. The South would be left prostrated with a formidable Indian foe "on our Southwestern borders, in order that the whole country north of the [Missouri] Compromise line should be kept exclusively for a white population." Where would the money come from, King asked, to pay for defense against Indian attacks? "We could not keep up a standing army sufficient to keep them in awe," he warned, noting that "the [Northern] States would not agree to it." For all of these reasons, King offered an amendment to the Territorial Bill calling for the establishment of a northern Indian territory to prevent the further emigration of Indians to the Southwest. He wanted to set aside all of the area east of the Rocky Mountains, north of the Missouri River and north and west of Missouri, for such a territory in order to balance the areas open to northern and southern expansion. Calhoun and Norvell immediately seconded the amendment. This proposal infuriated Lumpkin of Georgia, who warned that it gave a "sectional character" to the bill and threatened to prevent its passage. The Georgian, deeply committed to American wardship for the "incompetent" Indians, assailed Calhoun for "unnecessarily" agitating sectional strife over a measure which the South Carolinian had himself urged as secretary of war in 1825.[19]

Tipton of Indiana joined Lumpkin in pointing out that the bill already included a large area of land north of the Missouri Compromise line and that northern Indians would not be sent south of that line. Tipton, however, played into the hands of King and Calhoun. He admitted he was opposed to the extension of slavery and warned that nothing could block the "growing power" of the Old Northwest or "the emigration of the industrious, intelligent, and enterprising people from all parts of the United States to the Ioway Territory, west of the Mississippi river." This comment enraged Ambrose H. Sevier of Arkansas, an advocate of the Territorial Bill. "If the bill was good for the Creeks, the Cherokees, and the Chickasaws," he shouted, "it was good for the Sacs, Foxes, and Winnebagoes." Opponents of King's amendment were able to defeat it and secure the final passage of the original bill on May 3 by a margin of thirty-nine to six. Thus an overwhelming majority of the Senate favored the idea of an Indian territory with representation in Congress, in spite of the sectional questions that arose during the debates.[20]

The Senate bill went to the House for concurrence in May. The House Committee on Indian Affairs reported favorably on the proposal as well as on a similar one already pending before it. Whig Congressmen Horace Everett of Vermont, Ogden Hoffman of New York, and Caleb Cushing of Massachusetts ably supported the measure and worked vigorously to bring it to a final vote. The large southern tribes, however, again strenuously objected to the provision for a territorial council based on equal representation of all the tribes and urged Congress to defeat the bill. Cherokee agent Montfort Stokes warned supporters of the plan that "the Indians of the . . . great Nations may be deficient in political information, but they are not so ignorant as not to see the great inequality in the Representation provided for in the Bill." According to Isaac McCoy, many Indians feared that the bill was "a kind of treaty, in which the United States designed, in some covert manner, to defraud them of their present homes." The Choctaw General Council, for example, protested against any interference with their self-government and cautioned fellow tribesmen that the proposed measure would utimately lead to their "removal farther towards the setting sun." At the same time, the new head of the

Indian Office announced that he had reservations about the proposal. The combination of Indian opposition and the commissioner's lack of support led the House to postpone action on the bill.[21]

Newly appointed Indian Commissioner T. Hartley Crawford was not in sympathy with the Territorial Bill. He believed that the Indians had a right to receive "evidence" of legal title to their land, and he admitted that the assignment of agents to tribes did not provide them with adequate handling of their claims. Crawford's solution, however, was to issue the Indians land patents and to modify the existing agency system. He wanted to rotate agents so that they would become familiar with the problems of the various tribes, and he urged the creation of an annual or semiannual assembly of agents so that they could pool their knowledge and discuss common problems. The new commissioner also suggested that an Indian territory was unnecessary, since the government could easily manipulate and control tribal behavior by merely winning over influential chiefs and exerting pressure on the tribes through the licensed traders. Such tactics, he believed, were far superior to dealing with an intertribal Indian council.[22]

Crawford maintained that any attempt to form an Indian confederation would eventually prove futile. He asserted that the tribes had no common interests because they were at different stages of development along the path to civilization. The commissioner viewed the emigrant tribes as separate "colonies" which the "parent country" had to supervise and control. Congress should legislate for intertribal affairs while permitting the individual tribes to retain management of internal affairs which did not interfere with treaty provisions or American laws. An Indian confederacy would only "swallow up" the smaller tribes and place them at the mercy of larger ones.[23]

Crawford also had a more important reason for opposing the creation of an Indian territory. "We owe duties to ourselves," he cautioned. The commissioner was reluctant to provide the tribes "more concentration" on America's frontier than they already possessed. Finally, he warned that it would be foolhardy to adopt any system of government for the tribesmen as long as they retained the custom of communal land-holding. Crawford wanted to postpone the territorial scheme until a large number of Indians acquired private property. "The history of the world proves," he asserted, "that distinct and separate possessions make those who hold them averse to change." Their new interests would "dispose them to keep things steady," and they would become "the ballast of the ship." Until this occurred, Commissioner Crawford believed that agents could sufficiently handle any problems in the Indian country.[24]

Secretary of War Joel Poinsett concurred with Crawford's position and admitted to President Van Buren that his earlier support for the Territorial Bill was misguided. Poinsett now argued that the United States had to be extremely cautious in introducing principles of government to "a people who have hitherto lived with scarcely any knowledge of them!" He favored Crawford's suggestion of reforming the agency system and using white traders and friendly Indian chiefs to influence tribal behavior but broadened Crawford's suggestion of a regular council for agents. Poinsett advocated an annual council attended by the chiefs, agents, and American military officers. "In this manner," he told President Van Buren, "the Government would exercise a salutary influence over them, become acquainted with their wants, and heal their differences with each other." In addition, Poinsett recommended the establishment of more frontier posts, to be garrisoned with strong military detachments in order to protect American settlements in the West from "enemy" attacks. Van Buren was impressed with these proposals, and he urged Congress to substitute Poinsett's recommendations for the pending Territorial Bill.[25]

Senator Tipton, however, remained committed to the territorial plan. Exactly one week after the president's message to Congress, he reintroduced his bill. Once again Senators Calhoun and Norvell were unable to defeat it. The measure passed by an overwhelming majority on February 25, 1839, but the House took no action on it.[26]

Events in the Indian country in the late 1830s led the Van Buren administration to reaffirm its opposition to the territorial organization of the area. The forced removal of the Cherokees resulting from what antitreaty Indian leaders called the "pretended treaty" of 1835 led to strife between the new emigrants and old protreaty settlers. Continuing feuds between the National party and the Treaty party led to the brutal assassination of three leaders of the latter group, Major Ridge, John Ridge, and Elias

Boudinot, on June 22, 1839. The Van Buren administration, which felt a special obligation to the Treaty party, protested the impudence and perfidy of the National party and ordered that the assassins be immediately surrendered to American officials. This demand led National party leaders to remind the Van Buren administration that American courts had no legal jurisdiction under the Trade and Intercourse Act of 1834 in cases concerning a crime committed by an Indian against the person or property of another Indian. Secretary of War Joel R. Poinsett, however, thought otherwise. After warning the leaders of the National party that "the Government of the United States has a right to take all proper measures to preserve the peace of the [Indian] country," Poinsett dispatched a strong military detachment to the Cherokee country and ordered the immediate cessation of their annuity payments.[27]

To cope with the difficulties in the West, Secretary of War Poinsett suggested that the government offset the deficiences of the 1834 Trade and Intercourse Act by establishing tribunals in the Indian country for "the prompt trial and punishment of crimes" in order to prevent the Cherokees or other Indians from "treacherously murdering each other." Poinsett agreed with Commissioner Crawford that recent events had demonstrated that the formation of an Indian territory would involve "more hazard than benefit." Both men warned President Van Buren that a dissident Cherokee or some other "ambitious and daring chief" might use the proposed confederacy to promulgate his "desperate" designs and make the tribesmen his "blind instruments." Crawford conceded that the United States had an obligation under the Removal Act of 1830 to protect the emigrants "against all interruptions or disturbances" but argued that "beyond this . . . it would be impolitic to go." The commissioner favored legislating over the Indians rather than permitting them to become an integral part of the American Union as citizens of a territory. Both Crawford and Poinsett admitted that the United States owed a great debt to the emigrants, but they advised Van Buren that "we owe more to ourselves."[28]

Senator Ambrose Sevier of Arkansas was deeply concerned about the worsening situation in the Indian country bordering his state, and he continued to urge the adoption of an organic statute

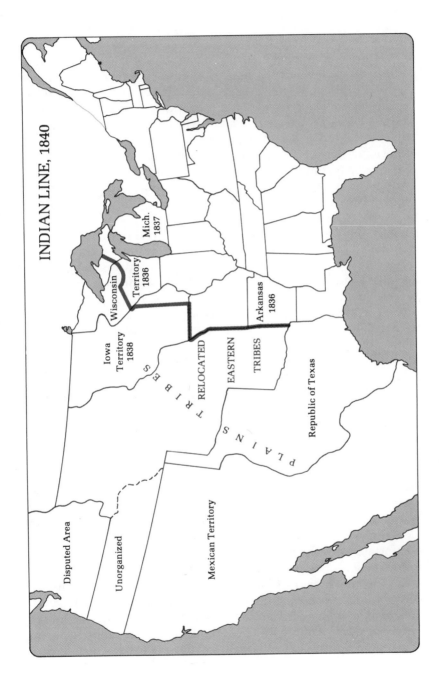

INDIAN LINE, 1840

for the area. Petitions from residents of Arkansas and Missouri opposing any additional influx of Indians on their western borders continually poured into Congress. At the same time, residents of the territories of Wisconsin and Iowa were clamoring for the extinction of Indian titles and the removal of indigenous tribes as well as the eastern ones relocated within their boundaries. The possibility of Indian-white conflict in the upper Old Northwest was of particular concern to the War Department, which was fearful that the British in Canada might exploit any hostilities for their own use. In order to placate residents of both the Southwest and the Old Northwest, the Van Buren administration began looking for a way to rid the area north of Missouri of its Indians without sending them west of the Arkansas-Missouri line.[29]

Indian Commissioner Crawford suggested that there were three possible solutions to the problem. The Indians could either assimilate into white society, seek refuge in Canada, or emigrate to a permanent northern Indian country established by the federal government. Crawford immediately dismissed the first alternative. "That a mass of wild and savage men should . . . quietly flow off in different channels into and through the social superiority around them, is what has never happened when both bodies were free, and never will happen," he advised. The commissioner warned that the second alternative was detrimental to national security. After receiving gifts and dallying in Canada, the Indians would undoubtedly return south with "more corrupted morals, and enervated bodies." Crawford called the prevention of a northern exodus "a leading object with this department." The third alternative was the "most beneficial" course open to the United States. Crawford proposed moving the Indians of the Old Northwest and Iowa to "a region hemmed in by the laws of the United States, and guarded by virtuous agents, where abstinence from vice, and the practice of good morals, should find fit abodes in comfortable dwellings and cleared farms, and be nourished and fostered by all the associations of the hearthstone."[30]

Commissioner Crawford's plan for the northern Indians received the support of the new Whig administration in 1841. Secretary of War John Bell, an old exponent of the virtues of Indian removal, joined hands with the commissioner to establish a northern Indian country. Bell hoped to remove approximately fifty thousand northern Indians to a permanent location north of the present Iowa-Minnesota border. "It is a point of national policy," Crawford acknowledged in mid-1841, "to prevent a farther increase of said [Indian] population to the South, and to separate it and the settlement contemplated in the North from each other, by the dense white population which will occupy the intermediate land." Crawford and Bell agreed that the location of "a hardy and efficient body" of citizens on the borders of the two Indian settlements would strengthen the security of the western frontier by preventing the possibility of an alliance between the northern and southern tribesmen. In order to provide sufficient land for the new Indian country, the Indian Office authorized Governor James D. Doty of Wisconsin Territory to negotiate treaties with the Sioux bands residing in the proposed location.[31]

Doty was a shrewd negotiator. By acknowledging all traders' claims and openly courting the assistance of these influential men, he was able to induce the Sioux to agree to a cession of thirty million acres of land in what is today northwestern Iowa, Minnesota, and the Dakotas. The treaty provisions asserted that all of the ceded land north of the present Iowa-Minnesota border and south of, roughly, the 46th parallel would form a territory open only to people of "Indian blood." Tribes emigrating to the new territory would have resident agents, schools, grist mills, saw mills, and various kinds of teachers to provide the necessary instruction to transform their people into "american farmers." The territory would be under the general supervision of a governor appointed by the president, and all residents would be under the jurisdiction of "such government, rules and regulations as shall be established by the Government of the United States therein." The governor would have authority to license traders and fix prices for goods sold to the Indians in order to prevent traders from charging exorbitant prices. Doty was perfectly correct when he informed Secretary Bell that his treaty called for "a radical change in the policy of the United States" toward the northern Indians.[32]

Doty's treaty contained the most far-reaching territorial proposal ever considered by the federal government up to that time. President Tyler urged the Senate to give its sanction to the document. Administration leaders claimed ratification of the treaty would provide four major benefits to the United States. They pointed out that the treaty would open vast areas of land in the Old Northwest to white settlement by providing an area for emigrants from states and territories with Indian population. It would also prevent the further accumulation of tribes in the Southwest, thereby reducing possibility of the "desolation" of neighboring white settlements. At the same time, it would provide a safe corridor for white expansion to the Pacific by freeing Iowa of Indian titles. Finally, Doty's treaty would convert the fierce Sioux Indians into "stipendiaries of the United States" and lure them away from British-Canadian influence. In spite of these advantages outlined by the Tyler administration, however, the treaty became the victim of the sharp political friction which developed in the Tyler administration by the summer of 1841.[33]

The treaty reached the Senate for consideration on September 3. Virtually all members of the Tyler cabinet, including Secretary of War Bell, resigned on the eleventh, after the president's break with congressional leaders of the Whig party. On the thirteenth, the closing night of the congressional session, the Senate hastily tabled the motion to consider the treaty. Henry Clay and other leading Whigs were responsible for this action. They saw the treaty as an administration proposal and sought revenge for the president's defection from their legislative program.[34]

In spite of this initial setback, President Tyler and the War Department continued to lobby for ratification of the treaty. Former Secretary of War John Bell secretly aided the administration by supplying information for a series of letters to the editor of the influential *National Intelligencer* outlining the benefits of the treaty. Governor Doty wrote numerous letters to senators advising them of the "security" value of concentrating the Indians of the Old Northwest in an area three hundred miles south of the Canadian border. Although residents of Iowa and the Old Northwest strongly supported Doty's treaty, the opposition to it in the Senate was overwhelming.[35]

In addition to Whigs seeking to harass President Tyler, Democrats generally opposed the treaty. Missouri Democrat Thomas Hart Benton joined the *Globe,* his party's leading organ in Washington, in labeling the treaty a Whig measure which established dangerous precedents by using the treaty-making process to secure what was really a legislative question and would cost millions of dollars. Other Democrats warned that the provision for the payment of traders' debts was evidence of "speculative villainy." Former secretary of war Joel Poinsett advised that "the plan if carried out will be permanently injurious to the United States, not only from the ruinous extravagance of the terms" of the agreement, but from "the location of the Indian tribes." Poinsett and former president Van Buren warned Senate Democrats that the treaty would seriously restrict white emigration to the Pacific coast and urged them to defeat the "iniquitous" document. Indian Commissioner Crawford, a Democrat of impeccable party loyalty, tried unsuccessfully to convince leading Democrats of the treaty's benefits. In spite of the strong support of the Tyler administration, Whigs and Democrats alike joined in defeating the ratification of the treaty when the president resubmitted it for consideration.[36]

After this unsuccessful effort to establish a northern Indian territory, the Tyler administration focused its attention on the southwestern frontier. Officials in the War Department and the Office of Indian Affairs were very dissatisfied with reports concerning existing conditions in the Indian country west of the Arkansas-Missouri line, where the policy of amalgamating "kindred" tribes initiated by Lewis Cass in the early 1830s had led to great intertribal tensions resulting in open hostilities by the late 1830s and especially in the early 1840s. At the same time, the antitreaty, or Ross, faction of the Cherokees was protesting the presence of American troops on their "sovereign" soil. The Seminoles and Creeks joined the Cherokees in complaining that they were not enjoying the independence the United States had promised them in the West. Opothleyola, a Creek chief, for example, asserted that "General Jackson told us, that if we would move to the West . . . that we should have our own laws here . . . and should not be interfered with." Yet Opothleyola noted that there were "bad white men" in the Creek nation without his people's consent. "There were two white men who knocked a woman on the head," he complained, adding that "we told the agent of it, but nothing was done about it." In addition to the ill feeling existing among many tribes in the Indian country, there were increasing reports of Indian attacks and rumors of alleged Indian plots against white settlements in Arkansas, Louisiana, and the Republic of Texas. These reports and rumors of Indian depredations forced government officials to seek new ways to promote better Indian-white relations in the trans-Mississippi West.[37]

Secretary of War John C. Spencer, an able jurist and the editor of the first American edition of Tocqueville's *Democracy in America,* advised President Tyler in 1842 that the government could only bring order to the Indian country by restructuring its relations with the tribesmen. "The present system of superintendents and agents is inadequate," he warned, "and the time seems to have arrived when we should turn our attention to devising some form of government which may secure peace and order among [the Indians] themselves and protection [for them] against others." Spencer observed that the existing system of bringing violators of the federal trade and intercourse laws to courts in Arkansas or Missouri was a complete farce. "The most atrocious offenders are seldom pursued, and more rarely brought to justice," he informed President Tyler. Under such conditions, it was no wonder that "the law of force and of retaliation is the only one recognized." Until the Indians felt safe in their persons and possessions, they could hardly make any advances in civilization. Spencer called the plan of organizing "something like a territorial government for the Indians" an object that was "worthy [of] the most deliberate consideration of all who take an interest in the fate of this hapless race."[38]

Spencer's interest in providing a territorial government for the Indians was not shared by Commissioner Crawford. Even before Spencer left the War Department early in 1843 to become secretary of the treasury, Crawford acted to prevent the possible confederation of the tribes in the Southwest. He informed field officials in November, 1842, that intertribal assemblages were "dangerous" and henceforth prohibited. In speaking of such gatherings, he observed that "they will probably conduce to no valuable end that may not be more safely and effectually reached thro' the agents and officers of the Department acting under its directions." Crawford advised agents that he alone would determine the "propriety and expediency" of holding any Indian councils. "Too much caution and prudence cannot be exercised," he warned, "in watching most vigilantly any movement on their part in originating or consummating such conventions or large meetings of them for any purpose or any occasion."[39]

In spite of the commissioner's warning, the Cherokees issued a call for an intertribal meeting at Tahlequah, their capital, in the summer of 1843. Agent Pierce M. Butler permitted the meeting to take place. Butler argued that the assemblage was merely an attempt to end the "confusion and commotion" in the Indian country caused by "the want of some common routine of domestic regulations." He agreed with Commissioner Crawford that the United States had to ultimately "govern" and "control" the tribes, but he believed that the Indian Office should allow such meetings, since it was easier to manipulate the tribes when they congregated together. "If we cannot control them in council," he wrote Crawford, "it will be impossible to do so out of council." The commissioner reluctantly permitted the council to finish its deliberations under the close scrutiny of Agent Butler and General Zachary Taylor.⁴⁰

The result of the council at Tahlequah was an intertribal compact of amity. The tribes agreed to abstain from the "law of retaliation," provide funds for education, prohibit cessions of land, suppress the use of "ardent spirits," and take other measures to ensure tranquility. Although the emigrant Indians had previously refused to join an "associated government" that would place them under the "civil yoke" of the United States, they were willing to work together themselves without such coercion.⁴¹

American reactions to the Tahlequah deliberations and similar meetings were mixed. The *United States Magazine and Democratic Review,* a leading Democratic party organ, agreed with Commissioner Crawford that such intertribal councils were "futile" because they led to the adoption of "mixed principles" which did not form the basis of a real government. "A law without a penalty is like a rope of sand," the *Review* argued, adding that only Congress, which had "full and complete jurisdiction" over the Indian country, could regulate intertribal affairs. Although a federal circuit court judge in Missouri had pointed out in 1843 that treaties expressly acknowledged the right of self-government to many tribes, most Americans tended to view the Indian country in terms similar to those expressed by the editor of the *Review.* Indeed, Chief Justice Roger B. Taney, a former advisor to President Jackson during the period when Indian emigration under the Removal Act commenced, decreed in 1846 that American legal jurisdiction extended over the Indian country. Even before Taney's pronouncement, however, Indians often found their freedom of action limited by the physical presence of the American military or by economic coercion. When difficulties persisted among the feuding Cherokees in the early 1840s, for example, the War Department imposed martial law upon these Indians and threatened to withhold their annuities and to disregard their "claims upon the country" unless they settled their differences on terms dictated by the United States. The government also used more subtle techniques to influence Indian behavior. Tribes wishing to unite politically found it expedient to receive the approval of American officials in order to guarantee that they would not lose part of their annuities. Government control of the purse strings to the Indian trust funds was a very effective form of social control and contributed to the emasculation of tribal sovereignty.[42]

During the Jacksonian era, the Office of Indian Affairs never permitted Indian emigrants the degree of independence it had promised them in order to secure their removal. The Indian commissioners, on the other hand, always upheld the tribesmen's right to the ownership of their new land. As early as the late 1830s, however, some congressmen listed the Indian country alongside Washington as federal territory when the question of abolishing slavery on federal soil came up in Congress. In the 1840s there was growing agitation for the extinguishment of "permanent" Indian title to the area included in present-day Kansas and Nebraska. The *United States Magazine and Democratic Review,* a leading exponent of expansionism, voiced the anxieties of a growing number of Americans in an editorial published in 1844:

> Our greatest apprehensions, we must confess . . . arise from the peculiar geographical position of the Indian territory with relation to our own. And this could not, perhaps, have been anticipated twenty years ago, when the plan was formed. Our population is on the broad move West. Nothing, it is evident, will now repress them this side of the Pacific. The snowy heights of the Rocky Mountains are already scaled; and . . . the path which has been trod by a few, will be trod by many. Now, the removed tribes are precisely in the centre of this path.

The *Review* claimed that it was uncertain as to the future fate of the congregated Indians. It refused to speculate on whether or not emigrants to the Pacific Coast would "trample on the red man" or permit an "Indian state" to block America's continental destiny. "Twenty years," the journal prophetically assured its readers, "will answer these questions."[43]

At the close of the Tyler administration, Secretary of War William Wilkins advocated the creation of a safe corridor to the Pacific Coast. Wilkins, a Democrat from Pennsylvania and an ardent expansionist, recommended the extension of the "blessings" of American institutions over the Indians, the organization of the Nebraska Territory, and the resettlement of the Indians in that area into a northern Indian country. Wilkins believed that the United States had an obligation to assure the safety of all travelers crossing the country en route to the Pacific Coast, and he wanted to increase the flow of white emigrants in order to strengthen America's claim to Oregon. He requested an appropriation of one hundred thousand dollars to garrison the Oregon Trail, pointing out that there were over 89,000 emigrant Indians and nearly 170,-000 indigenous tribesmen on the west side of the Mississippi River, excluding "the vast and numerous tribes that roam through the more distant forests of our own territory." In the Senate, Democrat Stephen A. Douglas of Illinois introduced legislation embodying Wilkins's proposals. The senator's action signaled the demise of the trans-Mississippi Indian country established in the 1830s.[44]

Between 1845 and 1848 the United States added nearly a million and a half square miles of territory to its national domain. Stephen A. Douglas and others who had supported Indian removal in the 1830s came to realize in the 1840s that they had created a barrier through the geographical center of the United States as it was constituted after the Mexican War. These former advocates of removal now recommended the relocation of some emigrant tribes from their "permanent" homes in order to provide a pathway to the Pacific Coast for white settlers. A chauvinist newspaper in Indian Commissioner William Medill's home state of Ohio voiced the sentiments of many advocates of continental expansionism in the late 1840s when it noted that the "Anglo-Saxon race" was destined to take possession of the entire North American continent. "If the people of these United States are true to themselves and to the institutions of the Pilgrim Fathers," asserted the editor of the *Cleveland Herald* in 1846, "the day is not far distant when the influence of the American name will redeem the world from tyranny of every kind, and cause the banner of Freedom to float in every breeze under the whole heavens." The *Cleveland Herald* evidently considered the Indian country a tyranny, because its call for expansion included "this whole continent."[45]

The clarion call of Manifest Destiny in the mid-1840s sent a shock wave of "distrust and alarm" among missionaries and other "sincere and disinterested friends of the Indians" who feared that the United States might not live up to its pledges to the transplanted tribesmen. Whig Congressman Charles S. Benton of New York spoke in behalf of the Baptist American Indian Mission Association of Louisville, Kentucky, when he cautioned Congress in June, 1846, that "we have approximated the point where this government must decide whether existing guarantees of treaties with those tribes [in the Indian country] shall be maintained in the spirit which dictated them." Benton's colleagues on the House Committee on Indian Affairs joined him in urging the government to consider "whether those guarantees are sufficient for the avowed object of providing a home for the red man forever in the country assigned him; or, whether those treaties are to be set at naught, the experiment of civilization arrested, and the red race again be driven and dispersed into the wilderness." The committee reported that it was sympathetic to the "benign policy" of removal to permanent western homes inaugurated by President Jackson in 1830 and urged Congress to reaffirm the "inviolability" of the Indian country. Nothing, however, came of Benton's bill asking Congress to specify "permanent" boundaries for the Indian country which, on paper at least, already had such boundaries since 1830.[46]

At the same time that the permanent title of the transplanted tribes was being questioned, the Polk administration was tampering with tribal sovereignty. In an attempt to protect Indians from avaricious whites who made a mockery of the Trade and Intercourse Act, the Indian Office asserted its right to oversee the expenditure of Indian funds. Indian Commissioner William Medill stated in 1847 that "it is unnecessary to inquire how far the Indians are capable of making contracts with individuals of a legal and binding nature, being considered in the light of wards under the guardianship of the government." Medill ordered that all con-

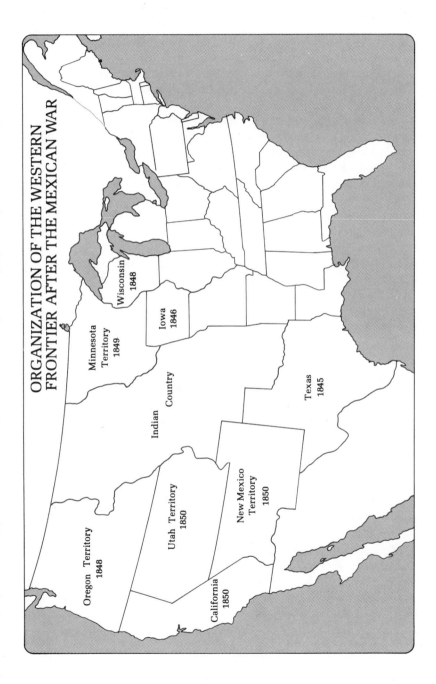

ORGANIZATION OF THE WESTERN
FRONTIER AFTER THE MEXICAN WAR

Oregon Territory
1848

Utah Territory
1850

California
1850

New Mexico
Territory
1850

Minnesota
Territory
1849

Indian   Country

Wisconsin
1848

Iowa
1846

Texas
1845

tracts made by the Indians calling for the payment of goods or money would henceforth be null and void. Although this decision was part of the Polk administration's effort to tighten up the federal prohibition against whiskey in the Indian country, it destroyed the Indians' right to deal with traders for goods without prior government approval. Efforts by the administration to alter the mode of distributing annuities by dividing the sum and issuing shares to individuals instead of to tribal treasurers undoubtedly reminded some contemporaries of a similar effort by Old Hickory in 1829 which had as its purpose the weakening of tribal authority.[47]

The Polk administration's tampering with Indian sovereignty to permit better enforcement of the trade and intercourse laws came under strong attack by Congressman Robert W. Johnson. The Arkansas Democrat argued that the net effect of the new policies would be to "destroy the salutary influence" of the chiefs over the "warriors" bordering his state. Such policies, coupled with Commissioner Medill's efforts to reduce the number of agencies by combining kindred Indian tribes, Johnson warned, would "light [at] once upon our frontier the torch of war," since the larger tribes almost universally opposed the schemes. Johnson told his western colleagues that the policies of Commissioner Medill, an Ohioan, clearly indicated that the Indian Office "should never again be placed in the hands of any man who resides east of the Mississippi." The security of the western frontier was more important to Johnson than the "miserable saving" that the reduction of agencies could produce, and stable tribal leadership, not the fragmentation of the tribes, would promote Indian-white tranquility. Johnson's attack on Commissioner Medill's programs was another manifestation of western concern about the possibility of a major conflagration between Indians and whites sparked by a minor incident or misunderstanding between the two groups.[48]

Meanwhile, growing anxiety in the East about the precarious condition of the tribes in the Indian country led Whig Congressman Abraham R. McIlvaine of Pennsylvania to introduce a territorial bill in 1848. McIlvaine's proposal called for the establishment of an Indian territory along the lines of the earlier proposals of the 1830s. He argued that the United States had reaped tremendous benefits from the removal policy but had accumulated a great moral debt to the Indians. "It remains for this government to carry out, in good faith," he remarked, "its obligations to the weaker and dependant party." The House Committee on Indian Affairs heartily agreed. "So undeniable is this obligation, that your committee consider it a question of *time* rather than *principle,*" the committee reported, adding that the time had arrived. The Polk administration, numerous congressmen, and the large southern tribes, however, stubbornly refused to support the bill, and it died in the House.[49]

President Polk cheerfully reported in December, 1848, that the removal policy had succeeded in extinguishing most of the Indian titles east of the Mississippi River. He undoubtedly questioned, however, the wisdom of one aspect of the removal policy—namely, the permanent resettlement of eastern tribes just west of the Mississippi River and the Arkansas-Missouri line. Even before the discovery of gold in California in 1848, petitions for railroad routes and overland trails which would transverse the permanent Indian country erected in 1830 were pouring into Washington. Several congressmen were calling for the purchase of Indian land in the trans-Mississippi West in order to provide a pathway to America's newly acquired possessions on the Pacific Coast. Indian Commissioner Medill admitted in 1848 that "material changes will soon have to be made in the position of the smaller tribes on the frontier, so as to leave an ample outlet for our white population to spread and to pass towards and beyond the Rocky mountains." The commissioner assured exponents of American continental expansion that the Polk administration had already begun work to establish a "northern [Indian] colony" on the headwaters of the Mississippi River and was planning to remove Indians from the "very desirable" land north of the Kansas River to the colony south of the river and west of Missouri and Arkansas. The two "colonies" of Indian concentration would be separated by "an ample outlet of about six geographical degrees" in order to provide "a wide and safe passage for our Oregon emigrants; and for such of those to California."[50]

By the close of the Polk administration, the future of the permanent trans-Mississippi Indian country was dim. During the winter of 1849, petitions from the state legislatures of North Carolina and Pennsylvania urged Congress to create a "permanent home" for the Indians to protect them from the rush of white emigrants to the Pacific Coast. The implication of these petitions was clear. Many Americans realized that it was just a matter of time before white settlers would inundate the Indian country. Early in 1849 Congress actually considered legislation to extend American laws over the tribes in the area northeast of the Missouri River, to allow an unlimited right of extradition of criminals from the southern Indian country, and to extinguish Indian titles in the area west of Missouri in order to build a national road from Saint Louis to San Francisco. The permanent Indian country created in 1830 was now clearly a major obstacle to continental development.[51]

President Jackson's removal policy had helped to establish by the mid-1840s what Napoleon in the 1790s and the British in 1814 had failed to accomplish—the construction of a barrier to American continental expansion stretching from Canada in the North to Texas in the South and from the Rocky Mountains in the West to the Arkansas-Missouri-Iowa-Wisconsin line. Once again, as in the 1820s, Indian title became an obstacle to American progress in the late 1840s. As in 1829, the Democratic president in the White House offered a convenient solution to the problem. The transfer of the Office of Indian Affairs to the newly created Interior Department and the organization of the Minnesota Territory during the last week of the Polk administration provided residents of the Indian country with a glimpse of what was to come. White settlers spilling onto the fertile prairies of present-day Kansas and Nebraska would ultimately provide the coup de grâce to the permanent trans-Mississippi Indian country established in the 1830s.[52]

NOTES

1. John Hope Franklin demonstrates in *The Militant South, 1800–1861* (Boston: Beacon Press, 1964), pp. 30–31, 214, that residents of the frontier areas bordering the Indian country continuously "remained nervous" about the prospect of Indian depredations against their communities and increasingly became critical of America's national defense posture.

2. Secretary of War, *Annual Report* (1829), p. 30, (1830), p. 29, (1832), p. 19; Arbuckle to Captain Jesse Bean, October 5, 1832, in McDermott, *Western Journals of Washington Irving,* p. 32; Macomb to Commanding Officer, Cantonment Gibson, November 5, 1832, Army Headquarters, LS,

4/2: 177–78, RG 108, NA; U.S., *Stat.*, 4: 652. For an excellent account of the efforts to establish a corps of mounted troops to patrol the trans-Mississippi West, see Prucha, *Sword of the Republic*, pp. 233–48. Also see the citations to studies of the operations of the dragoons in chapter 5, note 29.

3. Gaines to McComb, July 6, 1833, AGO, LR, Main Series, RG 94, NA; Memorial of Arkansas Territorial Assembly to Congress, October 23, 1833, November 8, 1833, in Carter and Bloom, *Territorial Papers*, 21: 808–9, 843–44; Macomb to Gaines, April 26, 1833, Macomb to Leavenworth, February 19, 1834, Army Headquarters, LS, 4/2: 258–59, 325–27; RG 108, NA; Commissioner of Indian Affairs, *Annual Report* (1834), pp. 240–41, (1836), p. 394; *Arkansas Gazette*, April 19, 1836; Gaines to Governor Cannon, June 6, 1836, in *Nashville Republican*, July 12, 1836; U.S., *Stat.*, 5: 67; Armstrong to Herring, June 23, 1836, Jackson Papers, Library of Congress; Census of the Indian tribes reported in 1836, IA, Misc. Records, 1: 276, RG 75, NA; McCoy to Tipton, December 10, 1836, in Blackburn, *John Tipton Papers*, 3: 322; Lieutenant Colonel William Whistler and Captain John Stout to Macomb, September 30, 1837, Quartermaster General's Report, November 7, 1837, *American State Papers: Military Affairs*, 7: 784, 978–80; *Niles' Register* 53 (December 2, 1837): 213, 53 (December 23, 1837): 257; Bowmar to Van Buren, August 29, 1836, Van Buren Papers. Also see *McCoy's Register* 1 (1835): 39–42; Henry H. Goldman, "A Survey of Federal Escorts of the Santa Fe Trade, 1829–1843," *Journal of the West* 5 (October 1966): 504–16; Beers, *Western Military Frontier*, pp. 94–149; C. C. Rister, "A Federal Experiment in Southern Plains Indian Relations, 1835–1845," *Chronicles of Oklahoma* 14 (December 1936): 434–55.

4. Richardson, *Papers of the Presidents*, 3: 173.

5. *Senate Journal*, 24th Cong., lst sess., p. 230; *House Journal*, 24th Cong., lst sess., pp. 369–70; S 159, HR 365, *Original Bills*, 24th Cong., 1st sess.; Report of Tipton, March 15, 1836, *Senate Document 246*, 24th Cong., 1st sess., pp. 1–8.

6. Commissioner of Indian Affairs, *Annual Report* (1836), pp. 393–94. Also see Bowmar to Van Buren, August 29, 1836, Van Buren Papers; *McCoy's Register* 3 (1837): 75.

7. Secretary of War, *Annual Report* (1836), p. 123. Also see *McCoy's Register* 3 (1837): 74–75.

8. Secretary of War, *Annual Report* (1836), pp. 123–25. Charles G. Sellers, Jr., notes Butler's deep religious convictions in his *James K. Polk, Continentalist: 1843–1846* (Princeton, N.J.: Princeton University Press, 1966), pp. 87, 286. Butler was a zealous public servant who was held in high esteem by the most renowned lawyers in the country. He was also

interested in humanitarian reform movements, especially the temperance crusade. George Bancroft claimed that Butler worked to assure that there was "as little of the element of evil in the [American] democracy as is consistent with the frailty of human nature." See Jesse Hoyt to Butler, December 2, 1836, plus enclosure, Story to Butler, July 30, 1838, Butler to E. C. Delevan, June 22, 1837, Bancroft to Butler, June 6, 1836, Benjamin F. Butler Papers. For Butler's views on representative government, see Benjamin F. Butler, *Representative Democracy in the United States: An Address* (Albany: C. Van Benthuysen, 1841).

9. Richardson, *Papers of the Presidents,* 3: 256.

10. S 15, HR 901, *Original Bills,* 24th Cong., 2d sess.; *Senate Journal,* 24th Cong., 2d sess., pp. 31, 42, 59, 160, 236; *Congressional Globe,* 24th Cong., 2d sess., pp. 146, 151, 185; Tipton to McCoy, December 18, 1836, in Blackburn, *John Tipton Papers,* 3: 326; Richardson, *Papers of the Presidents,* 3: 294.

11. Revised Regulations No. 2, April 13, 1837, IA, Misc. Records, 2: 237, RG 75, NA; Cross to Colonel S. W. Kearney, October 24, 1837, *House Document 278,* 25th Cong., 2d sess., p. 20; Poinsett to Secretary of State John Forsyth, April 14, 1837; Clipping from the *Natchitoches* (Louisiana) *Herald,* December 6, 1838, enclosed in R. Garland to Van Buren, January 3, 1838, DS, LR, Misc., RG 59, NA; *McCoy's Register* 3 (1837): 62–73, 4 (1838): 14; Correspondence on the subject of the protection of the Western frontier, February 14, 1838, *House Document 276,* 25th Cong., 2d sess., pp. 1–2, 4, 6–7, 13–16, 20–21; Van Buren's First Annual Message, December 5, 1837, in Richardson, *Papers of the Presidents,* 3: 392; Poinsett to Polk, June 16, 1838, *House Document 434,* 25th Cong., 2d sess., p. 1; Secretary of War, *Annual Report* (1838), p. 99; Correspondence of the *Chicago Democrat,* September 22, 1838, in *Army and Navy Chronicle* 8 (January 3, 1839): 12. Also see note 3; *Baptist Missionary Magazine* 18 (June 1838): 129.

12. McCoy to Tipton, May 29, October 9, November 22, 1837, in Blackburn, *John Tipton Papers,* 3: 407, 449, 468–69; *Niles' Register* 53 (September 30, 1837): 67–68; Commissioner of Indian Affairs, *Annual Report* (1837), p. 526; *McCoy's Register* 4 (1838): 11–13; *Arkansas Gazette,* April 20, 1830; Yeager, "Indian Enterprises of Isaac McCoy," pp. 483, 547, 562–63, 574. For evidence of McCoy's ambition to head the proposed Indian territory, see McCoy to Christiana McCoy, March 6, May 9, 1836, McCoy to Reverend S. N. Cone, March 12, 1836, McCoy to President [Jackson], March 14, 1836, McCoy to Cass, March 14, 1836, McCoy Papers. McCoy's opposition to the Indian agency system is evident in McCoy to Cass, February 1, 1832, *House Executive Document 172,* 22d Cong., 1st sess., p. 11; *McCoy's Register* 2 (1836): 48–51.

13. McCoy's comments are quoted in *Niles' Register* 53 (September 30, 1837): 67–68. For McCoy's decision to travel to Washington and his lobbying activities there, see Tipton to McCoy, September 20, December 11, 1837, McCoy to Tipton, November 22, 1837, in Blackburn, *John Tipton Papers*, 3: 439, 469, 472; George A. Schultz, *An Indian Canaan: Isaac McCoy and the Vision of an Indian State* (Norman: University of Oklahoma Press, 1972), pp. 188–90.

14. Commissioner of Indian Affairs, *Annual Report* (1837), p. 526; Schultz, *Indian Canaan*, pp. 188–89; William C. MacLeod, *The American Indian Frontier* (New York: Alfred A. Knopf, 1928), pp. 469–71; Secretary of War, *Annual Report* (1837), p. 184; *Congressional Globe*, 25th Cong., 2d sess., pp. 315, 335–36, 339–40, 345–48; *Niles' Register* 53 (February 10, 1838); 384, 54 (March 3, 1838): 3, 54 (April 21, 1838): 123, 54 (May 5, 1838): 156. Also see notes 3 and 11; Van Buren's First Annual Message, December 5, 1837, in Richardson, *Papers of the Presidents*, 3: 392.

15. *Congressional Globe*, 25th Cong., 2d sess., pp. 315, 335–36, 339–40, 345–48, appendix, pp. 269–74; *Niles' Register* 54 (April 21, 1838): 123, 54 (May 5, 1838): 156; Samuel Conner to Tipton, May 21, 1838, in Blackburn, *John Tipton Papers*, 3: 631–32. Tipton had reintroduced his Territorial Bill earlier in the winter. See S 75, *Original Bills*, 25th Cong., 2d sess.; *Senate Journal*, 25th Cong., 2d sess., p. 87.

16. *Senate Journal*, 25th Cong., 2d sess., p. 378; *Congressional Globe*, 25th Cong., 2d sess., p. 334; *Niles' Register* 54 (May 5, 1838): 155.

17. *Niles' Register* 54 (May 5, 1838): 156; *Senate Journal*, 25th Cong., 2d sess., pp. 380–81; *Congressional Globe*, 25th Cong., 2d sess., pp. 338, 339. For the significance of Calhoun's resolutions, see Van Deusen, *Jacksonian Era*, pp. 133–34.

18. *Congressional Globe*, 25th Cong., 2d sess., p. 340; *Senate Journal*, 25th Cong., 2d sess., pp. 380–81; *Niles' Register* 54 (May 5, 1838): 156.

19. *Congressional Globe*, 25th Cong., 2d sess., pp. 340–41, 345–48; *Niles' Register* 54 (May 5, 1838): 156–57; *Senate Journal*, 25th Cong., 2d sess., p. 383. For an early statement of Lumpkin's views on Indian affairs as reported by one of the leading opponents of the Removal Act, see Evarts to Greene, March 20, 1829, Papers of the American Board. Also see chapter 4, note 6. For Calhoun's views in 1825, see Report of Calhoun, January 24, 1825, *American State Papers: Indian Affairs*, 2: 542–44.

20. *Congressional Globe*, 25th Cong., 2d sess., pp. 345, 347–48, 352; *Niles' Register* 54 (May 5, 1838): 156–57, 54 (May 12, 1838): 172; *Senate Journal*, 25th Cong., 2d sess., pp. 385–86.

21. *Congressional Globe*, 25th Cong., 2d sess., pp. 147, 352, 405; *House Journal*, 25th Cong., 2d sess., pp. 330, 947; HR 495, *Original Bills*, 25th Cong., 2d sess.; *Niles' Register* 54 (June 2, 1838): 218; Tipton to

McCoy, May 29, July 5, 9, 1838, August 24, 1838, Tipton to Poinsett, July 12, 1838, Tipton to Harris, July 15, 1838, Harris to Tipton, August 7, 1838, McCoy to Tipton, September 13, 20, 1838, Stokes to Tipton, November 5, 1838, in Blackburn, *John Tipton Papers,* 3: 636, 653–56, 660, 672, 705, 722, 762–63; *McCoy's Register* 4 (1838): 11, 13; Secretary of War, *Annual Report* (1838), pp. 112–13; Commissioner of Indian Affairs, *Annual Report* (1838), pp. 451–52, 454–55. George A. Schultz erroneously asserts in his *Indian Canaan,* p. 191, that "the House of Representatives showed no intention of calling" for the Territorial Bill passed by the Senate.

22. Commissioner of Indian Affairs, *Annual Report* (1838), pp. 444, 451–52, 454–55.

23. Ibid., pp. 455–56.

24. Ibid., pp. 454–56. For a possible intellectual source of Crawford's ideas on private property, see Merle Curti, "The Great Mr. Locke: America's Philosopher, 1783–1861," *Huntington Library Bulletin* 11 (April 1937): 107–51.

25. Secretary of War, *Annual Report* (1838), pp. 99, 112–13; Richardson, *Papers of the Presidents,* 3: 500–501. Cf. Secretary of War, *Annual Report* (1837), p. 186.

26. S 23, *Original Bills,* 25th Cong., 3d sess.; *Senate Journal,* 25th Cong., 3d sess., pp. 35, 57, 272; *Niles' Register* 55 (December 15, 1838): 247. Senator Tipton's views on Indian affairs are conveniently summarized in Tipton to Gales and Seaton, [January 15, 1839], in Blackburn, *John Tipton Papers,* 3: 793–99. For information concerning Indian opposition to Tipton's bill, see Report of Armstrong, 1839, in Commissioner of Indian Affairs, *Annual Report* (1839), p. 474.

27. Resolutions of the Cherokee Nation, August 8, 1837, *House Document 82,* 25th Cong., 2d sess., pp. 8–9; Memorial of a Cherokee Delegation, December 15, 1837, *House Document 99,* 25th Cong., 2d sess., pp. 1–3; McCoy to Tipton, August 17, 1838, in Blackburn, *John Tipton Papers,* 3: 666; Commissioner of Indian Affairs, *Annual Report* (1839), pp. 338–40; Decree of the Cherokee Council, August 1, 1838, Poinsett to Arbuckle, November 9, 1839, Crawford to Armstrong, November 9, 1839, in Commissioner of Indian Affairs, *Annual Report* (1839), pp. 417–18, 425–26; Secretary of War, *Annual Report* (1839), p. 51. Cf. Poinsett to Cherokee Delegation, May 18, 1838, *House Document 376,* 25th Cong., 2d sess., p. 3. For a description of events leading up to the assassinations of the Treaty party leaders, see John A. Bell and Stand Watie to Editor, July 8, 1839, in *Arkansas Gazette,* August 21, 1839. Reverend John F. Schermerhorn, the negotiator of the Cherokee removal treaty of 1835, paid tribute to John Ridge in a letter to the *Utica Observer* in New York dated July 17, 1839. See *Arkansas Gazette,* October 2, 1839. Tennessee Whig John Bell

tried unsuccessfully to have the House of Representatives publish an Indian Affairs Committee report that was entremely critical of the administration's dealings with the Cherokees. See *Mr. Bell's Suppressed Report in Relation to Difficulties between the Eastern and the Western Cherokees* (Washington, D.C.: Gales & Seaton, 1840).

28. Secretary of War, *Annual Report* (1839), pp. 51–52; Commissioner of Indian Affairs, *Annual Report* (1839), pp. 347–48; Richardson, *Papers of the Presidents*, 3: 539.

29. *Congressional Globe*, 25th Cong., 3d sess., pp. 19, 22, 149, 210, 218, 26th Cong., 1st sess., pp. 126, 129, 130; *Niles' Register* 53 (February 10, 1838): 384, 54 (March 3, 1838): 3; Taliaferro to Dodge, July 4, 1838, enclosed in Dodge to Harris, July 25, 1838, in Carter and Bloom, *Territorial Papers*, 27: 1042–44; Dodge to Harris, August 16, 1838, IA, LR, Wisconsin Superintendency, Prairie du Chien Agency, RG 75, NA; Schoolcraft to Harris, October 4, 1838, Schoolcraft to Major General Winfield Scott, July 2, 1839, Schoolcraft to Crawford, September 30, 1839, IA, Michigan Superintendency, Mackinac Agency, LS, RG 75, NA; Crawford to Poinsett, January 15, 1839, *House Executive Document 107*, 25th Cong., 3d sess., pp. 2–4; Secretary of War, *Annual Report* (1840), p. 23; Commissioner of Indian Affairs, *Annual Report* (1840), pp. 232–33; Crawford to Poinsett, April 7, 1840, *House Executive Document 178*, 26th Cong., 1st sess., pp. 2–18; Crawford to Pilcher, March 1, 1841, IA, LS, 30: 146–47, RG 75, NA. Also see notes 3 and 11; Memorial of Gaines, December 31, 1839, *Senate Document 256*, 26th Cong., 1st sess., pp. 1–27.

30. Commissioner of Indian Affairs, *Annual Report* (1840), pp. 232–34.

31. Bell to Tyler, August 31, 1841, in Richardson, *Papers of the Presidents*, 4: 60–61; Crawford to Doty, May 10, July 16, 1841, IA, LS, 30: 260–65, 439–40, RG 75, NA; Commissioner of Indian Affairs, *Annual Report* (1841), p. 253. Also see B[ell] to Chambers, Doty, and Crawford, September 3, 1841, IA, LS, 21: 84, RG 75, NA. John Bell's concern about the burgeoning population in the Indian country is evident in *Mr. Bell's Suppressed Report*, p. 7.

32. Doty to Bell, August 4, 1841, Articles of a Treaty . . . between James Duane Doty . . . and . . . Bands of the Dakota (or Sioux) nation of Indians, [July 31, 1841], IA, LR, St. Peter's Agency, RG 75, NA; Meyer, *Santee Sioux*, pp. 73–74, appendix, pp. 377–88; Stephen R. Riggs to Samuel W. Pond, July 29, 1841, Pond Papers, Minnesota Historical Society, Minneapolis, Minn.; *Hawk-Eye and Iowa Patriot* (Burlington), October 28, 1841. Doty's role in negotiating the treaty and his subsequent efforts to lobby in its behalf are detailed in Alice E. Smith, *James Duane Doty:*

Frontier Promoter (Madison: State Historical Society of Wisconsin, 1954), pp. 257–62. The treaty of July 31, 1841, was the principal treaty negotiated by Doty. He also negotiated a supplementary treaty with other bands for about two million acres of land. See Articles of a treaty . . . between James Duane Doty . . . and . . . bands of the Dakota Nation, [August 11, 1841], IA, LR, St. Peter's Agency, RG 75, NA; Meyer, *Santee Sioux,* p. 74, appendix, pp. 388–89.

33. Bell to Tyler, August 31, 1841, Tyler to the Senate, September 1, 1841, in Richardson, *Papers of the Presidents,* 4: 59–63.

34. *Executive Proceedings of the Senate,* 5: 426–30, 439; *National Intelligencer,* September 14, 1841; Smith, *James Duane Doty,* p. 259. For the changes in Tyler's cabinet, see Oliver P. Chitwood, *John Tyler: Champion of the Old South* (New York: D. Appleton-Century Co., Inc., 1939), pp. 272–73.

35. *National Intelligencer,* October 1, 4, 6, 13, 23, 1841; *Hawk-Eye and Iowa Patriot,* October 28, 1841; Commissioner of Indian Affairs, *Annual Report* (1841), p. 253; C[rawford] to Doty, March 12, 1842, IA, LS, 32: 32, RG 75, NA; *Congressional Globe,* 27th Cong., 2d sess., p. 481; Smith, *James Duane Doty,* p. 260. Also see Morgan, *Whig Embattled,* p. 116.

36. Smith, *James Duane Doty,* pp. 260–62; Meyer, *Santee Sioux,* p. 75; Poinsett to Van Buren, October 30, 1841, Van Buren Papers; Van Buren to Poinsett, December 7, 1841, Poinsett Papers; C[rawford] to Benton, August 10, 1842, IA, LS, 32: 375, RG 75, NA; *Executive Proceedings of the Senate,* 6: 60, 141. Cf. William W. Folwell, *A History of Minnesota,* 4 vols. (St. Paul: Minnesota Historical Society, 1921–30), 1: 458–59.

37. Secretary of War, *Annual Report* (1842), pp. 190–91; Foreman, *Journal of Ethan Allen Hitchcock,* pp. 172–73, 182–83; [Hitchcock] to Major S. C., December 5, 1840, Hitchcock to Spencer, December 21, 1841, Sprague to Worth, July 12, 1841, Crawford to Hitchcock, January 27, 1842, Statement of Roley McIntosh, January 28, 1842, Hitchcock Papers; Talk of Opothleyola to Hitchcock, February 3, 1842, enclosed in Hitchcock to Secretary of War, May 30, 1842, Hitchcock to Spencer, April 7, June 1, 1842, IA, LR, Creek Agency, RG 75, NA; C[rawford] to Armstrong and Pilcher, January 27, 1841, Crawford to McCoy, May 17, 1841, Crawford to Cummins, March 25, September 29, 1841, IA, LS, 30: 47–48, 187, 226, 279–80, RG 75, NA; *National Intelligencer,* January 31, 1842; Governor Archibald Yell to Spencer, February 25, 1842, Louisiana and Arkansas Congressional Representatives to Spencer, March 29, 1842, Spencer to Congressmen, March 31, 1842, plus enclosure, *National Intelligencer,* April 4, 1842; Commissioner of Indian Affairs, *Annual Report* (1843), pp. 268–69; Crawford to Armstrong, April 10, June 17, 1844,

Crawford to Wilkins, May 20, 1844, in Commissioner of Indian Affairs, *Annual Report* (1844), pp. 329, 331–34; Butler to Davenport, February 10, 1843, Butler to Crawford, February 11, April 9, May 10, 1843, U.S. Miscellaneous MSS, 1840–60, Library of Congress, Washington, D.C. (hereafter cited as U.S. Misc. MSS); C[rawford] to Porter, July 26, 1843, IA, Report Books, 3: 468–70, 481, RG 75, NA. Also see notes 1, 3, 11, and 42; McKenney, *Memoirs,* 2: 130–33.

38. Secretary of War, *Annual Report* (1842), pp. 190–91. For biographical information on Spencer, see Pierson, *Tocqueville and Beaumont,* pp. 8, 216–25; chapter 9, note 49.

39. C[rawford] to Armstrong, November 29, 1842, Crawford to Butler, February 27, 1843, IA, LS, 33: 123–24, 325–26, RG 75, NA. Also see Armstrong to Butler, June 14, 1843, P. M. Butler Papers.

40. C[rawford] to Butler, February 27, 1843, IA, LS, 33: 325–26, RG 75, NA; Butler to Crawford, May 3, 1843, U.S. Misc. MSS; Foreman, *Advancing the Frontier,* pp. 205–15. Also see Foreman, *Journal of Ethan Allen Hitchcock,* p. 70; [Hitchcock] to Spencer, December 21, 1841, Hitchcock Papers.

41. McKenney, *Memoirs,* 2: 127–28; *United States Magazine and Democratic Review* 14 (February 1844): 184. For an account of intertribal councils in the trans-Mississippi Indian country, see Gail E. Boyle, "Emigrant Indian Tribal Policies as Indicated by Intertribal Councils, 1837–1853" (M.A. thesis, University of Chicago, 1941).

42. *United States Magazine and Democratic Review* 14 (February 1844): 184; *Anonymous,* 1 Federal Cases No. 447 (Circuit Court Missouri, 1843): 1004; *United States* v. *William S. Rogers,* 4 Howard 567 (1846): 572–73; McKenney, *Memoirs,* 2: 127–28; Beers, *Western Military Frontier,* p. 142; Gibson, *Kickapoos,* p. 118; Spencer to Taylor, March 28, 1842, in *National Intelligencer,* April 4, 1842. Also see Correspondence of the *Chicago Democrat,* September 22, 1838, in *Army and Navy Chronicle* 8 (January 3, 1839): 12; ibid. 9 (October 31, 1839): 286; U.S., *Stat.,* 9: 337–39, *United States* v. *Thomas Ragsdale,* 27 Federal Cases No. 16,113 (Circuit Court Arkansas, 1847): 685. For additional information concerning American interference in Cherokee tribal affairs during this period, see Bell, *Mr. Bell's Suppressed Report;* Foreman, *Five Civilized Tribes,* pp. 309–51.

43. *Congressional Globe,* 25th Cong., 2d sess., appendix, pp. 63–65, 69, 73–74; *United States Magazine and Democratic Review* 14 (February 1844): 184. Also see Washington *National Intelligencer* (triweekly), January 3, 1839; note 45.

44. Secretary of War, *Annual Report* (1844), pp. 125–27; *Congressional Globe,* 28th Cong., 2d sess., pp. 21, 41, 165, 173. Also see Tyler's

Third Annual Message, December 1843, Fourth Annual Message, December 3, 1844, in Richardson, *Papers of the Presidents*, 4: 258, 337–38.
    45. The quotation cited above is from the *Cleveland Herald*, July 15, 1846. The best account of the close tie between American expansionism and Indian policy during the Jacksonian era is James C. Malin, "Indian Policy and Westward Expansion," *Humanistic Studies of the University of Kansas* 2 (1921): pp. 251–358. For Douglas's earlier espousal of removal, see Douglas et al. to Democratic Republicans of Illinois, [December 31, 1835], in Robert W. Johannsen, ed., *The Letters of Stephen A. Douglas* (Urbana: University of Illinois Press, 1961), p. 29. Although Douglas's efforts to remove the Indian barrier to westward expansion spanned a decade, 1844 to 1854, historians have tended to ignore this aspect of his work to organize the territories of Kansas and Nebraska. See Ronald N. Satz, "The 1850's and the Need for Revision," *Maryland Historian* 1 (Spring 1970): 81–86. The General Land Office reported the number of "unsold" acres of land in the Indian country to Andrew Johnson in 1849 when he was preparing a speech in favor of a homestead bill. See Richard Young to Johnson, January 8, 1849, in Leroy P. Graf and Ralph W. Haskins, eds., *The Papers of Andrew Johnson, 1822–1851* (Knoxville: University of Tennessee Press, 1967), p. 488.
    46. Report on Memorial of American Mission Association, June 22, 1846, *House Report 751*, 29th Cong., 1st sess., pp. 1–6; *House Journal*, 29th Cong., 1st sess., p. 995; HR 490, *Original Bills*, 29th Cong., 1st sess.
    47. Commissioner of Indian Affairs, *Annual Report* (1846), p. 228, (1847), pp. 745–46, 750–51, (1848), pp. 400–2; Medill to Harvey, August 30, 1847, in Commissioner of Indian Affairs, *Annual Report* (1847), pp. 756–60; U.S., *Stat.*, 9: 203; *Congressional Globe*, 30th Cong., 1st sess., appendix, p. 774. For the need to revise the trade and intercourse laws and the government's concern with preventing the introduction of whiskey into the Indian country, see *United States Magazine and Democratic Review* 18 (May 1846): 333–35; Otto F. Frederickson, *The Liquor Question among the Indian Tribes in Kansas, 1804–1881* (Lawrence: University of Kansas Press, 1932). In order to provide more effective enforcement of the laws prohibiting the sale of liquor to Indians, Congress declared in 1847 that Indians were "competent witnesses" in court. The new legislation, however, did not guarantee the Indians a trial before a jury of their peers, and they still had to appear in courts in adjacent states or territories. U.S., *Stat.*, 9: 203.
    48. *Congressional Globe*, 30th Cong., 1st sess., appendix, pp. 773–74. For evidence that Johnson's attack on Medill's policies had little effect on the commissioner, see Commissioner of Indian Affairs, *Annual Report* (1848), pp. 392–93.

49. HR 579, *Original Bills*, 30th Cong., 1st sess.; Report of McIlvaine, June 27, 1848, *House Report 736*, 30th Cong., 1st sess., pp. 1–14; *Congressional Globe*, 30th Cong., 1st sess., p. 874. For an example of continued opposition by the large southern tribes, see Remonstrance of Peter Pitchlynn, January 20, 1849, *House Miscellaneous Document 35*, 30th Cong., 2d sess., pp. 1–4.

50. Richardson, *Papers of the Presidents*, 4: 636, 646, 651; *Congressional Globe*, 30th Cong., 2d sess., p. 182; Ira G. Clark, Jr., "The Railroads and the Tribal Lands: Indian Territory, 1830–1890" (Ph.D. diss., University of California, 1947), p. 17; Harmon, *Sixty Years of Indian Affairs*, pp. 176–81; Commissioner of Indian Affairs, *Annual Report* (1848), pp. 388–90.

51. Resolutions of the Legislature of North Carolina, January 29, 1849, *House Miscellaneous Document 39*, 30th Cong., 2d sess., p. 1; *Congressional Globe*, 30th Cong., 1st sess., p. 467, 30th Cong., 2d sess., pp. 68, 182, 448, 470–74, 484, 614, 615; HR 807, *Original Bills*, 30th Cong., 2d sess.

52. Malin, "Indian Policy," p. 262; Secretary of the Treasury, *Annual Report* (1848), p. 36; *Congressional Globe*, 30th Cong., 1st sess., p. 874, 30th Cong., 2d sess., p. 514; U.S., *Stat.*, 9: 395–97, 403–5. For early attempts by European powers to establish a western barrier to American expansion, see Samuel Flagg Bemis, *John Quincy Adams and the Foundations of American Foreign Policy* (New York: Alfred A. Knopf, 1949), pp. 116, 200–2. Secretary of the Treasury Robert J. Walker outlined the major reasons for shifting the Indian Office to a department concerned with "domestic relations" at the end of 1848. See Secretary of the Treasury, *Annual Report* (1848), pp. 36–37. The dissolution of the Indian country west of Missouri and Iowa is discussed in James C. Malin, *The Nebraska Question: 1852–1854* (Lawrence, Kans.: James C. Malin, 1953).

9 /

Civilizing the Indians

DURING THE TWO DECADES following the passage of the Removal Act of 1830, Indian Office agents and missionaries worked arduously in the new Indian country to transform the emigrants into "civilized" men and women.[1] Unlike President Jackson's assurances that the emigrants would be free to chart their own destinies in the West, his promises of large annuities and government subsidies for Indian education were basically fulfilled. Throughout the Jacksonian era, Democratic and Whig administrations alike espoused the virtue of Indian removal and praised the humanitarianism of the government's provisions for annuities and other educational benefits extended to the Indians. These programs, however, fully reflected the ethnocentrism of nineteenth-century Americans and, in addition to their humanitarian aspects, provided the government with a convenient means of undermining Indian culture and controlling Indian society.[2]

The annuities the Indian Office paid the tribesmen for their land served as an effective means of binding them closer to the will of the federal government. Indians received their payments either in specie, goods, or services—all part of the dominant white society and thereby a disruptive element in tribal life. American officials quickly recognized the potential inherent in the use of annuities as a device to weaken Indian cultural patterns, and they took full advantage of their opportunities. Field officials encouraged and oftentimes manipulated the tribesmen into applying their annuities toward the upkeep of educational and religious instruction by whites. Funds allocated by the Indians for education under such pressure went to the various missionary and benevolent societies which conducted religious and secular educational programs for most of the eastern tribes. Beginning in 1820 the government specifically earmarked portions of Indian annuities for educational programs. Thomas McKenney, the head of the old Indian Bureau, made a determined effort to siphon off as much of the annuity money as possible to support schools among the Indians. By the time Jackson had served his first year as president in 1830, Indian annuities for education amounted to approximately twenty-one thousand dollars.[3]

In addition to using annuities to finance educational programs for the Indians, the government also contributed its own funds. Since the administration of George Washington, the federal government had provided friendly tribes with clothing, implements of husbandry, and teachers to instruct them in "the arts of civilized life." Throughout the early years of the republic, Washington's successors stressed the need to instruct the Indians in Christianity, agriculture, and domestic trades. The House Committee on Indian Affairs reported in 1818 that "in the present state of our country, one of two things seems to be necessary: either that those sons of the forest should be moralized or exterminated." The committee advocated the former policy and suggested a program for moralizing the Indians. "Put into the hands of their children the primer and the hoe," the committee suggested, "and they will naturally, in time, take hold of the plough; and, as their minds become enlightened and expand, the Bible will be their Book, and they will grow up in habits of morality and industry ... and become useful members of society." The members of the House committee believed that education could provide a useful means of influencing future Indian-white relations by familiarizing the tribesmen with the ways of the white society which was rapidly encircling them.[4]

Congress responded to the committee's report and similar suggestions from Secretary of War John C. Calhoun by establishing a fund for Indian education in March, 1819. This "Civilization

Fund" consisted of an annual appropriation of ten thousand dollars for "the purpose of providing against the further decline and final extinction of the Indian tribes, adjoining the frontier settlements of the United States, and for the introduction among them of the habits and arts of civilization." Congress delegated to the president authority to "employ capable persons of good moral character, to instruct them in the mode of agriculture suited to their situation; and for teaching their children in reading, writing and arithmetic." Under explicit instructions from Secretary Calhoun, federal funds went to the various benevolent societies and individuals already engaged in missionary activities among the Indians. Calhoun established the policy of supporting only those endeavors which stressed agriculture and "mechanical arts" for boys and spinning, weaving, and sewing for girls. The object was to speed up the adoption of white trades by the Indians in order to advance them from their lowly place on the stepladder of civilization to a level approximating that of the American public.[5]

The Civilization Fund, like the annuities, provided a useful means of subordinating Indian society to white dominance. Calhoun, a fervent advocate of Indian removal, ruled in 1820 that all individuals or organizations receiving federal funds had to "impress on the minds of the Indians, the friendly and benevolent views of the government towards them, and the advantage to them in yielding to the policy of the government, and cooperating with it, in such measures as it may deem necessary for their civilization and happiness." The recipients of federal funds received notification that "a contrary course of conduct cannot fail to incur the displeasure of the government, as it is impossible that the object which it has in view can be effected, and peace be habitually preserved, if the distrust of the Indians, as to its benevolent views, should be excited." Thus, by the time Jackson entered the White House, the federal government had adopted at least two means of controlling or influencing the behavior of Indian societies—the annuities and the federally subsidized educational programs.[6]

While both of these programs remained in operation throughout the Jacksonian era, the government's educational endeavors for the tribesmen reveal most candidly the attitudes of federal administrators toward the American Indians. Educational programs receiving support from the government were coordinated by the head of the Indian Bureau before 1832 and by the commissioner of Indian affairs after that date. These officials synthesized suggestions from field personnel, congressional leaders, secretaries of war, and other administration leaders, and their annual reports on Indian education provide insight into the federal government's motivation and effectiveness in civilizing the Indians.

Thomas McKenney, the first head of the Indian Bureau during the Jacksonian era, had become an advocate of Indian removal before Jackson came to office. He claimed that the Indians, although they were making progress in the East, needed additional time to adapt themselves to the manifold complexities of white society and that Americans also needed time to accept the idea of civilized Indians receiving equal rights and benefits. During his brief tenure in the Indian Bureau under Jackson, McKenney became an outspoken defender of the president's contention that the Indians faced either extinction in the East or civilization in the trans-Mississippi West. While McKenney's support for Jackson's removal policy was undoubtedly based on political considerations, he did not find it an uncomfortable position. He had actually been thinking along similar lines in the past. While opponents of removal argued that the eastern tribes, especially the Cherokees and Choctaws, were making remarkable advances, McKenney replied that the relatively small number of educated Indians were merely "green spots in the desert."[7]

When Jackson began espousing the virtue of large-scale Indian removal during his first months in office, McKenney urged the president and administration leaders in Congress to give their full support to educational programs as a means of promoting emigration. McKenney pointed out that Pierre Juzan, a Choctaw educated at Richard M. Johnson's Choctaw Academy in Kentucky, had returned to his people and was urging them to heed the government's request that they leave Mississippi. "Suppose there were fifty Juzan's from different parts of the Choctaw Nation," McKenney suggested, "they would be the *lever* to lift the whole Tribe. And suppose the Creeks, and Cherokees, and Chickasaws &c. had among them young men thus educated, and informed on this great matter [;] who does not see the effect they would produce in getting their people to remove?"[8]

In order to promote the establishment of such a corps of "educated" Indian youth and to promote amity among transplanted Indians in the West, McKenney urged the administration to designate a central school for educating children from tribes throughout the United States. He argued that "common nurseries" would make lasting friendships between Indians from the diverse tribes and thereby aid the government in maintaining peace and amity among them as they came together in the area west of Missouri and Arkansas. "When the Tribes now scattered shall come to be neighbors," advised McKenney, "the influence of such early associations would tranquilize feelings that would otherwise arise among a people comparatively strangers to one another." Proper education of Indian youth would also provide an adequate base of support for the administration's removal policy. "Where can a more powerful auxiliary be found," he asked, "than in the Children of these people, whose views it is so easy to fashion after the plan which embraces the best interests of their families and friends?" McKenney worked unceasingly during the first year and a half of the Jackson administration to bring together as many youths as possible in a central location.[9]

McKenney proposed that the Choctaw Academy in Kentucky become the government's "*one School*" for the promotion of Indian education. The academy was already a successful business operation of Senator Richard M. Johnson, who was perhaps the greatest popular hero of the era next to Jackson. Although best known for his reputed slaying of the Indian chief Tecumseh during the War of 1812, Johnson was deeply interested in educational matters. He had served as an ordained Baptist minister and teacher before entering politics in the early 1800s, and he continued to manifest interest in education while serving in the United States Congress.[10]

Johnson was in the Senate in 1825 when his friend Choctaw agent William Ward suggested that the government use the senator's extensive plantation in Kentucky as a site for an Indian academy. The Choctaws had treaty provisions calling for funds for education and Ward wanted to isolate their children from the customs and practices of their parents. The Baptist Board of Missions drew up a working plan for the proposed school, and the Adams administration agreed to pay a fixed fee for other Indians attending the academy who were not covered by the Choctaw funds. The academy's curriculum, regulations, and even its menu received close scrutiny by the War Department, which ordered periodic inspections by field personnel. During the late 1820s the school became very popular among the Indians, and children from other tribes enrolled in its programs. Since Johnson received a fee from tribal annuities for each student attending the academy, as well as an allotment from the Civilization Fund, he was one of its most active supporters in Congress. Johnson was an intimate friend of President Jackson, who handpicked the Kentuckian to be Van Buren's running mate in 1836. It was no accident, therefore, that the decade of the 1830s marked the high tide of the Choctaw Academy's prosperity and influence.[11]

McKenney was aware of the close connection between Jackson and Johnson, and he was eager to advance the cause of the Choctaw Academy in order to secure his position with the new administration. The American Board of Commissioners for Foreign Missions and other benevolent societies, however, had long lamented that the academy attracted "the best scholars" and diminished interest among the Indians in missionary schools. While the Choctaw Academy received a fixed income from other tribes, the benevolent societies received only their alloted portion of the Civilization Fund from the government. But the societies could not always rely on the federal government. The "deranged" state of fiscal matters in the Indian Bureau in 1829 resulting from the counterwarrant system, for example, led the Treasury Department to divert money from the Civilization Fund. The result was that the American Board, the Baptist General Convention, and Indian youth at Kenyon College and academies throughout the United States received notification that their requests for aid had to "lay over" until Congress made up the loss in revenue. Meanwhile, McKenney encouraged field personnel to convince the tribes under their jurisdiction to use their annuities to send students to the Choctaw Academy.[12]

While the Jackson administration apparently centered its educational efforts around the Choctaw Academy, it did not neglect other avenues open to it. Agent Lawrence Taliaferro received administration support to establish a model agricultural community named Eatonville (located near Lake Calhoun in present-day

Minnesota) for the Santee Sioux of the upper Mississippi Valley region in the summer of 1829. Taliaferro and missionaries employed by the government to superintend the experiment made strenuous, albeit unsuccessful, efforts to transform the Sioux into Christian farmers and received an allotment from the Civilization Fund for this purpose. The fund, when fiscal mismanagement did not cripple it, subsidized many other similar endeavors.[13]

Federal control over the purse strings for Indian education provided the Jackson administration with a considerable amount of economic leverage over the benevolent societies. The American Board of Commissioners for Foreign Missions, one of the largest recipients of federal funds, was a strong opponent of Indian removal. Jeremiah Evarts, the board's chief officer, was one of the most prolific critics of the Removal Bill of 1830. One week after the passage of this legislation, Secretary Eaton terminated the American Board's allotment of nearly three thousand dollars for the southern Indians. Eaton reasoned that "the Government by its funds should not extend encouragement and assistance to those, who thinking differently upon this subject, employ their efforts to prevent removals." While Eaton acknowledged the benefits education would bring the Indians, he argued that it would be senseless to spend any more funds for tribes within states and territories claiming jurisdiction over them.[14]

This economic coercion and the necessity to bargain with the government for reimbursement for old school buildings in the East as removal got underway in the 1830s led the American Board and similar organizations to cease their opposition to removal. Isaac McCoy's efforts to secure the educational annuities provided in removal treaties for the financing of new Baptist missions in the Indian country awakened a competitive spirit among the benevolent societies, which soon began stressing the need to make the most of the possibilities presented by emigration. "To take up entire nations of men, and place them several hundred miles from their former seats, with the avowed intention of gradually amalgamating them into one homogeneous mass, or of amicably preserving their national peculiarities," asserted the *Biblical Repository and Quarterly Observor* in 1835, "is a measure, to say the least, which ought to be watched with the closest attention."[15]

The announced goal of federally subsidized education programs for the Indians during the Jacksonian era was the transformation of "savages" into "civilized" men who might eventually become a part of the great American experiment in democracy. Federal officials shared with many of their contemporaries an ethnocentrism which manifested itself in a disdain for Indian religious beliefs, kinship systems which stressed matrilineal descent and allowed children to grow up in an extremely permissive atmosphere, and economic systems which reversed the roles that males and females played in American society and stressed communalism over private ownership. The ethnocentrism of federal officials led them to exaggerate the hunting aspects of Indian society and to ignore the advances of many of the tribes in agriculture. While this misunderstanding of Indian culture may have resulted from a desire to give added credence to the removal policy, even the most sophisticated ethnologists of the period made the same error. As Roy Harvey Pearce observes, "The metaphysics of Christian, civilized progress not only distorted the facts of Indian life but *made* them."[16]

The personnel involved in the formulation of Indian policy in the 1830s and '40s believed that the Indians lacked the essentials of civilized society—Christianity, private property, and knowledge of agriculture and the mechanical arts. They argued that removal and segregation of the Indians in the trans-Mississippi West would provide the best means of introducing them to these prerequisites of civilization while protecting the easily manipulated tribesmen from unscrupulous traders, whiskey vendors, gamblers, prostitutes, and others who continuously fleeced them of their annuities in the East. Government officials warned that they could not protect the Indians from such people in areas where states claimed jurisdiction.[17]

Andrew Jackson and his successors concluded that the Indians faced the alternatives of extinction in the East or civilization in the West. This line of reasoning received the support of leading ethnologists. Henry R. Schoolcraft was just one of many who agreed that removal and education in the West under federal auspices would produce the necessary transition from the hunter to the agricultural state of society for the tribesmen. Interestingly enough, federal officials always claimed that their ultimate goal was the assimilation of the Indians once they reached the farming stage of development. This attitude was in marked contrast to the views of many of these same men concerning the status of the Negro and, later, the Mexican.[18]

While Indian Office personnel viewed the Indian as culturally inferior to the white man, most did not believe he was lacking in intelligence. They assumed that the Indians would willingly adopt American institutions, religious beliefs, and customs once they had an opportunity to see the tremendous benefits they would bring. More importantly, they admitted that the government had an obligation to redeem and assimilate the tribesmen.[19]

Indian Office personnel placed great faith in the power of education as a civilizing device. They held in common with many of their contemporaries the belief that man was perfectible through reason and that progress was inevitable. The missionaries they employed to educate the Indians also believed in the concept of progress. According to their particular version of this idea, the Indians were perfectible or capable of becoming civilized by accepting the teachings of the Gospel and acknowledging Jesus Christ as their redeemer. Unlike the schoolbook writers of this period, government agents and their missionary allies believed that the Indians need not suffer extinction. Indeed, these men claimed that they were eager to help the Indians become industrious and moral members of American society, and they argued that education was the means to that end.[20]

Federal support for Indian education went to several kinds of institutions and various individuals during the Jacksonian era. After removal commenced in earnest in the early 1830s, the government supported Indian youth at white colleges and academies, the Choctaw Academy in Kentucky, and other boarding and day schools in the United States and the new Indian country in the West. Treaty commissioners also included provisions in removal treaties for farmers and blacksmiths to teach the Indians their trades. At institutions receiving federal funds, Indian pupils received instruction similar to that obtained by white children of their age at common schools and academies throughout the United States. Depending on their age and level of achievement, Indians studied reading, writing, arithmetic, geography, history, algebra, astronomy, natural and moral philosophy, bookkeeping, and surveying according to the Lancaster, or monitorial, plan of instruction. Day schools in the Indian country usually had pattern farms and blacksmiths to demonstrate agriculture and the mechanical arts to the students. In addition to these subjects, however, Indian pupils spent considerable time studying the Bible and the religious doctrines of the missionaries, who usually served as their instructors.[21]

Baptist minister Thomas Henderson, superintendent of the Choctaw Academy, asked Secretary of War Lewis Cass in 1832 to permit the establishment of workshops for mechanically inclined students. The government had apparently backed away from requiring Indian students at the academy to attend manual trade classes because they were usually the children of chiefs who did not wish their offspring to do "menial industry" or to become the "negroes" of missionaries. Henderson, however, found that his students had a hard time keeping their minds on their books, and he thought they might find it more rewarding to learn the trades of "mechanicians."[22]

Henderson's suggestion received the support of Joseph Bourassa, a young Potawatomi who taught at the academy. Bourassa agreed that classical studies offered little to Indians and warned that the government was wasting its time and money providing the tribesmen with a classical education when "most any trade will prove more beneficial in the first settling of a country." The Indian teacher reminded Commissioner Herring that "it was not by the use of the pen and book [that America was settled by Europeans], but [by] the use of the axe and plough." Bourassa urged the government to teach young Indians trades so that they could support themselves in their new trans-Mississippi homeland and ease the hardships caused by their removal. "A useful trade," he observed, "will prove more beneficial among the Indians than the learning of the greatest professor in North America." He also argued that "an old Indian would be more pleased to get a knife or a tomahawk from his son than ten well ordered philosophical or historical lectures; for he will say, these lectures do not feed me nor clothe my children." Bourassa's appeal, together with Henderson's recommendation, led the War Department to rethink its position on mechanical education at the prestigious Choctaw Academy.[23]

Early in 1833 Commissioner Elbert Herring gave the academy permission to open, on a voluntary basis, a wheelwright shop, a shoe shop, and a blacksmith shop for its boys. He also ordered strict regulations to prevent the children from being overworked. These included the submission of records to the Indian Office of each boy's activities. The youths were to receive the proceeds of their labor according to the work they had actually performed after the government subtracted the cost of tools and the salaries of the mechanics who trained them. The academy was to forward quarterly reports of the progress of its pupils to the Indian commissioner.[24]

Early reports about student interest in the new programs at the academy gave added encouragement to the Indian Office. Commissioner Herring observed in 1834, "If the chase is to be abandoned, and war cease to be a favorite pursuit among them, it can only be effected by the substitution of other employments; and none so salutary, or so vital to the object, as the prompt introduction of such mechanical arts as are suited to the necessities of their condition, and adapted to the early stages of civilized life." Herring believed that mechanical education, together with an emphasis on "agricultural pursuits" and the "doctrines of christianity," would help the Indians move toward "the grand point of civilization." He encouraged other schools to add studies in mechanical arts to their curricula, and he became an avid supporter of these courses for the students at the Choctaw Academy.[25]

Herring hoped that the academy could provide a corps of "native teachers" who would be able to transmit their skills to other Indian youths. The Indian service reorganization act of 1834 specifically required that the government hire Indians, wherever possible, when treaties called for teachers, farmers, or mechanics, and Herring hoped that the tribes would agree to employ students who had learned to farm or had mastered a trade at the academy. Unlike his predecessor, Thomas McKenney, he did not encourage the separation of Indian youths from their parents. Commissioner Herring favored local schools over boarding schools. While he praised the remarkable progress of the boys at the Choctaw Academy, he believed that the majority of Indian children should remain with their parents so that "the strength of ties of kindred" could remain unimpaired. Local schools within tribal boundaries, he argued, would soon become "an object of common interest," while at the same time "the improvement and correct habits of the young often excite the more mature in years to exertion, and reform the vicious." In order to instill a deep interest in the local schools in the minds of the parents and the children, Herring ordered the agents assigned to tribes receiving educational assistance to make annual inspections of the schools, accompanied by a military detachment. These inspections included public examinations of the students. Herring hoped that such measures would convince the parents of the worth of the schools.[26]

Herring's faith in the ability of the Indian to adopt white agricultural practices and mechanical trades was shared by his successor, Carey A. Harris, who also believed that local schools were preferable to boarding schools. Schools situated within tribal boundaries, Harris observed in his first annual report in 1836, "become objects of common feeling and interest, and the ties of family and kindred are not separated or weakened." This position was in accord with the growing sentiment among the emigrant tribes to have their children remain with them and receive the education that the government had promised them in their new country rather than in the East. The Choctaws especially demanded that their children attend local schools. By the late 1830s this tribe had transformed its wilderness home into a prospering farm area and was extremely reluctant to see some of its finest young men leave for Kentucky or elsewhere. Harris encouraged the Indians in their support for local schools. His general philosophy, however, was that Indian schools should enroll only those students whose parents had sufficient influence with other tribesmen to shape their sentiment and conduct toward government programs.[27]

The ideas of Herring and Harris reflected the advice and reports from numerous field personnel throughout the country as well as suggestions from secretaries of war and congressional leaders. They provided Harris's successor, Thomas Hartley Crawford, with a solid framework upon which he could build. Crawford also brought some experience of his own in educational matters to the Indian Office when he became commissioner in 1838. Between 1833 and 1834 he had served as a member of the committee of the Pennsylvania legislature which established a new state system of general education. This committee had solicited information from educational leaders throughout the Union and had studied their replies carefully before making its own recommendations. It was perhaps no accident, then, that Crawford took such an active interest in educational programs for the Indians and in what ethnologists today refer to as acculturation, or the process by which one set of cultural traits is replaced by another.[28]

When Crawford took over the Indian Office in October, 1838, he made a careful examination of the educational reports of his predecessors and subordinates in the field service. He quickly discovered that the success of the civilization program was not very gratifying, in spite of general agreement among federal officials that the Indians were not inferior to whites in mental capacity. Crawford pondered this dilemma and decided that "there must be some defect in the course adopted."[29]

The commissioner believed that the error was the attempt of missionaries receiving federal funds to Christianize the Indians before civilizing them. He agreed with the teachings of the Puritan minister John Eliot, who had argued over a century earlier that aborigines had to be civilized before they could become Christians. Crawford observed that Europe had emerged from barbarism to civilization only after a great period of time, and he warned that missionaries and others living in the "full blaze" of civilization were aiming too high and attempting to civilize the Indians too hastily. "We ask untutored tribes of men and women (schooled as little by circumstance and time as by positive instruction)," he argued, "to discard habits that have existed from the creation of the world, and put on ours." The commissioner suggested that the government revamp its entire educational program for the Indians.[30]

Crawford agreed with his predecessors that manual arts and agriculture were vital subjects for Indian schools. He had, however, a more sophisticated understanding of the socialization and acculturation processes than McKenney, Herring, or Harris. While the commissioner recognized that white children mastered the arts of civilization "unconsciously and without knowing how or when," he realized that Indians would never do so by merely learning to read and write. As he explained it:

> If they do not learn to build and live in houses, to sleep on beds; to eat at regular intervals; to plough, and sow, and reap; to rear and

use domestic animals; to understand and practise the mechanic arts; and to enjoy, to their gratification and improvement, all the means of profit and rational pleasure that are so profusely spread around civilized life, their mere knowledge of what is learned in the school room proper will be comparatively valueless.

Commissioner Crawford lost little time in devising an educational program that would bring these rudiments of civilization to the Indian.[31]

Crawford's work with the educational system in Pennsylvania in the early 1830s had undoubtedly acquainted him with the curriculum of the manual labor academies and colleges that were sprouting up throughout the nation. Reformers, free Negroes, and some workingmen supported the establishment of such schools during the Jacksonian era because they wanted the indigent or their own children to acquire trades and, by receiving pay for their labor, learn habits of thrift and industry. Commissioner Crawford drew on the philosophy, experiences, and goals of the manual labor institutes to restructure federal educational programs for the Indians. Between 1838 and 1845 he constructed an educational system for the Indians that survived for generations.[32]

Crawford became a staunch defender of the manual labor school. Although he received encouragement and ideas from field officials and Secretary of War Joel Poinsett, the details of the program he developed were largely his. The commissioner realized that the civilization of the Indian would not occur overnight. "You must lay the foundations broadly and deeply, but gradually, if you would succeed," he advised Poinsett. He wanted to construct an educational system that would make the socialization of Indian youth more analogous to that of American children. While seeking to civilize the Indians, he was keenly aware that much of the learning and knowledge of white men could not yet be within their grasp or even useful to them. It was senseless to teach an Indian to read and write if he remained a savage in all other aspects of life. Precept, the commissioner argued, was not sufficient to improve morals, although it might do wonders for the mind. Indians had to learn to farm, to work in the mechanical arts, and to labor profitably before they could be truly civilized and secure their own welfare. Crawford believed that neither the belles lettres nor the academic wisdom of the scholar were going to save the Indian from extinction. Without training in manual labor, there would be no change in Indian habits.[33]

Crawford slowly worked out a blueprint for an entire educational system for the Indians. Clan or neighborhood schools with adjoining farms provided the cornerstone. The commissioner hoped that Indian youths would, over a period of time, begin to emulate American farmers and become tillers of soil on their own land holdings. Neighborhood schools offered many advantages. Teachers would not only mingle familiarly with their students, but they would meet and converse with their parents. The parents, in turn, would see their children engaged in studies and working on the farm. They would become "familiarized with the process, and observe (which even they must do) the change that is gradually but surely wrought upon the tempers, habits, and conduct of their children." While the parents and older brothers and sisters may be uneducated, he pointed out, "they will feel what they cannot explain, and unconsciously respect, by altered lives, what they do not understand." Crawford realized that changes in habits and values required time, but he believed his plan would provide benefits in the long run if the government would endorse it.[34]

While advocating the adoption of a neighborhood or clan school system, Crawford did not wish to withdraw support immediately from existing boarding schools. In fact, he hoped that larger boarding schools or perhaps even one central boarding school would provide a sufficient supply of native teachers for the clan schools. One advantage of such a dual system would be that Indians returning to their homes after receiving an education elsewhere would find peers with common interests. Heretofore, Indians returning from boarding schools received a hostile welcome from their brethren, who deprecated their mimicking of the white man. Speaking of the typical experiences of the Indian student who returned to his tribe from a white school, Crawford noted that "his knowledge is despised by the uncultured men around him, who value the capability of enduring fatigue, or of throwing a bullet or the tomahawk with accuracy, more than all he knows, while he, without association or interest, either relapses into savage habits, or is more likely to fall into vicious indulgence." By a plan providing for a central school or boarding schools for the more capable students in addition to smaller local schools, "the absentee will find, on his return, companions in those who have received local instruction, [and he will] be properly estimated, and communicate what the small institution did not teach."[35]

Crawford also suggested another innovation. Government educational programs for the Indians had always stressed education for the males, but Crawford believed this was one of the greatest errors federal administrators had made. "Unless the Indian female character is raised, and her relative position changed, such education as you can give the males will be a rope of sand, which, separating at every turn, will bind them to no amelioration," he warned. Ascribing to what one contemporary scholar calls "the cult of true womanhood," Crawford argued, "If the women are made good and industrious housewives, and taught what befits their condition, their husbands and sons will find comfortable homes and social enjoyments, which, in any state of society, are essential to morality and thrift." The commissioner wanted the largest proportion of Indian students to be female, for "the duties of wives and mothers [are] more important, as more to be extensively felt, than the education of the males." By providing their husbands with "all the delights that the word home expresses," good housewives would encourage the men to take pride in their homes and other private possessions.[36]

While Crawford admitted that the effect of teaching "housewifery" to the females would not be perceived immediately, he believed it would be reflected in the character and values of their children. Crawford argued that "without this ever-busy and ever affectionate auxiliary there can be no radical success." By combining manual arts and agriculture for the males and housewifery for the females, the government could create a sound educational system. Commissioner Crawford urged President Van Buren to adopt his plan. He acknowledged that "failure, substantially, so far, has marked the kind and beneficent agency of the Government and of good men and benevolent societies" in promoting the arts of civilized society among the Indians, but he maintained that his plan was feasible. "If the manual-labor system and a liberal extension of female instruction shall also prove unavailing after years of trial," he concluded, "then, but not until then, the hope of the philanthropist may be abandoned."[37]

Crawford's plan called for serious long-range planning as well as long-range financial commitments by the federal government. It received strong support from the Van Buren administration. Secretary of War Joel R. Poinsett fully endorsed the commissioner's proposals. Poinsett, one of the most cosmopolitan figures of his generation, was a firm advocate of compulsory public education. He had long believed that only an agricultural people could become civilized, and he urged the early adoption of Crawford's plan of Indian education.[38]

The commissioner went to work putting the system together in late 1840. He urged the establishment of primary schools in every district of the Indian country and selected abandoned Fort Coffee, located on the southern bank of the Arkansas River a few miles from the Choctaw Agency, as the site of a central manual labor school. The abandoned military fort offered many advantages. It had a sufficient number of buildings suitable for "an extensive school establishment," and "the farm is open, so as to connect the manual-labor and farm benefits with others." Crawford noted that while it was near the Choctaw country, it was "quite convenient to the Creeks, Cherokees, Senecas and Shawnees, Seminoles, and not very remote from the Chickasaws and Osages." The site was a healthy one, and generally "all the advantages that could be reasonably looked for seem to be here combined."[39]

Crawford planned to send promising male and female students from the clan schools to the new central school for advanced training. The central school would teach males to farm and instruct them in the mechanical arts, while introducing the females to sewing, spinning, weaving, and other domestic arts. He asked William Armstrong, the acting superintendent of the Indian country west of Arkansas, to search for "a man of irreproachable morals, and of capacity and acquirements far above what is usually sought for in an Indian tutor" to be principal of the new school. "He must . . . not be inferior to gentlemen placed at the head of academies in the populous states," Crawford warned. In addition to this presiding official, the commissioner hoped to hire a farmer to teach the boys agriculture and a matron who was a qualified seamstress to teach the girls housewifery. He insisted that the female student population should never be less than that of the males, for their education was of tremendous importance to the accomplishment of his program. "The foundation must be laid so broadly," he told Armstrong, "as to support the extended super-structure that it is hoped will be raised upon it."[40]

The commissioner sought to obtain money for the proposed manual labor school at Fort Coffee by channeling the funds that usually went to the Choctaw Academy in Kentucky to the new institution. The Whig administration that came to office in 1841 was not overly enthusiastic about subsidizing the academy which was operated by Van Buren's vice-president, and the Indians themselves favored moving the school closer to their country.[41]

Although the Choctaw Academy received over thirty thousand dollars annually from the annuities of various tribes, the Choctaws and others who sent their young there were increasingly becoming dissatisfied with the school. In early 1840, for example, Choctaw tribal leader Thomas LeFlore charged that his son had received terrible treatment at the academy and had learned only the vices of drinking and gambling. Similar reports by visitors to the school only strengthened the conviction of many full-bloods that Indian youths would only abandon their tribal customs and acquire indolent and other undesirable habits there. Methodist Episcopal missionary Henry C. Benson poignantly summed up the major grievances of the full-bloods:

> Their sons came home disqualified for usefulness. They were nei-ther Indians nor white men. They remained in Kentucky till they forgot their own people, their customs, and their traditions—in some instances even their native tongue. They came home stran-gers to their own parents and brethren, and wanting in attachment to their tribe and its national characteristics.

Indian leaders became particularly distressed when several stu-dents returning home from the academy committed suicide. These youths had found it impossible to cope with the fact that their education and new ways of life had estranged them from their kin in the Indian country. Meanwhile, serious discipline problems at the Choctaw Academy forced its owner, Vice-Presi-dent Richard M. Johnson, to agree in 1840 to terminate the school within a few years.[42]

Commissioner Crawford responded to the growing demand among the Choctaws for local schools by asking the Tyler administration to divert the funds expended at the Choctaw Academy plus an allotment from the Civilization Fund to a central school in the Indian country. While he eagerly awaited the approval of the new administration and the Indian tribes before putting his plans into operation, the commissioner also took other steps to assure better education programs for the Indians and to placate their grievances.[43]

Crawford encouraged Secretary of War John Bell to appoint Peter Pitchlynn, a mixed-blood chief educated at the Choctaw Academy in Kentucky, as superintendent of that institution. The commissioner told the Reverend Thomas Henderson, who had served as superintendent for almost a generation:

> The appointment of Col. Pitchlynn is to be considered in the light of an experiment being the selection of a native Choctaw, at the instance of the [Choctaw] nation, in the hope that from a better comprehension of the Indian character, he can judiciously manage the pupils at the Academy, give a more beneficial direction to their application to the branches of study they are prosecuting, and a moral tone to their conduct.

Crawford gave Pitchlynn virtually a free hand in running the academy, hoping that his presence would have a salutary effect on the student body. Since Pitchlynn had joined the full-bloods in their opposition to sending Indian youths to this distant school, his appointment to head it may have actually been part of Commissioner Crawford's overall strategy to divert the academy's funds to an institution in the Indian country.[44]

In an attempt to lay the groundwork for his broad educational plans for the Indian country, Commissioner Crawford supported the Methodist Episcopal church in its efforts to operate a manual labor academy at the Fort Leavenworth Agency. He promised the missionaries in charge of the school "liberal" aid but was disappointed to learn that they had enrolled twice as many boys as girls in their classes. "The conviction is settled," he told Methodist Episcopal church leaders, "that the civilization of these unfortunate wards of the Government will be effected through the instrumentality of their educated women, much more than by their taught men." He urged them to register more girls and suggested that they would be undermining their own effort if they did not do so.[45]

While working to establish an extensive educational system for the Indians in the trans-Mississippi West, Crawford did not neglect those in the Old Northwest and the East. He noted that "the present unsettled condition of the tribes . . . forbids any effort until they are permanently located beyond the primary schools, which are now established wherever they are likely to be useful, or tribes will consent to avail themselves of the advantages held out to them." When the Tyler administration considered creating a northern Indian territory as a counterpart to the southern Indian country in 1841, Crawford advised that "a plan of education on a broad foundation should be a part of the system that will be devised for it." Pending the establishment of the northern territory, however, Crawford urged that neighborhood schools among the northern Indians stress farming and manual arts.[46]

While the commissioner was working out the details for an elaborate Indian educational system, the House of Representatives threatened to cut off all federal funds for Indian education. Whig Congressman Samson Mason of Ohio introduced a resolution on January 25, 1842, adopted by the Committee on Ways and Means, calling for an investigation of the propriety of discontinuing the Civilization Fund and all appropriations for similar purposes stemming from treaties with the Indians. The country was still feeling the effects of the panic of 1837 in the winter of 1842, and retrenchment was the watchword in the House of Representatives. New York Whig Millard Fillmore, chairman of the Ways and Means Committee, had demanded convincing data and arguments for the huge expenditures in Indian affairs as early as 1841. Whigs were also looking for ways to embarrass the late Van Buren administration, and some apparently hoped that a careful examination of federal expenditures in Indian affairs would prove damaging to the Democrats. Pennsylvania Whig James Cooper, chairman of the Committee on Indian Affairs, took the resolution under advisement and began an investigation into the operation of the Civilization Fund and Indian appropriations stemming from treaty provisions.[47]

The Tyler administration quickly came to the defense of both types of federal expenditures. Secretary of War John C. Spencer joined Commissioner Crawford in defending the government's programs for Indian education. Spencer informed Congressman Cooper that there were thirty-seven schools and eighty-five teachers receiving federal funds to instruct nearly thirteen hundred pupils. "But very little of what is accomplished can be shown by figures," Spencer assured Cooper, adding that "the gradual advances in civilization, improvement in morals, and in the agricultural and mechanical arts, elevation of mind, and love of peace, cannot be measured. Yet, these have been attained, in a greater or less[er] degree, among all the Indian tribes, for whose benefit the civilization fund has been applied."[48]

Spencer's defense of the Civilization Fund was a manifestation of his commitment to America's debt to the Indians. One indication of his strong feelings for the tribesmen is that he fully endorsed the use of government funds to subsidize the work of the missionaries among them. Before joining Tyler's cabinet, Spencer had served as superintendent of the common schools in New York, where he had worked diligently to oppose the spread of sectarian education and the use of state money for religious schools. His bias against public support for religious schools did not, however, extend to the use of federal funds for the Christianization of the Indians.[49]

Spencer maintained that the United States had a tremendous moral obligation to the Indians. He responded to the House resolution with these queries:

> Who brought these Indians to their present condition? Who deprived them of the means of pursuing that mode of life to which they were fitted, and in which they were happy? Who enervated their bodies and degraded their minds by the contamination of the vices of the white man? And does not a fearful obligation rest upon us to mitigate, if we cannot arrest, the evils which our rapacious dominion has so profusely dealt to them?

Spencer found it difficult to believe that the House of Representatives seriously contemplated taking away "the poor pittance of an annuity of ten thousand dollars, to save them from utter degradation and wretchedness!" Such an act would be too ignoble. "It cannot be," he wrote, "that in this age, so distinguished for benevolent exertions to enlighten and improve our race, an American Congress can be found to tear this bright page from our statute book, and leave nothing but the records of oppression and injustice."[50]

Secretary Spencer also believed there were very practical reasons why Congress should not repeal the appropriation for Indian education. "In reference to our own interests, if an appeal so sordid be necessary," he asserted, "there can be no doubt of the wisdom of a just policy." Only acts of kindness would lead to the cultivation of friendly relations with the tribes inhabiting America's western borders. "Every step they take towards civilization removes them from the habits of the hunter life, and from the warlike dispositions which it engenders," the secretary cautioned, adding that "every advance towards Christian knowledge diminishes their ferocity, and disposes them to peace." The education of Indian youth was helping to promote tranquility on the nation's western boundaries. Educating the Indians was a means of controlling their behavioral patterns, for "every child among them who is instructed becomes a new ligament to bind them to the duties and obligations of civilized life." Spencer argued persuasively that money spent on educating the Indians was a wiser long-range investment than funds for military weapons. "No act could be more unjust, more hostile to the dictates of humanity and religion, or more impolitic," he asserted, "than a repeal of the noble act which admitted our obligations to the depressed and degraded Indian."[51]

Spencer also defended the continuation of treaty provisions for education. He pointed out that "they in truth are not dependent on the discretion of Congress." While treaty commissioners wrote treaties in such a way as to imply that Congress had authority to terminate funds for education, "the Indians never so understood the provisions referred to." Negotiators had assured the Indians that provisions for annuities were written in such a way in order to "conform to our Constitution, which gave to Congress the exclusive power of appropriating money; but that so long as the tribes existed, and were in a condition to require such aid, it would be granted." Spencer argued that the government had promised that the funds would be perpetual and that "the discontinuance of these annuities would be a palpable breach of the public faith."[52]

The secretary's eloquent defense of the Civilization Fund and annuities provided by treaties impressed chairman Cooper of the House Committee on Indian Affairs. After carefully examining data prepared for him by Spencer and Commissioner Crawford, Cooper defended both federal programs on the floor of the House. The Pennsylvanian admitted that the Indians had not made rapid progress along the path to civilized society, but he argued that "the first step towards the civilization of a barbarous people is the most difficult." The tribesmen, moreover, were laboring under severe handicaps. "In the case of the Indians," Cooper pointed out, "the difficulty was aggravated by extrinsic obstacles of the most formidable character, the greatest of which were their unsettled condition and the discontent occasioned by the effort necessary to compel them to quit their former abodes." Yet Cooper was optimistic about the future of the emigrants. He noted that many of the Indians were making "gratifying progress" in agriculture and the mechanical arts and, more important, that "several of the tribes have adopted forms of government and social institutions, framed upon the model of our own." Cooper concluded that the existing educational programs were "a good beginning" but warned that "fullest success" would come only "if the Government of the United States should persevere in a course of liberal policy towards them."[53]

The entire Committee on Indian Affairs responded favorably to these arguments and joined Cooper in recommending that "it would be both unwise and unjust to discontinue the [Civilization Fund] appropriation, when the object for which it was made is in so fair a way to be realized." The committee acknowledged that it had a duty to "retrench the expenses of the Government, in all cases where it is practicable to do so," but it argued that "no consideration of economy in the expenditures would justify the discontinuance of this appropriation at the present time." The committee agreed with Commissioner Crawford that the repeal of the Civilization Fund would be an act of "severity" which would "end in deeply injuring, if not blighting entirely, the prospects of the ignorant, poor, and dependent Indian." The Committee on Indian Affairs concluded that the repeal of the fund would be a deep stain on the nation's honor.[54]

After convincing Congress of the need to continue the Civilization Fund, Congressman Cooper and other members of his committee took up the defense of the appropriations for treaty provisions calling for funds for education, mechanics, farmers, and implements of husbandry for the Indians. There were over twenty treaties in existence containing such provisions, amounting to over forty thousand dollars annually. Members of the committee admitted that the treaties provided for the continuance of these funds at the discretion of the government, but they stated that "in construing treaties concluded between a powerful and enlightened nation and feeble savage tribes, the latter should have the benefit of a favorable interpretation; and perhaps it would be but right, in giving effect to the stipulations, to look beyond the letter, to what was the probable understanding of the weaker and less intelligent party." Cooper and his colleagues agreed with Secretary Spencer that "the Indians did not regard these provisions as mere gratuities . . . but as permanent annuities, to be paid to them in consideration of the cession of their lands." The committee believed that it would be unwise to discontinue these appropriations for the Indians. "They have suffered many wrongs, for which we owe them redress," Cooper reported, "and the only way to make such redress is to bestow upon them the means of education, and to instruct them in the arts of industry and peace."[55]

The fact that there were over ninety thousand Indians congregated on the frontier west of Arkansas and Missouri also made it unwise to tamper with the treaty provisions. The House committee warned that the probable effect of abrogating the provisions would be "an Indian war, in which all the tribes will unite." On higher moral grounds, however, the committee maintained that the American people would never object to spending federal funds to "elevate the condition of a people, who have, in many instances, received hard measure at the hands of the Government." A majority of the Congress apparently concurred with the Indian Committee's position that national honor, equity, humanity, and national security demanded the continuation of the appropriations, since nothing further came of the resolution from the Ways and Means Committee. Secretary Spencer, Commissioner Crawford, and members of Congress on Cooper's committee had saved the educational superstructure that had evolved since the early days of the republic from the attack of Millard Fillmore's retrenchment-conscious committee.[56]

With that crisis behind them, Secretary Spencer urged Commissioner Crawford to proceed with his elaborate plans for civilizing the Indians. Crawford also received some support from the Choctaws in the Indian country who, after meeting in general council in November, 1842, called for the establishment of neighborhood schools throughout their nation. The Choctaws, however, requested that Crawford change the site of the proposed central manual labor school from Fort Coffee on the periphery of their country to a location near Fort Towson, which was actually on their land. Crawford agreed to this request and forwarded seven thousand dollars to help erect permanent buildings for the new school and to support local schools throughout their country. He also promised to provide two thousand dollars annually from the Civilization Fund for this "important concern." Meanwhile, the Indian Office advised Richard M. Johnson, the proprietor of the Choctaw Academy in Kentucky, that "the obligations of the Government to furnish pupils" would cease in two years. Crawford, speaking for the Tyler administration, let it be known that henceforth it would be government policy to support "large schools of an elevated character" and "those of less pretension" within the Indian country.[57]

Crawford took other steps to invigorate the educational program in the Indian country. He hired John Bemo, a former Seminole "savage" and supposedly the nephew of Osceola who was brought up by a white family, to instruct his brethren in the West. Crawford hoped that his presence would remove the repugnance which Seminoles had for schools. When the commissioner discovered that the Choctaws did not particularly agree with his views on the education of females, he encouraged their agent to "persuade" them of the soundness of such programs and allotted a portion of their annuities specifically for this purpose "in anticipation" of the agent's success. Crawford tried to convince all of the tribes to spend their annuities on education instead of "wasting them" or converting them into "curses" like whiskey. He also arranged to send twenty of the best Indian "scholars" to college. Ten went to Asbury University in Indiana and the other half went to Lafayette College in Pennsylvania, where they could obtain a higher education while being situated near some of the best farmers in the country.[58]

Americans were pouring into Oregon in the early 1840s, and Crawford promoted the establishment of schools for the Indians in that area. The commissioner also forwarded funds to missionary groups among the Delawares, the Iowas, the Chickasaws, and many others. By the time Crawford left the Indian Office in 1845, he had made an indelible mark on federal educational efforts among the Indians. Throughout his tenure in office, he had held that "the fact of Indian capability to become all that education and Christianity can make man is incontestably established." He maintained, moreover, that education was "the great moral lever by which the Indian race is destined to be raised, as all other men have been lifted, from the miriness of idleness and vice, to the high ground of useful occupation and virtue." Only "perseverance" was needed to accomplish the task of transforming the savages into "all they are capable of becoming."[59]

The return of the Democrats to national power in March, 1845, did not perceptibly alter the educational policies established by Crawford under the Tyler administration. Crawford was a personal friend of President Polk, and when the commissioner left office his successor, William Medill, had only praise for his efforts. The new secretary of war, William L. Marcy of New York, joined Medill in supporting the measures Crawford had introduced. Manual labor schools, neighborhood schools, and training in agriculture and mechanical arts for the boys and domestic arts for the girls continued in vogue. Medill, however, directed in 1845 that all funds for education would thereafter be spent only on "manual labor and other schools in the Indian country." Up to this time, funds had also supported Indian youths at "literary institutions" in various states plus those preparing for learned professions. Medill and Marcy agreed that the training of Indians in their own country was so superior to any other plan of education ever suggested that the Indians would be wasting their time at schools "in the States." In July, 1848, Congress supported their contention by prohibiting the expenditure of government funds for Indian education in areas outside of the Indian country.[60]

At the end of the Polk administration, the Indian Office could boast that it was subsidizing sixteen manual labor schools, with over eight hundred students, as well as eighty-seven boarding and district schools, with nearly three thousand pupils. It could also claim that "no other Government has contributed so largely to schools and farming instruction among the Indians, or contracted for and paid, in like manner, annuities to tribes who have been removed from the land of which they originally held possession." Yet federal efforts to educate the Indians and transform them into mirror images of the white man during the Jacksonian era were not entirely successful. The acculturation of the tribesmen was uneven. As one critic of the Indian removal policy succinctly pointed out several decades later, "The result has been disappointing because the policy was inherently defective."[61]

Federal officials had envisioned the removal and segregation of the Indians in the trans-Mississippi West as the initial step in the civilizing process. They generally ignored or failed to recognize the achievements that many eastern tribes had already made in adopting the white man's ways. Before their removal, many of the southern Indians, for example, had benefited greatly from the Civilization Fund and treaty provisions calling for educational establishments, agricultural implements, and blacksmiths. Their land was already largely denuded of game animals, and they had made a remarkable transition from the hunting to the farming stage of development. The transplanting of such tribes into a strange environment across the Mississippi River actually retarded the advancement of some Indians in the so-called civilized arts.[62]

Tribesmen who had learned to farm in the East frequently had to hunt in the West in order to secure sufficient food for their families. Crops did not spring up overnight in their new homeland, and tardy shipments of farming implements promised by the government in removal treaties delayed planting. Hunting, therefore, was sometimes necessary to feed hungry mouths. The situation was particularly critical for many emigrants by the late 1830s because the influx of large numbers of eastern tribesmen to the trans-Mississippi Indian country caused an ecological imbalance which led to a scarcity of game. The propinquity of Indian emigrants to fierce plains Indians also made it necessary for some tribesmen who had buried the tomahawk and taken up the plow in the East to turn to the rifle in the West and to neglect the establishment of schools. The presence of "wild Indians of the prairies" in the district provided for the Chickasaws actually forced these Indians to take up temporary residence on Choctaw land. Although the Chickasaws were the wealthiest of all of the southern emigrants, they were exceedingly reluctant to build schools or churches or to make any costly improvements in the Choctaw district. Even some tribes receiving large annuities and government educational subsidies suffered initial setbacks in the acculturation process as a result of the trauma of removal and the manifold problems inherent in adjusting to a new environment.[63]

The situation in the Old Northwest demonstrates most clearly the wide gap between the announced goals of the removal policy and its actual effects. Although cultural factors played an important role in the reluctance of many of the tribes in this region to adopt white farming practices, the constant fear of future removals was also an impediment to attempts by the Indian Office to spread white civilization to these Indians. The government was continually reshuffling the tribes in the Old Northwest to new "permanent" locations. Indians were understandably reluctant to farm and improve their land. They were certain that a future removal was imminent and found it more convenient to live off their annuities than to labor in the fields. The tribes in the Old Northwest relied heavily on the fur traders for food and goods rather than labor on land which white men coveted and might claim tomorrow. Some officials, moreover, discouraged the "wasting" of federal funds on Indians not yet located west of the Mississippi River. Northeastern tribes transplanted in the Old Northwest often found that their new environment was not conducive to the patterns of farming they had developed in the East. The Oneidas of New York, for example, were as helpless in Wisconsin Territory, a critic of removal claimed, as they would have been on the streets of London.[64]

Federal officials often blamed the slow progress of the Indians in adopting the white man's ways on weakness of character. Indian Office personnel suggested that large annuities and the availability of whiskey also contributed to the Indians' refusal to take up farming or other aspects of civilized society. Although these factors certainly tended to discourage the interest of some Indians in educational programs, government officials failed to comprehend a more important deterrent to their efforts. Circumscribed in their thoughts and actions by the prevailing American values, officials were unwilling to concede the tribesmen a cultural distinctiveness and integrity worth preserving. Indeed, they interpreted the Indians' reluctance to abandon their old customs as evidence that they belonged to an "idle and dissipated" race. Even enlightened officials like T. Hartley Crawford could not fully appreciate the complexities of Indian culture and the acculturation process. Indian culture was, as Roy Harvey Pearce observes, "a delicately balanced system of attitudes, beliefs, valuations, conditions, and modes of behavior." Such a complex system is unlikely to reintegrate itself completely within a short period of time.[65]

The reluctance of many Indians to adopt the patterns of agriculture encouraged by the Indian Office often had very little to do with idleness or weakness of character. The refusal of Chickasaw mixed-bloods to work in the fields, for example, was actually an indication of their acceptance of the prevailing pattern of agriculture in the South. They had adopted slavery as an economic institution in Mississippi and saw little need to soil their own hands as long as their blacks could labor in the fields for them. The refusal of the Mdewakanton Sioux to use the plow, on the other hand, was not the result of any repugnance for physical labor. These semisedentary Indians were already agriculturalists, but their religion proscribed the use of plows, which would allegedly "injure" their fields. The Sioux, moreover, considered farming women's work. One perceptive agent noted that "their religion . . . does not allow a man, till he begins to decline with age, to labor in cultivating the earth or such other work as is usually performed by white men. The man who will do such work, is looked upon and treated like the hindoo who violates caste." The opposition of other tribesmen to government programs and the pervasive problem of drunkenness frequently noted by officials were often reactions to the deep trauma inflicted upon Indian society by the removal process and the iconoclasm of the missionaries employed by the government. The ethnocentrism of Indian Office personnel prevented them from understanding that not all Indians would prefer the "rewards" and "benefits" of American civilization to their ancient ways of life.[66]

Government officials sought to destroy the superstructure of Indian society by permitting the Indians virtually no avenues of continuity with old patterns. Unlike the situation in parts of nineteenth-century Latin America where creole governments permitted much of native culture to remain intact, American officials sought to devastate Indian culture and replace it entirely with American social and political institutions, religious practices, and kinship patterns. The result frequently approximated the condition contemporary sociologists refer to as social anomie, a situation induced by a tremendous conflict of norms which manifests itself in confusion, disorientation, disorganization, and antisocial behavior. Some Indians found that Christianity and the white man's ways provided a means of reorientating their lives and providing the order needed to stabilize their confused social state. The Delaware Indians, on the other hand, reverted to a strong nativism, or what social scientists call a revitalization movement, a deliberate effort of members of a society to reconstruct a more satisfying culture. Others found that whiskey made life more bearable and provided sufficient solace from the social conflict and insecurity wrought by the disruptive elements of white culture, while a few found their estrangement so unbearable that they committed suicide.[67]

The widescale employment of missionaries as civilizing agents often had a deleterious impact on the acculturation process. There was constant rivalry among the various Protestant denominations and between the Protestants and the Catholic missionaries. Tribal solidarity often suffered when members joined different churches or when Christian Indians sought to wrest control from "pagan" Indians. George Copway, a Chippewa chief, noted that "the *doctrines* which have been preached in this civilized country may be necessary for the purpose of stimulating various denominations to zealous labor, but in our country they have had a tendency to retard the progress of the gospel." Strenuous efforts by missionaries to defend doctrinal views prejudiced the minds of some of the Indians against Christianity. "When they preach love to God and to all men, and act otherwise toward ministers of differing denominations," Copway warned, "it creates doubts in the mind of the watchful Indian as to the truth of the word he hears."[68]

Some Indian emigrants demonstrated open hostility to missionaries and their preachings because they associated them with their removal from their ancient homes. Such antimissionary attitudes were particularly strong in tribes that had emigrated under duress. The Creeks, still bitter over the hardships and indignities they endured during their forced relocation, actually whipped anyone found attending Christian services. Not until the end of the Jacksonian era did official Creek opposition to Christian missionary work end. As long as Indians linked Christianity with their misfortunes, the acculturation process suffered. Similar difficulties occurred when some missionaries began agitating the question of the abolition of slavery among the slaveholding southern tribes.[69]

Another problem with the employment of missionaries as acculturative agents was that they represented only a small subculture of the larger white society. They stressed theology and moral taboos more than their fellow countrymen. Yet the Indians frequently saw other whites whom they came into contact with openly disregard the teachings of the Gospel. Many of the new traits the missionaries tried to implant, together with their emphasis on speedy conversions, weakened tribal bonds as well as social classes and otherwise disrupted Indian society without necessarily leading to the adoption of Christianity by the tribesmen. The missionaries, moreover, often remained totally oblivious of Indian culture, in spite of their long years of residence among the tribes. As Robert F. Berkhofer, the leading scholar of Protestant missions among the Indians in the antebellum period, notes, "The laborers in the Lord's vineyard were doomed not to reap the harvest they hoped because of their own cultural assumptions, the racial attitudes of their compatriots, and the persistence of aboriginal culture."[70]

The educational programs for the Indians throughout the Jacksonian era were merely devices to remake them in the image of the white man. Historian Timothy L. Smith asserts that there were four basic factors which helped to bring a sense of unity and order to American life in the early nineteenth century—the kinship group, religious and ethnic institutions, the neighborhood or town, and the nation itself. Indian removal and the educational programs financed by the government for the tribesmen confused or disorientated all of these unifying factors for the Indians and left their tribes in a socially weakened position. Many of the emigrants to the trans-Mississippi West had left their old homes only because they were told that they could not maintain their tribal identity in the East. Yet the government used missionaries, the Indians' own money in the form of annuities, the Civilization Fund, and other appropriations stemming from treaty provisions to wage a massive assault against the integrity of Indian culture in the trans-Mississippi West. Federal officials, like the missionaries and teachers they employed, were limited by parameters which conceived of society only in middle-class, Christian, and Lockian terms. Limited in their thinking by a narrow ethnocentrism, they were defrauding the Indians of their culture in the name of civilization and progress. They failed to comprehend that their programs only reduced the Indians from cultural maturity as members of tribal societies to cultural infancy as "civilized" men.[71]

In addition to problems stemming from the ethnocentrism of government officials, the education program suffered from the congressional parsimony and bureaucratic inefficiency that characterized other facets of federal Indian policy and administration in the Jacksonian era. While the Indian Office labored to educate and civilize the Indians, not until 1847 did it receive adequate funds to compile a census of the tribes and to undertake an intensive study of the history and customs of the various Indian societies. Even though the number of Indian youths attending school was only a fraction of their total population, the Civilization Fund remained at the original figure of ten thousand dollars throughout the period.[72]

Annuities and other funds provided by missionary groups aided the cause, but the civilization program suffered from insufficient finances. The annuities, moreover, often arrived late or remained in local banks while field personnel awaited tardy instructions from Washington. Treaty provisions calling for the establishment of education annuities from funds obtained by the sale of Indian land in the East often took years to go into effect. Land Office agents were notoriously slow in surveying such land and preparing it for sale. The economic problems stemming from the panic of 1837 and the drain on the field service caused by the Mexican War only aggravated these problems. Perhaps the most detrimental problem, however, was that many of the officials engaged in teaching the Indians received their appointments for political reasons. The teachers appointed by superintendents, agents, and subagents did not always bring altruistic intentions to their new positions.[73]

The civilization program eventually succumbed to the onslaught of American continentalism in the late 1840s. In 1848, for example, Superintendent Thomas H. Harvey at Saint Louis urged the Indian Office to allocate suitable farming land in the trans-Mississippi West for prairie Indians who lacked such land. Harvey pointed out that the buffalo herds were rapidly diminishing and that this situation provided the government with an excellent opportunity to transform the prairie Indians into Christian farmers. Commissioner Medill, however, unequivocally opposed the scheme, arguing that agricultural land in the trans-Mississippi West had to be kept open for "the egress and expansion of our own population."[74]

The Polk administration was extremely nervous about the Indian concentrations along the path of westward emigration to its newly acquired possessions in the Southwest and Pacific West. Commissioner Medill reported in 1848 that many of the tribes in the West had made considerable progress in adopting the patterns of civilized society, but he noted that some of them blocked the pathways to the Rocky Mountains. These tribes, the commissioner pointed out, would have to find new homes. "Else," he observed, "not only will they be run over and extinguished, but all [their accomplishments] may be materially injured." Once again, a Democratic administration called for the emigration of Indians to remove an impediment to American development and progress. Only this time the incumbent in the White House was looking not at land in the South but in the trans-Mississippi West, which he envisioned as a pathway to the Far West and the Orient beyond.[75]

NOTES

1. The terms *civilized, civilizing,* and *civilization* will hereafter appear without quotation marks. The usage of these words reflects a value judgment of Americans in the Jacksonian era, not of the author.

2. Francis Paul Prucha has recently attempted to refurbish Jackson's image in Indian affairs by stressing the national-security implications of his removal policy. Prucha, however, has neglected these aspects and concomitant proposals for social control in the government's educational efforts for the Indians in the trans-Mississippi West. Compare the following articles by Prucha: "Andrew Jackson's Indian Policy," pp. 527–39; "American Indian Policy in the 1840's: Visions of Reform," in *The Frontier Challenge: Responses to the Trans-Mississippi West,* ed. by John G. Clark (Lawrence: University Press of Kansas, 1971), pp. 81–110.

3. Strong, "Wardship," p. 109; Evelyn C. Adams, *American Indian Education: Government Schools and Economic Progress* (Morningside Heights, N.Y.: King's Crown Press, 1946), p. 32; Viola, "McKenney and the Administration of Indian Affairs," pp. 207, 209. George Dewey Harmon, whose study of "Indian Trust Funds," pp. 23–30, ignores the social-control implications of the program, contends that the government's handling of the annuities did much to "protect and promote the moral, social, financial, and general welfare of the Indians against the degrading influences of designing whites."

4. U.S., *Stat.*, 1: 329, 2: 139, 3: 516; House Committee Report, January 22, 1818, in *American State Papers: Indian Affairs*, 2: 151; Report of James Cooper, June 10, 1842, *House Report 854*, 27th Cong., 2d sess., p. 3; Prucha, *American Indian Policy*, pp. 213–21.

5. U.S., *Stat.*, 3: 516–17; Circular from Calhoun, September 3, 1819, IA, Data Book for the Civilization Fund, RG 75, NA; Calhoun to Clay, January 15, 1820, *American State Papers: Indian Affairs*, 2: 260–61; Calhoun to Barbour, April 11, 1822, *House Document 110*, 17th Cong., 1st sess., p. 2; Schmeckebier, *Office of Indian Affairs*, pp. 39–40. Calhoun's policy of funding established institutions remained in effect when Jackson entered office. See, for example, Herring to Reverend C. F. Quickenbourne, July 24, 1834, IA, LS, 9: 87, RG 75, NA. For a discussion of the cooperation between church and state in Indian affairs, see Beaver, *Church, State, and the American Indians.*

6. Regulations for the Civilization of the Indians, February 29, 1820, IA, Data Book for the Civilization Fund, RG 75, NA. Also see Strong, "Wardship," pp. 112–13, 276; Griffin, "Religious Benevolence as Social Control," pp. 423–44.

7. Viola, "McKenney and the Administration of Indian Affairs," p. 212; McKenney to Eaton, March 22, 1830, IA, LS, 6: 350–52, RG 75, NA. For McKenney's political motivation, see chapters 1 and 6.

8. McKenney to Richard M. Johnson, December 11, 1829, IA, LS, 6: 188, RG 75, NA. Juzan later signed the Choctaw removal treaty of 1830. See Kappler, *Indian Affairs*, 2: 316, 318.

9. McKenney to Johnson, December 11, 1829, McKenney to Street, April 13, 1830, McKenney to Clark, May 4, 1830, IA, LS, 6: 188–89, 385–86, 404, RG 75, NA.

10. McKenney to Johnson, December 11, 1829, IA, LS, 6:188, RG 75, NA. The standard biography of Johnson is Leland W. Meyer, *The Life and Times of Colonel Richard M. Johnson of Kentucky* (New York: Columbia University Press, 1932). Also see Shelley D. Rouse, "Colonel Dick Johnson's Choctaw Academy: A Forgotten Educational Experiment," *Ohio Archaeological and Historical Quarterly* 25 (1916): 88–117.

11. Kappler, *Indian Affairs*, 2: 135, 149; Ward to Barbour, June 26, 1825, McKenney to Johnson, October 12, 1825, McKenney to Kingsbury, October 20, 1825, McKenney to Choctaw Chiefs, October 21, 1825, Plan and Regulations of the Choctaw Academy, 1825, enclosed in McKenney to Secretary of War, December 9, 1825, Barbour to Henderson, September 11, 1826, plus enclosures, McKenney to Henderson, February 19, 1827, February 7, 1828, Abstract . . . of Choctaw and Other Pupils at the Choctaw Academy, 1827–1841, *House Document 109*, 26th Cong., 2d sess., pp. 4, 12, 14–16, 20–24, 33–36, 179; *Niles' Register* 29 (December 10, 1825): 226–27; Reverend Thomas Henderson to Eaton, May 1, 1829, IA, LR, Schools, RG 75, NA; McKenney to Johnson, December 11, 1829, McKenney to Street, April 13, 1830, McKenney to Clark, May 4, 1830, IA, LS, 6: 188–89, 385–86, 404, RG 75, NA; Porter to Jackson, December 15, 1833, Porter Papers; C[rawford] to Spencer, August 19, 1842, IA, Report Books, 3: 278, RG 75, NA; Rouse, "Johnson's Choctaw Academy," pp. 93–99, 111. There is evidence to indicate that Johnson's relationship with the inspectors of the academy during the Jackson and Van Buren administrations was a cozy one. See C[rawford] to Henderson, September 17, 1840, IA, LS, 29: 241–42, RG 75, NA; Porter to [Tyler], December 2, 1843, SW, LS, President, 6: 143–44, RG 107, NA. For examples of Johnson's maneuverings to increase the enrollment at the academy while he was vice-president, see Johnson to Tipton, October 27, 1838, in Blackburn, *John Tipton Papers*, 3: 757; Johnson to Milroy, March 8, 19, May 21, 1840, Milroy Papers.

12. Kingsbury to Barbour, June 26, 1825, plus enclosures, Kingsbury to McKenney, September 28, October 11, 1825, *House Document 109*, 26th Cong., 2nd sess., pp. 5–7, 12–13, 17–18; McKenney to Eaton, March 16, May 28, 1829, same to Evarts, March 23, 1829, same to Lincoln, March 23, April 7, 1829, same to Nathaniel Kendrick, April 1, 1829, same to Cass, May 29, 1829, same to Reverend Bishop Chase, May 29, 1829, same to Johnson, April 1, 1830, same to Street, April 13, 1830, same to Clark, May 4, 1830, IA, LS, 5: 346, 363, 367, 389, 399, 446–49, 451, 453, 6: 362, 385–86, 404, RG 75, NA; Bureau of Indian Affairs, *Annual Report* (1829), pp. 160–62. For evidence that McKenney did not go beyond the bounds of propriety in his dealings with Johnson, see McKenney to Johnson, June 13, 1829, IA, LS, 6: 13, RG 75, NA. See chapter 6 for a discussion of the counterwarrant system.

13. Meyer, *Santee Sioux*, pp. 49–50, 52–55, 62. For an analysis of government educational efforts among the Sioux, see Claude E. Stipe, "Eastern Dakota Acculturation: The Role of Agents of Culture Change" (Ph.D. diss., University of Minnesota, 1968). For examples of the wide variety of educational establishments supported with government funds,

see Commissioner of Indian Affairs, *Annual Report* (1836), p. 401, (1839), pp. 344–45, 471, (1841), pp. 349–52, (1842), p. 524; Secretary of War, *Annual Report* (1842), p. 191, (1846), p. 60; Doty to Lawe, August 24, 1843, Lawe Papers; Adams, *American Indian Education*, p. 40.

14. Eaton to McKenney, June 7, 1830, McKenney to Evarts, June 7, 1830, IA, LS, 6: 456, 459; Greene to Wirt, September 24, 1831, Wirt Papers, Maryland Historical Society. See chapter 1 for Evarts's opposition to removal. Even before Eaton cut off the appropriation to the American Board, McKenney advised missionary leaders that the best way to obtain funds for education was to have the Indians allocate a portion of the money "arising out of sales of land" to this purpose. See McKenney to Kingsbury, March 8, 1830, IA, LS, 6: 315, RG 75, NA.

15. Greene to Wirt, September 24, 1831, Wirt Papers, Maryland Historical Society; Isaac McCoy to Lewis Cass, April 10, 1832, McCoy Papers; *American Baptist Magazine* 14 (June, 1834): 208, 232–33; Ruby L. Culp, "The Missions of the American Board and Presbyterian Church among the Five Civilized Tribes, 1803–1860" (M.A. thesis, George Washington University, 1934), pp. 98, 143; Worcester to [Chandler], July 7, 1835, in Shirk, "Some Letters from the Reverend Samuel A. Worcester," p. 471; *Biblical Repository and Quarterly Observor* 5 (1835): 427–28, cited in Beaver, *Church, State, and the American Indians*, p. 114.

16. This paragraph is based on the official reports and the correspondence of the Indian Office. See Bureau of Indian Affairs, *Annual Report* (1829–31); Commissioner of Indian Affairs, *Annual Report* (1832–49); IA, LS, vols. 5–41, RG 75, NA; IA, Registers, LR, 2–37, RG 75, NA. The quotation is from Roy Harvey Pearce, "The Metaphysics of Indian-Hating," *Ethnohistory* 4 (Winter 1957): 34. For a discussion of ethnological thought during this period, see Robert E. Bieder, "The American Indian and the Development of Anthropological Thought in the United States, 1780–1851" (Ph.D. diss., University of Minnesota, 1972).

17. See notes 16 and 18.

18. See Richardson, *Papers of the Presidents*, 2: 438, 456–59, 554–55, 565–66, 597, 3: 33, 171–72, 294, 391–92, 498, 500, 561, 4: 80, 199, 348, 411, 505, 560–61, 651; Schoolcraft, *Memoirs*, passim.; Satz, "Federal Indian Policy," p. 217 n; also see note 16. Sociologists define assimilation as the process by which an outside group, like the Indians, becomes fully adjusted to another institutional order, like American society. See August B. Hollingshead, "Human Ecology," in *Principles of Sociology*, ed. by Alfred M. Lee, 3d ed. (New York: Barnes & Noble, 1969), p. 276.

19. See note 16. Also see *McCoy's Register* 1 (1835): 47–48.

20. See note 16; Elson, *Guardians of Tradition*, pp. 71–81. For an analysis of the concept of progress in antebellum America, see Arthur A.

Ekirch, Jr., *The Idea of Progress in America, 1815–1860* (New York: Columbia University Press, 1944). A penetrating analysis of missionary thinking during this period appears in Robert F. Berkhofer, Jr., *Salvation and the Savage: An Analysis of Protestant Missions and American Indian Response, 1787–1862* (Lexington: University of Kentucky Press, 1965).

21. This paragraph is based on an examination of the official reports and the correspondence of the Indian Office as well as the ratified treaties during the Jacksonian era. See note 16; Kappler, *Indian Affairs*, 2: 213–425. The government also furnished domestic animals and husbandry implements as gifts. See U.S., *Stat.*, 4: 738; Revised Regulations No. 3, June 1, 1837, IA, Misc. Records, 2: 264, RG 75, NA.

22. Henderson to Cass, May 8, 1832, same to Herring, April 18, 1833, *House Document 109*, 26th Cong., 2d sess., pp. 65–68; Henry C. Benson, *Life among the Choctaw Indians, and Sketches of the South-West* (Cincinnati: L. Swormstedt & A. Poe, 1860), p. 34; Berkhofer, *Salvation and the Savage*, p. 40.

23. Bourassa to General N. D. Grover, February 20, 1833, Bourassa to Cass, February 21, 1833, Bourassa to Herring, April 18, 1833, *House Document 109*, 26th Cong., 2d sess., pp. 61–65. For additional information on Bourassa, see Tipton to Henderson, October 20, 1831, Tipton to Cass, May 13, 1832, Bourassa to Tipton, August 3, 1832, in Blackburn, *John Tipton Papers*, 2: 448, 605, 672–73; Dorothy V. Jones, "A Potawatomi Faces the Problem of Culture Change: Joseph N. Bourassa in Kansas," *Kansas Quarterly* 3 (Fall 1971): 47–55.

24. Herring to Bourassa, March 25, 1833, Herring to Henderson, May 1, 1833, October 20, 1834, March 7, 1835, *House Document 109*, 26th Cong., 2d sess., pp. 64, 68, 84–85, 92–93.

25. Inspector's Quarterly Report of the Conditions of the Choctaw Academy, November 8, 1833, *House Document 109*, 26th Cong., 2d sess., pp. 69–70; Commissioner of Indian Affairs, *Annual Report* (1833), p. 169, (1834), pp. 241–42, 244–45, 262–63, (1835), pp. 273–74, 283. The idea of mechanical education as the Indian's door to civilization dominated the thinking of the Indian Office into the twentieth century. See U.S. Office of Indian Affairs, *Farm and Home Mechanics: Some Things that Every Boy Should Know How to Do and Hence Should Learn to Do in School* (Washington, D.C.: GPO, 1911).

26. Commissioner of Indian Affairs, *Annual Report* (1833), pp. 169–70, (1834), pp. 241, 262–63, (1835), p. 283; U.S., *Stat.*, 4: 737; Ward to Boyd, July 28, 1834, in Reuben G. Thwaites, ed., "Documents Relating to the Episcopal Church and Mission in Green Bay, 1825–1841," *Collections of the State Historical Society of Wisconsin* 14 (1898): 487; Kappler, *Indian Affairs*, 2: 252; Everett Dick, *Vanguards of the Frontier: A Social History of the Northern Plains and Rocky Mountains from the Earliest*

White Contacts to the Coming of the Homemaker (New York: D. Appleton-Century Co., 1941), p. 134. For the use of "native teachers" and the Choctaw Academy's success in supplying them, see Bureau of Indian Affairs, *Annual Report* (1831), p. 172; Report of Armstrong, 1837 and 1838, in Commissioner of Indian Affairs, *Annual Report* (1837), p. 542, (1838), p. 525. An effort to standardize the inspection process was made in 1837. See Revised Regulations No. 3, June 1, 1837, IA, Misc. Records, 2: 244–47, RG 75, NA. Cf. Hagan, *American Indians*, p. 91.

27. Commissioner of Indian Affairs, *Annual Report* (1836), p. 401; Report of Armstrong, 1838, ibid. (1838), pp. 524–25; Harris to Dodge, July 29, 1836, IA, LS, 19: 336–37, RG 75, NA; Armstrong to Harris, October 31, 1838, *House Document 109*, 26th Cong., 2d sess., p. 166; Debo, *Choctaw Republic*, pp. 78–79; Adams, *American Indian Education*, p. 39. Cf. Hagan, *American Indians*, p. 91.

28. Geo[rge] Smith, "How the Public School System was Established in Pennsylvania," *Pennsylvania Magazine of History and Biography* 37 (January 1913): 76–82. It is interesting to note that one of the major defects of the educational legislation Crawford helped to draft in Pennsylvania was the lack of sufficient administrative machinery to carry it into effect. Ibid., p. 79. For recent studies of the acculturation process, see Edward H. Spicer, "Acculturation," in *International Encyclopedia of the Social Sciences*, ed. David L. Sills, 17 vols. (New York: Macmillan Co., & the Free Press, 1968), 1: 21–27; Social Science Research Council, "Acculturation: An Exploratory Formulation," *American Anthropologist* 56 (December 1954): 973–1002; Edward M. Bruner, "Primary Group Experience and the Process of Acculturation," ibid. 58 (August 1956): 605–23. A brief general survey of Indian acculturation appears in Evon Z. Vogt, "The Acculturation of the American Indians," *Annals of the American Academy of Political and Social Science* 311 (May 1957): 137–46.

29. Commissioner of Indian Affairs, *Annual Report* (1838), pp. 450–51. The influx of large numbers of eastern tribesmen to the trans-Mississippi West caused an ecological imbalance which led to a scarcity of game. The Indian Office provided temporary subsistence to the emigrants, but this was a tacit admission of the demoralization which removal had inflicted on many tribal societies and of the government's failure to provide the Indians with sufficient provisions and training to survive in their new environment. See U.S., *Stat.*, 5: 298; Commissioner of Indian Affairs, *Annual Report* (1838), p. 450; Poinsett to [Harris], July 27, 1838, plus enclosures, in Commissioner of Indian Affairs, *Annual Report* (1838), pp. 473–75; Bert Anson, "Variations of the Indian Conflict: The Effects of the Emigrant Indian Removal Policy, 1830–1854," *Missouri Historical Review* 59 (October 1964): 82.

30. Commissioner of Indian Affairs, *Annual Report* (1838), p. 450, (1840), p. 242, (1842), p. 386, (1844), p. 313. Eliot's work among the Indians is discussed in Alden T. Vaughan, *New England Frontier: Puritans and Indians, 1620–1675* (Boston: Little, Brown, 1965). Francis Paul Prucha asserts in "American Indian Policy in the 1840's," p. 107 n, that "there was a controversy at the time among the missionaries about which should come first, civilization or Christianity, but the Indian Office did not enter into the dispute since it was agreed that both were needed."

31. Commissioner of Indian Affairs, *Annual Report* (1840), pp. 242–43, (1844), p. 313. Social scientists define socialization as the process by which individuals are incorporated into the customary and institutional order of a society. See Hollingshead, "Human Ecology," p. 276.

32. See note 28; *Niles' Register* 45 (November 2, 1833): 147; Petition of Citizens of Wisconsin Territory to Congress, [February 13, 1837], in Carter and Bloom, *Territorial Papers*, 27: 735; Gladys A. Wiggin, *Education and Nationalism: An Historical Interpretation of American Education* (New York: McGraw-Hill Book Co., Inc., 1962), pp. 369–71; August Meier and Elliot Rudwick, *From Plantation to Ghetto* (New York: Hill & Wang, 1966), pp. 99, 120. The work of the manual labor schools in Indian education before Crawford came into office is discussed in Robert F. Berkhofer, Jr., "Model Zions for the American Indian," *American Quarterly* 15 (Summer 1963): 176–90.

33. Commissioner of Indian Affairs, *Annual Report* (1838), p. 450, (1839), pp. 343–44, (1840), pp. 242–43.

34. Commissioner of Indian Affairs, *Annual Report* (1838), pp. 450–51, (1839), pp. 343–45, (1840), pp. 242–43. Also see ibid. (1844), p. 315. William T. Hagan contends in *American Indians*, p. 91, that government officials in the 1840s favored boarding schools over day schools.

35. Commissioner of Indian Affairs, *Annual Report* (1838), pp. 450–51, (1839), pp. 343–44, (1840), p. 243.

36. Commissioner of Indian Affairs, *Annual Report* (1838), p. 454, (1839), p. 344, (1840), p. 242. For the male image of women and their role in the antebellum period, see Barbara Welter, "The Cult of True Womanhood: 1820–1860," *American Quarterly* 18 (Summer 1966): 151–74. Ethel McMillan notes, in her study of "Women Teachers in Oklahoma," *Chronicles of Oklahoma* 27 (Spring 1949): 28–31, the presence of many women teachers in the Indian country during the Jacksonian era.

37. Commissioner of Indian Affairs, *Annual Report* (1839), p. 344.

38. Secretary of War, *Annual Report* (1838), p. 113, (1839), pp. 50–51, (1840), p. 28; Rippy, *Joel R. Poinsett*, pp. viii, 186–87, 207, 215 n; P[oinsett] to [Frances Tyrell], February 15, 1847, Poinsett Papers. Poinsett had

not always been optimistic about the prospect of educating the Indians in American ways. In 1832, for example, he told Alexis de Tocqueville that the Indians were "a race that will perish sooner than try to become civilized." Quoted in Pierson, *Tocqueville and Beaumont*, p. 652.

39. Commissioner of Indian Affairs, *Annual Report* (1840), p. 244; Crawford to Armstrong, July 11, 1840, ibid., p. 389. Also see Crawford to Poinsett, December 30, 1839, *House Document 103*, 26th Cong., 1st sess., pp. 7–8.

40. Crawford to Armstrong, July 11, 1840, in Commissioner of Indian Affairs, *Annual Report* (1840), pp. 389–90.

41. Ibid. (1840), pp. 243–44; Crawford to Armstrong, July 11, 1840, ibid. (1840), pp. 389–90; Armstrong to Crawford, October 6, 1841, ibid. (1841), pp. 318–20. Also see note 27 for Indian opposition to distant boarding schools.

42. Baird, *Peter Pitchlynn*, pp. 57–58; Benson, *Life Among the Choctaw Indians*, pp. 37–38; Josiah Gregg, *Commerce of the Prairies; or, The Journal of a Santa Fe Trader, During Eight Expeditions Across the Great Western Prairies, and a Residence of Nearly Nine Years in Northern Mexico*, 2 vols., 2d ed. (New York: J. & H. G. Langley, 1845), pp. 261–62; Foreman, *Five Civilized Tribes*, p. 59; Meyer, *Richard M. Johnson of Kentucky*, p. 367; Crawford to Armstrong, April 9, 1840, *House Document 109*, 26th Cong., 2d sess., p. 141; Crawford to Pilcher, June 27, 1840, IA, LS, 28: 475–76, RG 75, NA; Commissioner of Indian Affairs, *Annual Report* (1841): 263.

43. Commissioner of Indian Affairs, *Annual Report* (1841), p. 263. Also see note 41. Although Crawford hoped to transfer the funds spent on the Choctaw Academy to the Indian country, he continued to send pupils to the academy. Crawford and John C. Spencer, who replaced Bell as secretary of war in the fall of 1841, claimed that the government had an obligation to the Indians enrolled there to continue to support the school until it closed its doors. Crawford to Armstrong, April 9, 1840, *House Document 109*, 26th Cong., 2d sess., p. 141; Crawford to Pilcher, June 27, 1840, March 17, 1841, IA, LS, 28: 475–76, 30: 173–74, RG 75, NA; Secretary of War, *Annual Report* (1842), p. 192; Crawford to Armstrong, September 13, 1843, IA, Chickasaw Removal Records, LS, B, p. 323, RG 75, NA.

44. C[rawford] to Henderson, March 13, 1841, Crawford to Pitchlynn, March 13, 19, 1841, Crawford to Armstrong, March 17, 1841, IA, LS, 30: 168–69, 174–75, 177, RG 75, NA; Meyer, *Richard M. Johnson of Kentucky*, p. 375; Baird, *Peter Pitchlynn*, pp. 58–61. W. David Baird contends that Peter Pitchlynn deliberately "ruined" the Choctaw Academy. For Pitchlynn's conduct at the school, see ibid.

45. Commissioner of Indian Affairs, *Annual Report* (1838), p. 450, (1840), p. 243, (1841), p. 262; Adams, *American Indian Education,* pp. 36–37. Also see Commissioner of Indian Affairs, *Annual Report* (1844), pp. 313–15.

46. Commissioner of Indian Affairs, *Annual Report* (1841), p. 263. See chapter 8 for the attempt to establish a northern Indian territory.

47. Fillmore to Crawford, December 31, 1841, *House Report 75a,* 27th Cong., 2d sess., pp. 1–2; C[rawford] to Fillmore, January 4, 1842, IA, Report Books, 3: 75, RG 75, NA; *Congressional Globe,* 27th Cong., 2d sess., p. 169. For the activities of Fillmore's Ways and Means Committee, see White, *The Jacksonians,* pp. 129–30. The lingering effects of the panic of 1837 are described in Reginald C. McGrane, *The Panic of 1837* (Chicago: University of Chicago Press, Phoenix Books, 1965), p. 236; Peter Temin, *The Jacksonian Economy* (New York: W. W. Norton & Co., 1969), p. 155.

48. Spencer to Cooper, June 8, 1842, *House Report 854,* 27th Cong., 2d sess., p. 18. This printed letter is a corrected version of the copy in the Indian Office files. See IA, Report Books, 3: 196–97, RG 75, NA. Also see Commissioner of Indian Affairs, *Annual Report* (1842), pp. 385–86; Secretary of War, *Annual Report* (1842), p. 191.

49. Secretary of War, *Annual Report* (1841), p. 75. For Spencer's earlier career, see Glyndon G. Van Deusen, *William Henry Seward* (New York: Oxford University Press, 1967), pp. 68–70; Ray Allen Billington, *The Protestant Crusade, 1800–1860: A Study of the Origins of American Nativism* (Chicago: Quadrangle Paperbacks, 1964), pp. 150–51; chapter 8, note 38.

50. Spencer to Cooper, June 18, 1842, *House Report 854,* 27th Cong., 2d sess., p. 18.

51. Ibid., pp. 18–19. Cf. *Baptist Missionary Magazine* 17 (June 1838): 129.

52. Spencer to Cooper, June 18, 1842, *House Report 854,* 27th Cong., 2d sess., p. 19. Also see Secretary of War, *Annual Report* (1841), p. 75.

53. Report of Cooper, June 10, 1842, *House Report 854,* 27th Cong., 2d sess., pp. 1–4.

54. Ibid., pp. 4, 6, 15.

55. Ibid., pp. 7–9.

56. Ibid., pp. 13–15. The investigation of Indian expenditures in 1842 apparently led to a tighter supervision of the Civilization Fund and other appropriations for education. See Circular from Crawford, July 25, 1843, Doty to Lawe, August 24, 1843, Meade to Lawe, September 22, 1843, Lawe Papers.

57. Secretary of War, *Annual Report* (1842), pp. 191–92; C[rawford] to Armstrong, March 17, 1841, IA, LS, 30: 174–75, RG 75, NA; Commis-

sioner of Indian Affairs, *Annual Report* (1842), pp. 386–87, 526, (1843), p. 271; Report of Armstrong, 1842, ibid. (1842), p. 496; Crawford to Armstrong, September 29, 1842, ibid., pp. 524; Gregg, *Commerce of the Prairies,* 2: 261–62. While the Choctaws withdrew their students from the Choctaw Academy in 1845, the Indian Office continued to send Indian youths there until it closed its doors at the end of the Polk administration. Johnson to Medill, July 4, 1846, Medill Papers; Marcy to [Polk], February 13, 1849, SW, LS, President, 4: 386, RG 107, NA; Debo, *Choctaw Republic,* pp. 44–45; Meyer, *Richard M. Johnson of Kentucky,* p. 378.

58. Commissioner of Indian Affairs, *Annual Report* (1842), p. 387, (1843), pp. 271–72; Crawford to Armstrong, May 8, September 13, 29, 1843, ibid., pp. 370–73. Also see Crawford to Upshaw, April 29, 1844, IA, Chickasaw Emigration Records, LS, B, p. 349, RG 75, NA; Richard J. Bolling, *History of Catholic Education in Kansas, 1836–1932* (Washington, D.C.: Catholic University of America, 1933), pp. 29–30.

59. Commissioner of Indian Affairs, *Annual Report* (1840), p. 243, (1842), p. 385–86, (1843), pp. 270–73. Also see ibid. (1844), p. 317.

60. Ibid. (1845), p. 452, (1846), pp. 226–27, (1847), pp. 748–49, (1848), p. 386; Secretary of War, *Annual Report* (1845), p. 204, (1846), p. 60, (1847), p. 70, (1848), p. 84; U.S., *Stat.,* 9: 264. Contrary to his announcement that "literary institutions" would no longer receive government funds, Medill continued to send promising Indian youths to Eastern schools. See James P. Wilson to Medill, September 5, 1848, Medill Papers.

61. Secretary of War, *Annual Report* (1848), p. 84; Commissioner of Indian Affairs, *Annual Report* (1847), p. 735, (1848), p. 385, (1849), p. 956; *United States Magazine and Democratic Review* 18 (May 1846): 334–35; Hagan, *American Indians,* pp. 88–89. The quotations cited above are from Jefferson Davis, "The Indian Policy of the United States," *North American Review* 143 (November 1886): 439. For a discussion of the durability of Indian culture, see A. Irving Hallowell, "The Backwash of the Frontier: The Impact of the Indian on American Culture," Smithsonian Institution, *Annual Report* (1958): 447–71.

62. See notes 16 and 18; *Congressional Debates,* 21st Cong., 2d sess., pp. 774–75; Pearce, *Savagism and Civilization,* p. 66; Spoehr, "Changing Kinship Systems," pp. 160–62, 221–22; Norman A. Graebner, "Pioneer Indian Agriculture in Oklahoma," *Chronicles of Oklahoma* 22 (Autumn 1945): 232; Young, *Redskins, Ruffleshirts and Rednecks,* pp. 5–6; Anson, "Variations of the Indian Conflict," pp. 65, 67; Strong, "Wardship," pp. 84–85. For a convenient summary of the preremoval acculturation of many of the tribes that settled in Indian country, see Wright, *Guide to*

Indian Tribes of Oklahoma. Reginald Horsman contends, in "American Indian Policy," p. 136, that with the exception of the Cherokees, "the Indians apparently showed themselves unwilling or incapable of becoming American farmers." For evidence that the situation was more complex than Horsman indicates, see notes 65 and 66.

63. See note 29; Graebner, "Pioneer Indian Agriculture in Oklahoma," p. 235; Anson, "Variations of the Indian Conflict," pp. 65–67; Carolyn T. Foreman, "Education Among the Chickasaw Indians," *Chronicles of Oklahoma* 15 (June 1937): 140–41; Gibson, *Chickasaws*, p. 231; Bernice N. Crockett, "Health Conditions in Indian Territory: 1830 to the Civil War," *Chronicles of Oklahoma* 35 (Spring 1957): 85. Four books by Grant Foreman provide detailed information on the adjustment of many of the emigrants in the trans-Mississippi West: *Indian Removal; Five Civilized Tribes; Advancing the Frontier;* and *Last Trek of the Indians.*

64. Ge[orge] Copway, *Organization of a New Indian Territory, East of the Missouri River* (New York: S. W. Benedict, 1850), pp. 11–12, 16; Harris to Dodge, July 26, 1838, in Carter and Bloom, *Territorial Papers,* 27: 1045; Commissioner of Indian Affairs, *Annual Report* (1840), pp. 229, 232–34; Jas. P. Hays to Dodge, August 15, 1846, ibid. (1846), p. 258; *United States Magazine and Democratic Review* 18 (May 1846): 334–35; George M. Blackburn, "Foredoomed to Failure: The Manistee Indian Station," *Michigan History* 53 (Spring 1969): 37–50; Stipe, "Eastern Dakota Acculturation," p. 170. Adams, *American Indian Education,* p. 38; Davis, "Indian Policy," p. 441. For the adverse effect of the fur trade on attempts to civilize the Indians, see Report from Agent at Council Bluffs, 1837, in Commissioner of Indian Affairs, *Annual Report* (1837), pp. 547–58; Stipe, "Eastern Dakota Acculturation," p. 270; Victor Barnouw, *Acculturation and Personality among the Wisconsin Chippewa,* American Anthropological Association, Memoir Series, no. 72 (Menasha, Wisc.: 1950): 42–43.

65. This paragraph is based on an examination of the Indian Office correspondence and the reports of the Indian commissioners. The quotation cited above is from Pearce, *Savagism and Civilization,* p. 66. Also see Anson, "Variations of the Indian Conflict," p. 68; William T. Hagan, "Private Property, The Indian's Door to Civilization," *Ethnohistory* 3 (Spring 1956): 133–34; Strong, "Wardship," pp. 84–85. For examples of the arguments of government officials, see Cass to White, January 30, 1832, IA, LS, 8: 46–47, RG 75, NA; Commissioner of Indian Affairs, *Annual Report* (1843), p. 270, (1846), pp. 217–18.

66. Gibson, *Chickasaws,* pp. 140–41; Meyer, *Santee Sioux,* p. 63; Thomas S. Williamson to Amos J. Bruce, September 14, 1842, in Commissioner of Indian Affairs, *Annual Report* (1842), p. 486. Also see Hagan, *American Indians,* p. 87; Spoehr, "Changing Kinship Systems," p. 200;

Young, *Redskins, Ruffleshirts and Rednecks,* pp. 10–11; Debo, *Road to Disappearance,* p. 122; [Lawe] to [Doty], September 23, 1843, Lawe Papers.

67. Debo, *Road to Disappearance,* p. 122; Spoehr, "Changing Kinship Systems," pp. 210, 223–25; Harold S. Faust, "The Presbyterian Mission to the American Indian during the Period of Indian Removal (1838–1893)" (Th.D. diss., Temple University, 1943), pp. 2–4; Wilcomb E. Washburn, "Philanthropy and the American Indian: The Need for a Model," *Ethnohistory* 15 (Winter 1968): 49; Henry S. Commager and Richard B. Morris, Introduction to *Spain in America* by Charles Gibson (New York: Harper Torchbooks, 1966), p. x; Young, *Redskins, Ruffleshirts and Rednecks,* pp. 10–11; Hagan, *American Indians,* p. 91; note 42. For the acculturation of Indians in Latin America, see Eric Wolf's brilliant *Sons of the Shaking Earth* (Chicago: University of Chicago Press, Phoenix Books, 1959). Two excellent treatments of anomie are Marshall B. Clinard, ed., *Anomie and Deviant Behavior: A Discussion and Critique* (New York: Free Press of Glencoe, 1964) and Emile Durkheim, *Suicide: A Study in Sociology* trans. John A. Spaulding and George Simpson, ed. George Simpson (Glencoe, Ill.: Free Press, 1951), pp. 252–53. See the following articles by Anthony F. C. Wallace for additional information on revitalization movements: "New Religions among the Delaware Indians, 1600–1900," *Southwestern Journal of Anthropology* 12 (Spring 1956): 1–21; "Revitalization Movements," *American Anthropologist* 58 (April 1956): 264–81; "Stress and Rapid Personality Changes," *International Record of Medicine and General Practice Clinics* 169 (December 1956): 761–74. The following statement by a contemporary scholar provides a close parallel with the thinking of government officials in the Jacksonian era: "The Indian must be forced (if only by the process of education) into a different cultural mold from his earlier culture in order to live and survive within the larger society of which he is now merely a part." Washburn, "Philanthropy and the American Indian," p. 53.

68. Schmeckebier, *Office of Indian Affairs,* p. 40; Debo, *Road to Disappearance,* pp. 120–21; Copway, *Organization of a New Indian Territory,* pp. 8, 17; Schoolcraft, *Personal Memoirs,* p. 550; Bolling, *Catholic Education in Kansas,* p. 11; Berkhofer, *Salvation and the Savage,* pp. 125–41; Chief Bool to Walter Lowrie, May 13, 1838, in Faust, "Presbyterian Mission," pp. 6–7.

69. Culp, "Missions of the American Board," pp. 65–67, 122–23; Debo, *The Road to Disappearance,* pp. 118–20; Logan to Armstrong, September 20, 1845, in Commissioner of Indian Affairs, *Annual Report* (1845), pp. 515–16; Berkhofer, *Salvation and the Savage,* pp. 138–41; Foreman, *Five Civilized Tribes,* pp. 397–98. For an interesting account of how the anti-

slavery movement complicated missionary work in the Indian country, see Robert T. Lewit, "Indian Missions and Antislavery Sentiment: A Conflict of Evangelical and Humanitarian Ideals," *Mississippi Valley Historical Review* 50 (June 1963): 39–55.

70. G. Gordon Brown, "Missions and Cultural Diffusion," *American Journal of Sociology* 50 (November 1944): 214–19; Hagan, *American Indians,* p. 90; Copway, *Organization of a New Indian Territory,* pp. 4–7; Debo, *Road to Disappearance,* p. 122; Faust, "Presbyterian Mission," pp. 147, 150; Berkhofer, *Salvation and the Savage,* pp. 57, 69, 111, 122, 141, 159–60. Baptist missionary Isaac McCoy contended that "good sense" and "conciliating manners" were more essential to a successful mission among the Indians than preaching. *McCoy's Register* 1 (1835): 34–35. Some contemporaries noted that there was a shortage of young, energetic, and talented missionaries because foreign missionary work attracted much of the best talent. Schoolcraft, *Personal Memoirs,* pp. 490–91, 507, 515, 579. For an interesting account of Indian converts, see John F. Freeman, "The Indian Convert: Theme and Variation," *Ethnohistory* 12 (Spring 1965): 113–28.

71. Timothy L. Smith, "Protestant Schooling and American Nationality, 1800–1850," *Journal of American History* 53 (March 1967): 680. Also see Spoehr, "Changing Kinship Systems," pp. 205, 221–22, 224–25; Faust, "Presbyterian Mission," pp. 2–4; Lesser, *Pawnee Ghost Dance Hand Game,* p. 44. Alexis de Tocqueville observed, in *Democracy in America,* p. 331, that "living in freedom in the forest, the North American Indian . . . felt himself inferior to no man; as soon as he wants to penetrate the social hierarchy of the white man, he can only occupy the lowest rank therein."

72. *United States Magazine and Democratic Review* 18 (May 1846): 336; Commissioner of Indian Affairs, *Annual Report* (1846), p. 223, (1847), pp. 747–48, (1849), p. 950; U.S., *Stat.,* 9: 204; S[choolcraft] to Joseph Gales, enclosed in Circular from Medill, July 1847, Schoolcraft Papers; Hagan, *American Indians,* p. 88.

73. Clayton, "Impact of Traders' Claims," p. 314; Meyer, *Santee Sioux,* pp. 59–66; Bolling, *Catholic Education in Kansas,* p. 10; Foster, "Career of Montfort Stokes," p. 47; Herring to William Marshall, March 26, 28, 1833, Herring to Porter, March 28, 1833, C[rawford] to Chambers, September 25, 1841, IA, LS, 10: 150, 157, 159–60, 31: 219, RG 75, NA; Cass to Harris, Private, June 4, 1835, Lewis Cass Correspondence, Tennessee Historical Society, Nashville, Tenn.; *McCoy's Register* 1 (1835): 34, 36–37, 2 (1836): 38–39, 41; Lucius Garey to Schoolcraft, January 6, 1838, IA, Michigan Superintendency, Mackinac, LR, RG 75, NA; Dodge to Harris, August 16, 1838, in Carter and Bloom, *Territorial Papers,* 27: 1057; Lawe

to Doty, February 6, 1843, Lowe Papers; Lewis G. De Russy to Poinsett, October 10, 1844, Poinsett Papers; Old Settler Cherokees to Congress, December 8, 1848, *House Miscellaneous Document 40,* 30th Cong., 2d sess., p. 1; Commissioner of Indian Affairs, *Annual Report* (1846), p. 223; Wm. A. Richmond to Medill, October 30, 1846, ibid., p. 262.

74. Lesser, *Pawnee Ghost Dance Hand Game,* p. 13; Commissioner of Indian Affairs, *Annual Report* (1848), pp. 388–90; Adams, *American Indian Education,* p. 42. See note 29 for additional information concerning the ecological imbalance in the Plains area during the late 1830s and the 1840s.

75. Commissioner of Indian Affairs, *Annual Report* (1848), pp. 386–88.

Epilogue

ALL PRESIDENTIAL ADMINISTRATIONS and a majority of congressmen during the Jacksonian era espoused Indian removal as the best means of avoiding Indian-white conflict. "*Policy,* not *right,*" an easterner lamented in 1847, "has heretofore been the rule of our action" toward the Indians. "If they happened to be in the track of the 'March of Civilization' or their lands were wanted by a band of speculators, some pretext has always been found for removing them, willing or unwilling—right or wrong." In order to compensate emigrant tribesmen for their eastern land, the federal government promised permanent boundaries in the West, large annuities, and educational programs to civilize them so that they might later become a functioning part of American society.[1]

Year after year in the 1830s and '40s Indian commissioners noted with pride the improvement of the emigrants in the Indian country. While the federal government supported programs to transform the Indians into mirror images of white men, the tribesmen enjoyed neither the benefits of American citizenship nor the right of complete sovereignty in their new home. Secretary of War William L. Marcy inadvertently described the reality of American Indian policy throughout the Jacksonian era when he praised "our Indian system of control and management" in 1848.[2]

The desire of the chief executives to rid the area east of the Mississippi River of its Indian population without alienating public opinion explains the unique relationship between the government and the Indians that existed during the Jacksonian era. The Indians were the only minority accorded the status of wards during this period, and the Indian Office assumed considerable responsibility for their safety, education, health, and general well-being. Yet government officials were reluctant to commit themselves to more responsibilities for these wards than was absolutely necessary.[3]

While some efforts were made to provide the congregated Indians in the trans-Mississippi West with a territorial government, representation in Congress, and American citizenship, the federal government never carried out any of these programs. Constitutional arguments, sectional animosities, territorial expansionism, and the idea of white superiority always interfered with the plans of those who felt the Indians could be assimilated into American society. Federal Indian policy stressed acculturation rather than assimilation of the emigrants. The result was the development of an exceedingly paternalistic relationship which tended to lead the Indians toward dependency on annuities and government personnel and services, and worked to retard the development of community leadership and organization. Indian Office bureaucrats and field agents exercised considerable power over the tribes free from effective political pressure by the Indians because the tribesmen remained completely outside of the American political system. Indian Office personnel determined how, when, where, and to whom annuities and services guaranteed by treaties would be provided. With accessibility to Washington greatly limited by distance and the unwillingness of officials to meet unauthorized traveling delegations of Indians, emigrants had virtually no means of influencing policy formulation in their behalf other than through their agents. Thus the emigrants remained subject to but not part of the American government.[4]

The Indians themselves, however, were generally unwilling to assimilate or become incorporated into the American government. Many had come to appreciate the accouterments of American society, but they preferred to maintain their tribal identity. Choctaw Chief Peter Pitchlynn voiced the feelings of many emigrant tribesmen when he protested the formation of an Indian territory in 1849. Pitchlynn argued that "schools, [c]ivilization upon Christian principles, agriculture, temperance and morality are the only politics we have among us; and adhering to these few primary and fundamental principles of human happiness, we have flourished and prospered; hence we want none others." Pitchlynn feared that the creation of an Indian territory under American supervision would be a step towards the destruction of his tribe. "Bad men will use it as a means of introducing discord and confusion among our people," he warned, "and finally driving them from their present happy home to wander on the shores of the Pacific, or sink in its deep waters." Years earlier Winnebago Chief Whirling Thunder had issued a similar plea. "We wish to live like red men," he said, adding that "[we] hope the *fence* between us will continue forever." American ethnocentrism and the Indian desire to preserve their tribal identity combined to thwart the plans of those who wanted to transform them into Americans or at least to attach them closer to the "protecting arm" of the federal government.[5]

The opponents of the Removal Act of 1830 proved wiser prognosticators than its supporters. American cupidity, the desire for a transcontinental railroad, and the territorial organization of Kansas and Nebraska in 1854 ultimately provided an affirmative answer to a query posed by Jeremiah Evarts, an early critic of the Removal Act: "If Congress has the constitutional power to pass such an act, has it not the power of repealing the act?"[6]

NOTES

1. Reuben B. Warren to Crittenden, December 13, 1847, Crittenden Papers.

2. Secretary of War, *Annual Report* (1848), p. 84.

3. Ethnologist John C. Ewers notes, in "When Red and White Men Met," *Western Historical Quarterly* 2 (April 1971): 133, that "we have many ethnic minorities. But the Indians were and are different from any of the others. Not only is there a large and complex body of laws relating to Indians which spells out the responsibility of all of us for them, but those laws also define certain rights and privileges of Indians which are shared by no other groups in this country—either majority or minority."

4. The paternalistic relationship between the Indian Office and the Indians is analogous to that of the patron-client system found in traditional societies where the clientele remain virtually powerless. See Kathleen O. Jackson, "A Study of Changes in Authority Relations between American Indians and Government" (Ph.D. diss., University of Oregon, 1971), p. 66.

5. Pitchlynn to Congress, January 20, 1849, *House Miscellaneous Document 35*, 30th Cong., 2d sess., p. 3; Talk of Whirling Thunder, in *Niles' Register* 45 (August 31, 1833): 10–11.

6. Evarts, *Essays on the Present Crisis*, p. 99.

Appendix

The Removal Act of May 28, 1830[1]

An Act to provide for an exchange of lands with the Indians residing in any of the states or territories, and for their removal west of the river Mississippi.

Be it enacted by the Senate and House of Representatives of the United States of America, in Congress assembled, That it shall and may be lawful for the President of the United States to cause so much of any territory belonging to the United States, west of the river Mississippi, not included in any state or organized territory, and to which the Indian title has been extinguished, as he may judge necessary, to be divided into a suitable number of districts, for the reception of such tribes or nations of Indians as may choose to exchange the lands where they now reside, and remove there; and to cause each of said districts to be so described by natural or artificial marks, as to be easily distinguished from every other.

And be it further enacted, That it shall and may be lawful for the President to exchange any or all of such districts, so to be laid off and described, with any tribe or nation of Indians now residing within the limits of any of the states or territories, and with which the United States have existing treaties, for the whole or any part or portion of the territory claimed and occupied by such tribe or nation, within the bounds of any one or more of the states or territories, where the land claimed and occupied by the Indians, is owned by the United States, or the United States are bound to the state within which it lies to extinguish the Indian claim thereto.

And be it further enacted, That in the making of any such exchange or exchanges, it shall and may be lawful for the President solemnly to assure the tribe or nation with which the exchange is made, that the United States will forever secure and guaranty to them, and their heirs or successors, the country so exchanged with them; and if they prefer it, that the United States will cause a patent or grant to be made and executed to them for the same: *Provided always,* That such lands shall revert to the United States, if the Indians become extinct, or abandon the same.

And be it further enacted, That if, upon any of the lands now occupied by the Indians, and to be exchanged for, there should be such improvements as add value to the land claimed by any individual or individuals of such tribes or nations, it shall and may be lawful for the President to cause such value to be ascertained by appraisement or otherwise, and to cause such ascertained value to be paid to the person or persons rightfully claiming such improvements. And upon the payment of such valuation, the improvements so valued and paid for, shall pass to the United States, and possession shall not afterwards be permitted to any of the same tribe.

And be it further enacted, That upon the making of any such exchange as is contemplated by this act, it shall and may be lawful for the President to cause such aid and assistance to be furnished to the emigrants as may be necessary and proper to enable them to remove to, and settle in, the country for which they may have exchanged; and also, to give them such aid and assistance as may be necessary for their support and subsistence for the first year after their removal.

And be it further enacted, That it shall and may be lawful for the President to cause such tribe or nation to be protected, at their new residence, against all interruption or disturbance from any other tribe or nation of Indians, or from any other person or persons whatever.

And be it further enacted, That it shall and may be lawful for the President to have the same superintendence and care over any tribe or nation in the country to which they may remove, as contemplated by this act, that he is now authorized to have over them at their present places of residence: *Provided,* That nothing in this act contained shall be construed as authorizing or directing the violation of any existing treaty between the United States and any of the Indian tribes.

And be it further enacted, That for the purpose of giving effect to the provisions of this act, the sum of five hundred thousand dollars is hereby appropriated, to be paid out of any money in the treasury, not otherwise appropriated.

NOTE

1. U.S., *Stat.,* 4: 411–12.

Selected Bibliography

This is not an exhaustive bibliography on Indian policy in the Jacksonian era. Since the notes include brief bibliographical essays as well as specific references to sources of quotations and other pertinent data, this list indicates only the principal sources upon which my study is based.

1. Manuscript Sources

Government Manuscripts

National Archives, Washington, D.C.
Record Group 11: Government Documents Having General Legal Effect.
Ratified Indian Treaties, 1801–49.
Record Group 46: Records of the United States Senate.
Executive Messages Relating to Indian Relations, 1829–49.
Legislative Records of the Twenty-First Congress.
Record Group 59: Records of the Department of State.
Domestic Letters Sent, 1784–1849.
Miscellaneous Correspondence, 1789–1849.
Miscellaneous Letters Received, 1789–1849.
Record Group 75: Records of the Bureau of Indian Affairs.
Chickasaw Removal Records: Letters Sent, 1832–49.
Choctaw Removal Records: Census Roll, 1831; Records of Commissioners Pray, Murray, and Vroom, Choctaw Claims Journal; Register of Claims for Reservations, 1834–36.

Creek Removal Records: Records of the Commission of Crawford and Balch.

Documents Relating to the Negotiation of Ratified Indian Treaties, 1801–49.

Field Office Records: Records of the Michigan Superintendency and Mackinac Agency, Letters Received, 1829–49, Letters Sent, 1829–49.

Letters Received by the Office of Indian Affairs: Cherokee Agency, 1836–49; Cherokee Agency East, 1824–36; Cherokee Agency West, 1824–36; Choctaw Agency Emigration, 1826–49; Creek Agency, 1824–49; Creek Agency Emigration, 1826–49; Green Bay Agency, 1824–49; Indiana Agency, 1824–49; Miami Agency Emigration, 1842–49; Michigan Superintendency, 1824–49; Miscellaneous, 1824–49; Prairie du Chien Agency, 1824–42; Registers of Letters Received, 1824–51; Sac and Fox Agency, 1824–49; St. Peter's Agency, 1824–49; Schools, 1824–49; Seneca Agency in New York, 1824–32; Upper Missouri Agency, 1824–49; Wisconsin Superintendency, 1836–48.

Letters Sent by the Office of Indian Affairs, 1824–51.

Miscellaneous Records, 1836–49.

Records of the Civilization Division: Data Book for the Civilization Fund; Population Figures, 1800–53.

Records of the Commissary General of Subsistence: Letters Received, Choctaws, 1831–36; Letters Sent, 1830–36.

Records of the Employees Section: Register of Applications and Recommendations for Appointments, 1833–34, 1836, 1866–68; Register of Applications and Recommendations for Appointments, 1835–49.

Report Books, 1838–49.

Record Group 94: Records of the Adjutant General's Office.

General Order Books, 1829–49.

Letters Received, Main Series, 1822–49.

Orders and Circulars, 1797–1849.

Special Order Books, 1829–49.

Record Group 107: Records of the Secretary of War.

Letters Sent Relating to Military Affairs, 1800–49.

Letters Sent to the President, 1800–49.

Registers of Letters Received, 1800–49.

Reports to Congress, 1803–49.

Unregistered Letters Received, 1789–1849.

Record Group 108: Records of the Headquarters of the Army.

Letters Sent, 1828–46.

Record Group 233: Records of the United States House of Representatives.
Legislative Records of the Twenty-First Congress.

Personal Manuscripts

Chicago Historical Society, Chicago, Illinois
    Cyrus Bryant Papers
    Lewis Cass Papers
    William Clark Papers
    Gunther Broadside Collection
    Hardin Family Papers
    Horatio Hill Papers
    Elias Kent Kane Papers
    George W. Lawe Papers
    James K. Polk Papers
    George B. Porter Papers
    Henry Van der Bogart Papers
Detroit Public Library, Burton Historical Collection, Detroit, Michigan
    William Woodbridge Papers
Filson History Club, Louisville, Kentucky
    Orlando Brown Papers
Harvard University, Houghton Library, Cambridge, Massachusetts
    American Board of Commissioners for Foreign Missions Papers
Historical Society of Pennsylvania, Philadelphia, Pennsylvania
    Henry D. Gilpin Collection
    Simon Gratz Collection
    Richard Peters Papers
    Joel R. Poinsett Papers
    Roberts Vaux Papers
Huntington Library, San Marino, California
    Thomas L. McKenny–William D. Lewis Correspondence (microfilm edition in possession of Herman J. Viola)
Illinois State Historical Society, Springfield, Illinois
    Andrew Jackson Papers
    Black Hawk War Papers
    John Caldwell Manuscripts
    Lewis Cass Manuscripts
Indiana Historical Society Library, Indianapolis, Indiana
    John Dowling Papers
    Samuel Milroy Papers
Kansas State Historical Society, Topeka, Kansas
    Isaac McCoy Papers

Kentucky Historical Society, Frankfort, Kentucky
  Orlando Brown Papers
Lawson McGhee Library, McClung Historical Collection, Knoxville, Tennessee
  Thomas A. R. Nelson Papers
Library of Congress, Washington, D.C.
  John Jordan Crittenden Papers
  Franklin H. Elmore Papers
  Jeremiah Evarts Papers
  Ethan Allen Hitchcock Papers
  Andrew Jackson Papers
  John McLean Papers
  William L. Marcy Papers and Diary
  William Medill Papers
  Miscellaneous Manuscripts
    T. Hartley Crawford
  James K. Polk Papers
  Henry Rowe Schoolcraft Papers
  E. George Squier Papers
  U.S. Miscellaneous Manuscripts, 1840–60
    Pierce Mason Butler Papers
  Martin Van Buren Papers
  Daniel Webster Papers
  William Wirt Papers and Letterbooks
Maryland Historical Society, Annapolis, Maryland
  William Wirt Papers
Massachusetts Historical Society, Boston, Massachusetts
  Adams Family Papers (Typescript copy of Thomas L. McKenny material in possession of Herman J. Viola)
Minnesota Historical Society, St. Paul, Minnesota
  Samuel W. Pond Papers
  Henry Hastings Sibley Papers
Mississippi Department of Archives and History, Jackson, Mississippi
  J. F. H. Clairborne Collection
  Governors' Records
New-York Historical Society, New York, New York
  Philip Milledoler Papers (microfilm edition in possession of Herman J. Viola)
  Miscellaneous Manuscript Collection
    Henry Clay Papers
    Thomas L. McKenney Papers
Princeton University Library, Princeton, New Jersey
  Benjamin F. Butler Papers (microfilm edition at the University of Pennsylvania Library, Philadelphia, Pennsylvania)

Tennessee Historical Society, Nashville, Tennessee
  Lewis Cass Correspondence
  John Coffee Papers
  Carey Allen Harris Correspondence
University of South Carolina, South Carolinian Library, Columbia, South
    Carolina
  Pierce Mason Butler Papers
Yale University, Sterling Memorial Library, New Haven, Connecticut
  Evarts Family Papers

2. NEWSPAPERS

American Beacon and Norfolk and Portsmouth Daily Advertiser (Virginia). 1836.
American Spectator and Washington City Chronicle. 1830–31.
Arkansas Advocate (Little Rock). 1830.
Arkansas Gazette (Little Rock). 1829–39.
Arkansas Intelligencer (Van Buren). 1845.
Baltimore Republican and Commercial Advertiser. 1832.
Boston Courier. 1831–32.
Charleston Courier (South Carolina). 1836.
Columbian Gazette (Georgetown, D.C.). 1829.
Daily National Intelligencer (Washington, D.C.). 1829–42.
Daily Richmond Whig. 1829.
Detroit Daily Advertiser. 1843.
Georgia Journal (Milledgeville). 1824.
Georgian (Savannah). 1829–30.
Globe (Washington, D.C.). 1829–33.
Hawk-Eye and Iowa Patriot (Burlington). 1841.
Knoxville Register. 1830.
Liberator (Boston). 1841.
Madisonian (Washington, D.C.). 1841.
Mobile Commercial Register for the Country (Alabama). 1831.
Morning Courier and New-York Enquirer. 1832–33.
Nashville Daily Republican Banner. 1839–41.
Nashville Republican. 1836.
Nashville Republican and State Gazette. 1830–31.
Nashville Union. 1837.
Nashville Union (Semi-Weekly). 1841.
Nashville Whig. 1825–30.
Natchez Statesman and Gazette (Mississippi). 1829.
National Banner and Nashville Whig. 1830.
National Intelligencer (Washington, D.C. [triweekly]). 1839.
New Bern Spectator (North Carolina). 1832.

New-York Daily Advertiser. 1832.
New-York Evening Post. 1829–32.
New-York Evening Post for the Country. 1829.
New-York Observer. 1830–38.
North-Carolina Free Press (Tarborough). 1832.
Northern Standard (Clarkesville, Texas). 1844.
Pennsylvania Intelligencer (Harrisburg). 1825.
Pennsylvanian (Philadelphia). 1848.
Pittsburgh Gazette. 1832.
Poulson's American Daily Advertiser (Philadelphia). 1832.
Richmond Enquirer. 1830–41.
United States' Telegraph (Washington, D.C.) 1829–30.
Warrenton Reporter (North Carolina). 1825–32.

3. Periodicals

Advocate of Peace. Vol. 2 (1838).
American Baptist Magazine. Vols. 6–14 (1826–34).
American Quarterly Review. Vols. 8–11 (1830–32).
Army and Navy Chronicle. Vols. 8–9 (1839).
Baptist Missionary Magazine. Vols. 17–18 (1838).
Calumet. Vol. 1 (1832).
Columbian Star and Christian Index. Vols. 1–2 (1829–30).
McCoy's Annual Register of Indian Affairs within the Indian (or Western) Territory. Vols. 1–4 (1835–38).
Magazine of the Reformed Dutch Church. Vol. 4 (1829).
Missionary Herald. Vols. 26–29 (1830–33).
Niles' Weekly Register. Vols. 24–55 (1823–38).
North American Review. Vols. 30–63 (1830–46).
Prairie Farmer. Vol. 4 (1844).
Quarterly Register of the American Education Society. Vols. 3–5 (1830–32).
Southern Quarterly Review. Vol. 8 (1845).
United States Magazine and Democratic Review. Vols. 1–27 (1837–50).

4. Government Publications

Carter, Clarence E., and Bloom, John Porter, comps. and eds. *The Territorial Papers of the United States.* 27 vols. to date. Washington, D.C.: Government Printing Office, 1944–[69].
DeBow, J. D. B., comp. *Statistical View of the United States ... being a Compendium of the Seventh Census.* Washington, D.C.: Beverely Tucker, Senate Printer, 1854.

Georgia. State Legislature. *A Compilation of the Laws of Georgia Passed Between 1820 and 1829.* Milledgeville: Camack & Rayland, Printers, 1830.

Kappler, Charles J., ed. *Indian Affairs: Laws and Treaties.* 3 vols. Washington, D.C.: GPO, 1892–1913.

Richardson, James D., comp. *A Compilation of the Messages and Papers of the Presidents.* 10 vols. Washington, D.C.: GPO, 1896–99.

Thorpe, Francis Newton. *The Federal and State Constitutions.* 7 vols. Washington, D.C.: GPO, 1909.

U.S. *The Federal Cases Comprising Cases Argued and Determined in the Circuit and District Courts of the United States.* 31 vols. St. Paul, Minn.: West Publishing Co., 1894–98.

U.S. *Statutes at Large.* Vols. 1–10.

U.S. Bureau of Indian Affairs. *Annual Report.* Washington, D.C., 1828–31.

U.S. Commissioner of Indian Affairs. *Annual Report.* Washington, D.C., 1832–55.

U.S. Congress. *American State Papers: Indian Affairs.* 2 vols. Washington, D.C.: Gales & Seaton, 1832–34.

U.S. Congress. *American State Papers: Military Affairs.* 7 vols. Washington, D.C.: Gales & Seaton, 1832–61.

U.S. Congress. *American State Papers: Public Lands.* 8 vols. Washington, D.C.: Gales & Seaton, 1832–61.

U.S. Congress. *Congressional Globe.* 23rd Cong., 1st sess., to 30th Cong., 2d sess.

U.S. Congress. *Original Bills.* 22d Cong., 1st sess., to 30th Cong., 3d sess.

U.S. Congress. *Register of Debates in Congress.* 20th Cong., 2d sess., to 23rd Cong., 1st sess.

U.S. Congress. House. *Documents.* 17th Cong., 1st sess., to 28th Cong., 2d sess.

U.S. Congress. House. *Executive Documents.* 22d Cong., 1st sess., to 31st Cong., 2d sess.

U.S. Congress. House. *Journal.* 20th Cong., 1st sess., to 29th Cong., 1st sess.

U.S. Congress. House. *Miscellaneous Documents.* 30th Cong., 2d sess., to 42d Cong., 3d sess.

U.S. Congress. House. *Reports.* 21st Cong., 1st sess., to 31st Cong., 2d sess.

U.S. Congress. Senate. *Documents.* 20th Cong., 1st sess., to 28th Cong., 2d sess.

U.S. Congress. Senate. *Executive Documents.* 27th Cong., 1st sess., to 48th Cong., 2d sess.

U.S. Congress. Senate. *Journal.* 20th Cong., 2d sess., to 25th Cong., 3d sess.

U.S. Congress. Senate. *Journal of the Executive Proceedings of the Senate.* Vols. 4–6. Washington, D.C.: Duff Green & GPO, 1828–48.

U.S. Department of State. *Register of Officers and Agents, Civil, Military, and Naval in the Service of the United States.* Washington, D.C., 1827–49.

U.S. Office of Indian Affairs. *Office Copy of the Laws, Regulations, Etc. of the Indian Bureau, 1850.* Washington D.C.: Gideon & Co., Printers, 1850.

U.S. Secretary of the Treasury. *Annual Report.* Washington, 1848.

U.S. Secretary of War. *Annual Report.* Washington, 1828–49.

U.S. Supreme Court. *Report.* Washington, 1823–49.

5. PUBLISHED PRIMARY SOURCE MATERIAL

Adams, Charles Francis, ed. *Memoirs of John Quincy Adams.* 12 vols. Philadelphia: J. B. Lippincott & Co., 1874–77.

Ames, Herman V., ed. *The Reserved Rights of the States and the Jurisdiction of Federal Courts, 1819–1832.* Philadelphia: University of Pennsylvania, Department of History, 1901.

Bassett, John Spencer, ed. *Correspondence of Andrew Jackson.* 7 vols. Washington, D.C.: Carnegie Institution, 1926–35.

Blackburn, Glen A., comp. *The John Tipton Papers (1809–1839).* Edited by Nellie Armstrong Robertson and Dorothy Riker. 3 vols. Indianapolis: Indiana Historical Bureau, 1942.

Colton, Calvin, ed. *The Life, Correspondence, and Speeches of Henry Clay.* 6 vols. New York: A. S. Barnes & Co., 1857.

———. *The Private Correspondence of Henry Clay.* New York: A. S. Barnes & Co., 1855.

Croffut, W. A., ed. *Fifty Years in Camp and Field: Diary of Major-General Ethan Allen Hitchcock, U.S.A.* New York: G. P. Putnam's Sons, 1909.

Dale, Edward Everett, and Litton, Gaston, eds. *Cherokee Cavaliers: Forty Years of Cherokee History as Told in the Correspondence of the Ridge-Watie-Boudinot Family.* Norman: University of Oklahoma Press, 1939.

"Documents: Thomas Forsyth to Lewis Cass, St. Louis, October 24, 1831: Draper MSS. 6T152–164." *Ethnohistory* 4 (Spring 1957): 198–210.

Eaton, Margaret L. *The Autobiography of Peggy Eaton.* New York: Charles Scribner's Sons, 1932.

Fitzpatrick, John C., ed. *The Autobiography of Martin Van Buren.* Washington, D.C.: Government Printing Office, 1920.

Foreman, Grant, ed. *A Traveler in Indian Territory: The Journal of Ethan Allen Hitchcock.* Cedar Rapids: Torch Press, 1930.

[Gaines, George S.]. "Removal of the Choctaws." Alabama State Department of Archives and History, *Historical and Patriotic Series* 10 (1928): 9–24.

Graf, Leroy P., and Haskins, Ralph W., eds. *The Papers of Andrew Johnson, 1822–1851.* Knoxville: University of Tennessee Press, 1967.

Hamilton, James A. *Reminiscences.* New York: Charles Scribner & Co., 1869.

Johannsen, Robert W., ed. *The Letters of Stephen A. Douglas.* Urbana: University of Illinois Press, 1961.

Kellar, Herbert Anthony, ed. *Solon Robinson, Pioneer and Agriculturist: Selected Writings (1832–1851).* 2 vols. Indianapolis: Indiana Historical Bureau, 1936.

Kilpatrick, Jack Frederick, and Kilpatrick, Anna Gritts, eds. *New Echota Letters: Contributions of Samuel A. Worcester to the Cherokee Phoenix.* Dallas: Southern Methodist Press, 1968.

"Letters of Francis Scott Key to Roger Brooke Taney, and Other Correspondence." *Maryland Historical Magazine* 5 (March 1910): 23–37.

Lumpkin, Wilson. *The Removal of the Cherokee Indians from Georgia.* 2 vols. New York: Dodd, Mead & Co., 1907.

McDermott, John Francis, ed. *The Western Journals of Washington Irving.* Norman: University of Oklahoma Press, 1944.

McKee, Thomas Hudson, comp. *The National Conventions and Platforms of All Political Parties, 1789–1900.* 3d ed., rev. Baltimore: Friedenwald Co., 1900.

Merrill, Walter M., and Ruchames, Louis, eds. *The Letters of William Lloyd Garrison.* 2 vols. Cambridge: Harvard University Press, Belknap Press, 1971.

Oliphant, J. Orin, ed. *Through the South and the West with Jeremiah Evarts in 1826.* Lewisburg, Pa.: Bucknell University Press, 1956.

Powell, Fred Wilbur, comp. *Control of Federal Expenditures: A Documentary History, 1775–1894.* Washington, D.C.: Brookings Institution, 1939.

Prucha, Francis Paul, and Carmony, Donald F., eds. "A Memorandum of Lewis Cass: Concerning a System for the Regulation of Indian Affairs." *Wisconsin Magazine of History* 51 (Autumn 1968): 35–50.

Quaife, Milo Milton, ed. *The Diary of James K. Polk during His Presidency, 1845 to 1849.* 4 vols. Chicago: McClurg & Co., 1910.

Scott, Nancy N., ed. *A Memoir of Hugh Lawson White.* Philadelphia: J. B. Lippincott & Co., 1856.

Severance, Frank H., ed. *Millard Fillmore Papers.* 2 vols. Buffalo, N.Y.: Buffalo Historical Society, 1907.

Shirk, George H., ed. "Some Letters from the Reverend Samuel A. Worcester at Park Hill." *Chronicles of Oklahoma* 26 (Winter 1948–49): 468–78.

Steiner, Bernard C., ed. "Notes: Jackson and the Missionaries." *American Historical Review* 29 (July 1924): 722–23.

Story, William W., ed. *Life and Letters of Joseph Story.* 2 vols. Boston: Charles C. Little & James Brown, 1851.

Thwaites, Reuben Gold, ed. "Documents Relating to the Episcopal Church and Mission in Green Bay, 1825–1841." *Collections of the State Historical Society of Wisconsin* 14 (1898): 162–205.

Van Buren, Martin. *Inquiry into the Origin and Course of Political Parties in the United States.* Edited by his sons. New York: Hurd & Houghton, 1867.

Warren, Charles, ed. *The Story-Marshall Correspondence (1819–1831).* Anglo-American Legal History Series, vol. 1, no. 7 (1942): 1–29.

Weaver, Herbert, and Bergeron, Paul H., eds. *Correspondence of James K. Polk, 1817–1832.* Nashville: Vanderbilt University Press, 1969.

Webster, Fletcher, ed. *The Private Correspondence of Daniel Webster.* 2 vols. Boston: Little, Brown & Co., 1857.

Whittlesey, Charles. "Recollections of a Tour through Wisconsin in 1832." *Collections of the State Historical Society of Wisconsin* 1 (1855): 64–85.

6. BOOKS

Observations of Contemporaries

American Peace Society. *Eighth Annual Report.* Hartford, Conn.: William Watson, 1836.

Bell, John. *Mr. Bell's Suppressed Report in Relation to the Difficulties Between the Eastern and Western Cherokees.* Washington, D.C.: Gales & Seaton, 1840.

Benson, Henry C. *Life among the Choctaw Indians, and Sketches of the South-West.* Cincinnati: L. Swormstedt & A. Poe, 1860.

Benton, Thomas Hart. *Thirty Years' View; or, A History of the Working of the American Government for Thirty Years, from 1820 to 1850.* 2 vols. New York: D. Appleton & Co. 1854–56.

Combe, George. *Notes on the United States of North America during a Phrenological Visit in 1838–9–40.* 3 vols. Edinburgh: MacLachlan, Stewart & Company, 1841.

Copway, Ge[orge]. *Organization of a New Indian Territory, East of the Missouri River.* New York: S. W. Benedict, 1850.

Documents and Proceedings Relating to the Formation and Progress of a Board in the City of New York, for the Emigration, Preservation, and Improvement, of the Aborigines of America. New York: Vanderpoole & Cole, 1829.

[Evarts, Jeremiah]. *Essays on the Present Crisis in the Condition of the American Indians: First Published in the National Intelligencer, under the Signature of William Penn.* Boston: Perkins & Marvin, 1829.

————, ed. *Speeches on the Passage of the Bill for the Removal of the Indians, Delivered in Congress of the United States, April and May, 1830.* Boston: Perkins & Marvin, 1830.

Farnham, Thomas J. *Travels in the Great Western Prairies, the Anahuac and Rocky Mountains, and in the Oregon Territory.* 2 vols. London: Richard Bentley, 1843.

Gregg, Josiah. *Commerce of the Prairies; or, The Journal of a Sante Fe Trader, During Eight Expeditions Across the Great Western Prairies, and a Residence of Nearly Nine Years in Northern Mexico.* 2 vols. 2d ed. New York: J. & H. G. Langley, 1845.

McCoy, Isaac. *History of Baptist Indian Missions: Embracing Remarks on the Former and Present Condition of the Aboriginal Tribes, Their Former Settlement within the Indian Territory, and Their Future Prospects.* Washington, D.C.: William M. Morrison, 1840.

————. *Remarks on the Practicability of Indian Reform, Embracing Their Colonization.* Boston: Lincoln & Edmands, 1827, and 2d ed., New York: Graz & Bunce, 1829.

McKenney, Thomas L. *Memoirs, Official and Personal.* 2 vols. 1846. Reprint, vol. 1. Lincoln: University of Nebraska Press, Bison Books, 1973.

Mills, Robert. *Guide to the Capitol and National Executive Offices of the United States.* Washington, D.C.: Wm. Greer, Printer, 1847–48.

————. *Guide to the National Executive Offices and the Capitol of The United States.* Washington, D.C.: P. Force, Printer, 1842.

Morse, Jedidiah. *A Report to the Secretary of War of the United States, on Indian Affairs, Comprising a Narrative of a Tour Performed in the Summer of 1820.* New Haven: S. Converse, 1822.

Morton, Samuel George. *Crania Americana; or, A Comparative View of the Skulls of Various Aboriginal Nations.* Philadelphia: J. Dobson, 1839.

Peters, Richard. *The Case of the Cherokee Nation against the State of Georgia, with an Appendix.* Philadelphia: J. Grigg, 1831.

Schoolcraft, Henry R. *Personal Memoirs of a Residence of Thirty Years with the Indian Tribes on the American Frontiers.* Philadelphia: Lippincott, Grambo & Co., 1851.

Tocqueville, Alexis de. *Democracy in America.* Edited by J. P. Mayer, translated by George Lawrence. Garden City, N.Y.: Anchor Books, 1969.

Secondary Studies

Abel, Annie H. *The American Indian as Slaveholder and Secessionist: An Omitted Chapter in the Diplomatic History of the Southern Confederacy.* 3 vols. Cleveland: Arthur H. Clark Co., 1915–25.

Adams, Evelyn C. *American Indian Education: Government Schools and Economic Progress.* Morningside Heights, N.Y.: King's Crown Press, 1946.

Aronson, Sidney H. *Status and Kinship in the Higher Civil Service: Standards of Selection in the Administrations of John Adams, Thomas Jefferson, and Andrew Jackson.* Cambridge: Harvard University Press, 1964.

Baird, W. David. *Peter Pitchlynn: Chief of the Choctaws.* Norman: University of Oklahoma Press, 1972.

Barnouw, Victor. *Acculturation and Personality among the Wisconsin Chippewa,* American Anthropological Association, Memoir Series, no. 72. Menasha, Wisc., 1950.

Baxter, Maurice G. *Daniel Webster & The Supreme Court.* Amherst: University of Massachusetts Press, 1966.

Beaver, R. Pierce. *Church, State, and the American Indians: Two and a Half Centuries of Partnership in Missions between Protestant Churches and Government.* St. Louis: Concordia Publishing House, 1966.

Beers, Henry Putney. *The Western Military Frontier, 1815–1846.* Philadelphia: University of Pennsylvania Press, 1935.

Bemis, Samuel Flagg. *John Quincy Adams and the Union.* New York: Alfred A. Knopf, 1956.

Berkhofer, Robert F., Jr. *Salvation and the Savage: An Analysis of Protestant Missions and American Indian Response, 1787–1862.* Lexington: University of Kentucky Press, 1965.

Binder, Frederick M. *The Color Problem in Early National America as Viewed by John Adams, Jefferson and Jackson.* The Hague: Mouton & Co., 1968.

Biographical Directory of the American Congress, 1774–1949. Washington, D.C.: GPO, 1950.

Bolling, Richard Joseph. *History of Catholic Education in Kansas, 1836–1932.* Washington, D.C.: Catholic University of America, 1933.

Carroll, E. Malcolm. *Origins of the Whig Party.* Durham, N.C.: Duke University Press, 1925.

Chitwood, Oliver P. *John Tyler: Champion of the Old South.* New York: D. Appleton-Century Co., Inc., 1939.

Cohen, Felix S. *Handbook of Federal Indian Law.* Washington, D.C.: GPO, 1942.

Cotterill, R. S. *The Southern Indians: The Story of the Civilized Tribes Before Removal.* Norman: University of Oklahoma Press, 1954.

Debo, Angie. *The Rise and Fall of the Choctaw Republic.* 2d ed. Norman: University of Oklahoma Press, 1961.

———. *The Road to Disappearance.* Norman: University of Oklahoma Press, 1941.

DeRosier, Arthur H., Jr. *The Removal of the Choctaw Indians.* Knoxville: University of Tennessee Press, 1970.

Duckett, Alvin Laroy. *John Forsyth, Political Tactician.* Athens: University of Georgia Press, 1962.

Eaton, Clement. *Henry Clay and the Art of American Politics.* Boston: Little, Brown & Co., 1957.

Eaton, Rachel Caroline. *John Ross and the Cherokee Indians.* Chicago: Private Edition, 1921.

Eblen, Jack Erickson. *The First and Second United States Empires: Governors and Territorial Government, 1784–1912.* Pittsburgh: University of Pittsburgh Press, 1968.

Eby, Cecil. *"That Disgraceful Affair," the Black Hawk War.* New York: W. W. Norton & Co., Inc., 1973.

Ekirch, Arthur Alphonse, Jr. *The Idea of Progress in America, 1815–1860.* New York: Columbia University Press, 1944.

Elson, Ruth Miller. *Guardians of Tradition: American Schoolbooks of the Nineteenth Century.* Lincoln: University of Nebraska Press, 1964.

Fish, Carl Russell. *The Civil Service and the Patronage.* New York: Longmans, Green, & Co., 1905.

Foreman, Grant. *Advancing the Frontier, 1830–1860.* Norman: University of Oklahoma Press, 1933.

———. *The Five Civilized Tribes.* Norman: University of Oklahoma Press, 1934.

———. *Indian Removal: The Emigration of the Five Civilized Tribes of Indians.* New ed. Norman: University of Oklahoma Press, 1953.

———. *The Last Trek of the Indians.* Chicago: University of Chicago Press, 1946.

Franklin, John Hope. *The Militant South, 1800–1861.* Boston: Beacon Press, 1964.

Gammon, Samuel Rhea, Jr. *The Presidential Campaign of 1832.* Baltimore: Johns Hopkins University Press, 1922.

Gates, Paul W., and Swenson, Robert W. *History of Public Land Law Development.* Washington, D.C.: GPO, 1968.

Gibson, Arrel M. *The Chickasaws.* Norman: University of Oklahoma Press, 1971.

————. *The Kickapoos: Lords of the Middle Border.* Norman: University of Oklahoma Press, 1963.

Hagan, William T. *American Indians.* Chicago: University of Chicago Press, 1961.

————. *The Sac and Fox Indians.* Norman: University of Oklahoma Press, 1958.

Harmon, George Dewey. *Sixty Years of Indian Affairs: Political, Economic, and Diplomatic, 1789–1850.* Chapel Hill: University of North Carolina Press, 1941.

Hemans, Lawton T. *Life and Times of Stevens Thomson Mason: The Boy Governor of Michigan.* 2d ed. Lansing: Michigan Historical Commission, 1930.

Horsman, Reginald. *Expansion and American Indian Policy, 1783–1812.* East Lansing: Michigan State University Press, 1967.

Johnson, Allen, and Malone, Dumas, eds. *Dictionary of American Biography.* 22 vols. New York: Charles Scribner's Sons, 1956.

Lanman, Charles. *Biographical Annals of the Civil Government of the United States during its First Century.* Washington: James Anglim, Publisher, 1876.

Lesser, Alexander. *The Pawnee Ghost Dance Hand Game: A Study of Cultural Change.* New York: Columbia University Press, 1933.

MacLeod, William C. *The American Indian Frontier.* New York: Alfred A. Knopf, 1928.

McReynolds, Edwin C. *The Seminoles.* Norman: University of Oklahoma Press, 1957.

Mahon, John K. *History of the Second Seminole War, 1835–1842.* Gainesville: University of Florida Press, 1967.

Malone, Henry T. *Cherokees of the Old South: A People in Transition.* Athens: University of Georgia Press, 1956.

Meyer, Leland Winfield. *The Life and Times of Colonel Richard M. Johnson of Kentucky.* New York: Columbia University Press, 1932.

Meyer, Roy W. *History of the Santee Sioux: United States Indian Policy on Trial.* Lincoln: University of Nebraska Press, 1967.

Mooney, James. *Myths of the Cherokee and Sacred Formulas of the Cherokees.* 1900. Reprint ed. Nashville, Tenn.: Charles Elder, 1972.

Morgan, Robert J. *A Whig Embattled: The Presidency under John Tyler.* Lincoln: University of Nebraska Press, 1954.

Ostrogorski, M. I. *Democracy and the Organization of Political Parties.* Translated by Frederick Clarke. 2 vols. London: Macmillan & Co., Ltd., 1902.

Parks, Joseph Howard. *John Bell of Tennessee.* Baton Rouge: Louisiana State University Press, 1950.

Pearce, Roy Harvey. *Savagism and Civilization: A Study of the Indian and the American Mind.* Rev. ed. Baltimore: Johns Hopkins Press, 1967.

Pessen, Edward. *Jacksonian America: Society, Personality, and Politics.* Homewood, Ill.: Dorsey Press, 1969.

Phillips, Ulrich Bonnell. *Georgia and States' Rights: A Study of the Political History of Georgia from the Revolution to the Civil War, with Particular Regard to Federal Relations.* Washington, D.C.: GPO, 1908.

Pierson, George Wilson. *Tocqueville and Beaumont in America.* New York: Oxford University Press, 1938.

Poage, George Rawlings. *Henry Clay and the Whig Party.* Chapel Hill: University of North Carolina Press, 1936.

Prucha, Francis Paul. *American Indian Policy in the Formative Years: The Indian Trade and Intercourse Acts, 1790–1834.* Cambridge, Mass.: Harvard University Press, 1962.

_____. *Broadax and Bayonet: The Role of the United States Army in the Development of the Northwest, 1815–1860.* Lincoln: University of Nebraska Press, 1967.

_____. *Indian Peace Medals in American History.* Madison: Historical Society of Wisconsin, 1971.

_____. *Lewis Cass and American Indian Policy.* Detroit: Wayne State University Press, 1967.

_____. *The Sword of the Republic: The United States Army on the Frontier, 1783–1846.* New York: Macmillan Co., 1969.

Putnam, Herbert Everett. *Joel Roberts Poinsett, A Political Biography.* Washington, D.C.: Mimeoform Press, 1935.

Ray, Florence Rebecca. *Greenwood LeFlore: Last Chief of the Choctaws East of the Mississippi River.* Memphis: Davis Publishing Co., 1930.

Remini, Robert V. *Andrew Jackson.* New York: Harper & Row, 1969.

_____. *The Election of Andrew Jackson.* Philadelphia: J. B. Lippincott Co., 1963.

Royce, Charles C. *Indian Land Cessions in the United States.* Bureau of American Ethnology, Eighteenth Annual Report, 1896–1897, vol. 2. Washington, D.C., 1899.

Russo, David J. *The Major Political Issues of the Jacksonian Period and the Development of Party Loyalty in Congress, 1830–1840.* Transactions of the American Philosophical Society, New Series, vol. 62, pt. 5. Philadelphia, 1972.

Schmeckebier, Laurence F. *The Office of Indian Affairs: Its History, Activities, and Organization.* Baltimore: Johns Hopkins Press, 1927.

Schultz, George A. *An Indian Canaan: Isaac McCoy and the Vision of an Indian State.* Norman: University of Oklahoma Press, 1972.

Schurz, Carl. *Life of Henry Clay.* 2 vols. Boston: Houghton Mifflin Co. 1887.

Sellers, Charles Grier, Jr. *James K. Polk, Continentalist: 1843–1846.* Princeton, N.J.: Princeton University Press, 1966.

————. *James K. Polk, Jacksonian: 1795–1843.* Princeton, N.J.: Princeton University Press, 1957.

Silver, James W. *Edmund Pendleton Gaines: Frontier General.* Baton Rouge: Louisiana State University Press, 1949.

Smith, Alice Elizabeth. *James Duane Doty: Frontier Promoter.* Madison: State Historical Society of Wisconsin, 1954.

Sunder, John E. *Joshua Pilcher: Fur Trader and Indian Agent.* Norman: University of Oklahoma Press, 1968.

Tracy, E. C. *Memoir of the Life of Jeremiah Evarts.* Boston: Crocker & Brewster, 1845.

U.S. Office of Indian Affairs. *Indian Land Tenure: Economic Status and Population Trends.* Washington, D.C.: GPO, 1935.

Van Deusen, Glyndon G. *The Jacksonian Era, 1828–1848.* New York: Harper Torchbooks, 1963.

Van Every, Dale. *Disinherited: The Lost Birthright of the American Indian.* New York: Avon Books, 1966.

Wallace, Anthony F. *Prelude to Disaster: The Course of Indian-White Relations Which Led to the Black Hawk War of 1832.* Springfield: Illinois State Historical Library, 1970.

Ward, John William. *Andrew Jackson, Symbol for an Age.* New York: Galaxy Books, 1962.

Warren, Charles. *The Supreme Court in United States History.* 3 vols. Boston: Little, Brown & Co., 1923.

Weston, Florence. *The Presidential Election of 1828.* Washington, D.C.: Catholic University Press, 1938.

White, Leonard D. *The Jacksonians: A Study in Administrative History, 1829–1861.* New York: Macmillan Co., 1954.

Wilkins, Thurman. *Cherokee Tragedy: The Story of the Ridge Family and of the Decimation of a People.* New York: Macmillan Co., 1970.

Woodward, Grace Steele. *The Cherokees.* Norman: University of Oklahoma Press, 1963.

Wright, Muriel H. *A Guide to the Indian Tribes of Oklahoma.* Norman: University of Oklahoma Press, 1951.

Young, Mary Elizabeth, *Redskins, Ruffleshirts and Rednecks: Indian Allotments in Alabama and Mississippi, 1830–1860.* Norman: University of Oklahoma Press, 1961.

7. ARTICLES

Abel, Annie H. "The History of Events Resulting in Indian Consolidation West of the Mississippi." *American Historical Association, Annual Report for the Year 1906* 1 (1908): 233–450.

———. "Proposals for an Indian State, 1778–1878." *American Historical Association, Annual Report for the Year 1907* 1 (1908): 87–104.

Anson, Bert. "Variations of the Indian Conflict: The Effects of the Emigrant Indian Removal Policy, 1830–1854." *Missouri Historical Review* 59 (October 1964): 64–89.

Babcock, Willoughby M., Jr. "Major Lawrence Taliaferro, Indian Agent." *Mississippi Valley Historical Review* 11 (December 1924): 358–75.

Brannon, Peter A. "Removal of Indians from Alabama." *Alabama Historical Quarterly* 12 (1950): 91–117.

Berkhofer, Robert F., Jr. "Faith and Factionalism among the Senecas: Theory and Ethnohistory." *Ethnohistory* 12 (Spring 1956): 99–112.

———. "Model Zions for the American Indian." *American Quarterly* 15 (Summer 1963): 176–90.

Bidney, David. "The Idea of the Savage in North American Ethnohistory." *Journal of the History of Ideas* 15 (April 1954): 322–27.

Blackburn, George M. "Foredoomed to Failure: The Manistee Indian Station." *Michigan History* 53 (Spring 1969): 37–50.

Brown, G. Gordan. "Missions and Cultural Diffusion." *American Journal of Sociology* 50 (November 1944): 214–19.

Burke, Joseph C. "The Cherokee Cases: A Study in Law, Politics, and Morality." *Stanford Law Review* 21 (February 1969): 500–31.

Cain, Marvin R. "William Wirt against Andrew Jackson: Reflection on an Era." *Mid-America* 47 (April 1965): 113–38.

Clayton, James L. "The Impact of Traders' Claims on the American Fur Trade." In *The Frontier in American Development: Essays in Honor of Paul Wallace Gates*, edited by David M. Ellis, pp. 299–322. Ithaca: Cornell University Press, 1969.

Crockett, Bernice Norman. "Health Conditions in Indian Territory: 1830 to the Civil War." *Chronicles of Oklahoma* 35 (Spring 1957): 80–90.

Davis, Jefferson. "The Indian Policy of the United States." *North American Review* 142 (November 1886): 436–46.

DeRosier, Arthur H., Jr. "Andrew Jackson and Negotiations for the Removal of the Choctaw Indians." *Historian* 29 (May 1967): 343–62.

———. "The Choctaw Removal of 1831: A Civilian Effort." *Journal of the West* 6 (April 1967): 237–47.

Dillard, Anthony Winston. "The Treaty of Dancing Rabbit Creek between the United States and the Choctaw Indians in 1830." Alabama State Department of Archives and History, *Historical and Patriotic Series* 10 (1928): 25–31.

Doherty, Herbert J., Jr. "The Governorship of Andrew Jackson." *Florida Historical Quarterly* 33 (July 1954): 3–31.

Eriksson, Erik McKinley. "The Federal Civil Service under President Jackson." *Mississippi Valley Historical Review* 13 (March 1927): 517–40.

————. 'Official Newspaper Organs and Jackson's Re-Election, 1832." *Tennessee Historical Magazine* 9 (April 1925): 37–58.

Farnham, Wallace D. " 'The Weakened Spring of Government': A Study in Nineteenth-Century American History." *American Historical Review* 68 (April 1963): 662–80.

Faust, Harold S. "The Growth of Presbyterian Missions to the American Indians During the National Period." *Journal of the Presbyterian Historical Society* 22 (September 1944): 88–123, and 22 (December 1944): 137–71.

Fischer, LeRoy H., ed. "United States Indian Agents to the Five Civilized Tribes." *Chronicles of Oklahoma* 50 (Winter 1972–73): 410–57, and 51 (Spring 1973): 34–84.

Foreman, Carolyn Thomas. "The Armstrongs of Indian Territory." *Chronicles of Oklahoma* 30 (Autumn 1952): 292–308.

————. "Education Among the Chickasaw Indians." *Chronicles of Oklahoma* 15 (June 1937): 139–65.

Foster, William Omer. "The Career of Montfort Stokes in Oklahoma." *Chronicles of Oklahoma* 18 (March 1940): 35–52.

Gallaher, Ruth A. "The Indian Agent in the United States before 1850." *Iowa Journal of History and Politics* 14 (January 1916): 3–55.

Gates, Paul Wallace. "The Frontier Land Business in Wisconsin." *Wisconsin Magazine of History* 53 (Summer 1969): 306–27.

————. "The Role of the Land Speculator in Western Development." *Pennsylvania Magazine of History and Biography* 66 (July 1942): 314–33.

Govan, Thomas P. "John Berrien and the Administration of Andrew Jackson." *Journal of Southern History* 5 (November 1939): 447–67.

Graebner, Norman A. "Pioneer Indian Agriculture in Oklahoma." *Chronicles of Oklahoma* 22 (Autumn 1945): 232–48.

Guthrie, Chester L., and Gerald, Leo L. "Upper Missouri Agency: An Account of Indian Administration on the Frontier." *Pacific Historical Review* 10 (March 1941): 47–56.

Hagan, William T. "Private Property, the Indian's Door to Civilization." *Ethnohistory* 3 (Spring 1956): 126–37.

Harmon, George Dewey. "The Indian Trust Funds, 1797–1865." *Mississippi Valley Historical Review* 21 (June 1934): 23–30.

Hoffmann, William S. "Andrew Jackson, State Rightist: The Case of the Georgia Indians." *Tennessee Historical Quarterly* 11 (December 1952): 329–45.

Horsman, Reginald. "American Indian Policy and the Origins of Manifest Destiny." *University of Birmingham Historical Journal* [England] 11 (1968): 128–40.

Kellogg, Louise Phelps. "The Removal of the Winnebago." *Transactions of the Wisconsin Academy of Science, Arts, and Letters* 21 (1929): 23–29.

Knight, Oliver. "Fifty Years of Choctaw Law, 1834–1884." *Chronicles of Oklahoma* 31 (Spring 1958): 76–95.

Kroeber, A. L. "Nature of the Land-Holding Group." *Ethnohistory* 2 (Fall 1955): 303–14.

Lewit, Robert T. "Indian Missions and Antislavery Sentiment: A Conflict of Evangelical and Humanitarian Ideals." *Mississippi Valley Historical Review* 50 (June 1963): 39–55.

Lien, Arnold J. "The Acquisition of Citizenship by the Native American Indians." *Washington University Studies* 13 (1925): 121–79.

Lindley, Harlow. "William Clark—The Indian Agent." *Proceedings of the Mississippi Valley Historical Association* 2 (1908–1909): 63–75.

Lindquist, G. E. E. "Indian Treaty Making." *Chronicles of Oklahoma* 26 (Winter 1948–49): 416–48.

Longaker, Richard P. "Andrew Jackson and the Judiciary." *Political Science Quarterly* 71 (September 1956): 341–64.

Loos, John L. "William Clark: Indian Agent." *Kansas Quarterly* 3 (Fall 1971): 29–37.

Malin, James C. "Indian Policy and Westward Expansion." *Humanistic Studies of the University of Kansas* 2 (1921): 251–358.

Meserve, John Bartlett. "Governor Montfort Stokes." *Chronicles of Oklahoma* 13 (September 1935): 338–40.

Neil, William M. "The Territorial Governor as Indian Superintendent in the Trans-Mississippi West." *Mississippi Valley Historical Review* 43 (September 1956): 213–37.

Pearce, Roy Harvey. "The Metaphysics of Indian-Hating." *Ethnohistory* 4 (Winter 1957): 27–40.

Porter, Kenneth W. "Florida Slaves and Free Negroes in the Seminole War, 1835–1842." *Journal of Negro History* 28 (October 1943): 390–421.

———. "Negroes and the Seminole War, 1835–1842." *Journal of Southern History* 30 (November 1964): 427–50.

Prucha, Francis Paul. "American Indian Policy in the 1840's: Visions of Reform." In *The Frontier Challenge: Responses to the Trans-Missis-*

sippi West, edited by John G. Clark, pp. 81–110. Lawrence: University of Kansas Press, 1971.

———. "Andrew Jackson's Indian Policy: A Reassessment." *Journal of American History* 56 (December 1969): 527–39.

———. "Indian Removal and the Great American Desert." *Indiana Magazine of History* 59 (December 1963): 299–322.

———. "Thomas L. McKenney and the New York Indian Board." *Mississippi Valley Historical Review* 48 (March 1962): 635–55.

Ricciardelli, Alex F. "The Adoption of White Agriculture by the Oneida Indians." *Ethnohistory* 10 (Fall 1963): 309–28.

Rouse, Shelley D. "Colonel Dick Johnson's Choctaw Academy: A Forgotten Educational Experiment." *Ohio Archaeological and Historical Quarterly* 25 (1916): 88–117.

Satz, Ronald N. "The 1850's and the Need for Revision." *Maryland Historian* 1 (Spring 1970): 81–86.

Silver, James W. "A Counter-Proposal to the Indian Removal Policy of Andrew Jackson." *Journal of Mississippi History* 4 (October 1942): 207–15.

———. "Edmund Pendleton Gaines and Frontier Problems, 1801–1849." *Journal of Southern History* 1 (August 1935): 320–44.

Smith, Timothy L. "Protestant Schooling and American Nationality, 1800–1850." *Journal of American History* 53 (March 1967): 679–95.

Spoehr, Alexander. "Changing Kinship Systems: A Study in the Acculturation of the Creeks, Cherokee, and Choctaw." Field Museum of Natural History, *Anthropological Series* 33 (January 1947): 153–235.

Treacy, Kenneth W. "Another View on Wirt in *Cherokee Nation.*" *American Journal of Legal History* 5 (October 1961): 385–88.

Vogt, Evon Z. "The Acculturation of the American Indians." *Annals of the American Academy of Political and Social Science* 311 (May 1957): 137–46.

Wallace, Anthony F. C. "New Religions among the Delaware Indians, 1600–1900." *Southwestern Journal of Anthropology* 12 (Spring 1956): 1–21.

———. "Revitalization Movements." *American Anthropologist* 58 (April 1956): 264–81.

———. "Stress and Rapid Personality Changes." *International Record of Medicine and General Practice Clinics* 169 (December 1956): 761–74.

Washburn, Wilcomb E. "Philanthropy and the American Indian: The Need for a Model." *Ethnohistory* 15 (Winter 1968): 43–56.

White, Lonnie J. "Arkansas Territorial Indian Affairs." *Arkansas Historical Quarterly* 21 (Autumn 1962): 193–212.

Wilson, Major L. "Andrew Jackson: The Great Compromiser." *Tennessee Historical Quarterly* 26 (Spring 1967): 64–78.

_____. " 'Liberty and Union': An Analysis of Three Concepts Involved in the Nullification Controversy." *Journal of Southern History* 33 (August 1967): 331–55.

Wright, Muriel H. "The Removal of the Choctaws to the Indian Territory, 1830–1833." *Chronicles of Oklahoma* 6 (June 1928): 103–28.

Young, Mary E. "The Creek Frauds: A Study in Conscience and Corruption." *Mississippi Valley Historical Review* 42 (December 1955): 411–37.

_____. "Indian Removal and Land Allotment: The Civilized Tribes and Jacksonian Justice." *American Historical Review* 64 (October 1958): 31–45.

8. Theses and Dissertations

Alford, Terry L. "Western Desert Images in American Thought, 1800–1860." Ph.D. dissertation, Mississippi State University, 1970.

Bieder, Robert Eugene. "The American Indian and the Development of Anthropological Thought in the United States, 1780–1851." Ph.D. dissertation, University of Minnesota, 1972.

Boyle, Gail Elizabeth. "Emigrant Indian Tribal Policies as Indicated by Intertribal Councils, 1837–1853." M.A. thesis, University of Chicago, 1941.

Clark, Ira Granville, Jr. "The Railroads and the Tribal Lands: Indian Territory, 1830–1890." Ph.D. dissertation, University of California, 1947.

Culp, Ruby Lee. "The Missions of the American Board and Presbyterian Church among the Five Civilized Tribes, 1803–1860." M.A. thesis, George Washington University, 1934.

Faust, Harold S. "The Presbyterian Mission to the American Indian during the Period of Indian Removal (1838–1893)." Th.D. dissertation, Temple University, 1943.

Fogerty, Robert P. "An Institutional Study of the Territorial Courts in the Old Northwest, 1788–1848." Ph.D. dissertation, University of Minnesota, 1942.

Jackson, Kathleen O'Brien. "A Study of Changes in Authority Relations between American Indians and Government." Ph.D. dissertation, University of Oregon, 1971.

Leisure, Clara E. "Governmental Organization and Administration of Indian Affairs in the United States." M.A. thesis, Ohio University, 1948.

Mahoney, Marie Patricia. "American Public Opinion of Andrew Jackson's Indian Policy, 1828–1835." M.A. thesis, Clark University, 1935.

Montgomery, Dean Ray. "Jeremiah Evarts and Indian Removal." M.A. thesis, University of Maryland, 1971.

Peterson, John Holbrook, Jr. "The Mississippi Band of Choctaw Indians: Their Recent History and Current Social Relations." Ph.D. dissertation, University of Georgia, 1970.

Satz, Ronald N. "Federal Indian Policy, 1829–1849." Ph.D. dissertation, University of Maryland, 1972.

Somit, Albert. "The Political and Administrative Ideas of Andrew Jackson." Ph.D. dissertation, University of Chicago, 1947.

Stipe, Claude E. "Eastern Dakota Acculturation: The Role of Agents of Culture Change." Ph.D. dissertation, University of Minnesota, 1968.

Strong, Esther B. "Wardship in American Indian Administration: A Political Instrumentality for Social Adjustment." Ph.D. dissertation, Yale University, 1941.

Unger, Robert W. "Lewis Cass, Indian Superintendent of the Michigan Territory, 1813–1831: A Survey of Public Opinion as Reported by the Newspapers of the Old Northwest Territory." Ph.D. dissertation, Ball State University, 1967.

Van Hoeven, James William. "Salvation and Indian Removal: The Career Biography of the Rev. John Freeman Schermerhorn, Indian Commissioner." Ph.D. dissertation. Vanderbilt University, 1972.

Viola, Herman J. "Thomas L. McKenney and the Administration of Indian Affairs, 1824–30." Ph.D. dissertation, Indiana University, 1970.

Yeager, Randolph O. "Indian Enterprises of Isaac McCoy, 1817–1846." Ph.D dissertation, University of Oklahoma, 1954.

Index

Affairs; Committee on Ways and Means; Congress

"Housewifery," 261, 262. *See also* Schools, social role training in

Houston, Sam, 112, 156

Humanitarian concern for Indians, 2, 13, 18, 24, 28, 40, 51, 53, 55, 56, 64, 103, 108, 195, 232. *See also* Civilization program, motivation of; Indian rights; Public opinion

Illinois, 88 n.4, 113, 114, 115, 167, 231

Indiana, 88 n.4, 167, 183, 185, 213, 216, 270

Indian affairs. *See* Indian policy of the United States

Indian agents. *See* Agents

Indian allotments. *See* Allotment policy

Indian-black cooperation, fear of, 4. *See also* Blacks

Indian Bureau. *See* Bureau of Indian Affairs

Indian Commissioner. *See* Commissioner of Indian affairs

Indian confederacy. *See* Indian territory, west of Arkansas and Missouri

Indian country, east of the Mississippi River, 4, 18, 23, 47, 54

Indian country, northern, 224–25, 227, 231, 235, 265

Indian country, west of Arkansas and Missouri, 80, 107, 112, 115, 138, 143, 188–90, 265; controversy over the geographical and geological nature of, 26–27, 37 n.50, 41; investigations of conditions in, 79, 135–36, 137, 138–40, 161, 193, 211; the status of, 130, 134, 140, 216, 230–31, 232, 234, 235–36, 244 n.45; American interference in, 130, 132–34, 137, 138, 139, 142, 143–45, 150 n.40, 212, 213, 214, 221–22, 227–28, 229–30, 234, 236; boundary disputes in, 133, 136; McCoy's surveys of, 133, 137; accomplishments of emigrants in, 188, 292; communications problems between Washington and field officials in, 189–90; frauds against Indians in, 193; efforts to protect frontier settlements against attacks from, 211–36, 236 n.1, 269; number of emigrant Indians in,

97, 211, 212, 214, 231, 269; educational programs in, 246, 252, 254, 262, 263, 264, 270, 271, 272–73, 284 n.36, 285 n.43, 292; ecological imbalance in, 272, 283 n.29. *See also* Emigrants, Indian; Indian territory, west of Arkansas and Missouri; West, trans-Mississippi

Indian Department Organization Act of 1834: congressional action on, 140, 155; and the Indian field service, 155, 179–82, 183, 184–85, 191, 192, 195, 196–97, 207 n.37, 256

Indian depredations, efforts to protect the frontier against, 54, 55, 211–36, 236 n.1, 269

Indian emigrants. *See* Emigrants, Indian

Indian emigration, 65, 117 n.9, 166, 229. *See also* Emigrants, Indian; Removal policy

"Indian legislators," 142. *See also* Congress, efforts to provide Indian representation in

Indian medals. *See* Medals, for Indians

Indian Office. *See* Office of Indian Affairs

Indian policy of the United States, xii; conflicting goals of, 1–2, 16, 104, 165, 155, 178, 253–54; the administration of, 1, 10, 66, 112, 136–37, 151–68, 178–201, 277; and partisan politics, 53, 66, 163–64, 167–68, 186, 187, 265; becomes associated with frontier defense, 211; evaluation of, 292–94. *See also* Bureau of Indian Affairs; Civilization program; Congress; Federal officials; Frontier, efforts to protect; Office of Indian Affairs; Removal policy; United States

Indian removal. *See* Removal policy

Indian reserves. *See* Allotment policy

Indian rights, 40–41, 181, 195, 217, 220. *See also* Humanitarian concern for Indians; Land, titles of Indians; Treaty rights

Indians: dispossession of, 1, 2, efforts to civilize, 1–2, 246–78; remaining in the East after removal, 12, 55, 104, 198; American interference in affairs of, 64, 136–37, 182, 216, 231, 232–